STANDING BEFORE GOD

Studies on Prayer in Scriptures and
in Tradition with Essays

In Honor of
JOHN M. OESTERREICHER

STANDING BEFORE GOD

Studies on Prayer in Scriptures and
in Tradition with Essays

In Honor of
JOHN M. OESTERREICHER

Edited by
ASHER FINKEL and
LAWRENCE FRIZZELL

KTAV PUBLISHING HOUSE, INC.
NEW YORK
1981

© Copyright 1981
The Institute of Judaeo-Christian Studies
at Seton Hall University

Library of Congress Cataloging in Publication Data
Main entry under title:

Standing before God.

  Bibliography: p.
  Includes indexes.
  1. God—Worship and love—Biblical teaching—
Addresses, essays, lectures.   2. Prayer—Biblical
teaching—Addresses, essays, lectures.   3. Oester-
reicher, John M., 1904-   —Addresses, essays,
lectures.   I. Oesterreicher, John M., 1904-
II. Finkel, Asher.   III. Frizzell, Lawrence.
BS1199.W73S72   230'.2   80-21102
ISBN 0-87068-708-5

NIHIL OBSTAT: Rev. Msgr. John H. Koenig
                  Censor Librorum

IMPRIMATUR: Most Reverend Peter L. Gerety, D.D.
                  Archbishop of Newark

April 11, 1980

Manufactured in the United States of America

Table of Contents

Preface

On May 2, 1977, friends gathered with Msgr. John M. Oesterreicher to celebrate the fiftieth anniversary of his ordination to the priesthood. On October 29, 1978, the Institute of Judaeo-Christian Studies, which he founded, marked its twenty-fifth year with a scholarly convocation. On February 2, 1979, Msgr. Oesterreicher completed his seventy-fifth year. In conjunction with these events, this volume of studies by his friends and colleagues is offered as an enduring tribute to the man, the priest, and his work.

"Standing before God" expresses a consciousness that one's entire life unfolds in the divine presence. The human response to this realization involves words and actions which are dimensions of prayer. As the psalmist says: "I bless the Lord . . . (for) I keep the Lord always before me" (Ps 16,7-8).

To stand before God is a privilege of those who have been called to share in the Covenant. This bodily attitude shows a sense of reverence and an alertness to God's Word and his call to service. Thus the Levites stood before the Lord to minister to him and to bless his Name (Deut 10,8). As God's dwelling place with his people, the Temple was a place of perpetual prayer and praise. Another poet of Israel salutes those servants of the Lord who stand by night in his house (Ps 134,1).

Besides signifying prayer and obedient service, the upright position is assumed by those involved in judicial action. All the parties in the drama of the Israelite court—plaintiff and defendant, attorneys and witnesses—stand before the judge. The Hebrew term *tefillah* (prayer) means the presentation of a case in court, an act of intercession. In the synagogue such prayer is worded collectively and with an altruistic thrust. The individual, in profound sympathy with the community, stands as intercessor before the Creator and Judge of all the earth.

Within the Catholic tradition, the priest stands before the Lord in union with the praise and prayer of Jesus the High Priest (Heb 7,24-25; 9,24-25), making intercession for those entrusted to him.

Both traditions are rooted in the example of Abraham, who stood before God as intercessor (Gen 18,8.22), and in whose name the families

1

of the earth are blessed (Gen 12,3). Msgr. John M. Oesterreicher has lived by the example of Abraham, and above all has sought to bring reconciliation between Christians and Jews. In respectful recognition of his accomplishments, and their basis in a life of prayer, the editors selected the theme of spirituality and prayer for the *Festschrift* in his honor.

In most cases, the Jewish and Christian contributors offer original studies in this area. Their works are arranged under the headings "Worship in Scripture" and "Prayer in Tradition." The reader will find that certain articles deal with similar questions from different angles and approaches. We hope that these studies will advance scholarly discussion, and also provide a basis for personal reflection on the part of the reader. In the third section, the contributions deal with topics of Jewish and Christian thought of the medieval and modern periods. The cycle of Holocaust songs at the end of the volume reminds us of the extremely trying and dangerous times of Msgr. Oesterreicher's early literary work.

For the sake of uniformity, the contributions in German and French were translated; credit is given at the beginning of these articles.

The editors greatly appreciate the support given to this work by Dr. Robert T. Conley, former President of Seton Hall University, and Dr. Peter M. Mitchell, former Vice President for Academic Affairs. This encouragement has been continued by the new President, Father Laurence T. Murphy, M.M.

This project could not have developed without the financial assistance of the Foundation for Judaeo-Christian Studies. The editors express their gratitude to the members of the Board for their interest and collaboration in this work.

Mrs. Medora MacLaren, Mrs. Claude Seyler and Miss Mindy Levitt typed the manuscripts. Their careful attention to an arduous task is gratefully acknowledged.

Together with Monsignor Oesterreicher's many friends in the scholarly world, we congratulate him on his significant achievements and wish him many blessings in his continuing work for God and his people. *Ad multos annos!*

Asher Finkel
Lawrence Frizzell

Foreword

Many and diverse are the monuments that mark the memorable achievements of men and of civilizations. Not the least of these is the literary monument that serves to enshrine the reflections of sage and serious thinkers. The collection before us is such a monument, a significant literary memorial to the spirit and the intellect, the faith and the compassion of Monsignor John M. Oesterreicher. It is a testimony to the union of minds and hearts of Jewish and Christian scholars, their tribute to a brother, a fellow scholar and a friend, with whom they share the restless quest for truth, the understanding of the ways of God, and the effort to diminish the darkness of ignorance and the heat of hatred.

Time was, not long ago, when such a work as this could not have been conceived, much less written. The giant step it represents in Jewish-Christian relations is due in no little part to the first halting steps taken courageously by Monsignor Oesterreicher in Vienna in 1934. The change in Jewish-Christian relations, attitudes, and official statements that has taken place in the past forty-five years is a change of major importance in the history of religions and the sociology of human relations. It is not a leap, but a small step in the search for world peace, for the love of believers must come before the love of enemies and show the way.

My first meeting with Monsignor Oesterreicher was in New York City after the Second World War. He was resident at St. Peter's, Barclay Street at the time, where I was preaching a series of Lenten sermons. An affinity was present at our first encounter since I had pursued Old Testament studies at the Pontifical Biblical Institute, and was then professor of Scripture and Hebrew at the archdiocesan seminary at Darlington, New Jersey. I learned of his hope of continuing in this country the work in Christian-Jewish relations he had begun so auspiciously in Europe, and his desire to establish an institute in a university setting. I shared his hope and harbored a hope of my own, that Seton Hall University would extend to such an institute academic hospitality and "a local habitation." So it came to pass that the University received the institute and it was given a name, the Institute of Judaeo-Christian Studies.

3

In the intervening years Monsignor Oesterreicher and the Institute have brought valued scholarly prestige to the University. His service to the Church will be described in the pages that follow. In the forties we did not dream of an Ecumenical Council in the sixties, but when it came Monsignor was ready to serve and his imprint is stamped on an enduring conciliar document, *Nostra Aetate*.

—John J. Dougherty

Contributors

Dr. Jacob Agus, Rabbi of Beth El Congregation, Baltimore, Md.

Dr. Peter G. Ahr, Assistant Dean and Associate Professor (Religious Studies), Seton Hall University, South Orange, N.J.

Dr. Otto Betz, Professor of New Testament, University of Tübingen.

Dr. Alfons Deissler, Professor of Old Testament, University of Freiburg in Breisgau.

Bishop John J. Dougherty, Scholar in Residence, Seton Hall University, South Orange, N.J.

Father Willehad Eckert O.P., Prior of the Dominican Monastery in Bornheim-Walberberg, West Germany.

Dr. Asher Finkel, Professor of Judaeo-Christian Studies, Seton Hall University, South Orange, N.J.

Father Lawrence Frizzell, Associate Professor of Judaeo-Christian Studies, Seton Hall University, South Orange, N.J.

Prof. Dr. Arnold Goldberg, Director, Seminar für Judaistik an der J.W. Goethe-Universität, Frankfurt am Main.

Dr. Monika Hellwig, Professor in Department of Theology, Georgetown University, Washington, D.C.

Father Kurt Hruby, lecturer in Paris and Zürich.

Dr. Annie Kraus, 9 Maximilianstrasse, Münster.

Father Eugene H. Maly, Professor of Sacred Scripture, Mount St. Mary's of the West, Norwood, Ohio.

Father Richard M. Nardone, Assistant Professor of Religious Studies, Seton Hall University, South Orange, N.J.

Rabbi Jakob J. Petuchowski, Research Professor of Jewish Theology and Liturgy, Hebrew Union College, Cincinnati, Ohio.

Mr. Joseph Sievers, Adjunct Lecturer in Judaeo-Christian Studies, Seton Hall University, South Orange, N.J.

Dr. Lou H. Silberman, Professor in Department of Religious Studies, Vanderbilt University, Nashville, Tenn.

Father Gerard S. Sloyan, Professor of New Testament, Temple University, Philadelphia, Pa.

Dr. Walter Strolz, Herder Publishing Company, Freiburg in Breisgau.

5

Father Edward A. Synan, Professor at the Pontifical Institute of Medieval Studies, Toronto, Ontario.

Dr. Shemaryahu Talmon, J.L. Magnes Professor of Biblical Studies, Hebrew University, Jerusalem.

Father Clemens Thoma S.V.D., Rector of Theologische Fakultät, Lucerne.

Rabbi Herbert Weiner of Temple Israel, South Orange; Adjunct Associate Professor at Seton Hall University, South Orange, N.J.

Erika Weinzierl, Professor of the Institut für Zeitgeschichte, Universität Wien.

Dr. Michael Wyschogrod, Chairman, Department of Philosophy, Baruch College, City University of New York.

Dr. Dieter Zeller, Dozent of Sacred Scripture in the University of Freiburg in Breisgau.

Abbreviations

A.G.S.U.	—Arbeiten zur Geschichte des Spätjudentums und Urchristentums
Ant.	—Antiquitates Judaicarum of Josephus Flavius
A.P.O.T.	—Apocrypha and Pseudepigrapha of the Old Testament edited by R. H. Charles
b	—Babylonian Talmud
Bib. Vie Chr.	—Bible et Vie Chrétienne
B.J.R.L.	—Bulletin of the John Rylands Library
B.K.A.T.	—Biblischer Kommentar: Altes Testament (Neukirchen)
C.C.	—Corpus Christianorum (Series Latina)
C.B.Q.	—Catholic Biblical Quarterly
col	—column
Conc	—Concilium
D.A.C.L.	—Dictionnaire d'Archéologie Chrétienne et de Liturgie
D.J.D.	—Discoveries in the Judaean Desert (Oxford: Clarendon Press)
E.Th.L.	—Ephemerides Theologicae Louvaniensis
Ev. Th.	—Evangelische Theologie
F.J.B.	—Frankfurter Judaistische Beiträge
H.T.R.	—Harvard Theological Review
H.U.C.A.	—Hebrew Union College Annual
I.C.C.	—International Critical Commentary
j	—Jerusalem Talmud
J.B.L.	—Journal of Biblical Literature
J. Jew. St.	—Journal of Jewish Studies
J.P.S.A.	—Jewish Publication Society of America
J.T.S.	—Journal of Theological Studies
J.T.S.A.	—Jewish Theological Seminary of America
K.B.W.	—Katholisches Bibelwerk (Stuttgart)
LXX	—Septuagint
Lum. Vie	—Lumière et Vie
M	—Mishnah

M.G.W.J.	—Monatschrift für Geschichte und Wissenschaft des Judentums
M.V.A.G.	—Mitteilungen der vorasiatisch-ägyptischen Gesellschaft (Leipzig)
N.A.B.	—New American Bible
N.T.S.	—New Testament Studies
Nov. Test.	—Novum Testamentum
Onk.	—Targum Onkelos
P.A.A.J.R.	—Proceedings of the American Academy of Jewish Research
P.L.	—Migne, Patrologia Latina
rep.	—reprint
R.S.V.	—Revised Standard Version
S.B.	—Strack & Billerbeck, Kommentar zum Neuen Testament
SIDIC	—Service International de Documentation Judéo-chrétienne (Rome)
S.P.C.K.	—Society for the Promotion of Christian Knowledge
S.Th.	—Summa Theologiae
T.D.N.T.	—Theological Dictionary of the New Testament edited by G. Kittel
T.H.A.T.	—Theologischer Handkommentar zum Alten Testament (Berlin)
Th.Q.	—Theologische Quartalschrift
Th.W.A.T.	—Theologisches Wörterbuch zum Alten Testament edited by G. J. Botterweck
Th.W.N.T.	—Theologisches Wörterbuch zum Neuen Testament edited by G. Kittel
Z.A.W.	—Zeitschrift für die alttestamentliche Wissenschaft
Z.D.V.P.	—Zeitschrift des Deutschen Palästina-Vereins
Z.N.W.	—Zeitschrift für die neutestamentliche Wissenschaft
Z.R.G.G.	—Zeitschrift für Religions-und Geistgeschichte
Z. Theol. Kirche	—Zeitschrift für Theologie und Kirche

Biblical citations are made with chapter followed by a comma, verses separated by a period. A semi-colon separates two distinct citations.

John M. Oesterreicher: Cursus Vitae

Born on February 2, 1904 at Stadt-Liebau, Moravia (then part of the Austro-Hungarian Empire), son of Nathan and Ida (Zelenka) Oesterreicher.

Secondary education at Gymnasium (Liberal Arts School) Olmütz in Stadt Liebau (1914-1922)

University studies: Medical School, University of Vienna (Fall 1922-Spring 1924)

Theological College, University of Graz (Spring 1924-1926)

Theological College, University of Vienna (1927-1928)

Degrees: Licentiate in Sacred Theology, University of Vienna (1927)

Professor of Religion (1935), an Austrian degree entitling the bearer to teach in secondary school, equivalent to a doctoral degree. Dissertation: "The Christological Problem in Philippians 2,5-11."

Ordination: July 17, 1927 by Cardinal Prince-Archbishop Piffl

Parochial Assignments: (1) "Our Lady of the Snow," Gloggnitz, Austria (1928-1931),

(2) "Exaltation of the Cross," Vienna, 16th district, (1931-1934); Paulaner Kirche, Vienna, 4th district, (1934-1938)

First Editorial Assignment:

Missionsruf, ("Mission call") organ of Society of the White Cross (today, "Institute of Christ the King") a community founded by Max Joseph Metzger, and devoted to ecumenism, peace, and the proclamation of the gospel for people of our time.

Second Editorial Position:

Die Erfuellung. ("The Fulfillment"), Vienna, 1934-38, organ of *Opus St. Pauli*, purpose: to stand by the Jews in the hour of their need, to

denounce Nazi persecution of Jews and combat Hitler's glorification of race and hatred of
Jews.

Interrogation by Gestapo in March 1939

(shortly after invasion of Austria by German
troops). Left untouched because Nazi authorities kept arresting of priests to a
minimum; before the referendum (plebiscite)
on the "return" of Austria to the *Reich*, only
politically active priests, particularly declared
monarchists, were jailed.

Departure from Austria April 1939

by a bureaucratic blunder of the Gestapo.

By way of Switzerland (Basel, Fribourg) and Rome went to Paris. Lived
in Paris from Sept. 1939-June 1940

Left on Monday of the week the Nazi troops
entered Paris (Friday)

While in Paris worked against Nazi regime

(1) Limited cooperation with the politically
(politics meant party politics) engaged section
of Austrian emigration.

(2) Weekly broadcasts against Nazi ideology
as force that was not only anti-Jewish but, no
less, anti-Christian. Heard in various parts of
the Greater *Reich*. Nazi authorities protested
against this denunciation of their heresies, the
war, etc.

(3) Publication of first book: "Racisme, Antisémitisme, Antichristianisme," Paris, Editions du Cerf, 1939; major part of edition was
confiscated by Gestapo after fall of Paris, re-
published in 1943, by La Maison Française in
New York.

Departure from France: After several attempts and by circuitous routes
in France, crossing border into Spain and, after
3 days in jail (police-jail) in Barcelona, via Madrid into Portugal (Lisbon).

Arrival in USA: SS Exeter, Nov. 12, 1940

Parish Assignments: (1) Church of the Assumption, West 49th St.,
NYC, April-Oct. 1941. (2) Church of St.
Joseph, East 83rd St., NYC, Fall 1941-1944,
return to Church of the Assumption, 1944-

1949. Church Rosa of Lima, South Bronx, NYC, 1949-50, St. Peter's, 1950-52 with interval of several months at the Augustinians, Riverdale—to Seton Hall University in 1953.

Research Professor, Manhattanville College, Purchase, N.Y., 1944-53.

Foundation of Institute of Judaeo-Christian Studies, Seton Hall University, March 25, 1953.

Participation in the work of the Secretariat for Christian Unity, in preparation during Council session.

Attendance of second, third, and fourth sessions of the Council.

Danforth Committee Lecturer, Columbia University (1962) and Miami University (1963)

Papal Chamberlain (1963)

Honorary Prelate (1966)

L.L.D. honoris causa bestowed by Incarnate Word College, San Antonio, Texas in 1967.

D.H.L. honoris causa bestowed by Canisius College, Buffalo, N.Y. in 1968.

Chairman of the M.A. program of Judaeo-Christian Studies, Seton Hall University from 1975-1979.

D.L. honoris causa bestowed by Seton Hall University, South Orange, N.J. in 1977.

Distinguished University Professor, Seton Hall University, 1978.

Scholar in Residence, Seton Hall University, 1979.

The Beginnings of John M. Oesterreicher's Work for Christian-Jewish Understanding*

ERIKA WEINZIERL

In early 1960, John M. Oesterreicher, the Director of the Institute of Judaeo-Christian Studies at Seton Hall University in New Jersey, together with John J. Dougherty, Professor of Sacred Scripture at the Seminary in Darlington, N.J. and thirteen fellow priests, wrote a petition to Cardinal Bea, which was presented at Fordham University on June 8, 1960. The authors hoped that the coming Vatican Council II would continue the reconciliation of the Catholic Church with the Jews, which had begun with Popes Pius XI and Pius XII but above all by John XXIII. It requested that "if the Council were to inquire into the nature of the Church in the course of its deliberations, it should proclaim that the call of Abraham and the deliverance of Israel out of Egypt belong to the genesis of the Church, so that she can fittingly and rightly be called 'the Israel of God' (Gal. 6,16), the Israel renewed and exalted by Christ's word and blood."

The Council should also express "the unity of salvation history, which comes especially to life in the prayers surrounding the administration of the sacraments. This could be achieved if the Masses now peculiar to the patriarchate of Jerusalem were made into votive Masses of the whole Church, or if a universal feast of all the just of the Old Testament were introduced."

Finally, the signatories asked—"for the love which Christ had for his kinsmen—that misleading phrases, above all the readings of the Office, which distort the true teaching of the Church and her real attitude towards the Jews, should be changed. If the Council were to turn its attention to the problems of our own time, the Church should, as in the

---

*Translation from the German by L. Frizzell.

past, judge and condemn hatred of the people whose 'is the human stock from which Christ came; Christ who is God over all, blessed for ever. Amen.' (Rom. 9,5)."[1]

This petition constituted an important impulse for the plan of a special declaration of the Council on the Jews, for whose preparation Oesterreicher was called in February 1961 as a consultor in the Secretariat for Christian Unity. Together with Abbot Leo Rudloff and Father Gregory Baum O.S.A., he served as a member of the "subcommission for the Jewish questions."

Therein Oesterreicher played a central role and at its order drafted a basic study which, in its presentation before all the co-workers of the Secretariat, Bea received with applause. He was active also on the further drafts (Decretum de Judaeis, chapter IV of the schema on ecumenism, introduction to the schema on ecumenism, fourth draft) which had to be made because of opposition by the Arab world and deliberations within the Council. Finally the "Statement on the Bond of the Church to the Jewish People" found its place in the "Declaration on the Church's Relation to the Non-Christian Religions" and with this was accepted by an overwhelming majority in the last session of the Council (1965). Oesterreicher collaborated untiringly in this work and fought for it in the front lines.[2] Its acceptance was the summit and crown of the decades-long efforts of Oesterreicher. They began in Austria, where he was born in 1904.

Coming from Judaism himself, he became Catholic during his medical studies and dedicated himself to the priesthood. In 1927 he was ordained to the priesthood by Cardinal Piffl[3] and quickly placed himself in the very difficult service of reconciliation between Christians and Jews, for which during the 1930s he found a generous sponsor in the often misjudged Cardinal-Archbishop Dr. Theodor Innitzer. He was the director of "Opus Sancti Pauli" which sought to present the so-called Jewish question as a question addressed by God to Jews and Christians, a question demanding faith of Jews and love of Christians. Faith here meant faith in Christ. Oesterreicher readily admits that in those early days quite a few of his approaches were like the halting steps of one learning to walk, like the gropings of a beginner. He was also editor of *Die Erfüllung* (Fulfillment), which first appeared in 1934. The foreword of Cardinal Innitzer, which certainly must be attributed to Oesterreicher, reads: "In these confused and dismal times, *Die Erfüllung* will be a voice of the Spirit and of truth. Its goal is to present to Jews and Christians the *religious* version of Jewish existence. So it is summoned to lay low the walls which people have erected between one another through ignorance and dissension, through error and sin. Thus it will serve peace, and nothing is more important today—however, not a false but rather the true peace, which comes from the truth, which is from God." This foreword bears the date July 17, 1934. Eight days later the Austrian Chancellor, Dr. Engelbert Dollfuss (who on his part in February 1934, after civil strife had eliminated the Austrian Social Democrats from legal political life) fell to the bullets of National Socialist rebels. Although their insurrection was put down quickly and Hitler immediately distanced himself from it, Austria was very far from inner and outer peace in this very time. Thus, the goal which *Die Erfüllung* set forth in its preface, which certainly comes from Oesterreicher's pen, is to be the more highly esteemed.

"*Die Erfüllung* acknowledges the primacy of the Spirit. It knows that the decisions of history belong to the Spirit and nowhere else, that from our need there is no escape except a spiritual rebirth.

"Our journal takes its starting point from the Jewish question. It sees therein not a question of the times, but a question of eternity; a question on which minds are divided. It desires to serve an encounter of Jews with the Spirit of Jesus Christ and an encounter of Christians with the mission of Israel. Finally, it desires the fulfillment of Christ's petition, which is the interest of true humanity, 'That they all may be one!'

"*Die Erfüllung* desires to bring the hidden existence of Judaism to light. It will speak of the divine truth and human sublimity of the Bible; of wisdom in the Talmud and of Hasidic piety. To a great extent, it will also examine contemporary Judaism as modern spiritual life.

"This Jewish thought and activity of our time regards people above all. However the present manifests it clearly: Whoever proclaims nothing as humanity, directly loses it and himself. From this insight, 'that the human being, who desires no more than only a human being, does not once fulfil the human' (Joseph Bernhart), *Die Erfüllung* speaks of Christ, the God-Man.

"Such a periodical in such a time as ours is a hazardous venture. It can succeed only with the full cooperation of our readers. There will not be very many, for the new, the coming will always be borne only by the few. But we cry out to them!'

To the not so many, who bear the new, the coming, *Die Erfüllung* offered the following significant articles during its first year of publication (1934-35): Gertrud LeFort, "Israel and the Church" (the beginning of her novel, *The Pope from the Ghetto*); Karl Thieme, "The Jews and we Christians from the Gentiles"; Otto Maria Karpfen, "Franz Kafka, or the Breakthrough"; Josef Dillersberger, "On the Nature of the Gospel"; Olga Lau-Tugemann, "Church and Synagogue," Otto Maria Karpfen, "The Jews and Socialism"; Dietrich von Hildebrand, "The Yearning for

Truth"; Robert John, "I.N.R.I."; Josef Dillersberger, "His Own" (John 1,11); Walther Eidlitz, "Struggle on behalf of the People of Moses"; Waldemar Gurian, "Judaism and nineteenth century Enlightenment"; Otto A. Marbach, "Life from the dead" (Rom 11,15); Bernhard Steiner, "The Witness of Biology"; Karl-Borromäus Heinrich, "A Confession: Letter to the Editor of *Die Erfüllung*"; Otto A. Marbach, "Life in the Old Covenant (an Interpretation of Salvation History according to Romano Guardini)"; Otto Maria Karpfen, "Church and Culture"; Rudolf Fanta, "The Jews and Socialism."

The documentation, as well as reviews of books and periodicals found in each issue come almost exclusively from the pen of Father Oesterreicher. With these and the authors he gained for *Die Erfüllung*, it manifested a distinctive intellectual tone and an alertness to the signs of the times in conjunction with value and permanence. Among the most interesting are indeed his articles, the first of which, "The Jewish question" should be reprinted because of its significance and its moving commitment. His other articles in the first six issues of *Die Erfüllung*, which appeared from 1934-36, bear the titles "Sinai" (Israel's Sinai is the glory and blessing, its law is the law of humanity . . .); "Solowjew's Vision of the Antichrist"; "Franz Rosenzweig: a Jewish Destiny";[4] "Hominem non Habeo"; "Jews and Socialism" as an answer to Rudolf Fanta's letter on this question. "Hominem non Habeo"[5] dealt with the German Reich's law "For the protection of German blood and honor," promulgated on September 15, 1935 (the so-called "Nuremberg laws"), with which the existential deprivation of Jewish rights began: They declared juridically that the Jews are inferior human beings, and thus the first step toward the "final solution" had been taken. Oesterreicher protested in the name of justice, the Spirit, the Gospel, and the Church.[6] At the beginning of his passionate protest, he cited words of the Church Father Ambrose to Caesar Theodosius: "For a priest, nothing is so dangerous before God, so ignominious before men as the lack of courage. Who would risk to speak the truth if the priest does not so risk?" After reproducing the text of the laws, Oesterreicher states that until this time *Die Erfüllung* had never uttered a word on political events. "We have refrained from expressing a reaction to the exclusion of German Jewry from the economic and social life of Germany. This, however, is no longer possible; we can no longer look on the anti-Jewish measures as if they were not our concern. Now it is our duty to take a public stand. All of the measures which placed the existence of German Jewry within German society in grave perils had been passed over in silence. But here is a decree which shatters any political framework, which no longer attacks only the external positions but strikes at

German Jewry in the depth of its being, desiring to annihilate it in its inner existence. This decree threatens not only the Jews but the West, not only the West but humanity as such. This law concerns each and every individual and no one can shirk the responsibility of taking a stand." These are prophetic words, which—as always in history—were believed by only a few . . .

Moreover, John Oesterreicher did not limit himself only to "his" periodical in regard to this responsibility. Wherever it was possible, in word and writing, he pleaded for the reconciliation of Christians and Jews. That this had become increasingly more difficult to maintain in "the Christian Corporative State" is shown by incidents that took place during a lecture series organized by the *Pauluswerk* in the Spring of 1937.[7] It began with a lecture by the German Dominican Franziskus Straatmann, Apostolic Penitentiary in Saint Mary Major in Rome, and Germany's leading pacifist, on "The Jews and we Christians."[8] At the end of the lecture, "in the midst of the enthusiastic applause, some youths in the gallery suddenly yelled and hurled down pieces of paper upon which these words were written: For the solution of the Jewish question there is still time. What is threatened today is Christianity, Heil Innitzer!"[9]

This incident led some Vienna newspapers to the assumption that the demonstrators were National Socialists, whereas they were defended by the organ of the Christian Corporative government, *Reichspost*: "Demonstrating National Socialists like other cries and are wont to announce their presence with stink-bombs. The opinion that the 'Jewish question' is not the most urgent of all questions and that events in the world should draw Christians' attention above all to threats concerning themselves is an opinion held widely in Austria too. Hence it is not a sign of an inclination towards National Socialism, which indeed has itself gone among the foes of the Church and Christianity. Moreover, as we hear, in their interrogation with the police, the arrested demonstrators have firmly denied any link with National Socialism. That they were immediately called 'Nazis' by some of the nervous participants at the lecture is no convincing evidence, given the known tendency of certain circles."[10]

This "defense" caused the weekly edited by Professor Dietrich von Hildebrand *(Der Christliche Ständestaat)* to make a sharp critique of the *Reichspost* under the title: "Have we sunk so low?" "Does the *Reichspost* not note how deplorable for us Catholics is the position that it was not National Socialists but Catholics who so behaved?"[11]

In that series of lectures Professor von Hildebrand spoke next, then Senator Pant and finally John Oesterreicher spoke. According to the

Neuigkeits-Weltblattes the young demonstrators, who did not want to "put up with the blemish" of being suspected and criticized as Nazis, consulted with "esteemed members of the Catholic clergy," and following their advice, chose another form of protest. "They agreed to refrain from any interference during the lectures, but afterwards, before leaving the hall, to make the sign of the cross and to add the words: 'Christ conquers, Heil Innitzer.' " The *Reichspost* maintained that one ought to pardon the demonstrators because excessive applause at passages overly friendly towards Jews "provoked" them. *Der Christliche Ständstaat* showed this defense to be absurd because Oesterreicher's presentation "in its lofty, purely religious character gave absolutely no occasion for applause, except for an attempt that was stifled as soon as it began." Besides, some listeners heard "Heil Hitler" instead of "Heil Innitzer." Thus was a mental abberation and a perversion of taste revealed, which Catholic papers still defended . . .[12]

In 1961 the periodical *Wort und Wahrheit* asked Catholics of Germany, Switzerland and Austria the question: "What do you expect of the Council?" John Oesterreicher began his response with the sentence: "Were the Council Fathers to come to me as in the fairytale and grant me only one wish, then I would request without hesitation a declaration concerning human dignity." The reason for this, as he develops in his statement, is anti-Semitism and the disturbed relationship of Christians and Jews.[13] That the Council indeed fulfilled this wish as indicated in the introduction, was in real part the work of Oesterreicher. The first step towards this he made decades earlier in Austria.

NOTES

1. John Oesterreicher, "Introduction and Commentary: Declaration on the Relationship of the Church to Non-Christian Religions," *Commentary on the Documents of Vatican II* (ed. Herbert Vorgrimler), New York: Herder & Herder 1969 III p. 10-11.

2. Ibid. p. 1-136.

3. *Wort und Wahrheit* 16 (1961) p. 646.

4. This response to Rosenzweig, the religious thinker and model of a sufferer was probably the first Catholic voice drawing attention to the importance of this Jewish theologian. (Editor)

5. The reference is to John 5:7 (Vulgate), where the paralyzed man at the Pool of Bethesda laments: "I have no man to put me into the pool . . ." (Editor)

6. (1) In the name of justice: One of the regulations of the laws brands Jews implicitly as sex-criminals—an obvious injustice.

(2) In the name of the Spirit: The culture of the West has been largely fashioned by the biblical message that man was created in the image and likeness of God. The laws are a violation of this human dignity.

(3) In the name of the Gospel: Christ's message has done away with the old divisions of humanity into races; it has robbed them of their significance. The Nuremberg Laws seek to foster racial superiority instead of evangelical love.

(4) In the name of the Church: The Nuremberg Laws forbid marriages between a Jew and an "Aryan"—a prohibition entirely unnecessary. After two years of Nazi domination few, if any, would have dared enter a mixed marriage. Hence, the purpose of that law is therefore to strike at the Church, her freedom in administering the sacraments, in conveying God's grace without discrimination. (Editor)

7. By this time the *Pauluswerk* had become part of the Catholic Action of the day.

8. *Reichspost,* May 6, 1937.

9. *Der christliche Ständstaat,* May 16, 1937.

10. *Reichspost,* May 9, 1937.

11. *Der christliche Ständstaat,* May 16, 1937.

12. *Der christliche Ständstaat,* May 23, 1937.

13. *Wort und Wahrheit* (1961) p. 646-648. This wish was fulfilled in the "Message to Humanity" released by the Council on October 20, 1962 (nine days after the Council had opened). The text may be found in *The Documents of Vatican II* (edited by Walter M. Abbott), New York, America Press 1966 p. 3-7. (Editor)

Worship in Scriptures

"... The Highest Heavens Cannot Contain You..." (2Kgs 8,27): Immanence and Transcendence in the Deuteronomist

EUGENE H. MALY

In January of 1975 a group of Christian theologians issued what came to be known as "The Hartford Appeal."[1] It consisted of thirteen theological themes, stated and briefly discussed, which the signers felt were "false and debilitating to the Church's life and work."[2] "The focus was on the less than satisfactory condition of contemporary Christian thought, the apparent loss of a sense of the transcendent, and the debilitating influence of a number of themes that were judged to be both pervasive and false."[3]

The Appeal obviously "struck a live theological nerve" (J. Finn), since it was followed by a series of debates and symposiums in which many of the best known theologians in the country took part. In this writer's view, the one issue which can be seen as underlying the majority of the themes condemned is that of divine transcendence. Can we really speak of God as the "wholly Other"? Does an insistence on the divine transcendence lead to an undue concern for an "other-worldly" existence and to a denigration or a slackening appreciation of social and other "this-worldly" concerns?

The other divine characteristic which is set in paradoxical complementarity to his transcendence is referred to as "immanence."[4] By this is meant God's intimate association with the world and humankind, his loving concern to bring creation to fulfillment, the intimate revelation of himself to men and women as their Savior and Redeemer. Christians see in the Incarnation of the Son of God the fullest manifestation of this divine immanence. Although the term was not used by the signers of the Hartford Appeal, it is clear that they felt that an undue emphasis on this aspect of God could lead to the denial of transcendence altogether.

It is not my purpose here to attempt a resolution of the paradox of a transcendent and immanent God. Rather, the contemporary debate simply serves as a catalyst for the examination of one biblical tradition in terms of the paradox. Most commentators would agree that a number of biblical passages emphasize the holiness or transcendence of God, while others reflect a strong conviction of his immanence. This does not mean that any of the biblical authors would deny the other aspect of God; rather, it is a matter of emphasis made by reason of the particular situation that the writer was addressing or the personality of the author himself.

Perhaps the most powerful presentation of the holy God[5] is in Isa 6,1-13 where the prophet's call to ministry is recorded. Here the over-powering note of transcendence is met in what Otto calls "an unsurpassable form . . . there there is sublimity alike in the lofty throne and the sovereign figure of God, the skirts of His raiment 'filling the temple' and the solemn majesty of the attendant angels about Him."[6] It is this experience of transcendence that evoked in Isaiah the consciousness of his own sinfulness: "Woe is me, I am doomed! For I am a man of unclean lips, living among a people of unclean lips; yet my eyes have seen the King, the Lord of hosts!" (Isa 6,5). Otto notes the striking similarity between the reaction of the prophet and that of Peter on witnessing Jesus' first miracle (Luke 5,8). The experience of transcendence is not one of the Old Testament period alone.

Illustrations of divine immanence abound in the Scriptures. In the Old Testament they seem to be best represented by the boldly anthropomorphic presentations of God. The Yahwist's story of origins, for example, speaks of God forming man out of the clay of the ground and blowing into his nostrils the breath of life (Gen 2,7). Even more vividly God is pictured as moving about in the garden, apparently prepared to engage in friendly conversation with the man and woman (Gen 3,8). All these suggest that God is a loving God, concerned with his creatures and ready to associate with them. Still another strong illustration of this immanence is had in Gen 18, the scene of the visit of the Lord and two companions with Abraham and of their sharing a meal together. This is continued in the sequel when Abraham argues, or better, bargains with the Lord for the safety of the people of Sodom. A note of transcendence is introduced when Abraham admits his presumption in speaking to the Lord, "Though I am but dust and ashes!" (v 27).

What I have tried to do so far is simply to set up the biblical context in which our analysis can be made. I think the majority of scholars recognize the presence of these two aspects of God in the Scriptures. It is generally agreed, for example, that the Elohist (E) presents a more transcendent God than the Yahwist (J), and that the Priestly writer (P) stresses that transcendence more than the other two. Our question concerns the role of the Deuteronomist (D) in this spectrum of presentations of the God of Israel.[7] Chronologically, it would seem that the later the tradition, the more transcendent is the presentation of God.[8] If age were the sole determinant, then the God of D would be expected to be as transcendent as P, at least in its final, exilic or post-exilic, form. But, while religious growth would normally lead to a more sophisticated concept of divinity and thus to a more transcendent picture, there are other factors that influence religious convictions, factors which are not necessarily or exclusively determined by time. These must also be considered.

There are several reasons for claiming that D's picture of God is a strongly immanent one, in the sense that we have defined that term, that is, one of intimate association with the world and mankind. The striking hortatory character of Moses' address in Deut can only be explained by a conviction about such a divine concern. This is no God who is aloof from his people, unaffected by their conduct. The emphasized "you" as the object of the address is a telling mark of personal care.

Many of the phrases that have been determined to be characteristic of D, while not as boldly anthropomorphic as J's, still reveal the "humanness" of D's picture of God. Thus, in Deut the word "to love" (*ʾahab*) is used five times of God's attitude toward Israel. The Hebrew word expresses a passionate love that goes out to the object of the love; in the cases in Deut it is always election love. It is not found elsewhere in the Pentateuch in this sense. Similar is the use of *bahar*, "to choose," applied several times to Israel, to the priests, and to the place where God will "make his name to dwell." Again, the word is not found before this of God's choice of his people. The phrase "so that the Lord, your God, will bless you," clear evidence of loving concern, is characteristic of Deut. The "strong hand and outstretched arm" of God are mentioned at least five times in Deut, always in the context of God's liberation of his people from Egypt.[9]

In Deut 30,11-14 we have an exquisitely presented piece on the nearness of God's word to his people, probably in exile. The author is at pains here to emphasize that it is not an inaccessible word, something "too mysterious and remote for you," something "up in the sky" or "across the sea." "No, it is something very near to you, already in your mouths and in your hearts . . ." (v 14). There is a Wisdom substratum here,[10] but the remarkable point is that, unlike Wisdom in so much of the Wisdom literature, it is one that human beings not only have access to but even possess within themselves. And, of course, it is a divine

Wisdom. Thus the author is saying something tantamount to the divine presence in the people's lives.

Paul has taken over this passage and interpreted the command of God as being Christ (Rom 10,6-8). Of course, this is an accommodation by Paul, but it provides at least an analogue for the interpretation of Deut. The word of God, his command, is inseparable from God himself. "As God in the Deuteronomic covenant is very near to his people, so God in Christ, the living Lord of his people is always near."[11]

That such an interpretation of Deut is justified is confirmed by the passage in 4,7 where the closeness of God to his people is explicitly stated: "For what great nation is there that has gods so close to it as the Lord, our God, is to us whenever we call upon him." While the nearness of God is presented here in the context of answering prayers, it need not be restricted to that function. It is evident from the context that the author is attempting to counteract the influence of the Canaanite worship on Israel. Yahwism, with its stress on the divine spirituality (in the sense of non-fleshly or non-material existence), could prove a scandal to the weak who needed a more corporeal divinity within their reach. In fact, it was the gross materialism of these pagan gods that was one of the strongest factors in explaining their popularity. We can recall the story of the golden calf where the idol was commanded to be made by the people precisely because of the prolonged absence of Moses, God's representative among them (Exod 32; see v 1). Deut was well aware of this "original sin" of Israel in the desert (9,7-21).

In view of all this we can readily understand why the author would want to express the closeness of God to his people as strongly as he can without compromising his spirituality or non-corporeality. It is true that the nearness of God was expressed in the older traditions by the Ark which manifested the divine presence in varying ways according to the various traditions. Deut is not unaware of the Ark which is called "the ark of the covenant of the Lord" (10,8) and which is seen as containing the two tablets of the Law (10,1-8). But it is significant that in this passage in 4,7 where he wants to emphasize the presence of God to his people, he does not mention the Ark, though he does mention the just "statutes and decrees" (4,8) which give evidence of God's love. Deut wants to avoid a possibly materialistic understanding of that presence. More positively he would want to affirm a much more dynamic presence which implicitly acknowledges the divine transcendence.

When we reflect on all these indications of divine immanence in D, it is difficult to avoid the conclusion that this characteristic of God is affirmed as strongly here, if not in the same way, as it is in J. Yet we must also say, on the basis of evidence to be presented, that no other tradition presents the divine transcendence as forcefully as D. In fact, there is some reason for arguing that D's conception of the transcendent God is even more sophisticated than that of P.

The passage in the whole of the D corpus that must take pride of place in this respect is one found in Solomon's prayer, made on the occasion of the dedication of the newly built temple: "Can it indeed be that God dwells among men on earth? If the heavens and the highest heavens cannot contain you, how much less this temple that I have built!" (1Kgs 8,27). Almost all scholars agree on the D provenance of the prayer, although there is some variation in fixing the time of its composition. J. Robinson[12] holds that, while there is reference to exile (vv 46-48), this must be the exile of the Northern Kingdom since nowhere does the prayer make reference to the destruction of the temple. Some see this verse 27 as interrupting the logic of the prayer and so as a later insertion to counteract any false concept of the presence of God in the temple.[13] This may be, but the whole "name" theology of D, which is also involved here (see v 29), has the same purpose. We can, accordingly, proceed with our discussion without the necessity of fixing the exact time of composition.

Does this verse say that God is in no way present in the temple? The answer to the question is necessarily linked up with the meaning that D intends for the phrase that is characteristic of the tradition: "the place he has chosen to make his name dwell there" (see Deut 12,11; 14,23; 16,2. 6. 11; 26,2; also 1Kgs 8,16. 29; 2Kgs 23,27).[14] It could be asked whether the word "contain" in v 27[15] means to enclose as in a box or merely to possess in some way without suggesting a denial of the divine presence elsewhere. D would certainly exclude the first meaning. The question is whether the second meaning is also being excluded. And that can only be answered, again, by the meaning of God's name dwelling in the temple.

Almost all the scholars see in D's use of this phrase a reaction to a gross conception of God's presence being limited, or at least bound, to the material temple.[16] "To the Semitic mind, the name expressed and represented the person: God was present in a special way wherever the 'Name of Yahweh' was. The last development of this theology came when Judaism evolved the notion of the Shekhinah, 'the dwelling,' which is an attempt to express *the gracious presence of God amid Israel without taking anything away from his transcendence.*"[17] The italicized words illustrate the tension between divine immanence and divine transcendence which is our present concern. Thus, even though we read in v 30 that

God is asked to listen to Solomon's prayers "from your heavenly dwelling," this would not preclude, in de Vaux's view, a special presence in the temple.

De Vaux, of course, recognized that this is a more "spiritualized" conception of the divine presence than was had by many of D's compatriots. Jeremiah's famous temple address (7,1-15) clearly presupposes, on the part of the Judaeans, the dogma of the inviolability of the temple and probably also presupposed, as the basis of the dogma, some kind of conviction of a binding presence of God there. The prophet reminds them that only if they thoroughly reform their ways and deeds will God "remain with you in this place" (vv 5-7). These last words do imply a divine presence of some kind in the temple, even though it is in no way a binding presence.

This more "spiritualized" conception of the divine presence, suggested by the "name" theology, is accepted by other scholars. A very explicit expression of this is found in Robinson's commentary on 8,27-30:[18] "God was not to be thought of as being present in the temple in any sense which implied that he was absent from the rest of the world. God cannot be circumscribed, only approached. Our relationships with him are essentially personal. Yet God has accepted the limitation of an earthly dwelling place . . . So, God truly dwelt in the temple. Israel, in the person of the king, could meet him there and offer prayer."

A nuanced interpretation of this presence is offered by Gray.[19] "The Temple, as the sequel makes clear, is but the meeting-place of man and God, from where and to where man can address his prayers to the divine presence, which has been realized upon the invocation of his 'name.' God's 'name' is the extension of his personality from the remote sphere which is the proper dwelling place of the Lord transcendent ('heaven'), and it is there that he ultimately receives ('hears') prayer." Here, then, the presence is realized when the "name" is invoked. But it is difficult, in this writer's view, to think that D associated the *dwelling* of the "name" only with its invocation by the worshiper. If that were the case, would not some other term than "make to dwell" or "put" have been used?

Other scholars have taken a still more radical direction in the interpretation of the "name" theology. G. von Rad had written on this subject that "Deuteronomy is replacing the old crude idea of Jahweh's presence and dwelling at the shrine by a theologically sublimated idea."[20] What precisely is meant by "theologically sublimated" is not made clear, but E. W. Nicholson, in referring to von Rad's remark, understands it in an almost completely transcendent way.[21] "What is new in Deuteronomy . . . is the radical definition of this ("name") concept whereby not

Yahweh himself but his name is present in the sanctuary. In other words, Deuteronomy is concerned with emphasizing the distance between God and the sanctuary . . ." Later, in commenting on 1Kgs 8,27-30, he says: "This peculiar name-theology must therefore be seen as the theological background to the radically 'demythologized' view of the Ark in Deuteronomy 10,1f. and 31,24f. where it is no longer conceived of as the throne of Yahweh, he who is 'enthroned above the Cherubim' (see 2Kgs 19,15) but is merely the receptacle for the tables of the Law."[22] In this interpretation, then, the dwelling of God's "name" does not involve the divine presence itself, thus apparently voiding the notion that the name represents the person (de Vaux) or even that it is an extension of his personality (Gray).

Weinfeld, too, appears to take the same position. First of all, he argues that there is no difference between Deut's phrase "the place where I put My name" and Dtr's phrase "the place where My name shall be,"[23] as some had argued. He then goes on to say that the "most definitive expression" of the "name" theology is found in Solomon's prayer in 1Kgs 8: "According to this prayer, in which the functions of the temple are elaborately defined, the temple is not God's place of habitation, but serves only as a house of worship in which Israelites and pagans alike may deliver their prayers and their oaths to the Lord who *dwells in heaven.*"[24] Weinfeld, therefore, sees D's "name" theology as a rejection of the Priestly anthropomorphism which considered God as "enthroned upon the cherubim" and which "derives from early sacral conceptions."[25]

This review has certainly not resolved the question of D's precise conception of the divine presence in the temple. In this writer's view, Nicholson's and Weinfeld's contention of a radical break between God and his name[26] is difficult to integrate with the concreteness of the Semitic mind. Also, it is difficult to integrate with the evidences of D's conviction of the divine immanence discussed above. In view of that evidence it seems that Robinson's position is more balanced.

At any rate, what the review has done, it is hoped, is to show that the overall picture of God which D presents is one which passionately affirms the love and concern of God for his people and his desire to be associated with them in a special way. At the same time, D has taken a firm new step in upholding the transcendence of the Lord. Perhaps nowhere else in the Hebrew Bible are these two characteristics of immanence and transcendence so happily combined. It can be said that because D has asserted the divine transcendence so clearly (1Kgs 8,27 is the strongest affirmation), divine immanence can have the powerful meaning that it does.

NOTES

1. See *Worldview*, Summer, 1975, pp. 3-5.
2. Art. cit., p. 3.
3. J. Finn, art. cit., p. 2.
4. The term is not particularly relished by some scholars because of its suggestion of a form of panentheism. Some would prefer simply to speak of God's "presence."
5. The word "holy" in Hebrew, *qadoš*, probably has the root meaning of "apart" or "separated from."
6. R. Otto, *The Idea of the Holy*, New York, 1958, p. 63.
7. We are not primarily concerned here with the stages in the development of the Deuteronomic tradition but with the work as it now stands, including both the book of Deuteronomy, which we abbreviate "Deut", and the Deuteronomic History, which we abbreviate "Dtr." If the distinction of the stages of development is important for the point being made, it will, of course, be mentioned.
8. This follows from the chronological order of J, E and P.
9. For other characteristic words and phrases of Deut, see S. R. Driver, *Introduction to the Literature of the Old Testament* (9th ed., Edinburgh 1913) p 99-102.
10. M. Weinfeld, *Deuteronomy and the Deuteronomic School* (Oxford 1972) p 258f.
11. H. Cunliffe-Jones, *Deuteronomy* (London 1951) p 166.
12. *The First Book of Kings* (Cambridge 1972) p 98f.
13. T. Charry, "Une Demeure pour Dieu sur la Terre," *Bib Vie Chr*, 20 (1957-8), p 77.
14. It is interesting to note that *N.A.B.* translates the phrase in 1Kg 8:16, which reads literally "that my name may be there," as "to my honor." Again, in v 29, which reads literally "the place of which you said, 'My name shall be there,' " *N.A.B.* has "the place where you have decreed you shall be honored." This clearly takes the emphasis off the divine presence and suggests that God's name is present simply in the worship of the people.
15. In Hebrew it is the pilpel form of the root *kul*.
16. See R. de Vaux, *Ancient Israel* (New York 1961) p 326.
17. De Vaux, op. cit. p 327; italics added.
18. Op. cit. p. 102f.
19. J. Gray, *I & II Kings* (2nd ed. London 1970) p 221.
20. *Studies in Deuteronomy* (London, 1953) p 39.
21. *Deuteronomy and Tradition* (Philadelphia 1967) p 55f.
22. Op. cit., p 71.
23. Op. cit., p 194f.
24. Ibid. Italics are his.
25. Op. cit. p 192f.
26. This seems also to be the position of the *N.A.B.* translation in the two verses mentioned; see n. 14.

The Theology of Psalm 104*

ALFONS DEISSLER

Psalm 104 is held simply to be a Psalm of Creation. In its over-all design it portrays the creative rule of Yahweh in all spheres commonly called "the cosmos." It does this graphically; often it becomes nature poetry, for example v 12: "Beside them (the gushing springs) the birds of the air make their nests and sing among the branches." In the final stanza, however, the psalm assumes an historical dimension, that of salvation history, depicting a future world without evil. This is often unnoticed by readers and worshipers alike.

It is worthwhile not only to inquire into the theology of our psalm, but also to determine the significant meaning of how creation and history in their interdependence were evaluated in Israelite belief. The study of Psalm 104 can also provide an important contribution to our current reflections and discussions on the theme "Man and Nature."[1] Finally, it will be seen that our psalm is eminently qualified to be an ecumenical prayer for Jews and Christians especially in these times of deteriorating relationship between human beings and the rest of creation. We offer this contribution in the *Festschrift* honoring Msgr. Oesterreicher, with heartfelt good wishes.

I. *Preliminary Questions*

In light of textual criticism Psalm 104 does not pose special problems. The lack of agreement between the pronominal suffix of "kissito" with the gender of the object (v 6) is insignificant.[2] In place of the unique phrase "Trees of Yaweh" (v 16) the *Vorlage* of the Greek seems to have read "Trees of the field" (*šadday* connotes also "Almighty"). In v 17 the term *berošim* (cypresses) in the Massoretic text can remain even though the Greek reads *"be-rošam"* ("in their crowns"). In v 19 perhaps the

---

*Translation from the German by Mrs. Nora Quigley and the editors.

verbs should be vocalized as participles and it is unnecessary to amend " *'oniyyot"* (ships) in v 26 with *tanninim.*

From the perspective of motif and tradition history, our psalm certainly has been influenced by the "Hymn to the Sun" of Akhen-Aton, especially vv 19-24. However, it seems to have been transmitted in a Canaanite (i.e. Phoenician) world, where the motif of "The Battle of Baal with the Sea" obviously comes through in v 26. The influence of the encyclopedic wisdom lists of Egyptian natural science can also be presumed. Within the biblical tradition the relationship to Gen.1 is to be noted. It may be questioned, however, whether the priestly creation story serves as a model for the psalmist (so Gunkel). It could also be related to a tradition common to both texts.

The dating of the Psalm raises certain questions. In the past most commentators thought that the psalm originated in post-exilic times. H. -J. Kraus[3] dissociates himself from this position. M. Dahood opts for a pre-exilic date,[4] mostly because of the "numerous typically Phoenician forms, expressions and parallelisms." Moreover, Dahood's points are doubtful in several cases and the 'Phoenician influence' is also evident in post-exilic times, as reflected in the Book of Kohelet. In view of the elaborated development of the creation theme in exilic and post-exilic times (so Second Isaiah, Gen 1, Job 38-42) it would be difficult to ascribe a pre-exilic date for our psalm. It seems rather that it represents a hymnic echo of the already developed teaching about creation.

The question whether Psalm 104 had been written expressly for cultic use can be answered in the negative. The concluding Alleluyah could have been added later. "Bless Yahweh, my soul" at the beginning and the end indicates a hymnic structure for the individual, whereas the content offers indisputable evidence of wisdom tradition. Therefore it seems reasonable to include the psalm among the "Spiritual Songs"[5] which were written for both non-cultic and cultic (i.e. synagogal devotion) usage.

II. *The Structure of the Psalm*

It is difficult to discern a formal arrangement of this hymn which employs a 3 + 3 meter throughout. In the Massoretic text v 5 changes to a finite verb from the previous use of participles. V 10 again starts with a participle (with the article!), which is followed by finite verbs. Similarly it appears in v 13ff. In the Massorah v 19 begins with a perfect tense. V 24 is characterized with the exclamation *"mah"* (= how). With v 13 begins a series of wish-forms with jussives which ends only in v 32 with a descriptive form.

This formal study reveals a division of stanzas which vary in length: I. 1-4, II. 5-9, III. 10-12, IV. 13-18, V. 19-23, VI. 24-26, VII. 27-30, VIII. 31-35. This arrangement can be corroborated by the contents. Stanza I concerns the Creator of the heavens and Stanza II the Creator of earth. In Stanza III Yahweh sustains his creatures with water from the springs and brooks. Stanza IV glorifies the "Dispenser of Rain" who creates a viable environment of the plant world for men and animals. Stanza V depicts Yahweh as the Arranger of cosmic time. Stanza VI praises Yahweh as the Ruler over land and sea, Stanza VII as the Lord over life and death. Stanza VIII takes as a final theme the psalmist's joy over Yahweh's rule and kingdom.

The eight fold arrangement is not accidental. In the post-exile time it was considered as the "filled-out seven" (the symbol of perfection) as reflected for example, in the extension to eight days (Lev 23, 36) of the feast of Tabernacles (Deut 16, 13) which originally lasted seven days. Such eight fold division is seen in Psalm 119 with its 8 verses in each stanza. This relationship to the number seven is especially obvious in our psalm which relates the whole story of creation in seven steps until the eighth stanza, where the psalmist introduces himself as a committed believer.

III. *The Theological Theme of the Psalm*

1. God as Creator of the World

The God of the Covenant is the Creator of the world. In Gen. 2 the Yahwist already introduces the covenantal Name "Yahweh" as the most fitting term for the Creator, closely linking creation and salvation history. Our psalmist assumes this perspective and deepens it; this is closely related to Second Isaiah. Eight times he uses the covenantal name for the ruling Creator[6] (v 1 (twice), v 24, v 31 (twice), v 33, v 34, v 35). On the second occasion he even adds "Elohay" (= my God) as a responsive echo of the self-revelation of God in the covenant-charter of the Decalogue: "I am Yahweh your God, who brought you out of the land of Egypt, out of the house of bondage" (Exod 20, 2). It therefore follows that the psalm, pointing obviously to Yahweh's historical rule in v 4, 7, 9, 19, 31, 32, "moves" toward the *eschaton*, which Isa 66, 22 described as the "new heavens" and the "new earth". All of God's acts which are realized in the eternal munificence to the world and to men, as reflected in the name Yahweh, erect one continuous great arch for the psalmist. This "arch of the covenant" (K. Barth, J. Oesterreicher) spans and holds together all space and time. This view is extremely important also for Christian theology and faith-consciousness. "Order of creation" and "order of redemption" are usually separated from each other even though one cannot logically overlook their differences in the theology of grace. It leads to the conception of God the Creator in terms of power and wisdom but ignores the fact that creation and all its riches are gifts of the Covenant-God who lovingly turns toward us. The intention of Psalm 104 is to proclaim and inscribe this on the hearts and souls of God's people and the individual believers.

2. God the Creator as King

The idea of God's kingship originally belonged to the non-biblical concept of the origins of the world as, for instance, demonstrated by the Babylonian myth of the creation "Enuma elish." In it Marduk becomes the king of the gods and the world because he vanquishes the powers of chaos and out of them forms the cosmos. Baal also receives the title of king in Canaanite mythology because he defeated the sea-god *Yam*.

In Israelite religious history it took a long time to ascribe to Yahweh[7] the title of King perhaps because of the Molech-cult in Canaan which required the sacrifice of children to the king-god. The earliest reference to Yahweh as king appears in Isa 6,5. Isaiah views Yahweh as *"Melek"* both as "Creator of the cosmos" (6, 3) and—this becomes the specific Israelite idea—as the Lord of History who prevails over the chaotic powers with his plan for salvation (see Isa 52, 7), ushering in the eschatological kingdom of God. Both perspectives are interwoven in the Yahweh-King hymns (see Pss 93, 95, 96) even though they differ in emphasis.

Our psalm uses neither the title *Melek* nor the related verb form *malak*. It nevertheless praises Yahweh quite clearly as "King of the cosmos." The "greatness," which is predicated to God in the beginning of the hymn, is a favorite characterization for a king (see Gen 41, 10; 2 Sam 5, 10; Mic 5, 3; as to God [= King!] Ps 47, 3; 95, 3; 96, 4). Even clearer is the designation *hod wehadar* (highness and honor) which expresses the royal majesty (see Ps 21, 6; 45, 5; as to God—Ps 96, 6). God's royal raiment (see Isa 6, 1) is light itself, which was perceived by the Israelites as independent from the sun and the stars and specifically designates a closeness to God (see Gen 1, 3; Isa 60, 19). The "high dwelling place" (*'aliyyot*) above the heavenly waters is the palace of the King of heaven (see Amos 9, 6; Ps 29, 10). The "clouds as a chariot" remind one of the chariot of Yahweh in Ezek 1; the "wings of the wind" of the cherubim are also described there. The "fiery flames" (v 4) of the seraphim surround the throne of God the King in Isa 6. The subduing of *tehom* (v 6-9) corresponds to the mythical idea of the battle of the gods against the

Chaos (Enuma elish), i.e., against the primeval ocean (myth of Baal). Thereby the victorious God is designated with the title of king. Here, as in Ps 29, extra-biblical ideas concerning Yahweh are included. The extent to which the myth is suppressed can be established from v. 26: "There the ships are going to and fro and Leviathan whom you made to amuse you." In Canaanite mythology Leviathan is a powerful primeval dragon (see Job 3, 8) but here it is a sea creature formed by the Creator, obedient as a pet, with whom Yahweh jests and plays. At the end of the psalm God's royal power *(kabod, v 31)* reappears this time in a historical sense, with the elimination of all ungodliness from this earth (see Ps 96, 13; 97, 10ff.; 98, 9).

This pronouncement of "Yahweh as King" was a joyful message for Israel. It meant not only that he was an "absolute ruler" but that he was the God who used his might to subdue chaotic powers in the universe and in history. It is a message relevant to our times when the image of God as King is not only fitting but also meaningful and offers great promise: Neither the world nor humanity is drifting toward a final chaos, but a lasting reward is guaranteed to them in the Kingdom of Yahweh.

3. The constantly creating and ruling God.

God's royal rule is at once powerful and redemptive. This is the basic theme for our psalm. Therefore it presents not only a "creatio prima" as in Gen 1; from the third stanza onwards it introduces the "creator continuus." This "creatio continua" we sometime refer to as "preservation of the world" or "providence." All occurrences in nature and in the lives of men are continuing works of God. The participles in v. 10, 13, 14, 32 convey a durative function. In v 20, 28, 29, 30, 32 God's actions are even described with imperfect verb forms which emphasize continuous action. Contextually the twelfth stanza is most impressive: "All beings look to you, to give them food in due season; you provide for them and they gather. You open your hand and they are satiated with goodness. When you turn your face away, they are dismayed; when you take away their breath, they die and revert to dust. When you send out your breath, they are created, and you keep renewing the *face of the earth*" (v 27ff.).

Is such a notion of a continuous divine action in this world not simply naive and completely unacceptable to our modern scientific way of thinking? It is necessary to raise the question, for to respond with a simple affirmative answer is not sufficient. Our psalmist knows quite well about the relative independence of the created world. Therefore he relates the effects of God's works with examples of natural actions of his creatures, for example verses 8, 11-12, 14[b]-18, 21-23, 25-27. His view of God's created world is obviously dialectical: God is omnipotent, but his limitless power and wisdom (v 24) liberate his creation in such a way that dependence and independence do not negate each other. Is such a dialectical position compatible with human reason? If reason remains open to various "dimensions of being" while not deciding to reduce all reality to an unproven "single dimension," it may conceive of an almighty Creator and a creature (in this "vertical" relationship) having "horizontal" autonomy, as both are understood as working together *(concursus)*. In such a perpective, the psalmist's words (v 24) are refreshing: "The earth is full of your creation" (*qinyan* is well rendered by M. Buber as "Stiftung," establishment). This act of creation (v 30 uses *bara꜄*) does not involve physical work as far as the psalmist is concerned (in spite of the concrete terms!) but, at least in regard to living beings, it is accomplished through his *ruaḥ* (that is, his creative breath, v 29f, see Job 33, 4). Psalm 33, 6 links this *ruaḥ* with the idea of a divine creative word: "By the word of Yahweh the heavens were made, all their hosts by the breath of his mouth." This is surely how our psalmist conceives of God's creation as creative speaking since he is familiar with the tradition found in Gen 1 and Second Isaiah. It is a common idea in the Orient that God utters a powerful word and this word is consolidated into matter (see Ps 33, 9).[8] This is a grand concept which through its powerful imagery surpasses our abstract definitions of "creatio." It precludes any pantheistic explanation of the world. Only those unfamiliar with Hebrew Scriptures sense a pantheistic idea in Psalm 104, 29f. God's word and spirit emanate from him, and are simultaneously distinct from him. Yet one should avoid an extreme dualism: the act of creation, through word and spirit, unites the created world intrinsically with its Creator.

Our psalm certainly presents the created world in light of the old world view *(Weltbild)* which corresponds to a concrete preception. The contemporary *Weltbild* is different even though our language still functions within the dimension of our sense preceptions and daily experiences. For this reason can Ps 104 address us. It appears that our psalmist is not primarily concerned with the exact description of creation or even with its scientific explanation, but essentially with the relationship between God and the world, that is, the "creatio prima et continua." Whoever wishes can without difficulty integrate our modern macrocosmic and microcosmic *Weltbild* with the perspectives of Ps 104. According to the psalm's basic principle, all existence and its qualities are God's work and establishment. Thus a clearer light is shed on the Creator and creation, so one can declare enthusiastically: "Glory for ever to Yahweh. Yahweh rejoices in his works!" (v 31).

In contrast to Paul's expression: the "groaning of the entire creation" (Rom 8, 22)—(such sensitivity is expressed by many in our times)—Ps 104 is saturated with open optimism. Is it possible that our psalmist was not attentive to the suffering of this world? We note that v 29-30, within the realm of living things, explicitly refers to the painful experience of death. Still the writer does not question this phenomenon in the manner of Job, although he was familiar with this work. For our psalmist life and death "correspond" to the sovereign order of the omnipotent God. In this dark realm of human experience the psalmist acknowledges God as God. At the same time he believes that God's final ordering word does not apply to death but to life. In the seventh stanza he intentionally selects the rhythm of life: living—dying—living, and significantly stresses the final line: "You sent forth your spirit (M. Buber: Geistbraus) and all are created and you renew the face of the earth" (v 30). This thrust demonstrates that the psalmist did not intend to describe the cycle of life and death but focuses on the God of life. The final verse corroborates this future-oriented view, which points to the renewal of the present while the old is not destroyed but transformed.

4. Man as "Crown of Creation"

Gen 1 and 2 emphasize, each in its way, that man is the supreme creature, even that he is the goal of creation. According to Psalm 104 man seems to be rooted in, even totally absorbed by, the world. With the exception of Ps 104 there is no other text in the Hebrew Bible viewing humans and animals on even footing. Here God's living breath, which is applied in Gen 2 to man alone, refers equally to animals. Is the author approaching the skepticism of Kohelet? "Both (humans and animals) have one and the same breath *(ruaḥ)*. . . . Who knows whether the spirit of the human being indeed goes upward while the spirit of the animals goes down to the ground?" (3, 19-21). It seems that the optimistic tone of our psalm refutes such an idea. In v 29 the author simply adopts a view that the Creator implanted the drive for survival in his creation. On closer inspection, we find a profound difference between man and animal: an animal exists and goes on living in the world but man has a definite influence on his environment. *Adam* is closely related to *ʾadamah*, because he engages in cultivation (*ʿabodah*, v 14 and 23). In this capacity he is in a certain way an "imitator of God": Yahweh is the supreme ruler but man is commissioned in God's name to be the "overseer in the world." In this instance our psalm is closely akin to Gen 1 and 2. According to Gen 2 *Adam* himself is commissioned for the Garden of Eden, "to cultivate it (*ʿabad*) and to safeguard it" (Gen 2, 15).

In Gen 1, 26 man is put into this world as the "image of God" so that he can dominate it and rule it. This form of human rule, according to Ps 104, points to a realization of all possible properties intended by the Creator for nature. For instance God is the dispenser of earth's productivity as a whole, yet the ultimate forms of bread, wine and oil rely on man's extension of God's creative intention.

In the non-biblical myths of creation, the person was created to serve the gods (with food-, drink- and fragrant sacrifices). In the Bible, as exemplified by our psalm, the accent is on transforming the "service to the world" into "service to God." This is why scholars speak of the secularization of the biblical image of the human being. In a way this is correct, but one should not let the "service to God" be eliminated in the "service to the world." The creation of man in God's image (see Gen 1, 26.28) is evident in his delegated control over the rest of creation, but the deeper meaning of this image-relation of God and man is achieved only in the intimate dialogue between them. The psalmist himself realizes this relationship in his great hymn, when he expresses the wish: "May my meditation be pleasing to him (Yahweh)!" (v 34). At the same time he acknowledges: "I will sing to Yahweh all my life; I will give praise to my God while I exist." (v 34). The exclamation: "Bless Yahweh, my soul" which forms a framework for the psalm expresses the highest potentiality of a person turning to God: the human being can address the God of glory and goodness. The dialogue with the Creator bespeaks human responsibility for creation: the "horizontal posture" of his existence in this world is maintained by the "vertical posture" of his relationship with God. Man is a doer and an overseer but, at the same time, he is a believing suppliant with prayers and praise.

Man is portrayed against an agricultural background in Ps 104, but he is certainly not diminished thereby. The "governing in this world" embraces all human activities and conduct. Therefore, this psalm is relevant even in our technical and industrial era. The creative actions of man have ushered in this age. Psalm 104 supports the theological validity of this fact, although we might be going too far in seeking a "charter for technology" in the Bible. Nevertheless we find the command in Genesis: "Subdue the earth!" (Gen 1, 28), which is echoed by our psalm. Thus, it is rooted in the religious grounds of Judaism and Christianity. This leads to the conviction that the laws of nature have to be investigated scientifically to be placed at the service of man. This is to be evaluated positively. The Biblical view of "service to the world" is not responsible for excessive developments in the technical subjection of nature which endanger both nature and human life. So Psalm 104 offers an instrumental example that the commission for human beings to dominate the earth is a mandate to administer all as intended by the Creator. The perfecting of nature by humanity must be within the context of a "dialogue" with God. Only with the emergence of a technological civilization, and the resulting promotion of human "emancipation from God" were the given limits and measures of his outlook erased. On the other hand Psalm 104 opposes any self-glorifying control by man of the natural world entrusted to him (in this psalm v 10-30 stress nature's independent right to exist) and, on the other hand, it opposes the false promises of an "emancipation from God". The poet's God is Yahweh, a God of deliberate munificence, which comes to light in its luminous glory (*kabod*, v 31 see Ps 19, 2; 29, 9; 150, 1). It does not subjugate mankind like the sun makes it possible for life on earth in a state of dependence. Our psalmist can, therefore, formulate his thought as a wish: "May he (Yahweh) rejoice in his works!" This joy is manifested as an element of existence and the author is so convinced that it possesses him: "I rejoice in Yahweh!" (v 34). Here is a God who "plays" with the powers of creation, and who invites poetic singing and playing (*siah* v 34).

Our psalm is a magnificent human testimony of the fact that joy and freedom are intrinsically related.

IV. *Summary*

1. Psalm 104 is a significant testimony of the biblical message on creation. It is noteworthy that the doctrine of creation is expressed as a hymn. Israel did not employ abstract formulae in its teaching. There is a lesson for Christianity here.

2. Our psalm widens the view of the faithful suppliants from regional and ethnic limitations to a universal dimension. It incorporates cultic and sapiential traditions whose center was, apparently, the Jerusalem of the monarchial period. Apparently the concept of a royal Creator was integrated with the early dominant historical character of Yahwism, which Psalm 104 developed poetically in post-exilic times.

3. Psalm 104 knows and celebrates God of the covenant as the God of creation. Then all his works of creation are testimonies and signs not only of his power and wisdom but also of his munificence and his convenantal will. In this way creation and history fuse into "one arch of the covenant".

4. God the Creator not only establishes the beginnings but he is also present temporally and spatially as the guardian of his creation. All living things are indebted to him and to his creative breath and word, while they are subject to death which he decreed.

5. Man as the "crown of creation" should perceive himself as divinely

appointed to royal stewardship in the world. He is responsible for the further development of nature. This has to occur in a "dialogue" with God the King and through an ongoing apprehension of the incomprehensible order of the creation. Therefore nature must never be considered as man's "stone quarry" with which resources man can selfishly decide to build a self-glorifying, and therefore "God-less," world.

6. Psalm 104 summons all believers to a "secular piety" which is determined by a reverence to the Creator as well as by the joy in his works and gifts. This positive view of the world characterizes the piety of Jesus also. Like our psalmist he sees the Father affecting all his works. "He causes the sun to rise on evil men as well as good, and his rain to fall on righteous and unrighteous alike" (Matt 5, 45). "He feeds the birds in the sky" (Matt 6, 26), and "clothes the grass in the fields" (Matt 6, 30). Jesus said of the flowers that "not even Solomon in all his glory was robed like one of these" (Matt 6, 29). He must have observed them at length and drew them into his very being.

NOTES

1. Compare with this question O.H. Steck, "Zwanzig Thesen als alttestamentlicher Beitrag zum Thema: Die jüdischchristliche Lehre von der Schöpfung in Beziehung zu Wissenschaft und Technik", in *Kerygma und Dogma* 23(1977) p 277-299.

2. Aquila, Theodotion, Jerome, and Targum read third person singular feminine.

3. "The time of origin of this psalm cannot be determined. A pre-exilic date is not to be excluded from consideration" (BKAT [1] 1960, p. 709).

4. *The Anchor Bible,* Psalm III (1970) p. 33.

5. In spite of the possibly anachronistic terminology, H. Gunkel has observed this correctly.

6. The specific title in v. 16 is dubious.

7. Exod 15,18; Num 23,21; Deut 33, 5. These are not "archaic places," contrary to Soggin in *THAT* (1971) p. 916. The same holds true for Martin Buber's earlier use.

8. Compare L. Dürr, "Die Wertung des göttlichen Wortes im AT und im antiken Orient" (*MVAG* 42, 1) 1938.

A Hymn of Creation in Daniel

LAWRENCE FRIZZELL

Foremost among the areas suggested by Vatican Council II for fraternal dialogue among Catholics and Jews is the study of Sacred Scripture (*Nostra Aetate* 4). Fortunately this was already common among scholars investigating the Hebrew text and its ancient translations, and contacts were developing among exegetes. It is but the first step to learn what the human author intended. Each passage takes on an extended life when incorporated into the larger context of book and Testament. Differences will persist between Jewish and Christian interpretations of the total message, but we can profit from the insights offered by the other tradition.

In New Testament studies we try to discern which passages of the Hebrew Scriptures were applied by Jesus to his own life and ministry, and which were developed by the preacher-theologians of the early Christian communities.[1] The Qumran scrolls indicate that the application of biblical passages to persons as well as situations of a later period was part of the Jewish heritage, especially appropriate to a liturgical and/or prayer-study setting. To quote Dom Hubert Zeller, "More has gone into the Scriptures than man will ever take out of them"; knowing the hermeneutical tools employed by each tradition, Christians and Jews together can plumb the depths of God's gifts in the Word.

The incorporation of texts from the Hebrew Bible into the New Testament and the teachings of Christian communities is noticeable to even a casual reader. It is important also to recall that the Church took large sections of the Bible as they are and inserted them into the liturgy, where they became a vehicle of instruction and inspiration for the community of believers. The Psalter is the most obvious example of this

---

This essay is dedicated to Monsignor John M. Oesterreicher who, as a priest of the Latin rite, prayed the hymn of the three youths countless times as part of the Divine Office. This study appeared with an examination of Daniel by Asher Finkel in *SIDIC* (Rome) volume 11 (1978).

process. In certain manuscripts of the Greek Bible, a number of hymns are collected and placed after the 151 psalms attributed (for the most part) to King David. In Rahlfs' edition of the Septuagint they are called the nine odes of the Greek Church (Exodus 15, 1-19; Deut 32, 1-43; Samuel, 2, 1-10; Habakkuk 3, 2-19; Isaiah 26, 9-20; Jonah 2, 3-10; Daniel 3, 26-45, 52-88 and Luke 1, 46-55.68-79).[2]

The first known commentator on these odes in such a collection is Verecundus, bishop of Junca, who died in 552 A.D. He states that Ezra gathered these canticles, presumably for liturgical use.[3] O. Rousseau argues that Verecundus had no reason to invent this allusion to Ezra's work. Hilary of Poitiers credits Ezra with collecting the Psalms into one book, so perhaps Verecundus had access to a psalter with the canticles attached which alluded to Ezra.[4]

I. The present study is limited to Daniel; as the Prayer of Azariah (3, 26-45) has been subject of an essay by M. Gilbert,[5] we limit ourselves to the hymn of the three young men in the furnace (3, 52-90), considered first in itself and then as used by the Church.

Many scholars think that this hymn was composed in Hebrew.[6] The Aramaic text recording the account of the trial by fire ends with Nebuchadnezzar blessing the God of the three youths, and decreeing that no one may blaspheme him with impunity (3, 28-29). The prayerful recognition of God's presence and gifts complements this very beautifully.

In a recent commentary, Carey Moore divides the passage into an ode (3, 52-56) and a hymn (3, 58-90). He notes that God is addressed in the former, creatures in the latter.[7] Matthias Delcor describes the entire piece as a hymn, with introduction (v 51), praises to God (v 51-56), invitation to creatures (v 57-87) and the praises of the three youths for particular motives (v 88-90).[8]

We shall follow the division suggested by Moore, but will quote the Revised Standard version. Differences in order of verses between the Greek text of Theodotion and the Septuagint will not be discussed.

A. *The Ode*
>51 Then the three, as with one mouth
>praised and glorified and blessed God
>in the furnace, saying:
>52 "Blessed are you, O Lord, God of our fathers,
>and to be praised and highly exalted for ever;
>And blessed is your glorious, holy
>name
>and to be highly praised and
>highly exalted for ever;

53 Blessed are you in the temple of your
    holy glory
    and to be extolled and highly
    glorified for ever.
54 Blessed are you, who sit upon cherubim
    and look upon the deeps,
    and to be praised and highly
    exalted for ever.
55 Blessed are you upon the throne
    of your kingdom
    and to be extolled ar d highly
    exalted for ever.
56 Blessed are you in the firmament
    of heaven
    and to be sung and glorified for ever."

B. *The Hymn*
1. *Heavenly creatures are called to praise God*
57 "Bless the Lord, all works of the Lord,
    sing praise to him and highly
    exalt him for ever.
58 Bless the Lord, you heavens,
    sing praise to him and highly
    exalt him for ever.
59 Bless the Lord, you angels of the Lord,
    sing praise to him and highly
    exalt him for ever.
60 Bless the Lord, all waters above the heaven,
    sing praise to him and highly
    exalt him for ever.
61 Bless the Lord, all powers,
    sing praise to him and highly
    exalt him for ever.
62 Bless the Lord, sun and moon,
    sing praise to him and highly
    exalt him for ever.
63 Bless the Lord, stars of heaven,
    sing praise to him and highly
    exalt him for ever.

2. *Elements from heaven should praise God*
64 Bless the Lord, all rain and dew,
    sing praise to him and highly
    exalt him for ever.
65 Bless the Lord, all winds,
    sing praise to him and highly
    exalt him for ever.
66 Bless the Lord, fire and heat,

sing praise to him and highly
    exalt him for ever.
67 Bless the Lord, winter cold and
        summer heat,
    sing praise to him and highly
    exalt him for ever.
68 Bless the Lord, dews and snows,
    sing praise to him and highly
    exalt him for ever.
69 Bless the Lord, nights and days,
    sing praise to him and highly
    exalt him for ever.
70 Bless the Lord, light and darkness,
    sing praise to him and highly
    exalt him for ever.
71 Bless the Lord, ice and cold,
    sing praise to him and highly
    exalt him for ever.
72 Bless the Lord, frosts and snows,
    sing praise to him and highly
    exalt him for ever.
73 Bless the Lord, lightnings and clouds,
    sing praise to him and highly
    exalt him for ever.
3. *Earthly creatures should praise God*
74 Let the earth bless the Lord;
        let it sing praise to him and
        highly exalt him for ever.
75 Bless the Lord, mountains and hills,
    sing praise to him and highly
    exalt him for ever.
76 Bless the Lord, all things that
        grow on the earth,
    sing praise to him and highly
    exalt him for ever.
77 Bless the Lord, you springs,
    sing praise to him and highly
    exalt him for ever.
78 Bless the Lord, seas and rivers,
    sing praise to him and highly
    exalt him for ever.
79 Bless the Lord, you whales and all
        creatures that move in the waters,
    sing praise to him and highly
    exalt him for ever.
80 Bless the Lord, all birds of the air,

sing praise to him and highly
exalt him for ever.
81 Bless the Lord, all beasts and cattle,
sing praise to him and highly
exalt him for ever.
4. *The human race should praise God*
82 Bless the Lord, you sons of men,
sing praise to him and highly
exalt him for ever.
83 Bless the Lord, O Israel,
sing praise to him and highly
exalt him for ever.
84 Bless the Lord, you priests of the Lord,
sing praise to him and highly
exalt him for ever.
85 Bless the Lord, you servants of the Lord,
sing praise to him and highly
exalt him for ever.
86 Bless the Lord, spirits and souls of
the righteous,
sing praise to him and highly
exalt him for ever.
87 Bless the Lord, you who are holy
and humble in heart,
sing praise to him and highly
exalt him for ever.
88 Bless the Lord, Hananiah, Azariah,
and Mishael,
sing praise to him and highly
exalt him for ever;
for he has rescued us from Hades
and saved us from the hand of death,
and delivered us from the midst of the
burning fiery furnace;
from the midst of the fire he has
delivered us.
89 Give thanks to the Lord, for he is good,
for his mercy endures for ever.
90 Bless him, all who worship the Lord,
the God of Gods,
sing praise to him and
give thanks to him,
for his mercy endures for ever."

The relation between creation and history is clear in the phrase "God of our fathers" (v 52) and in the last stanza. The hymn draws heavily upon the psalms (especially 103; 148) and breathes a liturgical fragrance. From approximately the same period, a Qumran text "The words of the heavenly lights"[9] ends with a fragment under the rubric "Hymns for the Sabbath Day" which touches the same themes (see Ps 92, 1-5).

> "Give thanks. . .
> (Bless) his holy Name unceasingly
> . . . all the angels of the holy firmament
> . . . (above) the heavens,
> the earth and all its deep places,
> the great (Abyss) and Abaddon
> and the waters and all that is (in them).
> (Let) all his creatures (bless him) unceasingly for everlasting (ages).[10]

Delcor suggests that v. 53 refers to the Jerusalem Temple rather than to the heavenly Temple, because the expression "You sit upon the cherubim" indicates God's presence above the Ark of the Covenant.[11] However, another Qumran text[12] describes an angelic liturgy followed by a description of the *merkabah* (see Ezekiel 1-3). "The cherubim bless the image of the Throne-Chariot above the firmament, and they praise the majesty of the fiery firmament beneath the seat of His glory" (Vermes, p 212). Since all in the Temple is patterned after the heavenly prototype (see Exod 25, 9.40; Wis 9, 8, etc.), this Ode concentrates on the celestial reality. The phrase "You look upon the depths" (54) is understood better in this interpretation. The New American Bible transposes v 54 and 55; this gives an additional emphasis to the interpretation suggested here.

Following the Ode, it is natural for the poet to call first the heavenly creatures and the waters above the firmament (60) to bless God. God's creative activity has the same movement and, to some extent, the six-day structure of Genesis 1 is background for the hymn. The last section (82-90) is not only the culmination of creation in the human being and the Chosen People, but it also represents the community possessing the authority to call all works of the Lord to the duty of blessing him. Behind this must be the theology of man and woman created in God's image (see Psalm 8).

Jesus ben Sira's reflection on Gen 1, 26-28 articulates a theological background for this hymn in Daniel. It dates to approximately 200 B.C.

> "The Lord created man . . . and granted (human beings) authority over the things on earth.

He endowed them with strength like his own, and made them
in his own image.
He placed the fear of them in all living beings, and granted
them dominion over beasts and birds . . .
He set his eyes upon their hearts to show them the majesty of
his works.
And they will praise his holy name, to proclaim the grandeur of
his works."
(Sir 17, 1-10, see 39, 14-16; Wis 9, 2).

God reveals himself through creation (see Wis 13, 1-5); the acknowledgment of his attributes leads those made in his image and likeness to praise the manifestation of his person (the Name). Because God's Name is revealed at Sinai (Exod 3, 14; 34, 6-7), Jesus ben Sira moves immediately from creation to Covenant:

"He bestowed knowledge upon them, and allotted to them the
law of life,
He established with them an eternal Covenant, and showed
them his judgments." (17, 11-12).

In the same way, both Ps 148 and the hymn of the three young men come to a climax with the Chosen People, constituted because of the promise to the patriarchs (83, see 52 "God of our fathers"), represented by the priests and Levites ("Servants of the Lord"—Ps 135, 1-2, 20; 1Chr 9, 33) and exemplified by the righteous, defined as "holy and humble in heart." Typical of the righteous are the three youths, members of the tribe of Judah (Dan 1, 6).[13]

Usually, blessing is considered in its descending and ascending aspects: God's gifts and human acknowledgment (thanks for the gifts, praise to the Giver). It is striking that this entire prayer is pure praise until v 88, when motives for the ascending blessing are given. There seems to be a movement from the general response of creatures to their *raison d'être* to the specific deliverance of the martyrs. King Nebuchadnezzar intended to kill them, but fire did not harm them, even though their executioners died in the flames (3, 22.48). The Creator controls the forces of nature, placing them at the service of the righteous. The Book of Wisdom reflects thus on the plagues and the Exodus experience:

"For the whole creation in its nature was fashioned anew,
complying with your commands, that your children might be
kept unharmed . . . Fire even in water retained its normal

power, and water forgot its fire-quenching nature. Flames, on the contrary, failed to consume the flesh of perishable creatures that walked among them." (Wis 19, 6.20-21).

The finale (89-90) reverts to the litany formula (Ps 106, 1; 136) of the Temple liturgy as the theme which unites all worshipers of the one God:

"Give thanks to the Lord, for he is good, for his mercy endures forever."

The goodness of God manifests itself in forgiveness (Prayer of Azariah) and in other forms of mercy towards those caught in the ambiguities of the human order.[14]

II. Christian interpretations of the hymn consider it first within the context of Nebuchadnezzar's persecution, indeed as a source of inspiration to the Church in a similar trial.[15] Hippolytus, priest of Rome, wrote the first extant Christian commentary on the Book of Daniel about the year 202-204 A.D.[16] It deserves our attention.

The Greek texts of Daniel 3, 1 note that it was in the eighteenth year of his reign that Nebuchadnezzar made the golden statue. The first two letters of the name Jesus in Greek add up to the number eighteen. So, according to Hippolytus, Nebuchadnezzar "imitated Jesus, the Son of God, who when he lived in the world, raised up his own statue from among the dead, that is the man that he was, and manifested it, pure and irreproachable (as if from gold), to his disciples. The sixty cubits in height imitate the sixty patriarchs who prefigured, according to the flesh, the statue of God, the Word . . . The six cubits in width imitate the six days of creation, for it was on the sixth day, molded in dust, that man was created" (II, xxvii).

The theme of resurrection develops also from the fact that fire burned the bonds but not the clothes of the martyrs (Dan 3, 25.27). God's power can restore the corruptible body just as he preserved the clothes which shared the holiness of the young men (II, xxviii).

As in the Köln papyrus 967,[17] Hippolytus attributed the prayer of Azariah to all three youths. After confessing their sins and those of Israel, they invited all creatures to join them in praising, blessing and glorifying God. In his summary, Hippolytus adds after v 63: "Bless, all you elements who move in the heavens, sing praise to him and exalt him for ever." After, "sons of men" (82), Hippolytus named the beings of the underworld, the *spirits* of the angels of Tartarus (see 2Pet 2,4; James 2, 19) and the *souls of the just*. Thus, he interprets v 86 as referring to demons and the dead; the litany should be all-inclusive. "After making the rounds of all creatures, they name themselves as the smallest, the most humble" (II, xxix).

Then Hippolytus speaks directly to the youths, requesting their prayers so that he may obtain the reward of martyrdom.[18] He asks them to describe the fourth person in the furnace (Dan 3, 25). "Who is this man who, by your mouth, reviewed all creation without forgetting any creature that exists or existed? You only spent an hour in the furnace, but you learned all the creation of the world. It was the Word which was with you, and who spoke by your mouth, because he alone knows the way in which the world was created . . . They named everything: celestial, terrestrial, and subterranean beings, proving thus that everything created by God's Word is his servant." (II, xxx).

Hippolytus identifies the angel who brings a dew-laden breeze to the furnace (Dan 3, 49-50) with the one who drowned the Egyptians and punished the Sodomites. He is the "Angel of great counsel" (Isa 9, 6 Septuagint, see Rhabanus Maurus, P.L. CXIII c. 1152) and therefore is related to Jesus as the Messiah (II, xxxii).[19]

Chromatius, bishop of Aquileia (387-407?) relates the rescue of Paul and Silas from prison (Acts 16, 23-26) to the three youths and notes that when two or three are gathered in common prayer, the Lord will be with them (Matt 18, 20) to rescue them (C.C. IXa p. 492-493).

The canticle of the three young men entered the Christian liturgy at an early date. Writing about 406 A.D., Rufinus noted that it was sung by Christians throughout the world (P.L. XXI c. 612-614). In the seventh century the council of Toledo expressed concern: "The hymn of the three youths, in which all creatures of heaven and earth praise God, and which the Catholic Church celebrates everywhere, is neglected by certain priests in Sunday Masses and martyrs' feasts" (canon 14). The Roman Missal used the canticle as a text on Ember Saturday, and suggested it for the priest's thanksgiving after Mass. The fourth biblical prayer of Lauds in the Divine Office was always a canticle of the Old Testament. The song of the three youths was selected for Sunday Lauds (followed by Ps 148). This relates to the commemoration of creation on the first day of the week.

As the word "Benedicite" (the common title of the hymn as used in the Office) indicates, the liturgical text begins with v 57. Instead of the motives given after the names Hananiah, Azariah and Mishael (v 88), the Church inserts "Let us bless the Father and the Son with the Holy Spirit; let us sing praise to him and highly exalt him forever." As with many of the psalms, Christians considered this hymn to be "open" to a reading in the light of the way in which revelation developed through Jesus' teaching. The interpretation of the experience in the furnace to

Christ's redemptive work goes back to Hippolytus, if not earlier. The inclination to seek hints of the Trinitarian mystery throughout the Old Testament provided the basis for this addition. It is, of course, a variant of the usual prayer ("Glory be to the Father . . .") which terminates each psalm.

" 'The three, as with one mouth . . . praised God' (v 51). These three men . . . symbolize the elect of God who, united in belief of the Holy Trinity, adore, worship and proclaim one God, Father, Son and Holy Spirit. . .".[20]

The ecclesiastical use of this hymn ends with v 56, addressing God directly in his eternal dwelling-place. This would seem to be the Church's expression of a desire to unite worship of the earthly community with that of the heavenly court, as in the *Sanctus* and the *Te Deum*.

Often an additional note of interpretation is found in the antiphon recited before and after a given psalm or canticle. The antiphon for the ordinary Office throughout the year reads: "The king commanded, and the three children were cast into the furnace, fearing not the flame, but saying: Blessed be God." The duty of creatures to praise God in word and deed is placed within the context of the total response which is martyrdom. At Easter, there is an explicit link with the resurrection of Christ: "He who delivered the three children from the burning fiery furnace, Christ is risen from the grave." The antiphon for the feast of Jesus' Baptism (the Sunday after the Epiphany) is of particular interest: "The fountains of water were hallowed when Christ appeared in glory on earth. Drink water from the fountains of the Savior (see Isa 12,3); for now Christ our God has sanctified every creature."

The recent reform of the Office places the "Benedicite" at Lauds of the first and third Sundays in the four week cycle and at Lauds of major feasts; it uses Dan 3, 52-57 at Lauds on the second and fourth Sundays. The antiphon for Easter Sunday now reads: "Our Redeemer has risen from the grave: let us sing a hymn to the Lord our God."

The Church uses this canticle to express her vision of creation's response to God, both in his creative activity and provident presence to all levels of nature and in the coming renewal which is the Kingdom, whose first-fruits are found in Christ's resurrection (1Cor 15, 20-28). Although one may wonder whether this prayer developed from a Jewish theology of the human being as high priest of creation (recalling the cosmic symbolism in Philo's description of the High Priest's vestments), this is certainly present in the Christian vision of reality. The two components of the phrase "kingdom of priests and holy nation" (Exod 19, 6) may have been applied to the entire people of Israel, at least in Hasmonean times, and this is the Christian understanding. "You are a chosen race, a royal priesthood, a holy nation, God's own people, that you may declare the wonderful deeds of him who called you out of darkness into his marvellous light" (1Pet 2, 9).

Like the leaven in the dough (Matt 13, 33), the movement of creatures through history towards the Kingdom consists in a presence orienting and co-ordinating all things to serve God. Those created anew in Christ (2 Cor 5, 17) conform themselves ever more to his image (Gal 4, 19) so that they can help bring the inanimate world to the service of love (Matt 25, 31-46), wherein the image of God is recognized in all human beings. It is singularly appropriate that the "Benedicite" is suggested as a prayer after the celebration of the Holy Eucharist. Having elevated bread, wine and other elements of daily life to the mediation of God's highest gift to his people, the Christian community recognizes that every level of creation is straining toward the same goal (Rom 8, 19-23), and through Christ is more and more integrated into the crescendo of thanks-and-praise which is a response, in time and beyond, to God's gift of himself.[21]

NOTES

1. See, for example, the forthcoming monograph by Asher Finkel *Vigilance in the Gospel of Mark*.
2. Some manuscripts add Isa 5, 1-9; 38, 10-20; the Prayer of Manasseh; Luke 2, 29-32; "Glory to God in the Highest." See H. Schneider, "Die biblischen Oden in christlichen Altertum" *Biblica* 30(1949) p 28-65; 432-453.
3. The commentary is edited in *Corpus Christianorum* (Latin series) XCIII. No manuscript of the Hebrew Psalter exists with the Odes attached; see Schneider, p 33.
4. O. Rousseau, "La plus ancienne liste de cantiques liturgiques tirés de l'Ecriture" *Recherches Sciences Religieuses* 35(1948) p 129.
5. M. Gilbert, "La prière d'Azariah" *Nouvelle Revue Theologique* 96(1974) p 561-582.
6. Winfried Hamm, *Der Septuaginta-Text des Buches Daniel Kap. 3-4 nach dem Kölner Teil des Papyrus* (Bonn: Rudolf Habelt 1977) p 57, 249. (I thank Father Arthur McCrystall for use of this text). For a revision back to Hebrew, see Curt Kuhl, *Die Drei Männer im Feuer, Beihefte ZAW* 55(1930). In 1894 Moses Gaster published "The unknown Aramaic original of Theodotion's additions to the Book of Daniel". This essay has been reprinted in *Studies and Texts in Folklore, Magic, Medieval Romance, Hebrew Apocrypha and Samaritan Archaelogy.* (New York: Ktav 1971) volume I p 39-68; volume III p 16-21.
7. Carey Moore, *Daniel, Esther, and Jeremiah: the Additions* (Garden City; Doubleday 1977) p 75. We follow his division of the hymn on the same page.
8. M. Delcor, *Le Livre de Daniel* (Paris: Gabalda 1971) p 103.
9. M. Baillet, "Un receuil liturgique de Qumran, Grotte 4: les paroles des luminaires" *Revue Biblique* 68(1961) p 195-250.

10. G. Vermes, *The Dead Sea Scrolls in English* (Harmondsworth: Penguin[2] 1975) p 205.

11. Delcor, p 104.

12. John Strugnell, "The angelic liturgy at Qumran" *Oxford Congress Volume*, Supplements to *Vetus Testamentum* 7(1960) p 318-345.

13. Moore, p 73, considers the names in v 60-88 as listed "in ascending order of importance". This judgment fails to take into account the all-inclusive nature of the phrase "sons of men", and the parallelism of the succeeding verses. In the last centuries of the second Temple period, it was recognized that belonging to the Chosen People included an explicit call to righteousness and holiness on the part of the individual. This was accompanied by a sense of unworthiness and sinfulness exemplified in the Qumran *Hodayot* (1QH). Thus, the truly righteous are recipients of gifts and must be "humble in heart". They would not be considered the "most important" but the Israelites who have lived the vocation for which all have been chosen.

14. Probably the stories of the three youths and Daniel in the lions' den were circulated among Palestinian Jews during the persecution of Antiochus IV Epiphanes. In 2Macc 6-7, the martyrs give witness by their blood and God's triumph is in terms of resurrection and final retribution in the new life. Note the valiant mother's speech: "I beseech you, my child, to look at the heaven and the earth and see everything that is in them, and recognize that God did not make them out of things that existed. Thus also mankind comes into being. . . Accept death, so that in God's mercy I may get you back again with your brothers" (7, 28-29). The allusion to the Maccabean martyrs in relation to Dan 3 is made early in the third century (Hippolytus of Rome, *Commentary on Daniel*, II, xx; see xxxv on the reason God does not act thus to save the Christian martyrs). St. Augustine asks this question in *Sermo* 32 (*C.C.* XLI p 406) and *Enarrationes in Psalmis* 32 and 136 (*C.C.* XL p 1277, 1988).

Earlier, Tertullian discussed the power of prayer in spirit and truth (John 4, 23) with reference to Daniel. "Of old prayer delivered from fire, beasts and famine (Dan 3, 93; 6, 24; 14, 33-39) and yet did take its form from Christ. . ." Christian prayer transforms the individual so that he understands the mystery of suffering for God's name (De Oratione 29, C.C. I p 274).

15. See Margaret Schatkin, "The Maccabean Martyrs" *Vigiliae Christianae* 28(1974) p 97-113, for use of other texts.

16. G. Bardy, *Hippolyte: Commentaire sur Daniel* Paris Editions du Cerf, (1947) p 17.

17. Hamm, p 249.

18. Sermons in the early Church frequently draw a parallel between the three youths and St. Lawrence of Rome, who was burned alive.

19. Because St. Jerome cannot understand how the wicked Nebuchadnezzar could have seen the Son of God, he follows Symmachus, who translates "son of God" by "angel"; see Commentary on Daniel Book III (*C.C.* LXXVa p 807-808).

20. Rhabanus Maurus, *P.L.* CXII c 1152; see Cyprian, De Dominica Oratione 29, *C.C.* IIIa p 111, Rupert von Deutz, In Daniele liber unus *P.L.* CLXVII c 1505-07; John Beleth, Summa de Ecclesiasticis Officiis, *C.C.* (continuatio medievalis) XLIa No. 30d, 85a, 92c.

21. Although the Jewish liturgy does not make use of prayers preserved in the Greek additions to Daniel, many of the themes found in the "Benedicite" are developed in the later "Pereq Shirah" (see *Encyclopedia Judaica* 13 c. 273-275.)

"To Worship God in Spirit and in Truth": Reflections on John 4, 20-26*

OTTO BETZ

a) The problems of the text and previous attempts at solution.

"God is spirit, and those who worship him must worship in spirit and in truth" (John 4, 24) — this dogmatic sounding utterance represents a high point in the conversation between Jesus and the Samaritan woman at Jacob's well near Shechem (Sychar). It confirms the Solomonic judgment concerning the dispute about Gerizim and Jerusalem:

> "Woman, believe me, the hour is coming when neither on this mountain or in Jerusalem will you worship the Father. You worship what you do not know; we worship what we do know, for salvation is from the Jews. But the hour will come, and is now, when the true worshipers will worship the Father in spirit and truth, for such the Father seeks to worship him" (John 4, 21-23).

One must ask what such a worship in spirit and truth means. Furthermore, how is this strange aspect of time, the juxtaposition of present and future, to be understood? Finally what is this search by God for the true worshiper? V22 is full of problems: Who are those who know about the true worship? On what is their knowledge that salvation comes from the Jews grounded and what does this salvation mean concretely? It is also astonishing that in v25 the Samaritan woman was not satisfied with Jesus' statement and referred to the Messiah who "will tell us everything." Yet this seemingly skeptical response, which Jesus rejects, leads to the messianic self-revelation: "I who speak to you am he" (John 4, 26). At this point one could ask: What does the Messiah

---

*Translation from the German by Mrs. Nora Quigley and the editors, with corrections by the author.

have to do with worship in spirit and in truth? How could the Samaritan woman expect a full explanation from the Messiah after just having experienced and acknowledged Jesus as a prophet (John 4, 18f) and after having asked his opinion on the true place of worship (4, 20)?

R. Bultmann has attempted to solve this problem in light of literary criticism: In this chapter, with its many inconsistencies, the evangelist has utilized and commented on various sources such as written *Vorlagen*, and his work was finally published by an ecclesiastical redactor who added several insertions.[1] A so-called *"Semeia-Quelle"* (Sign Source), which offers the "signs" of Jesus to the evangelist, contains among others a conversation with a Samaritan woman.[2] Bultmann includes the verses (4) 5-9. 16-19. 28. 30. 40 in this basic source and considers v 25f as belonging to it also. In this source which derives from the Hellenistic Church Jesus is depicted according to the ideal "Divine Man" (*Theios Anēr*, i.e. *Theios Anthrōpos*), miraculous power and supernatural knowledge of human nature establish messiahship.[3]

The evangelist provided the story of Jesus' conversation at the well with an introduction and with ample commentary by developing it further through theological reflections. He is responsible for the verses 1-3 (4). 10-12. 15. 20-22a. 27. 29. 31-39.

Bultmann assumes that some sentences from the non-Christian source of Gnosticizing *"Offenbarungsreden"* (revelatory discourses) were also added, for instance, vv 13-14 and 24, and probably v 23.[4] Finally v 22b appears as a gloss from the pen of the ecclesiastical redactor, because this verse is not compatible with the otherwise negative assessment of the Jews in the Fourth Gospel. Also, v 22a should be considered a gloss; in any case it refers to the contrast between Samaritans and Jews; however, it is likely that John, employing "we", places these two groups, which are labeled as uncomprehending, in contrast to Jesus and his disciples.[5]

This literary criticism concluded that the particular, questions-provoking verse about true worship stems from the evangelist. He deliberately inserted the mention of it into Jesus' conversation and supplied the answer with the help of the pre-Christian Gnostic revelatory discourses. According to Bultmann, John intended to elevate the stories from the *Semeia*-source, which usually reflects a primitive, objectifying *theologia gloriae,* to the level of his own Christology. According to it, the revelation of the Son of God is to be believed in contrast to his appearance, namely that as a "pure human being" Jesus of Nazareth claimed that he was the Saviour sent by God and the all-decisive eschatological event. In accord with this Christology the cultic veneration for God in vv 20-24 is not only something spiritual, internal but stands in relation to eschatology. It is appropriate to God's being because it is unworldly: The spirit manifests itself as God's marvelous deed for human beings, which occurs in the word of proclamation, and the truth as the reality of God, which lifts the believer up from worldly existence and places him in the eschatological, truly free way of being.[6]

Recently, in articles on John 4,22, F. Hahn and K. Haacker have refuted Bultmann's interpretation.[7] After a good summary of the divergent opinions in exegesis, F. Hahn proposed that in chapter 4 John reworked an old *Vorlage*, which in essence is identical to the stories of the *Semeia-Quelle* reconstructed by Bultmann. He designates it form-critically as a *"Mission Legend"* which originally did not relate to the Messiah but to the Samaritan *Ta'eb*, the "returning" redeemer (p. 73). The evangelist resolved the tension-filled relationship between Samaritans and Jews as given in the *Vorlage* by proclaiming Christ as the one who brings universal salvation, he who opened the way to a proper worship of the Father and to a unity of all true worshipers of God (p. 74). According to F. Hahn, verses 20-26 form a unit to which v 22, rejected by Bultmann, also belongs: The intrinsic connection of these verses becomes apparent when the whole unit is left in its present form (p. 75). Hahn proves convincingly that v 22b fits very well into the overall theme of chapter 4. One notices that in v 9 Jesus is addressed as a Jew and, as such, he is an opponent of the Samaritans, but in v 42 he is acknowledged as the "Savior of the world." The statement in the middle— "Salvation is from Jews" (v 22)—appears a necessary pointer which allows for the bridging of the contrasts, the linking of the two poles (p. 76); John 4,22b is genuinely Johannine (p. 82). Hahn thinks that the tension between the salvation history role of the Jews and the critique of their unbelief is established throughout the fourth Gospel and evident in its theological validity (p. 76-83). Salvation comes from the Jews because they are the bearers of the witness to divine promises, as "descendants of Abraham and followers of Moses who pointed to Christ", and "God has bound himself to his promise" (p. 82). From this Hahn also explains v 22a: The Jews know about the God promising salvation. Thus, insofar as they reject Jesus, can they be reprimanded concerning their unbelief and the offense of their disposition coming to expression therein (p. 82). Hahn has made good observations, but the reason given here for the salvation history role of the Jews is not convincing. The Samaritans too are sons of Abraham and have, like the Jews, Jacob for their father (v 12: the evangelist!). They also have Moses who points to Christ in his Law (John 5,46). Why should they not also know the proper worship of God?

The essay of K. Haacker[9] goes further concerning these points. He demonstrates the value of the literary critical analysis of John 4 through the verification of religion-history elements in it. Above all, this holds true for verse 22a, which criticizes the ignorance of the Samaritans: see Sir 50, 25f, according to which "the foolish people live in Shechem", and T. Levi 7, where Shechem is mentioned as "the city of the ignorant." To these can be added the message sent to Antiochus Epiphanes by the Samaritans, according to Josephus (Ant 12,258-264), which supports such criticism. Already in the second century B.C. this reproach about foolishness plays a role in the dispute between Jews and Samaritans, and in this context John 4,22a finds its place (p. 111-119). Haacker likewise offers an exegetical basis for the dogmatic sounding statement of John 4,22b in the messianically interpreted passage Gen 49,10. According to the blessing given by Jacob (see John 4,5f), the tribe of Juda assumes a key role for Israel's salvation (p. 120-122). As a consequence of this literary critical judgment it follows that v 22 as a unit is, as it were, a sectarian yet a Jewish *("judaistische")* answer to the question in v 20, while vv 21.23f transcend the historical conflict between Jews and Samaritans. Haacker considers that v 22 is more primitive, the section vv 21.23f being a reflective insert by the evangelist. When one leaves it out, a close relationship results: Jesus' remark on salvation being from the Jews (v 22b) is echoed by the reference to the coming of the Messiah attributed to the Samaritan woman in v 25 (p. 123).

Still, Haacker's worthwhile suggestions do not offer a fully satisfying explanation to the questions posed above. It seems to me that there is no difference between a partial, more primitive concept of salvation and a later, universal one, especially no different literary strata. One must begin methodically from the unity of the text and understand it in its inner logic. This entails going back to its spiritual foundations in the Old Testament and in the Jewish traditions. Haacker failed to do this for John 4,22a, and he did not see the full influence Gen 49,10 had on John 4, 22b.

b) The difference between Samaritans and Jews: the influence of 2Kings 17,24-41 (see Josephus, Antiquities 9,288f).

The fundamental text on the origin of the Samaritans and their cult is found in 2Kings 17,24-41. It would be strange if the evangelist who was so fully aware of the difference between Jews and Samaritans had neglected this. It mentions specifically the ignorance of the Samaritans with regard to the true worship of God and also the disastrous results: "They do not know (*lo' yad$^{e\varsigma}$u,* LXX = *ouk oidasin,* see John 4,22a: *ouk oidate*) the law of the god of the land; therefore he has sent lions among them (according to Ant 9.289, an epidemic) which are causing havoc, because they do not understand how to give due worship to the god of the land. So the king of Assyria gave the following order: 'Send back one of the priests whom you carried away from there; let him go and live there and teach them how to give due worship to the god of the land' " (2Kgs 17,26f). The proper worship brings redemption, according to Josephus, salvation (*sōtērion* 289). With this background, we can notice that in John 4,22a, Jesus compares the ignorance of the Samaritans to the knowledge of the Jews (Jews and not Christians are meant) regarding the true worship of God. The reference to John 4,22b also becomes clear: salvation for the Samaritans came from the Jews. One can go a step further and ascertain the place of v 22 in the whole of John 4. Even Jesus' revealing statement to the Samaritan woman, "You have had five husbands and he whom you now have is not your husband" (v 18) is dependent on 2Kgs 17. It describes not only the woman's unsuccessful married life but also symbolically the perverted service of God by her people, as 2Kgs 17,29-33 (and Ant 9,288ff) described. The five Samaritan tribes worshiped each a strange god on the high places, as well as God, the Lord. While seven strange gods are mentioned in 2Kgs 17,29-31, Josephus stated that each of the five Samaritan tribes brought its own god, so thus the impression of five gods arose. "The Samaritans feared the Lord, but also worshiped (*ʿabᵉdu*, LXX = *elatreusan*) their own gods with the practices of the nations from among whom they had been carried away" (2Kgs 17,33). In John this syncretistic joining of worshiping strange gods and the one true God is transposed into a chronological succession: The Samaritan woman had five husbands and the one she has now is not her husband. This succession can be explained from 2Kgs 17,34 a statement that is also important for John 4,22a, because it attests to the continuing ignorance of the Samaritans: "To this day they do according to the former practice. They do not fear the Lord in the right way and do *not* abide[10] by their statutes or ordinances or the law or the commandment which the Lord had commanded the sons of Jacob, whom he named Israel." From this one can surmise that the Samaritans had abolished the worship of idols and worshiped only Yahweh but "they worship what they do not know" (John 4,22a) for only the Jews had knowledge.

From this biblical background Jesus appears in John 4 first of all in the role of the Jewish priest who once had taught the true worship of God to the Samaritans. The Samaritan woman recognizes him as such as she asks him about the proper way to worship (v 20). He is, as it were, a traveler from foreign lands, the Jewish prophet who sees into her problem-filled life and as a prophet like Moses (Deut 18,18) knows an answer to all the questions of her people. She awaits this teacher in the Messiah, too (v 25). He may be compared to the returning Elijah in Judaism or to the awaited Prophet who will tell them what must be done with the stones from the defiled altar of the Temple (1Macc 4,46). Finally, he is reminiscent of the unnamed man who, according to Josephus, wanted to show to the Samaritans on Mount Gerizim the holy vessels which should be buried there where Moses placed them.[11] Just as Jesus wished to gather the lost sheep of Israel (see Matt 15,24) so he sought out the Samaritans (John 10,16) because, according to God's historical decree, they were the sons of Jacob (2Kgs 14,34). Thus, he wants to restore the unity of the people of God. As previously mentioned, K. Haacker has pointed to polemics between Jews and Samaritans behind John 4,22 and he mentions especially Sir 50,25f and T. Levi 7 wherein the Samaritans are depicted as foolish people, and Deut 32,21, serving as scriptural background for this (p. 111f). But in John 4,22 the direct reference is to 2Kgs 17, whereby the evangelist wants to show how Jesus tries to do away with Jewish-Samaritan ignorance and polemics. The Jews must prove themselves as helpers to the Samaritans.[12] The unity of the section John 4,18-22 becomes clear. But the question concerning the true worship of God in John 4,23-24 remains open. Does it also have a basis in the Old Testament?

c) The overcoming of opposition: The commitment to true worship at Shechem (Josh 24).

In 2Kgs 17,34-41, the obligation of the Samaritans for proper worship is shown explicitly: They too belong to the "sons of Jacob" (v 34, see John 4, 12) to whom God gave his Law. With them too he made his covenant in which he commanded them not "to fear, to bow down to any other gods (*hištaḥawah*, LXX = *proskynein*, Targum *s^egad*), not to serve them (*ʿabad*, Targum *p^elaḥ*), nor to sacrifice to them, but you shall fear Yahweh, who brought you out of the land of Egypt with great power and with an outstretched arm; you shall bow down to him, and to him you shall sacrifice" (2Kgs 17,35f). From this the background of the Johannine verb *proskynein* becomes clear: it corresponds (in the strict sense) to the Hebrew verb *hištaḥawah* (LXX *proskynein*) central to 2Kgs 17,35f. This text also contains the related concepts fear of God and especially worship (service) of God, *ʿabodah*, which according to Aboth 1,2 is one of the three pillars of the world. Also important in 2Kgs 17,35-38 is the covenant and the reference to God as he who brought Israel out of the land of Egypt. From this the road leads to another biblical tradition which is also important for John 4. It is the making of the Covenant at Shechem (Josh 24) whereby Israel is exhorted to abandon idol worship and to choose the worship of the one true God, who delivered them from slavery in Egypt. In this pericope we find a firm scriptural basis for John 4,23-26.

Before we explain the details, there must be a brief comment on the concepts of "spirit and truth" which, according to John 4,23f, describe the character and manner of the new eschatological worship of God. Of the indications mentioned in v 24 on the being and action of God, only the mark of the Spirit is to be expected for the new worship of God, for God is spirit. The word "truth" gives the impression of being a later insert since it is not the exact equivalent of "spirit" as indicated, for instance, in the expression "the Spirit of truth" for the Paraclete (John 14,16f). The "spirit" is the power of God's creative work, which can "beget a human being from above" and which prepares him for God's kingdom (John 3,3-6); the opposite of the spirit is the flesh. "Truth" is the essence of God's revelation which comes through the Word made flesh (John 1,17), but also is predicated of human action inasmuch as it is performed "in God" and therefore does not have to fear God's light and the final judgment (John 3,21). The opposite of truth is not only falsehood, but also the evil and the reprehensible which are manifested in the deeds of the "old person" (John 3,20). The definition that God is spirit can be drawn from the Bible[13] but there is no scriptural basis for worship in "spirit and truth" (John 4,23f). This does not apply to the Johannine expression "grace and truth", which is well attested biblically (Gen 32,10; Hos 4,1; Ps 40,11, etc.). How does the link between spirit and truth come about, and why as the sign of worship is spirit completed by the concept "truth?"

We find an important indication for this in Joshua 24, a chapter to which we must turn from 2Kgs 17,24-41 in any case. Joshua appears at the assembly at Shechem as the representative of God (Josh 24,2) who reveals himself to the Israelite congregation as the Lord of history: He led Abraham into the Land (v 3); then by his marvelous helps he freed the people from the domination of Egypt (vv 4-7) and after a long wandering in the desert he brought them into the land of Canaan where he helped to vanquish their enemies (vv 8-12). In all these events God showed himself to be the "Redeemer" (v 10) and as a gracious Lord he gave Israel a land not acquired by their own labor to be their possession (v 13). In response to this merciful guidance God expects proper worship, an unequivocal decision by the people for Yahweh and a definite denial of other gods: "So now, *(weʿattah)* fear Yahweh and serve *(ʿibedu)* him in sincerity and truth *(betamim ubaʾ emet);* put away the gods which your fathers served beyond the Euphrates and in Egypt and serve Yahweh (alone!)" (v 14). Joshua places before them the alternative choice of idol worship but clearly renounces this for himself: "But as for me and my house, we will serve Yahweh!" (v 15). The people follow his example and ceremoniously reject the other gods, acknowledging the

God who led them in history and saved them from oppression (vv 16-18): "We will serve Yahweh our God and his voice we will obey" (v 21. 24). That day Joshua made a covenant with the people, and made statute and ordinance for them at Shechem (vv 25-28).

The relationship between Joshua 24 and Jesus' conversation in John 4 is immediately evident. Obvious points of contact are the place Shechem, and, the similarity of persons (there it is Joshua, here Jesus (= Jehoshua) who are both representatives of God). But above all, the theme of Joshua 24 is like that of John 4, 20-26: the decision to worship the true God in contrast to the gods of their fathers[14] which has to be made "now."[15] Thus the making of a covenant at Shechem with the obligation to worship God "in truth" was binding on all of the Israelites including the tribes of the Samaritans later. In Joshua 24, 14, as well as in John 4, 23f, we find a dual characterization of proper worship, namely "in sincerity and truth." In John 4, 23f this formula is introduced again and explained. It is likened to the being of God which is defined as spirit. This emphasizes that true worship is correspondence, reaction and answer to the revelation of God's being; as is shown in Shechem to be the grateful acceptance of God who revealed himself to his people as a helper and redeemer. Thus, the definition of God in John 4, 24 is seen as a summary of the historical revelation of the gracious God; "in spirit and truth" are experienced as his ways of acting, as a gift bestowed on human beings. The spirit is the power that will be given to the elect in End-time. In "spirit and truth" the eschatological and the historical, traditional dimensions of proper worship are united. With "truth" the Samaritan woman, who asks about true worship, is reminded of the ancient promise made by her forebears, sworn in the community of Israel to serve God in truth (Josh 24, 14). She is guided through the dark episode of Samaria's history in 2Kgs 17, through the cloud of ignorance and syncretistic cult to the covenant of Shechem and its commitment: The "must" (dei) of true worship of God (John 4, 24) has its basis in this emphatic reminder. However, Jesus is not only a prophetic preacher as Joshua once had been, but is also the Christ, the one anointed by the Spirit (v 25f). He ushers in the End-time, which bears the mark of the eternal and therefore is also the era of the Spirit, corresponding fully to God's being and actions. For this reason, worship of God is now qualified by the concept of "spirit" and is thus eschatologically oriented. Joshua too was a "man in whom the Spirit dwells" (Num 27, 18) and resembles the Johannine Jesus "on whom the Spirit rested" (John 1, 32f). The Samaritan woman saw in Jesus a successor of Moses and therefore a man like Joshua, who was the immediate successor of Moses. In John 4, 19, she calls Jesus a "prophet", thinking of the reference in Deut 18, 15-22 according to which a prophet like Moses = Joshua will arise. Her messianic expectation is also influenced by this promise: The coming Messiah should proclaim everything as the new Moses who, according to Deut 18, 18 will relate to Israel what God puts into his mouth. Finally, we must mention Joshua's exemplary and decisive confession to God, whom he will serve with his entire household (Josh 24, 15). According to John 4, this has a correspondence in Jesus. In contrast to the disciples, who are concerned about food for the body (John 4, 31-33), Jesus says that his food is to do the will of him who sent him and to accomplish his work (John 4, 34). This statement by Jesus reminds us of the rabbinic play on words: *maṣṣot* and *miṣwot*. But the unity of Jesus with God is not only that of the pious, who do God's will, and that of the prophet, who possesses God's Spirit, but also that of the Son, who carries out what he sees the Father doing (John 5, 19f) and collaborates in creation and new creation (John 1, 3; 5, 21); the Son not only possesses the Spirit, but he also gives it (John 20, 22). Thus, worship in spirit is the activity of those who are begotten by God through the Spirit (John 3, 5f) and called his children (John 1, 12f). Therefore, they pray in the Spirit to God as their Father (John 4, 23f) and listen to Jesus who tells them the truth as does the Samaritan woman.

It is significant in this reminiscence of Joshua 24 in John 4 that the covenant of Shechem united the now separated tribes of Jews and Samaritans into one Covenant- and worship-community. Secondly, at that time no precise place of cult was designated for divine worship in truth. The conflict which broke out later whether Gerizim or Jerusalem should be that place seems from this perspective to have been introduced historically and improperly. Not the place, but the form of divine worship is decisive, namely, full concentration upon the one God which guarantees a response to his works. As characteristics of divine reality, spirit and truth have the power to transcend human discord and to create eschatological unity. The dispute between Jews and Samaritans had been ignited because of terrestrial perspectives on the place for revelation and divine worship.

A second Old Testament passage which may shed light on John 4, 23f, is Ps 42 and 43, which form a unit. The suppliant who is abroad, in the area of the Jordan's source and Mt. Hermon (Ps 42, 7), and seems oppressed because of his loyal devotion to God so far away (Ps 42, 10f), remembers the pilgrimages to the house of God (Ps 42, 5). But he is now deprived of these, being far from God in a foreign land. Earlier, in the company of pilgrims he had experienced the blessings of God's presence. Now in his desperate situation he prays:

> Send out your light and your truth! Let them lead me, let them bring me to your holy mountain and to your dwelling! Then I

will go to the altar of God, to God my exceeding joy; and I
will praise you with the lyre, O God, my God (Ps 43, 3f).

Here the desired goal is divine worship in the Temple. The physical
distance makes a pilgrimage impossible but God's light and truth are
called powers which eliminate the dividing might of space and, as it
were, allow for a spiritual divine worship. The prayer from afar finds its
way to God, and divine worship in light and truth consists of praise of
God, whom one trusts as Savior (Ps 43, 4; 42, 12). The waters of the
Jordan are not life-giving but rather frightening, recalling the power of
Tehom (Ps 42, 8), whereas light and truth are sought as helping powers.
With this text in mind one can understand the statement in John 4, 23b:
God seeks those who worship him; his initiative is emphasized here. He
gives them light, truth and the holy Spirit which will lead people to him.
God's benevolent approach makes true divine worship possible. The
eschatological view of Jubilees 1, 15-17 is also important for this statement. There God promises the ingathering of Israel and the building of
his temple. He desires to live with them and they will be his people in
truth and faithfulness. They "will seek me, and I shall be found by
them" (Jub 1, 15-17). God must be sought and spirit and truth are God's
gifts for the seekers. This becomes clear in the texts that stand between
the Old Testament basis for true divine worship and its eschatological
re-establishment by Jesus, namely, the writings of the Qumran community.

d) Divine worship in spirit and truth at Qumran.

The Qumran texts are pertinent to our theme not only because the cult
of that community was separated from that of the Temple in Jerusalem,
but also because in them the close association of spirit and truth occurs.
Here the concept "truth" occupied the foreground in divine worship.
The waiting for God's revelation in Hab 2, 3 is fulfilled (according to
1QpHab 7, 10-12) in the attitude of the pious and the "men of truth",
"whose hands shall not tire in the service of truth *(me'abodat ha'emet)*
when the final age is prolonged." Service of truth means divine worship
in a comprehensive sense. In the Community Rule (1QS, *Serekh ha-*
Yahad) it is stated that the "foundation of the spirit of holiness for eternal
truth" *(y'sod ruah qodeš l'emet 'olam* 9, 3-5) is established in Israel
through the council of fifteen men. This atones for the sins of the people
and obtains God's benevolence for the Land. The community in whose
life the holy spirit and truth are embodied[16] understands itself as a
living, spiritual sanctuary (1QS 8, 5f; 9, 6f) which replaces the defiled,
malfunctioning Temple in Jerusalem. Their life in spirit and truth effects

forgiveness better than any sacrifices. "The proper offering of the lips shall be as an acceptable fragrance of righteousness, and perfection of way is a delectable free-will offering" (1QS 9, 5). The phrase "foundation of the spirit of holiness for eternal truth" means also that God himself is the builder of this spiritual house and fills it with his power (see 1QH 6, 25f). Thus it is founded in truth (1QS 8, 4) and its living stones become witnesses of truth at judgment (1QS 8, 6). In the Hymns *(Hodayoth)* this worship, oriented toward the consummation of history, is performed; they give an example for a "thanksgiving offering of the lips." It joins in the spiritual worship of the angels, with whom the community knows it is already invisibly united. There is a second place in the Community Rule where spirit and truth are mentioned as the foundation of the new, eschatological existence. 1QS 3, 6ff speaks of the sanctification of human beings: One is not purified through rites of atonement and immersion alone, not even the waters of seas and rivers can accomplish this. Only through the "spirit of God's true counsel" can the ways of a person be expiated of all failings, so that he can behold the light of life (3, 6f). Through the holy spirit, who is given to the community by God's truth, man will be cleansed of all his sins (1QS 3, 8). Water and spirit should not exclude each other any more than in John 3, 5ff, but belong close together. The holy spirit, which here too is united with truth, is the power which purifies and renews old, sinful human beings. Thus the context makes clear how the cleansing and life in spirit and truth come about: Through the humble submission to God's precepts (1QS 3, 8) and through perfect conduct in the ways of God as he commanded concerning times appointed for him (1QS 3, 9f). The Qumran community stands in the tradition of the Covenant on Mount Sinai, and also in that of Shechem when it strives for a perfect and true divine worship. It is a "house of perfection and truth" in Israel *(beth tamim we'emet,* see Joshua 24, 14) wherein one brings an offering of pleasant fragrance and where the covenant is established according to the eternal precepts (1QS 8, 9f). The members of the community are told to "do truth and righteousness, and justice and loyal love and to walk humbly each with his neighbor." Into these words, taken from Micah 6, 8, the "doing of truth" is inserted; we find this expression in John 3, 21, too. Truth is given in the Torah insofar as it is understood and interpreted correctly and one encounters the holy spirit in the holy Scripture which is revealed by the spirit (1QS 8, 15f). The Teacher of the community too is graced by the spirit (1QH7, 6f). Both ideas are somewhat burdened by a sectarian narrowness and a polemical intent since only the community actualizes them in the present. On the other hand, even it is still imperfect. The complete purification of the elect through the spirit and God's truth is awaited in a baptismal act which God himself will accomplish from heaven. Only then will knowledge and conduct become irreproachable like that of the angels (1QS 4, 20-22). The promises of Ezekiel 36, 25-27 stand in the background of both Jesus' statement in John 3, 5-8 and 1QS 4, 20-22.

In Qumran we find also the familiar expression "Spirit of truth" of the Johannine farewell discourses,[17] but the statement "God is spirit" is missing. Instead God is defined as truth (IQH 4, 40; 15, 25), where it is clear that this expression wishes to emphasize the character of God's historical deeds in relation to human beings: his mouth (1QH 11, 7) and especially his actions are truth (1QH 14, 12; 1QH 1, 30; 1QS 10, 17). God's truth proves itself in his loving attention toward men, and "he judges with great pity and forgiveness" (1QH 11, 8f). Thus it becomes possible for the actions of a purified person to be in "his truth" (1QH 6, 8f). The benedictions (1QSb) show clearly that proper divine worship represents the human response to God's benevolence. He is the Source of all blessings (1, 5). "He opens from heaven an eternal fountain which (shall not deceive)." He will "(not withhold the waters of life from) the thirsty" (1, 6). This means that God is merciful with the holy spirit and grace (2, 24), merciful with eternal truth (2, 28). The blessing of Aaron is thereby furnished with the gifts of spirit and truth. Ultimately a priestly worship with the angels is made possible through the power of such blessings. We find that in these blessings the themes of John 4 also appear. The fountain which gives water for eternal life (see John 4, 14) plus the gifts of Spirit and truth make an eschatological worship possible (John 4, 23f).

In the Temple Scroll from Cave 11, recently published and richly commented on by Y. Yadin,[18] a program for an "unspiritual," that is, for a real cult in the Temple is offered. Here the concepts of "spirit and truth" appear only rarely with a different meaning.[19] Instead of this, the design, the buildings, courtyards and implements of the Temple, which God commanded Moses to build, are described in detail (Columns 3-12; 30-45) and also the various sacrifices and gifts for the feasts (16-30). Further, we find descriptions of instructions for the purification of the Temple and the holy city (45-47), the laws for the holy life of the people, where especially the second part of Deuteronomy serves as a basis. It is obvious that this scroll describes a sanctuary that Israel should have built, and not a temple erected by God at the end of time.[20] In the scroll God Himself announces: "I will sanctify my Temple through my glory because I will let my glory dwell upon it until the day of blessing (i.e. the last day), when I will create my Temple in order to establish it myself forever according to the Covenant which I made with Jacob at Bethel" (29, 8-10). The building of a new temple is promised also in Ethiopic

Henoch 90, 27 and in Jubilees 1, 15-17. God declares: "And I shall build my sanctuary in their midst and I shall dwell among them. I shall be their God and they shall be my people in truth and in faithfulness" (Jub 1, 17). In Jub 1, 23 the gift and the purification of the holy spirit is promised to God's people of this time with the filial relationship. God will be their father "in truth (uprightness) and faithfulness" and he will love them (Jub 1, 25). Again we find Johannine motifs: the dwelling of God among men (see John 1, 14), the truth as one of the two basic powers of eschatological existence (see John 4, 23f) and the giving of the Spirit, whereby the Israelites become true children of God (John 1, 12f; 4, 23f). The recollection of the Covenant which God made with Jacob at Bethel[21] concerning the eschatological sanctuary which God himself will build is important. The eschatological Temple represents the redemption of the promise which God made to Jacob at Bethel.[22] This throws some light on the obscure remark in John 1, 51 according to which Jesus' disciples will see the heavens open and the angels of God ascending upon the Son of Man (see Gen 28, 12). According to John 2, 19-21, the Son of Man is the sanctuary which is destroyed on Good Friday and is rebuilt on Easter Sunday in which eschatological glory dwells (John 1, 14). So he himself is the fulfillment of what Jacob saw at Bethel, he is the place declared holy by angels. This is also important for the conversation at Jacob's well: Jesus is the true wellspring and the sanctuary of God (John 4, 14). The worship in spirit and truth is therefore not tied to a localized temple, to a mountain chosen by God, but to a person, the "Holy One of God" (John 6, 69) from whom salvation comes. This is why the teaching about the true worship is placed in a messianic framework (4, 19, 25f) and is concluded with the self-revelation of the Messiah (4, 26). Therefore the statement about salvation coming from the Jews is central to the teaching (4, 22). This no longer means salvation which is due to the knowledge of Jews but specifically the redemption that Jesus the Messiah brings.

e) The messianic basis for true worship: salvation comes from the Jews (John 4, 22b).

In light of tradition history, the statement in John 4, 22b is determined by Jacob's blessing of Judah (Gen 49, 10): "The sceptre shall not depart from Judah, nor the ruler's staff from between his feet until Shiloh (to whom it belongs? the ruler?) comes, and to him shall be the obedience of the peoples." This prophecy, which probably applied to David originally, has three different concepts, namely the "sceptre" *(meḥoqeq)*, "Shiloh"[23] and the obedience *(yiqqehah)* of the peoples. How were they interpreted in the New Testament times? The Septuagint looks upon the sceptre as a leader *(hēgoumenos)*, upon Shiloh as "the things stored up for him" (ta apokeimena autō for seloh), and upon the obedience as the expectation (prosdokia) of the nations. In the so-called "Patriarchal Blessing" from the Qumran Cave 4 (4Q Patr 1-7) the sceptre is applied to the covenant of kingship which God made with the house of David (obviously reading $m^eḥuqqaq$, a Pual). Shiloh is interpreted messianically, and precisely in connection with Isa 11, 1.4 and 2Sam 7, 12f as "the Anointed (Messiah) of righteousness, the offshoot from David, for to him and his offspring is given the covenant of kingship for eternal generations" (4QPatr 4). The obedience of the peoples does not receive comment. In the Targums to Gen 49, 10[24] the sceptre is understood to be the scribe (Onkelos), or collectively, as the scribes who teach the Torah (Jerusalem Targum I and II). Accordingly, the Jews are the teachers. Shiloh is the Messiah to whom kingship belongs. The nations will obey him (yištame ʿun Onkelos), i.e. serve him (yišta ʿb^edun Jerusalem Targum II). Gen 49, 11 was understood as indicating the military subjugation of the nations because the blood of the grapes applied to the blood of enemies. In the Apocalypse of John, Christ is portrayed as the victorious Lion from the tribe of Judah, but his victory over his foes is achieved on the cross (Rev 5,5). Christ is also the lamb that was sacrificed (Rev 5, 6) and the believers have washed their robes in his blood (Rev 7, 14; see Gen 49, 11). Paul plays on Gen 49, 10 in Rom 15, 12 but relates it also to Isa 11, 1.10: "A shoot springs from the stock of Jesse, . . . rising up to rule the nations, and in him shall the nations trust" (LXX). According to Paul the coming of this Messiah will lead the Gentiles to true worship of God (Rom 15, 8-12). In the conversation with Jesus in John 4 the Samaritan woman understands that he alludes to Gen 49, 10 in speaking of salvation from the Jews. She responds to him in v 25: "I know that the Messiah comes (= is coming)." This knowledge is based on Gen 49, 10, whereby like the Jewish exegesis, she understands the coming Shiloh messianically. The evangelist too presents this interpretation as correct when he explains the pool of Siloam to mean "sent." He is thinking not only of the root šalaḥ = to send, but also Gen 49, 10 (Shiloh). For him Jesus as the Messiah is the Son sent from the Father. This concept is central to Johannine theology.[25] The awaited didactic activity of this coming Messiah is also an interpretation of Gen 49, 10 for the Samaritan woman (4, 25). "To whom shall be the obedience of the people" means that they will listen to him as an authoritative teacher (see Targum Onkelos yištam^eun), as the woman listens to him and later on her fellowmen (4, 42). In John 4, 22b the expression about the coming of Shiloh is described as the salvation (sōtēria l = y^ešuʿah) which will come to human beings through the Messiah Jesus (Y^ehoshuʿa). He is the Saviour of the world (John 4, 42).[26] Even for the Samaritan woman he is more than simply a teacher of salvation. His "declaration" (anaggellein, v 25) points to the realization, the coming of salvation. The woman grasped this after Jesus' self-revelation in v 26. In v 29 she proclaims Jesus as the one who told her everything she had done, and thus the Christ, the one who has been sent, who forgives her sin in the name of God. The word of forgiveness establishes the community of salvation; in other words, fellowship with Jesus means salvation. For this reason the Samaritans declare after Jesus had stayed with them for two days (John 4, 40): "We have heard for ourselves and we know that this is indeed the Savior of the world" (John 4, 42).

The Messiah of the Jews, from the tribe of Judah, brings salvation not only to the Jews but to the nations. John 4, 22b is to be understood in a universal sense. The conversation with the Samaritan woman in John 4 has an intent similar to that with Nicodemus in chapter 3. There the discussion concerning the new creation through God's Spirit develops into testimony about the Son of Man Who will be lifted up on the cross so that everyone who looks at him believing will have eternal life (3, 3-16). So in John 4, the discussion about the living water and proper divine worship leads to the Messiah who, by his coming will give not only instruction but also his life for the salvation of all. In John 3, through cross and exaltation of the Son of Man, Ezekiel's prophecy about the new creation through God's Spirit is realized (Ezek 36, 25-27). So too, these events constitute a prerequisite for life in the forgiveness by God (4, 19), for divine worship in spirit and truth (4, 23f), and for the salvation of the world (4, 42). God comes to the world in his Son and seeks people who will worship him. In contrast to Jewish tradition, John 4, 23 reverses the direction of this search: it is not that human beings should seek God, but God seeks them by sending his Son; therefore he talked with a Samaritan woman; this was surprising to her and to the disciples (4, 9.27). Indeed, with Jesus the Messiah is already here and salvation is already present. On the other hand, his hour has not yet come inasmuch as worship in spirit and truth belongs to the post-Easter future.

This worship is connected also with Gen 49, 10 and the Jewish tradition of interpretation. It indicates the Johannine understanding of the obedience of the nations. The Samaritan woman interprets it to be attentive listening (*š^ema‘*, so Onkelos), Jesus understands it as service (*yišta^b^edun*, Jerusalem Targum II). By this he does not mean the enslavement of subjugated nations to the Messiah, but the service of all people for God whom they see as their Father. The word *w^elo* = "and *him* (shall they obey)" (Gen 49, 10) now refers to God; the service of the nations becomes divine worship (see also Rom 15, 8-12). Thus the concept "truth" takes a new meaning. Referring to God, it indicates the unity of word and deed, promise and fulfillment, which will become evident in the final age. The truth of God's love for the world emerges especially in salvation through Christ (John 3, 16) and therefore belongs together with God's grace (John 1, 17). For this reason, the worship oriented to God in truth is not offered properly if the new law of love (13, 34f) is not fulfilled with it.

Conclusion

The examination in light of tradition-history makes it clear that from its biblical basis John 4,20-26 (or for that matter, the entire chapter 4) is so closely intertwined that any literary critical division appears to be arbitrary and its assignment to various sources seems unlikely. It is not possible that the same scriptural texts serve as the basis for a part of the revelatory discourse (v 23f), the *Semeia Source* (v 25), the commentary of the evangelist (v 21) and a gloss of the redactor (v 22b). Such coincidences do not occur. In the Fourth Gospel we have before us the uniform work of John, the seamless robe of Christ. Moreover verses 4,20.22 are not a particular Jewish answer to the Samaritan woman's question in contrast to a universal one in verses 21,23f. Rather verse 22b interprets Gen 49,10 in a universal way. The *Messias Judaeorum* is the salvation for all nations.

Does this exposition belong to the evangelist alone, or is it rooted in Jesus' legacy and in early Christian tradition?

1) In Acts, Luke narrates how the promise of the eschatological gift of the Spirit was fulfilled at Pentecost. From heaven Christ poured upon the disciples the Spirit which, as the exalted One, he had received from the Father (Acts 2,33). In the power of this Spirit the Apostles proclaimed in various languages to an international crowd God's great saving deeds (Acts 2,4-11). It is clear that God seeks men, making worship in the Spirit possible, and also that this worship consists in praise of God's great deeds. As Peter said in his Pentecost sermon, the prophecy of Joel was fulfilled with the outpouring of the Spirit. God manifests his truth in the last days by transforming his word into action (Acts 2,17). The Spirit is given to all human beings without distinction (Acts 2,17f, quoting Joel 3,1-2), and salvation is realized on the day of the Lord. For "whoever calls on the name of the Lord shall be saved"

(*sōthēsetai* Acts 2,21 quoting Joel 3,5). In calling upon this name the Christian appeals to the great saving events of cross and resurrection, which bestowed on him forgiveness and new life in the power of the Spirit. Joel 3,5 plays an important role in early Christianity and indeed with both meanings possible in the Hebrew form *yiqra'*, the active and passive (or reflexive) Niphal *yiqqare'*.[27] Christians are those who call upon the name (Acts 9,14.21), and who acknowledge this Jesus as the Christ (11,26). In the power of the Spirit, whom they received at baptism, they confess Jesus as the Lord (1Cor 12,3), and thereby his saving power. On the other hand, all nations upon whom God's name is called will search for the Lord (Acts 15,17). As in John, the new worship is based on God's saving action in Christ. One proclaims this event and acknowledges Jesus as the redeeming Lord. This tradition appears also in Paul's writings: worship consists of confession, the invoking of the name in which salvation is guaranteed (Rom 10,9-13).

What about the role of Jerusalem? In Acts 2, Luke thinks of the unquoted continuation of Joel 3,5: "For in Mount Zion and in Jerusalem, shall the Savior appear . . . and they who have glad tidings, whom the Lord has called" (LXX 2,32). For Luke, Jerusalem is the place where the history of Christ as the revelation of salvation was manifested (Acts 1,4) and therefore the origin of the Christian mission (Acts 1,8). What the prophets Isaiah and Micah said about the central, enlightening role of Zion at the end of time (Isa 2,2-4; Mic 4,1-4) is fulfilled in the Church's mission. Luke was thinking especially of Isaiah 2,3. "Out of Zion shall go forth the Law, and the word of the Lord from Jerusalem." This is the main theme of Acts and for this reason the gospel there is called the "Word of God" (of the Lord). For Christians the "instruction" goes out from Jerusalem as shown by the apostolic council (Acts 15). Yet nothing can be found there about the most important statement of this Isaiah text, namely, the promised pilgrimage of the nations (Isa 2,2-3a). "Come, let us go up to the mountain of Yahweh, to the house of the God of Jacob; that he may teach us his ways and that we may walk in his paths." For Luke, Jerusalem is the place of the Word, which goes forth to the nations, but not the goal of a pilgrimage, and not the only place where God is worshiped in truth. The Jerusalem community worshiped in the Temple (Acts 2,46), but this was not required of Gentile Christians. Prayer in the name of Jesus and in the power of the Spirit, the praise of God, took place in distant, widely scattered communities (see 1Cor 14; Col 3,26). Forgiveness and sanctification are no longer linked to Jerusalem. Peter emphasizes in his sermon at the apostolic council that God gave the Holy Spirit to the Gentiles and purified their hearts through faith (Acts 15,8f). Advocating God's grace and the freedom from the Law for the Gentiles, Peter influences the council as a guide to Shalom (Petros is linked with the Hebrew word *paṭar* = to declare free).

2) As at last we go back to *Jesus*, we find that he proclaimed the universal salvation brought to pass by the Messiah. "For the Son of Man came not to be served but to serve, and to give his life as a ransom for many (i.e. for all)" (Mark 10,45). The Evangelist John interpreted this statement of Jesus anew in 3,16 and made its universal meaning very clear.[28] Jesus purified the Temple of Jerusalem because he saw it as a house of prayer for all nations (Mark 11,15-17), but he also proclaimed the building of a new sanctuary not made by human hands (Mark 14,58). As the reference to a period of three days indicates, he meant by this the repentant Israel (see Hos 6,2), the community of the Messiah which defies the assault of the power of chaos (Matt 16,18; see 1QH 6, 25ff). This spiritual house of God signifies also a spiritual worship introduced with the gospel of "Today," the fulfilled prophecy and God's great year of liberty, as Jesus once proclaimed it in Nazareth (Luke 4, 16ff, quoting Isa 61, 1f).[29]

3) Worship in spirit and truth, as it occurred at Qumran and even more strictly among Christians, especially the circle around Stephen, represents an important innovation in antiquity. This worship without a sacrificial cult can also be taken for granted for the synagogues of the Greek-speaking Jews in Egypt, as indicated by the name "prayer house" *(proseuchē)* for the synagogue.[30] It also appears in the Stoa.[31]

The spiritualization of worship was further advanced in Christian gnosis. In the logion 76 of the Gospel of Philip from *Nag Hammadi* there appears a spiritual explanation of three chambers in the Jerusalem Temple structure. They refer to the three sacraments: the "holy" (house) points to baptism, the holy of the holy (one) to redemption, the holy of the holy ones to the bridal chamber, which is the symbol for the divine world of the pleroma (col 117,14; 118,4). It seems that column 117,30-36, which is a very damaged section, mentions those who do not worship in Jerusalem but rather in spirit and in truth.[32] Here too, the tearing of the veil in the Temple is mentioned which is elaborated further in logion 125. The veil. . . . "was rent from top to bottom (see Matt 27,51). Those above opened to us who are below in order that we might go into the secret of the truth" (col 133, 10.13).[33] This entering means the passing through the worthless symbols and weaknesses of earth to the perfect heavenly glory (col 133, 14-17).

These statements are closely related to Johannine thought but are further expansions. Worship in spirit and truth is celebrated as praise of the heavenly world but also as overcoming the earthly, illusionary world of an evil demiurge. The Holy Spirit, received in the gnostic sacrament, is the power of the world-conquering gnosis and the awaited salvation is found in the return of the individual soul to its heavenly abode. This is no longer the truth as John proclaimed it.

NOTES

1. *Das Evangelium des Johannes,* (Göttingen, Vandenhoeck & Ruprecht, 1964[10],) p. 127-142.
2. Assignment to this source is not totally certain, any more than to the section John 1,35-50. In this regard, see D. M. Smith, *The Composition and Order of the Fourth Gospel,* (New Haven: Yale University Press 1965) p 38.
3. Op. cit. p 131, see my article "The Concept of the So-Called Divine Man in Mark's Christology", in A. P. Wikgren Festschrift, Suppl. to *Novum Test* 33 (1972), p 229-240.
4. Op. cit. p 127f.
5. P 139 note 6.
6. P 140. For a critical analysis see also H. M. Schenke, "Jakobsbrunnen-Josephsgrab—Sychar. Topographische Untersuchungen und Erwägungen in der Perspektive von Joh 4; 5; 6", *ZDVP* 84(1968) p 159-184. Schenke finds four layers in our chapter, the *Vorlage* has the verses 5-7, 9, 16-23, 28-30, 35f, 40.
7. In *Wort und Wirklichkeit: Festschrift für Eugen Ludwig Rapp* (Meisenheim 1976).
8. "Das Heil kommt von den Juden. Erwägungen zu Joh 4, 22[b]", p 67-84.
9. "Gottesdienst ohne Gotteserkenntnis. Joh 4, 22 vor dem Hintergrund des jüdisch-samaritanischen Auseinandersetzung", op. cit. p 110-126.
10. Differently in LXX and the Targum: They practise fear of God and live by their laws and justice and thus also according to the justice and the commandment, which the Lord gave to the sons of Jacob.
11. Ant 18, 85-87. Behind this promise stands the view that a valid proof can be brought forward that Gerizim was a sacred mountain chosen by God. This event took place under Pilate who saw it as a rebellious action *(thorybos)* taken by the mob of assembled Samaritans, whom he opposed by force of arms.
12. Compare Rom 10, 19, where Paul cites Deut 32, 21 with the question: "Did Israel not understand?" They did; however, they remained stubborn and, as a result, God turned to the Gentiles in order to make the Israelites jealous. See also Rom 11, 11.
13. See Isa 31,3: "The Egyptians are men, not God; and their horses are flesh, and not spirit." The domain of the creaturely, perishable, human is the flesh; that of the creative, eternal and divine is the spirit.
14. Compare Joshua 24,15: "Your ancestors served the gods" with John 4,20: "Our fathers worshiped on this mountain."
15. Compare Joshua 24,14: And *now (weʿattah)* with John 4,23: "And now" *(kai nyn),* also Joshua 24, 15 "today" *(hayyom).*
16. Compare here the explanation by J. Licht, *Megillath Ha-Sᵉrakhim* (Jerusalem 1965) p 189.
17. See my book, *Der Paraklet* (AGSU II, Leiden: Brill 1963).
18. Y. Yadin, *Megillath Ha-Miqdash* (Jerusalem 1977-78) 3 volumes.

19. Truth col. 55, 5.20; 56.4 echoing texts of Deuteronomy. "Men of Truth" (57,8) as counsel to the king: *Ruah* represents "direction toward heaven" (Col 30-40 on the building of the Temple).

20. Comp. Y. Yadin,op cit., vol. I, p 140f.

21. Y. Yadin points to the meaning of the covenant at Bethel in the Book of Jubilees (27, 19ff; 31-32, also T. Levi 7,4; 8; 9,3), op. cit. I, 142; II, p 92. See also the fragment *DJD* III, No. 13, p 181ff, where God "revealed to Jacob at Bethel (the covenant? secrets?)."

22. God commands Jacob not to build a temple at Bethel (Jub 32, 22).

23. According to S. Mowinckel, *He That Cometh* (Oxford Blackwell² 1959) p 13, note 2, it is derived from the Accadian *šelu* or *šilu* = Ruler and it translates "his (Judah's) ruler."

24. Arranged in the critical edition by G. Dalman, *Aramäische Dialektproben,* 1926 (rep. Darmstadt 1960) p 6f.

25. See the important work of Jan A. Bühner, *Der Gesandte und sein Weg im 4. Evangelium,* (WUNT 2,2 Tübingen 1977).

26. See 4QFlorilegium, line 11-13: the Davidic shoot will arise at the end of time to save Israel.

27. See P. Billerbeck, *Kommentar zum Neuen Testament,* II p 615-617. The passive form is used already in Acts 2, 39, where the subject is God; see Phil 2, 10-15.

28. See W. Grimm, *Weil ich Dich liebe. Jesus und Deuterojesaja* (ANTI I, Bern-Frankfurt 1976).

29. See A. Finkel, *The Pharisees and the Teacher of Nazareth* (AGSU IV, Leiden: Brill 1964, reprinted 1974).

30. W. Schrage, "Synagogē" in *T.W.N.T.,* vol VIII, p 810ff. Also M. Hengel "Zwischen Jesus und Paulus", *Z. Theol. Kirche* 72 (1975) p 182f. Yet Prov 16,6: "By grace and truth sin is atoned for."

31. E. Norden, *Agnostos Theos* (rep. Darmstadt 1956) p 129f.

32. So the emendations by H. M. Schenke and M. Krause. Compare line 30f *ne netshlel. . . . tierosolyma. . . .,* also O. Hofius, *Der Vorhang vor dem Thron Gottes* (Tübingen 1972) p 129f.

33. R. McL. Wilson, *The Gospel of Philip* (New York: Harper and Row 1962) p 189.

"He Loved Them to Completion": The Theology of John 13-14

PETER G. AHR

John, unlike the Synoptics, dates the Last Supper (and thereby the death of Jesus) on Passover Eve, the 14th of Nisan. Brown[1] summarizes the argument on the historical accuracy of this date; although this question does not directly affect the thesis of this paper, I agree with his conclusion that John's chronology is in fact to be preferred on this issue.

In dating the Last Supper and Jesus' death on Passover Eve, however, John is making a theological point as well as a chronological one: a point which is part of the theological pattern which I believe underlies Jesus' discourse in chapters 13 and 14. The nature of this pattern can be clearly seen by contrasting it with the alternate, more familiar, pattern created by the Synoptic dating of Jesus' death.

Both the Johannine and the Synoptic theologies of the meaning of the death of Jesus rest on the original tradition that Jesus died at Passover. The historical and theological significances of Passover are accessible to all believers in Jesus, both those who come from Judaism and those who do not. Accordingly, the symbolic significance of Passover quickly impressed itself on the story of Jesus' death. The version of that significance most familiar to Christians is the one, implicit in the Synoptic chronology, which sees the death of Jesus as the new Exodus event, the salvation-historical inauguration of a new age and the creation of a "new people". The Lord's Supper is seen as a repetition of Jesus' Passover meal, and therefore to be ritually celebrated, as the Passover meal is in turn a ritual commemoration of the meal the Hebrews ate on the eve of that day which marked the beginning of their status as God's people, the day on which they experienced God's decisive favor in their behalf. Jesus' death is the Exodus event, the decisive break between the old and the new, the ultimate experience of God's lovingkindness towards his people. This basic theological understanding dominates Christian thinking because it is Paul's understanding: Paul gives the Synoptic account of the Last Supper (1Cor 11,23-26), and his preaching begins with the assertion that "Christ died for our sins according to the scriptures . . ." (1Cor 15,3-8). It is worth noting here that this latter text begins Christian belief with Jesus' death and continues, in effect, to the present by leading up to Paul's vision of Jesus and his commission to preach as he is doing in this letter. Another point to notice in the ancient formula of faith Paul is quoting here is that the resurrection takes a second place, sandwiched between the burial and the appearances to Peter and the others. For all Paul's zeal to defend the reality and significance of the resurrection (1Cor 15,12-58), he does not ascribe causal significance to it: Christ's resurrection is the "first fruits" of the resurrection we all expect, not the cause of ours. The cause is found in Christ's death "for our sins".

A similar emphasis is visible in the symbolism Christianity has evolved to give plastic expression to its self-understanding: conspicuously absent from the basic repertory of Christian symbols is any common representation of the resurrection. Neither the medieval image of the Harrowing of Hell nor the resurrection paintings of the Renaissance nor any other attempt to give pictorial form to the doctrine of the resurrection have attained anything like the general symbolic resonance of the cross-image: the cross figures in the earliest-known pictorial reference to Christianity, and it is the single constant visual form of the central doctrines of Christianity.

This theological and symbolic weight ascribed to the death of Jesus is visible in the Synoptic dating of Jesus' death. By superimposing the death of Jesus on the sequence of events in the Passover story and on the festal reenactment of that story as it does, the Synoptic tradition invites us to see the death of Jesus as another, more perfect, Exodus. Such an interpretation allows a clear transition from Judaism to emerging Christianity by using the central events of the older tradition to illuminate the newer; but it also affects the newer story by imposing on it the rhythm of the older. In the story of Passover (both the Exodus and the Paschal meal), there are several key moments in the sequence of events. There is the preparation of the meal, including the killing of the lamb on the afternoon of Nisan 14; the eating of the meal, which inaugurates the main sequence of events; the intervention of God to bring about the end result; and finally the saving event itself. All subsequent history is the working out of the consequences of that event. The Synoptic tradition follows this sequence: on the day when the lamb is killed, the disciples prepare the meal (Mark 14,12-16); the Passover meal is eaten (Mark 14,17-25); Jesus is betrayed in the garden and tried (Mark 14,26-15:20), and finally killed (Mark 15,21-39). The parallelism is, indeed, so close that the narrative of the crucifixion itself is introduced by a verb which recalls the Exodus: "they led him out" (Mark 15,21); "on coming out" (Matt 27,32); "and as they were taking him away" (Luke 23,26). It is clear that, in the minds of the Synoptic evangelists, the death of Jesus is the new Exodus, the saving event which begins the new covenant, and that the chronology of that event fits the pattern of the earlier event which is its type.

John, on the other hand, works with an alternate reading of the chronology which yields a quite different symbolic significance. By dating the Last Supper and the death of Jesus "before the feast of Passover" (13,1; see 18.28; 19.14. 31.42), he removes the Last Supper from the ritual context of the Passover meal and synchronizes the death of Jesus (the "lamb of God", 1,29) with the slaughter of the paschal lambs. The absence of ritual motifs in John's account of the supper has long been noticed; most striking is the absence of any eucharistic account, despite the prominence of this narrative in all the other accounts of the meal. Indeed, John's account of the supper with the extended sermon of Jesus resembles nothing in first-century Judaism so much as the regular meal of the rabbi with his disciples; this similarity, in turn, may give some clue to the ritual practice of John's own community, whose regular gatherings were likely to have centered around the sort of teaching represented here rather than around a ceremonial eating. (Given the discourse on the Bread of Life in ch. 6, of course, it seems likely that John's community did know and practice a eucharistic ritual, but that they did not accord it the central place it had in, for example, Paul's practice.)

The meal and the subsequent betrayal and trial of Jesus being taken out of the Passover context, the story of Jesus' death joins the Passover sequence only at the point of the crucifixion. Pilate condemns Jesus to death "on the day of preparation for the Passover, about the sixth hour" (19,14); Jesus' death thus takes place in the afternoon of Passover Eve, the time when the lambs for the Passover festival are slaughtered in the Temple.[2] Because it is the preparation day, the Judaeans ask Pilate to hurry the executions along so that the coming great Sabbath will not be desecrated. Since Jesus is already dead when the soldiers come, however, they do not break his legs, but instead stab the corpse to allow the blood and water to flow out. The importance of this detail is underlined by the emphatic claim to eyewitness testimony on this point (19,35): Jesus dies according to the laws for ritual slaughter, and specifically according to the prescription for slaughtering the Passover lamb which is explicitly quoted (19,36). The allusion can hardly be clearer.

But if Jesus' death is chronologically and symbolically linked with the slaughter of the Passover lamb, what does John make of the rest of the

Passover symbol? The slaughter of the lambs in the Exodus story, after all, is not the saving event, nor is it even the cause of the saving event; it is only the occasion, the beginning of the sequence of events which leads to the deliverance of the people. The whole sequence of divine causality is still ahead in the story. John certainly knows the story, and he is quite clear as to how Jesus' death fits the story; but where is his equivalent of the Exodus, since Jesus' death is not it? The only remaining part of his story which can carry this symbolic weight is the twentieth chapter, which consists of the stories of how, first, the "other disciple" — presumably John himself (but, curiously, not Peter), then Mary Magdalene, then Thomas "saw and believed." That it is the believing and not the seeing which is decisive is clear from Jesus' own last words at what was originally the climax and conclusion of the gospel: "Blessed are those who have believed without seeing" (20,29). It is, then, what John calls "believing" that is his equivalent of the Exodus, the saving event — an event which is occasioned by, prepared for, but not caused by the death of Jesus.

This theological pattern, in which Jesus' death is seen as the necessary precondition of salvation, underlies the teaching which Jesus imparts to his disciples at the supper: it is the explanation of what believing is, "so that when it happens you may believe that 'I am' " (13,19). The explanation begins, as John's explanations generally do, with an action on Jesus' part: the washing of the disciples' feet. The significance of this episode is usually missed by commentators, who generally see in it some form of sacramental reference[3] or exhortation to humility[4]. That these explanations are beside the point is evident from the fact that the ensuing discourse of Jesus does not center on these subjects. It is a characteristic of John's narrative style to begin an episode with an action of Jesus, whose elucidation is the subject of the ensuing discourse; it is not evident that he is departing from this stylistic pattern here by introducing a fundamentally irrelevant (to what follows) story as the beginning of Jesus' last words.

Rather, we must recognize this episode as the point on which the action of the entire gospel hinges: the action which is a dramatization of the principal theme to follow, and thus of the disciples' (readers') preparation for what will happen when Jesus is "glorified". It begins with the solemn announcement that Jesus knows "that the Father had given all things into his hands, and that he had come from God and was going to God" (13,3), a description not only of Jesus' psychological state, but of his ontology. Several elements in John's narration allow us to understand his sense of the significance of this action. The first of these is the verbs he uses to begin and end the story: Jesus "puts off" *(tithēsin)* and "takes up" *(elaben)* his clothes—the same verbs John uses earlier (10,17-18) for Jesus' "laying down" and "taking up" his life. A second is the fact that Jesus takes off "his clothes": as Brown notes[5], one would expect the singular here, since the outer robe is "obviously" meant; *pace* Brown, however, the unexpected plural is surely not an error, but what the author intends to say, and any attempt to understand him must start with what he says. The third element is, of course, the footwashing itself; its importance is signalled by Jesus' insistence on it over Peter's protests. Finally, there is Jesus' own explanation of the significance of this action.

John's use of the verbs "put off" and "take up" clearly suggest that he understands this action as an acting out of the crucifixion/resurrection of Jesus, who "knows . . . that he is going to God." To understand the meaning of this action, therefore, is to understand the meaning of Jesus' death/resurrection. The reference to the crucifixion is even more clearly present in the statement about Jesus' nakedness: anyone familiar with the story of Jesus' death can grasp the reference to the removal of clothes[6], and, indeed, it is the very unexpectedness of this statement which points the reader to this reference. To take off one's clothes in the middle of a dinner was as unexpected an action in the first century as it would be now; least of all does one expect the guest of honor (as Jesus is here) to act this way. To compound this strange behavior by undertaking the menial act of washing the feet of others at table is to commit a social impropriety of the first order, one which is bound to produce just the sort of shocked indignation exhibited by Peter. To wash the feet of others is a task ordinarily assigned to the lowest of one's household slaves; we hear occasionally of zealous disciples doing the same for their teacher as a mark of extraordinary respect. But Jesus' action is unheard of, as the wording of Peter's reaction makes clear: *"You* are going to wash *my* feet? *You* will never wash *my* feet!"* Jesus' response to Peter tacitly acknowledges the strangeness of his behavior, and the propriety of Peter's reaction: Peter does not know yet what Jesus is doing (nor could he be expected to); but he will know later. When will Peter know? After he has seen something still more shocking than Jesus stripping himself and acting as a common slave: when he understands what he has seen at the tomb of the Messiah executed as a common criminal.

It is because the footwashing is a parable-in-action of the crucifixion that Jesus must insist on it so forcefully. Given the seating arrangement John has in mind at 13,34, where Jesus is reclining on the middle of the couch at the head of a horseshoe-shaped arrangement of couches and tables, with the "disciple whom he loved" to his right and Judas to his left, and Peter in a position to confer privately with the Beloved Disciple, we can take it that Peter, at the head of the places to Jesus' right, is one of the last to be approached. He has thus had ample opportunity to register his outrage at Jesus' behavior, as the vehemence of his response indicates. Jesus, however, is equally insistent that he must do what he proposes to do: "If I do not wash you, you have no part with me." The force of this insistence is seen in Peter's utter collapse: "Lord, not just my feet, but my hands and my head as well." As so often in John, Jesus' interlocutor takes him literally, only to have Jesus turn what is being talked about into a metaphor of something else. Jesus' reply dismisses Peter's assumption that this washing has to do with bodily cleanliness: what Jesus is doing is all that needs to be done. That being done, they are all clean—except, of course, for the yet-unidentified one for whom the footwashing leads to no result.

John's understanding of the meaning of the footwashing is clear, not only from his narrative details, but from the explanation which Jesus himself proceeds to give. He begins with the rhetorical question, "Do you know what I have done to you?" (13,12). His answer to the question, however, begins with a reference, not to what he has done, but to the disciples' estimation of him as teacher and master, an estimation which he confirms. The terms of this estimate are essentially relative and not absolute: the titles he refers to are titles which describe his relation precisely to *them*, as the argument *a maiore ad minus* in 13,16 indicates. It is therefore this relation which is being depicted in the footwashing: "If I, the master and teacher, have washed your feet, then you also should wash each other's feet" (13,14). The force of the argument rests on the fact that it is the *master* and *teacher* who has done the footwashing: it is the very one who should not be the one to wash feet who has in fact done so. The listener's attention is drawn to the impropriety of the action, with the injunction to do likewise. In what does this impropriety consist? It consists in the reversal of expected roles: the master does the slave's work; the teacher does what the disciple might be expected to do. This is the example which he sets for the disciples: the master becomes the slave, the teacher the disciple. But if Jesus is, in this action, not the master and teacher, who is the master and teacher? The master and teacher is the one whose feet are being washed: the one who has hitherto been servant and disciple. The example, then, is not one of humility, but of replacement. What is being acted out here is the situation which the disciples will find themselves in after the crucifixion: with Jesus gone, where is the teacher? Jesus' answer is that they are to be masters and teachers after him—with the injunction that they are in turn to yield that place to others, as he has done. For if he, their teacher and master, has done so, then they have no claim to exemption from this necessity (13,16). The importance of this command is indicated both by the solemn introductory phrase, "Amen, amen I say to you," and by the beatitude invoked on those who obey it.

That the point of the command is not merely humble service but the teacher's abdication of his place and his replacement by the disciple, is also borne out by the phrasing of the argument. The first antithesis is the slave-master relationship, corresponding to the title "master" used above. But the second antithesis ("nor is the one sent greater than the one who sent him", 13,16) does not follow verbally from the title "teacher" used in Jesus' explanation, although it fits into the pattern of the argument where the teacher-disciple pair belongs. The shift to the verbal idea of "sending", while it appears to be a simple paraphrase of "teaching", is in fact a significant expansion of the argument. Throughout the gospel, Jesus has described his own relation to the Father in terms of "sending" (*apesteilen ho theos ton hyion*, 3,17; *hon gar apesteilen ho theos*, 3,34; *ho patēr me apestalken*, 5,36; *ho pempsas me patēr*, 5,37; *hon apesteilen ekeinos*, 5,38; *hina pisteuete eis hon apesteilen ekeinos*, 6,29; *to thelēma tou pempsantos me*, 6,39; *ho patēr ho pempsas me*, 6,44; *kathōs apesteilen me ho zōn patēr*, 6,57; *hē emē didachē . . . tou pempsantos me*, 7,16; *estin alēthinos ho pempsas me*, 7,28; *kakeinos me apesteilen*, 7,29; *hypagō pros ton pempsanta me*, 7,33; *egō kai ho pempsas me patēr*, 8,17; *ho pempsas me patēr*, 8,18; *ho pempsas me*, 8,26 and 29; *ekeinos me apesteilen*, 8,43; *ta erga tou pempsantos me*, 9, 4; *hon ho patēr hēgiasen kai apesteilen eis ton kosmon*, 10,36; *hina pisteusōsin hoti sy me apesteilas*, 11,43; *eis ton pempsanta me*, 12,44; *ho pempsas me patēr*, 12,49), a sending which is in turn the source of Jesus' teaching; he has been "the one sent", and the Father "the one who sent him". Now, however, the positions change: Jesus is now the one sending and the disciples are the ones sent: the disciples (hitherto always described as *mathētai*) are now "the sent" (*apostoloi*). This new status of the disciples is explicitly confirmed by the risen Jesus in 20,21: "As the Father has sent me, so I send you." Jesus' status in the world has its origins in his being sent by the Father; from now on, the disciples have that status by virtue of their being sent by Jesus.

The sending, however, demands the absence, the abdication of the sender: while Jesus speaks in theory and explanation of the disciples' being sent before his death, they are actually not sent until after Jesus' death and resurrection. If the disciples are also to "wash one another's feet", then their sending of others will also demand their abdication of the role of teacher in their turn. It is by this continuing process of the teacher's abdicating before his disciples who become teachers in their turn that the problem of the continuity of the community and the teaching is resolved.

This shift in the theology of sending also portends for John an alteration in the status of Jesus: while he has hitherto been the one sent by the Father, he now becomes, like the Father, the sender. If the disciples have taken his place, he in turn takes the Father's place. But this taking of the Father's place can happen only by his becoming the "slave", by his abdication, by his death. The disciples can be sent only by the Jesus who has died, who has "gone to the Father", who "is glorified". It is primarily in this sense that John speaks of Jesus' death as, paradoxically, his "glorification"; it is this equation that explains the double sense of the "lifting up of the son of man" (3,14; 8,28).

This sending is yet in the future as Jesus speaks (although it has already occurred for John and his audience); it is being explained in advance, "so that when it happens you may believe that 'I am' " (13,19). For John and his listeners, the reality of which Jesus speaks is already an element in their lives: they already believe that "I am". The importance, for John, of this believing is seen in his original conclusion of the gospel at the end of chapter 20: "these things are written that you may believe that Jesus is the Messiah, the son of God, so that, believing, you may have life in his name" (20,31). The content of this belief is variously expressed by John: it is a belief *about* Jesus, as in the just-quoted text; it is a response to the person of the risen Jesus, as the story of Thomas in chapter 20 shows; it has to do with what Jesus reveals about himself, as in the revelatory "I am" statements throughout the gospel (I am the light of the world; I am the resurrection and the life; I am the good shepherd; I am the way and the truth and the life; etc.); it refers to what may be called Jesus' *identity*. This identity of Jesus, it has been abundantly made clear throughout the gospel, is not understood abstractly or ontologically, but is rather a function of Jesus' relation to the Father, on the one hand, and to the disciples, on the other. It is perhaps most succinctly expressed in the saying in 8,28: "When you lift up the son of man[7], then you will know that 'I am', and that I do nothing on my own, but speak just as the Father has taught me." "That 'I am' " and "that I . . . speak just as the Father has taught me" are not two separate things that the disciples will learn, but two ways of expressing what the listeners will know at Jesus' "lifting up". What they will understand is that Jesus is what he is because he relates himself to the Father as he does.

What it means to understand Jesus' identity is summed up in the solemn saying which concludes this explanation of the foot-washing: "Amen, amen I say to you, he who receives anyone I send receives me, and he who receives me receives him who sent me" (13,20). The disciples are being "sent", as Jesus himself is "sent"; he sends them as the Father has sent him. But just as he has been the full revelation of the

Father to them (to receive him is to receive him who sent him), so they, in turn, are to be the full revelation to others of what Jesus is, and thus of what the Father is as well (to receive them is to receive Jesus). They are to be to others what Jesus has been to them. Once Jesus has been "lifted up", he will no longer be there to reveal the Father to others, to "do the Father's works"; that work will thenceforth belong to the listeners. But if the identity of Jesus is to do the Father's works, then the listeners will share that identity. To "believe that 'I am' ", then, is not only to believe about Jesus, but also to understand one's own identity as well: to understand that one is now what Jesus has been.

This understanding underlies the discourse which begins after Judas' exit and continues to the end of chapter 14. With Judas' departure into the "night" (13,30), Jesus is now speaking only to the assembly of believers: the disciples, in the story, and the gospel's listeners, in the author's intention (the "you" of 20,31). This dual audience, which is always present to the author[8], requires that the Jesus who speaks, speak in two different time frames: there is the Jesus who is a character in the story who speaks to other characters in the story, and there is the Jesus who is speaking through the voice of the storyteller directly to the community for whom the book is written. We must remember that the gospel of John, like every literary work of antiquity, was written to be read aloud either to oneself or to an audience: there were no "readers" in the modern sense of the term, who discern the meaning of the book by visual inspection of the writing on the page. Jesus' teaching in the gospel is written to be heard by John's audience as it was heard by the disciples years before; the "Jesus" of the gospel, then, is always two voices speaking to the two audiences. Indeed, to the extent that the evangelist conceives of himself as "sent" by Jesus (to receive him is to receive Jesus), his voice, too, appears in the character of "Jesus"[9], as well as in his literary work of organizing the remembered sayings into the discourses in the text.

The present discourse (13,31-14,31), which at one stage in the writing of the gospel led directly into the story of Jesus' arrest (as the easy transition from 14,31 to 18,1 shows), is spoken for two parallel esoteric audiences. With Judas gone, the room is filled only with the faithful disciples to whom Jesus explains the meaning of what is to happen; John's room is likewise filled only with the believers, for whom the revelatory act is no longer future, and who are present precisely to have the meaning of that event unfolded to them. That meaning begins with the assertion that "now is the son of man glorified, and God is glorified in him" (13,31). The "now" is the event which begins with Jesus' death (shortly to follow in the story) and culminates in the disciples' (believers') believing that "I am". In that "now", Jesus, the son of man, is revealed as what he is: his identity is fully disclosed; and God, Jesus' Father, is also made visible in him. But this final, exhaustive, manifestation of the Father's presence to him cannot take place without a change in Jesus himself: God will glorify him, and indeed shortly will do so (13,32). No longer will Jesus be the medium through whom the Father is manifested to others: he will share in the status of the Father and will, like the Father, be the object of manifestation to others. He will be what the Father is, and will be related to by others as the Father is: as has already been said, he who has been sent will thenceforward be the sender. Jesus will no longer be the empirical person in whom others see the Father, his source; he will now be the source made visible in the revelatory actions of others who have taken his place.

Jesus' impending departure from the world of the disciples' empirical experience (of which the disciples are still ignorant) prompts him to warn them of the imminent end of their present mode of access to him (13,33): the Jesus they have known up to now will no longer be available to them: he will no longer be their master and teacher, and they cannot follow him to where he is going. What they have from him is no longer his presence, but his commandment (as he has a commandment from the Father: 12,49): that they love one another as he has loved them (13,34). John has a clear and specific understanding of what that love is: he has already described it as a love "to completion" (eis telos, 13,1), a love which lasts the whole of Jesus' life and which is qualitatively ultimate and fruitful, so that he reports Jesus' last utterance as "it is completed" (tetelestai: he has arrived eis telos), after which he "handed over the Spirit" (19,30). That this love is more than mere sentiment or general benevolence appears from a later discussion of this theme. In what is apparently another redaction of this saying (15,12-17), Jesus gives the commandment to love and immediately follows it with the amplification, "no one has greater love than this, that one lay down his life for his friends." That this theoretical formulation is clearly meant as applying first of all to Jesus is evident in the story of his arrest: John (who seems to be giving eyewitness testimony of this episode: see 18,15) records that, when the cohort came to arrest Jesus, he bargained with them to secure the escape of his followers at the price of his own capture. When Jesus dies the next day, those who had been with him at the time of his arrest cannot escape the knowledge that he has died in the most literal sense for them. In commanding his disciples to love each other, then, the Jesus who speaks to John's audience is enjoining on them an attitude of service which knows no limits to the self-sacrifice it is prepared to offer. It is presumably because John sees this attitude as underlying Jesus' action that he makes no mention of Jesus' having to struggle within himself before his arrest in the garden.

But the love which Jesus exemplifies and commands is not only a general disposition to be of service to others (although it certainly is at least that); it is specifically a matter of the teacher's obligation to his disciples, as the sequence of ideas in this passage shows. The passage began with a discussion of the "glorification" of the son of man, moved from there to the disclosure that Jesus, and Jesus alone, is going away, and then introduced the commandment to love as Jesus loved. The commandment to love, however, is apparently bypassed in the ensuing discussion, which revolves around Jesus' going away (13,36-38). Peter's question and objection again take Jesus' words at face value, assuming that Jesus is speaking of a simple geographical transfer; Jesus' replies point to a different universe of meaning: "You cannot follow me now, but you will follow later. . . . *You* will lay down your life for *me*?". It is clear why Peter cannot follow now; but why does Jesus say he will follow later? Certainly, John (or at least his school) knows of Peter's death (21,18-19); but Jesus' death is not merely a physical event to be imitated physically: it is an exemplary event, which Peter is not yet in a position to imitate, as Jesus' ironic answer to Peter's protest indicates. On the one hand, coupled with the prediction of Peter's denial, Jesus' question simply calls into question the plausibility of Peter's profession of zeal. But Jesus is also questioning Peter's assumption that he *could* lay down his life for Jesus. The emphasis in the question is: You will lay down your life *for me*? It is the moral impossibility of that suggestion that prompts Jesus' irony: it is not the disciple's place to die for the teacher. The teacher, rather, must die for the disciple, for only in this way can he complete his work of bringing the disciple to the full understanding of the Father. If Peter were to die for Jesus at this point, Jesus' work in his regard would be forever incomplete. Once Jesus has died, however, and Peter in his turn has been the teacher, it will then be his place to follow Jesus; but at that point he will be laying down his life, not for Jesus, but rather for his own disciples. This, then, is the love that Jesus commends to his disciples: the love which serves the other by revealing to him the Father which is its source, and then abdicates its mediatorial role so that the other may discover that source for himself.

It is because Jesus' death will have this meaning that the disciples are admonished not to be troubled by his death (14,1): their attitude is to be one of believing in him as they believe in God. The point of this last admonition is not that they are to trust him or to trust his word that all will work out for the best; rather, the emphasis is on the parallel between God and Jesus: their attitude toward Jesus is to be that which they have toward God. Whether one reads the verb as indicative or imperative, the focus of the sentence is on the object: Jesus stands in the place of God, for what he is, is what God is.

But while there is a complete relational unity between Jesus and the Father (a point John returns to several times in this discourse), that unity allows for a multiplicity of realizations; hence the shift to a discussion of the "many dwelling places in the Father's house" (14,2). Whether the image be that of the complex structure of the Temple ("my Father's house", 2,16) or, more probably, the more general image of the extended agricultural household with its provision for several generations of family along with the retinue of household servants and laborers, the language of this statement clearly suggests that there are many different ways of relating to the Father, many places to dwell within the one household. Jesus' reassurance on this point ("were it not so, I would have told you") serves to emphasize the fact that his own relation to the Father is exemplary and not unique. His own going away will make it possible for them to enter into such a relation with the Father for themselves ("I am going to make ready a place for you", 14,2); but that going away will also be a coming back to them, a taking them to where he is. While on the empirical plane Jesus will disappear, in their entering into their own relation with the Father, the disciples will again encounter Jesus, for then they will be where he is. Jesus can speak of this encounter as "I will take you", for their encounter with the Father will happen only because Jesus has made it possible: it will be experienced by them as a gift of Jesus, the fruit of his work in their regard.

The topographical language of the "Father's house" and of the project of encounter with the Father enables Jesus to say, "and whither I am going you know the way" (14,4). That this language is understood by John as metaphorical is evident from Thomas' question, "Lord, we do not know where you are going; and how can we know the way?" (14,5). Thomas' misunderstanding consists precisely in his assumption that Jesus is speaking of a real place, heavenly or earthly, to which there is a road which is describable in spatial terms (or even in the moral terms of ethical injunctions). What he is asking for is the specific instructions which will bring him to that place.

Jesus' answer, however, does not come in the terms of Thomas' question, but rather undercuts the presuppositions of the question. The "way" is not a set of instructions that Jesus or anyone can give, and Jesus is not in possession of secret information that Thomas is not yet privy to: what the way is, is simply what Jesus is, just as what truth is, is what Jesus is, and what life is, is what Jesus is (14,6). Way, truth and life are all symbolic expressions of the object of the religious quest; Jesus' answer to Thomas is that these symbols are not objects in themselves, but serve only as heuristic tools for grasping the identity of Jesus and, for the believer, of oneself. For the disciples have already been told that they know the way (14,4); while they do not yet recognize the way at this point in the story (for Jesus has not yet "gone to the Father"), the other audience of Jesus' words (John's congregation) is here being reminded of what they already know.

As Bultmann notes[10], the "I" of this answer is the predicate, not the subject, of the sentence. Jesus does not say, *I* am the way, but rather: if you are looking for the way, here I am, not as the "it" you are looking for, nor as the empirical individual whose biography you must strive to imitate, but as a subject whose subjectivity you must learn to grasp intuitively and use as the guide to your own subjectivity. It is this intuition which is the attainment of your quest for truth, and which is a living in comparision to which all other existence is as death. In the same way, Jesus has previously said that the bread which nourishes one for real life (6,35), the light by which one sees the world for what it truly is (8,12) and the resurrection and life (11,25) are not objective entities or empirical events to be searched for in themselves but symbolic ways of grasping what he is.

The sense of the rest of Jesus' answer to Thomas must also be understood in light of the meaning of the first part. If the "I" in question is not the person of Jesus as subject of the assertion, but the identity of Jesus as its predicate, then the "me" through whom is the only access to the Father is also the *what* Jesus is: "through me", then, is not an assertion of the uniqueness of Jesus as sole mediator who carries believers to the Father as a bridge, but rather the assertion that the kind of union with the Father which is at the core of Jesus is the only kind of union with the Father that is possible, so that this is also the kind of union which the believer must have. "If you knew me," Jesus says, "you would also know the Father. From now on, you know him and have seen him" (14,7). The condition contrary to fact reflects the fact that, as Thomas' incomprehension shows, the disciples have not yet understood what Jesus is; for to understand him is to know the Father. "From now on," however (in the time of John's audience), from the "now" of Jesus' glorification, once Jesus has gone to the Father, the listener does know him and has seen him.

The disciples' continuing incomprehension is voiced in Philip's question: "Lord, show us the Father and that is enough for us" (14,8). Philip's error is similar to Thomas': he assumes that Jesus is speaking of a "Father" who can be seen or known in himself, and that Jesus is holding back from giving them the definitive vision of that Father. Jesus' somewhat impatient answer rejects that assumption. He who has seen Jesus has seen the Father (14,9); there is nothing more to see. While Jesus' language speaks of the Father as separate from Jesus, in reality that concretization of the "Father" is as metaphorical as the rest of Jesus' vocabulary. The Father is the object, not of sight, but of insight, an insight that one has on one's own, having been brought to the point of inseeing by the guidance of one who already sees. This insight (intuition, understanding, knowing) is what characterizes Jesus, what makes him what he is, what constitutes his relation to the Father. To see Jesus, to know him, then, is to confront one already in possession of that understanding; to understand him is to be ready for that insight on one's own, provided that one see that what is looked for is not a *what*, but a *how* and *why*: "The things I say to you I do not speak on my own; it is the Father remaining in me who is actually doing the works" (14,10). Jesus directs the listeners to notice that "I am in the Father and the Father in me" (14,10): I am in the Father as in an environment, a context; and the Father is in me as a principle implicit in all I do and say. There is nothing Jesus does that is not a revelation of the Father; if the disciples will not accept Jesus' word for this, let them look at what Jesus does (14,11), for what he does reveals why he does it and whence it comes.

The works which reveal the presence of the Father are not, however, the exclusive prerogative of Jesus; they will equally be done by the believer (14,12). The one who believes in Jesus will do the same works, and will do even greater ones, "because I am going to the Father" (14,12). To "believe in Jesus", then, is not a matter of looking back on the once-and-for-all accomplishment of the revelation of the Father in Jesus' lifetime, but a doing what he did, a continuation of the knowing and manifesting the Father that constituted his identity. Since this further manifestation of the Father will not be limited by the horizons of Jesus' own lifetime, the disciples will be able to do even "greater" works, to reveal the Father even more widely than Jesus himself was able to do. They will do these "greater" works, he says, "because I am going to the Father"; they will be enabled to manifest the Father because they will themselves know the Father once Jesus is no longer present as the object of their attention and they have seen the completion (13,1; 19,30) of Jesus' manifestation of the Father.

While Jesus is henceforth no longer to be physically present to the disciples, he will not be wholly absent, as the following section of the discourse shows. Whatever the believer asks in his name, Jesus will do, that the Father may be glorified in the Son (14,13-14). Because Jesus will now be with the Father, sending the disciples, they can rely on him who sends them for all that they need to accomplish their mission of revealing the Father. To this end, they are admonished to love Jesus, that is, to keep his commandments (14,15); if they do so, the Father, at Jesus' request, will give them "another Paraclete" to be with them always (14,16). This "other Paraclete"[11] will henceforth be their Guide, as Jesus has been their Guide up to now. What Jesus is pointing to is the experience of John's community: they have not been left orphans (14,18), but are in continuing dynamic contact with the Father, and know that that knowledge of the Father is theirs as a gift of Jesus; it is traced back to him, and is experienced as a continuation of the Father's presence to him. The Guide is how they know the Father now; it is "another" Guide, for Jesus is the first way in which they knew the Father. Jesus can couple the promise of the Guide with his promise to return (14,17-18) because what the believer experiences in the presence of the Guide is what Jesus is: the knowledge of the Father. For it is not the empirical individual, Jesus of Nazareth, who will return, except for a brief and ultimately irrelevant time ("Have you believed because you saw me? Blessed are those who have believed without seeing", 20,29); the Jesus who returns and dwells with the believer is the essential Jesus whose identity it is to manifest the Father. In describing the Guide as the "spirit of truth" (14,17), Jesus is saying that, like the wind (*pneuma*), it is known only by its presence (3,8), but what is known in its presence is truth, as what Jesus is, is truth (14,6). This knowledge of the Father in the Guide is not the sort of empirical information that can be grasped by the "world", those outside the experience of belief; it can be known only by its presence. The circularity of this argument (14,17) is deliberate and instructive: John's whole perspective is that of two opposed circles of belief, each with its own center and its own horizon. The one, the "world", consists of those who do not know Jesus and the Father and are consequently "from below" (8,23), in the darkness (3,19-21); the other consists of those who believe, who know the Father, who are thus "from above" and of the light. These two circles are mutually exclusive, and John does not even discuss the possibility of change from one to the other except to speak of it as a being born over again from above (3,3). The circle of interest to him is that of the believers: they know the Guide by his presence in them.

Just as the world will not know the Guide, so it will be able to see Jesus for only a short time longer (14,19): with his death, he will no longer be accessible to all. To the disciples, however, what he is will be seen (inseen), in that they will live as he lives. Life is what Jesus is (14,6); when they experience themselves as living (as Jesus does, 6,57), they will experience the presence of what Jesus is. It is that insight, "on that day", that will disclose to them that Jesus is in the Father, that they are in him, and he in them (14,20). The relation that exists between Jesus and the Father (14,11) will then be experienced as the core of their lives as well.

This insight comes about because the believer "loves" Jesus, "keeps his commandments", his "word", which is not Jesus' but that of the Father who sent him (14,21-24). If one does this, he does what Jesus himself has done; Jesus will reveal himself to him; Jesus and the Father will love him and remain with him. The believer will thus, indwelt by Jesus and the Father, be what Jesus has been. The understanding of this presence is the work of the Guide, who will continue the teaching of Jesus and continually bring to mind what Jesus has already prepared the disciples to see (14,25-26).

The conclusion of the discourse (14,27-31) sums up the main points Jesus has been making: his impending death, gruesome though it will be, will paradoxically leave with them a profound peace (neither the English word nor the Greek *eirēnē* conveys adequately the sense of fulfillment in the *shalom* which presumably underlies this text) rather than disturbance; his death is a going away, a going to the Father, but that going away will entail a return which will be the cause of rejoicing, for he will return in such a way that the disciples will find him as the Father, as their own source. All of this is being explained in advance, "that when it happens you may believe."

This being said, Jesus has little more to say to the disciples; the ruler of the world is coming (not that he has any power over Jesus), but Jesus fulfils the Father's command, that the world may know that he loves the Father. There is nothing more to do but to go out to complete the Father's work.

With this, the early draft of the Farewell Discourse leads directly to the story of Jesus' arrest, trial and execution, the meaning of which has been laid out in advance. From Jesus' side, these events mark the completion of his work and his going to the Father. But the Discourse lays far greater emphasis on the effect of Jesus' work in the lives of the disciples, an impact which does not, however, occur at Jesus' death, for it is not then that they believe. The meaning of Jesus' death lies in the disciples' discovery that what Jesus is, is now what they are; that discovery is told in the stories of the disciples' coming to belief in chapter 20, for John's word for that discovery is "believe". The telling of these stories brings to its real conclusion the story of the saving event: for these stories are, for John, the new Exodus, the beginning of the people to which he belongs. In this context, Jesus' death is not the cause of this new people, by effecting a cosmic change in human nature or in the Father; it is the ultimate manifestation of the Father, an example (13,15) of what the disciples are to do and to be. But this manifestation requires an audience: it must be seen and grasped if it is to have any effect. In the story as it is told, it is the disciples who come to the realization of the meaning of Jesus' work, after his tomb is found empty, and they have no empirical presence of Jesus to hang on to (20,17); for John, however, the readers are the ultimate audience to whom Jesus' manifestation of the Father is directed. They are being encouraged to respond to that manifestation by believing, by recognizing in their lives the presence of Jesus' Father, that insight which was at the center of what Jesus is, and which it was his purpose to bring them to understand, so that, believing, they "might have life in his name" (20,31).

NOTES

1. R. E. Brown, *The Gospel according to John* (Anchor Bible 29a) (New York: Doubleday, 1970) p. 555-6. On the related question of the authorship of the gospel (and hence its plausibility), see J. E. Bruns, *The Art and Thought of John* (New York: Herder & Herder, 1969).

2. Brown, p. 883.

3. For example, C. H. Dodd, *The Interpretation of the Fourth Gospel* (Cambridge University Press, 1963), p. 401.

4. Brown, p. 558-569.

5. Brown, p. 551.

6. The same word *(himatia)* is used in the crucifixion story (19,23).

7. Note the reference to the paradoxical significance of the crucifixion.

8. For example, 4,23: "the hour is coming, and now is, when the true worshippers will worship the Father in spirit and truth."

9. Most commentators, for example, agree that the monologue of Jesus in 3,11-21 shifts at some point to a narrator's gloss, although the location of the shift is not clearly visible.

10. R. Bultmann, *The Gospel of John* (Philadelphia: Westminster Press, 1971), p. 605, note 3.

11. See Brown, p. 1135-1143 for a full discussion of the meaning of the word.

Prophets/Angels: LXX and Qumran Psalm 151 and the Epistle to the Hebrews

LOU H. SILBERMAN

In the Hebrew text 11QPs^a 151, the word corresponding to *angelon autou* of LXX is *nby'w* rather than *ml'kw* as may have been expected.[1] If the text at hand represents in some way that lying behind LXX, then it offers the only instance in which the work *nby'* is rendered *angelos* in LXX. There is, however, a midrashic tradition reported in *Wayyiqra Rabba* 1,1 that understood such an equation to reflect biblical usage. The verse under discussion is Ps 103,20; "Bless the Lord, his angels . . ." and the question asked is, who is thus designated, celestial or terrestial beings? The second response to the query reads:

> The prophets are called angels as it is written: "and he sent an angel and he brought us forth from Egypt" (Num 2,16). Now was it an angel? Was it not Moses? Why was he called "an angel"? From this it is evident that prophets were called angels. Similarly: "and the angel of the Lord went up from Gilgal to Bochim" (Judges 2,1). Now was it an angel? Was it not Phineas? Why was he called "an angel"? Said R. Simon: at the moment that the holy spirit rested on Phineas, his face glowed like a torch. The rabbis said: what did Manoah's wife say to him? "Behold a man of God came to me, his appearance like that of an angel of God" (Judges 13,6), for she thought he was a prophet, not an angel. Said R. Yohanan, the principal passage from which they learn that prophets are called angels is Haggai 1,13, "then Haggai, the angel of the Lord, spoke to the people with the Lord's message". Here one necessarily learns that this is their principal passage proving prophets are called angels.[2]

This equation of *nby'* with *angelos* apparent in the Hebrew and Greek texts of Ps 151 raises new questions about the time and place of the composition of the psalm and the relationship between the two texts. M.

Noth in his discussion of the Syriac text of the psalm emphasized its non-canonical nature and expressed doubts about a Hebrew Vorlage, seeing it as a product of Alexandrian Jewry.[3] J. A. Sanders, on the other hand, while denying that LXX is a translation of the Q text, has argued that the latter is the original and the former "depends ultimately on (it)". He did not, however, examine the issue raised by the point here under discussion.[4]

It may be asked, therefore, does *nby*ʾ = *angelos* represent the impact of a midrashic tradition upon Greek translations, thus offering an early witness to that tradition? Again, are there other evidences for this tradition? It is to provide an answer to this second question that this paper is, in the first instance, addressed. May it not be that the occurrence of *tois prophētais* in Heb 1,2 and of *angelōn* in 2,2 to designate the "mediators" between God and Israel reflects this tradition? The theme of these two verses, indeed, of the whole section is the speaking of God to the fathers: *ho Theos lalēsas tois patrasin en tois prophētais* (1,1) and *ho di'angelōn lalētheis logos* (2,2). Thus viewed, it seems clear that the two words *prophētais* and *angelōn* are easily understood to be synonymous, referring to one group of spokesmen. The shift to the second term in 2,2 was, it may be conjectured, occasioned by the intervening discussion of the superiority of the Son over "angels", defined in 1,14 as *leitourgika pneumata*. This quite different theme was introduced by the theological concern of the author to prove the superiority of the Son and his message over the "messengers" and their message, on the basis of the interpretation of a series of biblical quotations, an undertaking that could be accomplished only by means of texts involving the term *angelos/angeloi*, there being no texts dealing with *nby*ʾym that could provide the required contrast between them and the Son or Lord. Thus Heb 1,5 shifts to the synonym *angelōn* in order to make possible the introduction of a Christian midrash based on Ps 2,7; 2Sam 7,14; Deut 32,43 (LXX); Ps 104,4; Ps 45,6-7; Ps 102,25-27; Ps 110,1; that exhibits the superiority of the Son. Having accomplished this, the author returned to the central theme, divine communication and the superiority of the new word, now established by the midrashically demonstrated superiority of the Son over all previous messengers. Now only if there was a tradition already in circulation equating *nby*ʾym/*prophētai* with *mlʾkym/angeloi* could the necessary transition in v 5 have been taken place.

Unfortunately the structure of this section with its central theme and its subordinate midrashic proof has not been recognized, although an unnamed commentator, uneasy over the apparent thematic disjuncture, suggested that " 'angels' should be read . . . for "prophets' (in 1,2) since in the rest of the chapter there is a contrast between the Son of God and angels, not prophets"[5]. However, as has been suggested here, the required unity is to be found not in textual emendation but in the recognition of the structure of the argument:

1. the word of God was in the past transmitted by messengers;
2. these messengers are inferior to the Son who is the ultimate messenger, this demonstrated by a midrash;
3. therefore, the Son's message is the true means of salvation, displacing the message of the previous messengers.

The Epistle has, however, been read as though 1,5-14—the contrast between the Son and the angels—was the central theme rather than a Christian midrash used to support the major interest of the author, (item 3 above) the appearance of a new and definitive message conveyed by a superior messenger. In keeping with this understanding of the structure, the meaning of *angeloi* as a synonym for *prophētai* in this context has been ignored and its more limited meaning, *leitourgika pneumata*, growing out of the biblical citations used, has been emphasized. Thus 2,2 *ho di'angelōn lalētheis logos*, "the word spoken by angels", is understood to refer to "angels" in the second sense. But what is this "word spoken by angels"? Although recent translations tend to leave the matter hazy, RSV rendering *logos* as "message" and the Jerusalem Bible[6] as "promise", many commentators are less inhibited. Moffatt explains his translation unequivocally: "the reference in *logos* is to the Mosaic code . . ."[7] H. Montefiore states flatly that the doctrine of Torah mediated by angels was "a common belief in first century Judaism"[8]. W. D. Davies points to "the well-attested traditions that the Law as given by angels"[9]. If this claim is correct then, of course, the entire previous argument that we may have a witness to the tradition that equates *nby'* with *ml'k* = *angelos* fails. But if, on the other hand, it turns out that the doctrine of angelic mediation is a chimera, then the claim being made that Hebrews is a witness to the tradition equating these two may indeed survive. More than this, however, it may be added to the evidence previously educed by others concerning a relationship between the author of Hebrews and the Qumran community and may thus shed some light on the *Sitz-im-Leben* of Ps 151.

The evidence for the position, here being challenged, has been drawn from two traditions, extra-rabbinic/hellenistic and rabbinic, and is reported with varying degrees of assiduity in commentaries and handbooks.[10] It is, therefore, necessary to examine it, if one is to challenge the contention that angelic mediation of *Torah* was a common belief in first century Judaism and make at least plausible the counter-suggestion here offered.

Extra-rabbinic/hellenistic sources

There are three items brought forth regularly under this heading: Jubilees 1,27; Deut 33,2 in LXX; Josephus, *Antiquities* XV, 136.

1. The Jubilees passage reads: "And he said to the angel of the presence: write for Moses from the beginning of creation till my sanctuary has been built among them for all eternity. . . ." To this, Charles commented: "In New Testament times the ministry of angels has become the universal means of approaching or hearing from God." The evidence he adduced for this claim includes Philo, *de somniis* 1,22; the Josephus passage noted above; Galatians 3,19; Acts 7,53; the passage in Hebrew under discussion; some references to Samaritan sources. He concluded, however, that "hostility to Christians caused the Rabbis to revert to older view in Shabb 88b, Shemot Rabba 28. The angel here writes, not the Pentateuch, but a history up to the Messianic kingdom, but Deut XXVIII-XXX may be meant."[11] Montefiore, too, finds the passage a doubtful expression of the view that the Law was given through angelic mediation.[12] Indeed, more than half a century ago Louis Ginzberg argued the impossibility of making Jubilees support such a view since, as he pointed out, 1,4ff. expressedly states that God himself taught Moses.[13] Even were the claim to be upheld, one may ask whose position within the range of Jewish ideas does Jubilees represent? At all events, references to the angel of the presence, understood within the total context of Jubilees, indicate his having played some special role, but they do not serve, seen within that context, as evidence for angelic mediation of *Torah*.

2. The second extra-rabbinic proof offered is LXX of Deut 33,2 where in place of the notoriously difficult reading *mymynw ʾšdt* one reads *ek dexiōn autou angeloi met'autou*, "at his right hand were angels with him". Bruce comments: "This associates angels more closely with the law-giving, but does not make them mediators." Indeed, he appears to be in agreement with Calvin whom he cites in a note: "It is probable that both Paul and Stephen derived from this passage their statement that the Law 'was ordained by Angels in the hand of a mediator' (Gal iii, 19; Acts vii, 53) for its authority was greatly confirmed by its having so many witnesses *(obsignatores)*."[14] Which, of course, is something quite other than a "common belief . . . that the Law was given through angelic mediators", and leaves us with a diminished collection of evidence.

3. The most important proof generally cited is the passage in Josephus *(Antiquities* XV, 136) which reports Herod's exhortation of "the masses" after a defeat at the hand of the Arabs. The foe had "seized and destroyed the envoys of the Jews who had come to make peace with them". Herod, referring to this action in order to stir up the people,

pointed out that the Greeks held the person of the herald—*kērykos*—
"sacred and inviolable", and the Jews, too, he argued, understood this
since they had "learned the noblest of our doctrines and the holiest of
our laws, *di' angelon para tou Theou*". Ralph Marcus in his note to this
passage wrote: "Most scholars take *angeloi* here to mean 'angels' but it
seems to me that the prophets or priests are meant", hence, he translated it "messengers".[15] The meaning of the word is certainly crucial, for
the phrase in which it occurs, *nomois di'angelōn para tou Theou* comes
close to that in Heb, *di'angelon lalētheis logos*.

The whole question has been examined by W. D. Davies who, having
first suggested that "the well-attested traditions that the Law was given
by angels" makes it "natural to find the idea here in Josephus", goes on
to suggest five major considerations that "*may* justify our finding a
reference instead to the prophets as ambassadors of God."[16] Ginzberg,
too, had argued that the passage is "ein Wortspiel mit *ml'k*, das heb-
räisch sowohl Engel wie Gesandter bedeutet; Gott, sagt dieser, offen-
barte die wichtigsten Lehren und Gesetze durch Moses und die Prophe-
ten, die er—nach biblischen Sprachgebrauch Chaggai I, 17—als 'Engel'
bzw. "Gesandte'—bezeichnet."[17] Clearly the intent of the passage is to
argue the sacred nature and the inviolability of messengers by reference
to their function. Thus *kēryx* and *angelos* must be thought of as parallel
terms if the argument is to have meaning. Josephus portrays Herod as
discussing international law, not theology.

With this the extra-rabbinic/hellenistic evidence all but vanishes. At
most one may say that on the basis of the material cited there was a
belief, among some hellenistic Jews, in the presence of angels at Sinai;
further, that the term *angelos* was used to refer functionally to a messenger between God and man without any indication of his nature,
semi-divine or human. But it is impossible to claim on the basis of these
materials that there was a "well-attested tradition that the Law was
given by angels". Neither the existence of angels, nor their presence at
Sinai, nor their function as messengers allows for such a conclusion. We
are thus made dependent upon rabbinic materials if the case is to be
proved.

Rabbinic sources

Strack-Billerbeck have gathered together *ad* Galatians 3,19 all of the
material, including that just examined, that have been used by commentators to support the idea of angelic mediation of *Torah*. The authors
themselves are, however, quite cautious: "Die Anwesenheit von Engeln
bei der Gesetzgebung ist altjüdisches Traditionsgut . . . Über die Auf-
gabe der Engel bei Gesetzgebung gehen die Meinungen auseinander."

Unfortunately, those who have depended upon Strack-Billerbeck or who have found the material elsewhere have not been so cautious; hence, a seriatim examination of the material is called for.[18]

1. *Pesikta rabbati* 21. The verse commented on is Ps 68,18:

rkb ʾlhym rbwtym ʾlphy shnʾn ʾdny bm syny bqdsh

The words under discussion are *ʾlphy shnʾn*, variously understood. R. Jose b. Halafta (c. 140-165 C.E.) states that the angels referred to by these words are "the princes (i.e., the guardian angels) of the nations of the world."[19] Strack-Billerbeck suggest in their comment, "Damit soll wohl gesagt sein, dass diesen die Torah ebenso bekanntgegeben sei wie den von ihnen vertretenen Volkern selbst," which is certainly irrelevant to our problem.

2. *Pesikta de Rab Kahana*. Here, too, Ps 68,18 is under discussion. R. Eleazar b. Pedat explaining *ʾlphy shnʾn* said: "They came down (with) sharpened (swords) to consume Israel's enemies (a euphemism for Israel); if they did not accept the Torah, they would destroy them."[20] Strack-Billerbeck render this correctly. There is no reference to angelic mediation of Torah.

3. *Mekilta* to Ex 20,18. The words commented on are "and they stood afar off." The Mekilta explains: "more than twelve miles" and goes on to report that the Israelites fled when they heard the ten words being spoken and return to their original place after each word, so that by the time all the words had been spoken they had travelled two hundred and forty miles and were quite exhausted. Therefore God sent the ministering angels to support the weary people.[21] Strack-Billerbeck sum up this reference and its parallels with these words: "Engel unterstützen die Israeliten, das sie die körperlichen Anstrengungen, die für sie mit der Gesetzgebung verbunden waren, ertagen könnten." Again, we have a report of the presence of angels but not of mediation of *Torah*.

4. Babylonian Talmud, *Shabbat* 88a. Again the text commented on is Ps 68,18, and while the angels are said to accompany God to Sinai, their activity is confined to the period following the giving of *Torah* and consists in crowning each Israelite with two crowns as a reward for Israel's double declaration: "We will do and we will harken," (Exod 24,7). Strack-Billerbeck's summary is clear: "Die Engel schmücken die Israeliten zum Lohn für die Annahme der Tora. Nach einer andern Ansicht würde diese Ehre nur den Stamm Levi zuteil."

5. Even a cursory examination of the material thus far cited, together with the parallels reported by Strack-Billerbeck, makes it unmistakably evident that none of it supports anything more than the idea that angels

were present at Sinai and had some secondary role in the events surrounding the giving of Torah. However, the sixth section of Strack-Billerbeck's collection of material is introduced by the statement: "Die Engel setzten den Israeliten das Gesetz u. die Tragweite seiner einzelnen Bestimmungen auseinander." This is, of course, a crucial claim. The principal evidence educed is the passage from Josephus discussed above and, in addition, another citation from *Pesikta Rabbati* 21. This latter text reads:

> *bmswrt s'lh bydm mn hgwlh mṣ'u ktb trtyn rbwn d'lphy shn'n dml'kyn yrdw 'm hqdwsh brwk hw' 'l hr syny lytn twrh lyśr'l*

The translation offered reads: "In einer Überlieferung, die in ihrer Hand (mit der Zurückgekehrten) aus dem Exil heraufgekommen ist, fand man geschrieben: Zwei Myriaden von den unter der Engel führen mit Gott hernieder auf den Berg Sinai, um Israel die Torah zu geben." This seems a clear statement that the angels did indeed give *Torah* to Israel. However, before a conclusive claim be made, it would be well to examine the pericope beginning at the top of 102b in the Friedmann edition and continuing to the top of 105a. The whole section is devoted to interpretations of Ps 68,18 and the several words or phrases that compose it are understood to refer to the event at Sinai and its *dramatis personae*.[22] The phrase *'lphy shn'n*, as we have seen above, is taken to denote various groups of angels while *rbwtym* is interpreted variously to indicate the number present. The phrase *'dny bm syny* is understood to mean: "the Lord (was) with them (on) Sinai", the "them" referring to the angels mentioned in the previous words. The concluding word *bqdsh* is also variously explained. What we have before us is a midrashic structure at whose center is the phrase "descended with God to Mt. Sinai." To this is added, either before or after, mention of which angels and of their number. One example of this, with mention of the angels and their number following the set phrase, is found beginning with the last words at the bottom of 102b and continuing at the top of 103a: "Said R. Yohanan, on the day the Holy One blessed be he revealed himself upon Mt. Sinai to give Torah to Israel, there descended with him 60 myriads of angels." At the top of 102b the angels are mentioned before the set phrase: "Said R. Abudimi of Haifa, I learned in a mishnaic collection I have, 22,000 ministering angels descended with the Holy One blessed be he upon Mt. Sinai."

In the case at hand, the interpretation begins with the mention of the number, 2 myriads, followed by the specification of the kind of angels, *'lphy shn'n*, then the set phrase, "descended with the Holy One blessed be he upon Mt. Sinai." This is followed by the clause, "to give Torah to Israel." Now it is possible to argue that the plural subject of the finite verb "descended" is to be carried over as subject of the infinitive "to give," indicating that the angels came to give Torah to Israel, but in the face of the structural analysis here offered and the parallel phrase noted above "the Holy One blessed be he revealed himself upon Mt. Sinai to give Torah to Israel", it is indeed doubtful.[23] At any rate it seems highly unwise to make a possible ambiguity arising out of the use of a formal literary phrase bear too great a burden of proof. And what is more, when one reads on a few lines further one encounters the question "why did they come down? to honor the Torah or to honor Israel?" which does not suggest that there was any intention of teaching that they came to give Torah.

In this same section, Strack-Billerbeck cite another passage, this from Midrash Song of Songs Rabbah 1,2, to support the suggestion made in their introductory remark that the angels also explained the significance of the individual items of Torah to the Israelites. The verse commented upon in *yshqny mnshyqwt pyhw*, understood to mean "he kissed me with the kisses of his mouth." R. Yohanan (c. 279 C.E.) explained the verse in this fashion: "An angel would bring forth each of the words from the divine presence and carry it around to each individual Israelite asking, 'do you accept this word? Thus and so are the decrees implicit in it . . . ' To which each Israelite would respond: Yea! He would further ask, 'do you accept the divinity of the Holy One blessed be he?' To which the individual would respond, Yea! Yea! Immediately he kissed him upon his mouth as it is written: 'to you was it shown that you might know' (Deut 4,35) by a messenger." The majority of scholars, however, held that the "word" itself approached each Israelite and asked acceptance.[24]

This passage, of all examined, does suggest angelic mediation, particularly R. Yohanan's addition of the words "by a messenger" to the quotation from Deut 4,35. However, it must be noted that the statement comes from the end of the third Christian century and represents the opinion of one expositor. In the absence of an intervening chain of tradition carrying it back to earlier teachers and of parallels in earlier Midrashim, it can hardly be expected to establish by itself the claim that angelic mediation of Torah was a widely accepted view in the first century C.E. Further, when one pays attention to the theological concern of the passage, one sees that the problem under discussion is the subject of the verb *yshqny*, "he kissed". Given the general allegorical nature of the exposition of Song of Songs, one may expect it to be God. However, R. Yohanan and his opponents are loathe to make that assumption. Rather, they sought a substitute: either an angel or the word itself bestows the kiss.

With what then are we left? A possible ambiguity explicable as arising out of a formal literary structure, and a single opinion of a late third century teacher whose focus is elsewhere. This is hardly sufficient evidence upon which to base the ubiquitous claim that there was a widespread belief in angelic mediation of *Torah* in the first Christian century. Which brings back our original suggestion that *ho di' angelōn* of Heb 2,2 is a reference back to *tois prophētais* of Heb 1,1 and taken together they support the tradition reported in *Wayyiqra Rabba* that prophets are called angels / messengers, a tradition that lies behind LXX's rendition of *nby'w* in the Qumran text of Ps 151 as *angelōn autou*. This, of course, points to the suggestion frequently made concerning a connection between the Epistle to the Hebrews and the community at Qumran. It may even suggest something about the authorship of Ps 151 and raises questions about its appearance in LXX.

NOTES

1. J. A. Sanders, *The Psalm Scroll of Qumran Cave 11* (11QPs[a]), Discoveries in the Judaean Desert of Jordan, IV (Oxford, 1965) p 54-60; *The Dead Sea Psalm Scroll* (Cornell University Press, 1967) p 96-97.
2. Mordecai Margulies, *Midrash Wayyiqra Rabbah: A Critical Edition based on manuscripts and Genizah fragments with variants and notes* (Jerusalem, 1953) I, 2ff. See below note 15.
3. Martin Noth, "Die fünf syrisch überlieferten apokryphen Psalmen," *ZAW*, 48(1930) p 1-23.
4. *Op. cit., loc. cit.*
5. For the bibliographical reference see below, note 10(b), Montefiore.
6. But see note a *ad loc.*: "The Law given through the intermediary of angels, cf. Gn 3,19+, . . ." The reference is, of course, not to Genesis but Galatians. The note there, "k", reads: "In Jewish tradition angels were present at Sinai when the Law was given. The 'intermediary' is Moses, cf. Acts 7,38+."
7. For bibliographic reference see below, note 10(1), Moffatt.
8. See below note 10(b) for bibliographical details.
9. See below note 16.
10. (a) F. F. Bruce, *The Epistle to the Hebrews* (Grand Rapids, Michigan: Eerdmans, 1964), p 28. (b) Hugh Montefiore, *A Commentary on the Epistle to the Hebrews* (New York: Harper and Row, 1964), p 52. (c) C. Spicq, O. P., *L'Epitre aux Hebreux* (Paris: Gabalda, 1953), p 54. (d) Otto Michel, *Der Brief an die Hebräer* (Göttingen: Vandenhoeck & Ruprecht, 1966) p 125. (e) Heinrich Schlier, *Der Brief an die Galater* (Göttingen: Vandenhoeck & Ruprecht, 1951) p 109ff. (f) G. Kittel, *ThWNT* I p 82. (g) Hans Windisch, *Der Hebräerbrief* (Tübingen, 1931, 2nd ed). (h) Hans Kosmala, *Hebräer-Essener-Christen* (Leiden: Brill, 1959) p 77. (i) Martin Dibelius, *Die Geisterwelt im Glauben des Paulus* (Göttingen: Vandenhoeck & Ruprecht, 1909) p 278ff. (j) F. Weber, *Jüdische Theologie* (2te Aufl., 1897) p 269ff. (k) Bousset-Gressmann, *Die Religion des Judentums* (3te verb. Aufl., 1926) p 120. (l)

Jas Moffatt, *ICC, Epistle to the Hebrews* (1924). (m) E. Burton, *ICC, Galatians* (1920). (n) O. Everling, *Die paulinsche Angelologie und Dämonologie* (1888). (o) Strack-Billerbeck, *Kommentar zum Neuen Testament aus Talmud und Midrash* (München: C. H. Beck, 1926) III p 554 et seq.

11. R. H. Charles, ed., *The Apocrypha and Pseudepigrapha of the Old Testament* (Oxford, 1913) II, "The Book of Jubilees," *ad* 1,27. The Philo passage is referred to by Spicq but it is most tenuous and is ignored by the other commentators.

12. *Op. cit., loc. cit.*

13. Louis Ginzberg, *Eine Unbekannte Jüdische Sekte* (New York, 1922, p 246-247. The long note beginning on p 246 brings together considerable evidence challenging the idea of angelic meditation of *Torah*. It has been uniformly ignored by the commentators. In addition it should be noted that Jub. 1,26, immediately preceding the verse in question, reads: "And do thou write down for thyself all these words which I declare unto thee on this mountain, . . .", a clear reference to Moses as mediator. In the English edition of this work, *An Unknown Jewish Sect* (New York: *JTSA*, 1976), this note is found on p 172-173.

14. See note 10 (a) for bibliographical details.

15. F. Josephus, *Jewish Antiquities,* ed Ralph Marcus (Cambridge and London, 1963) XV, 136 (p 66, note a). Marcus refers to Ginzberg, see above note 13. He also refers to the passage in *Wayyiqra Rabbah,* see above note 2, an item I had connected with the problem independently, and to the essays cited in the following note.

16. W. D. Davies, "A Note on Josephus, Antiquities 15, 136," *HTR* 47(1954) p 135-140. Marcus cites this paper in the note cited above, together with that of Francis R. Walton, "The Messenger of God in Hecataeus of Abdera," *ibid.* 48(1955) p 255-257. Not only must Davies' evidence and arguments be given careful attention but one must as well keep an eye open for the circular argument that besets the whole discussion. The "well-attested tradition" making it "natural to find the idea (of angelic mediation of Torah) in Josephus", itself depends in part for attestation on Josephus. When the Josephus passage is removed, an important element in the argument that there was a widespread belief in angelic mediation of Torah falls out. Montefiore, Spicq, Michel, Schlier, Charles, Bousset-Gressmann, Moffatt, Burton, Kosmala, Strack-Billerbeck all take Jos. as evidence for the angelic mediation of Torah. So does Morton Smith in his review of W. D. Davies, *Torah in the Messianic and/or Age to Come JBL* 72(1953), p 192.

17. See note 13.

18. See note 10 (o) for bibliographical details. References to St.-B. are found in Spicq, Michel, Schlier, Kittel, Davies. See notes 10 and 16 for bibliographical details.

19. M. Friedmann, *Pesikta Rabbati: Midrasch für den Fest-Cyclus und die aus-gezeichneten Sabbathe* (Wien, 1880). The passage referred to here is found on page 103b. See too, *Pesikta Rabbati: Discourses for Feasts, Fasts and Special Sabbaths,* translated from the Hebrew by William G. Braude (Yale University Press, New Haven, 1968) 2 vols. See Vol. I, 425-428.

20. The edition from which St.-B. cite (the correct reference is 107b-108a) is that of Sol. Buber, *Pesikta, die alteste Hagada, redigirit in Palastine von Rab Kahana* (Lyck, 1868). See too, B. Mandelbaum, *Pesikta de Rav Kahana* (New York, 1962) 2 vols; Vol. I p 219-220; the statement is made by R. Eleazar b. Pedat (c. 270 C.E.).

21. There are three modern editions of this work. That of J. Z. Lauterbach (Philadelphia, 1933) in 3 vols has an English translation. The passage cited is

Bahodesh IX, (Lauterbach, II p 269). Bruce, above note 10 (a), cites this passage as an allusion to angelic mediation. Spicq, above note 10 (c), refers to St.-B.

22. *Op. cit.* note 19. Chapter 21 begins on p 98b and continues to p 110b. The relevant citations, i.e., the interpretation of Ps 68,18, begin at the top of page 102b and continue to the bottom of page 103b. English translation, p 425-428.

23. I would translate the passage in a slightly different fashion: "in a tradition they received from the Exile (= Babylonia) they found written (*KTYB* =*KTB*, see Bacher, *Die Exegetische Terminologie der Jüdischen Traditionsliteratur*, II, 93): two myriads of *'lphy sn'n*, i.e., of angels, descended with the Holy One blessed be he upon Mt. Sinai to give Torah to Israel." See, too, Braude's translation, I p 428. In *Pesikta de Rab Kahana*, 107b (Mandelbaum, I p 220), and *Midrash Tehillim* to Ps 68,10, the clause "to give Torah to Israel" is lacking.

24. *Midrash Rabbah, Song of Songs* (London: Soncino Press, 1939) IX, *ad loc.*

Who Are the People of God?

GERARD S. SLOYAN

The obvious answer to the question, "Who Are the People of God?" is that in the strict theological sense God alone knows. Peoples are not lacking, however, who say that he has revealed himself to them on this subject. The claim is widespread. Surprising numbers of peoples and groups have identified themselves as the objects of the divine predilection. From an inspection of the notion of God, one might deduce that the human race was his people and that any restriction of the idea had to be a confusion on the nature of deity. From the standpoint of the people in question, its consciousness of chosenness by him and fidelity to him is the distinctive feature.

A fairly sophisticated theodicy might see the dispossessed as the people of God. The reality of human freedom alters the case somewhat, with its introduction of the idea of free response to the providential purpose or plan. Still, the concept of God's antecedent choice of some over others of his creatures—however the divine will may be viewed—is fraught with so many difficulties that it gives the appearance of being a cloak for human ignorance of the mysteriousness of his ways.

The question of a people of God would not be consequential for Jews or Christians or groups deriving from either except that it has come to the fore strongly in Catholic usage at that point in history when ecumenical reaching out in a conciliatory spirit is being fostered by Jews and Christians. The period in question, the decades immediately following the Second Council of the Vatican, are at the same time the *floruit* of John M. Oesterreicher. The term needs examining to see whether a counterproductive usage begins to flourish at just that time when a truly productive conversation has been inaugurated.

It is possible to capsulize the concept "people of God" for purposes of dismissing it—as segments of the worlds of sociology and psychology do—by calling it psychic grandiosity or imperialism of the spirit. A less emotive approach would be to describe the phenomenon as the reported experience of God's elective presence to a people, however wide or narrow the ethnic, geographic, or other extension of peoplehood may be, and let the matter go at that. A descriptive discipline like anthropology does just this. Philosophy tends to examine truth claims, while religions are in the business of both making truth claims and exploring them reflectively. The matter cannot, therefore, be left to the psychic distancing attempted by anthropology, from which a faintly patronizing tone as regards religious matters is not always absent. Despite the dispassion claimed for this social science, student and teacher, expert and layperson alike inhabit a world where claims are made for the exclusive possession of religious truth. Part of this larger claim is the claim that God has made special choice of a people or peoples. The notion cannot be dismissed lightly. It has to be examined with the same seriousness with which it is put forward. Moreover, great respect not only for persons but for the claim itself must mark the inquiry since it comprises for many a penultimate value short of the worship proper to godhead. With varying degrees of intensity, religious peoplehood is close to the heart of the religious reality.

The present writer does not have the capacity to explore the concept of the people of God by a comparative anthropological method. It is clear that similar skills would be required for a religious taxonomy of all the groups that have sprung from Christianity as new religions with whom the claim, if not the precise term, is associated—like the Latter Day Saints and Jehovah's Witnesses. The writer does know something of how the Christian church acquired the title from the Jews, via an accommodation of phrases in the Septuagint Greek Bible, and what it made of it in subsequent centuries. This usage the present essay shall try to explore.

The gospels are a record of the terms of discipleship of Jesus, who in turn is thought to be the son of man, the Lord, the son of God, the Christ. "Come after me" (Mark 1,17) and "Follow me" (Mark 2,14; 10,21) are invitations that dot its pages. Response to the challenge is made in a trustful state of mind described as *pistis*, faith. This faith is primarily lodged in God but a component of it is trust in Jesus: that he is God's man, that he speaks the truth, that under God he is capable of deeds of power. The words for "faith" and "believe" occur fairly infrequently in the first three gospels, so we must look for the concept of discipleship there in another vocabulary as well. Indeed, the evidence seems to be that the primitive church, for which faith was centrally significant, expanded several of Jesus' original sayings in this direction.

Thus, the praise of Jesus directed to a Canaanite in Matthew, "O woman, great is your faith," is an addition to a Marcan original (Matt

15,28 = Mark 7,29), while Luke adds the verb for faith twice to his telling of the parable of the seed spread randomly by the sower (Luke 8,12f). Jesus may well have said things like, "Your faith has healed you" to the menstruous woman, but that it has come down to us with the vocabulary *pistis* and *sesōken* from *sōzein*, "to save" (Mark 5,34), is noteworthy. Similarly, Jesus says to a Roman centurion, "Even as you trusted *('episteusas)*, (so) shall it be done to you" (Matt 8,13). J. Jeremias warns against too great suspicion, however, since the Aramaic family *hemin, hemanuta²* could easily underlie the *pisteuein/pistis* group without the overtones of later church belief in Jesus as savior. Since more than half the words for faith in the first three gospels occur in a context of miracle stories or sayings dealing with miracles, and all are put on Jesus' lips with very few exceptions, they convey both an unqualified confidence in his power and his attitude toward that confidence. When this group of words is applied to the disciples it implies a recognition of Jesus as the prophet of the time of salvation, the vanquisher of Satan, and the messenger of good news for the poor. The disciples' faith "includes readiness to sacrifice family, possessions and even life."[1] Faith is not the only New Testament vocabulary of discipleship but it is an important one.

A group of disciples accompanies Jesus on his travels (Mark 2,14; Acts 1,21), including women (Luke 8,1-3; Mark 15,40f). The nucleus is described as a certain twelve whom he sends out, the traditions on whose names differ as is evidenced by the gospel listings. Only in two places does the word *ekklēsia,* usually rendered "church," occur in the gospels (Matt 16,18 and 18,17 (twice)). It is probably a Greek rendition of *'edah,* a congregation. While *ekklēsia* clearly came into use in Pauline circles as a description of a local community or of believers in Jesus taken globally, the Matthew who wrote some three decades after Paul could have been reporting a primitive Jesus-use of the term like that found in Qumran scrolls. In Cave IV, a commentary on Ps 37 has been found which says that v 23-24 of that psalm speaks of "the Priest, the (Teacher of Righteousness . . . whom) he established to build for himself a congregation of. . ."[2] This seems to be the closest verbal parallel to Matthew's "building a congregation" of 16,18, establishing it as a possible Jesus-saying even though the later usages of *ekklēsia* in ch 18 seem clearly to be church-sayings.

'Edah, when used favorably in Qumran, at times means the heavenly host but most often the Essene community itself—members of the people of salvation rather than the reprobated others. Hence the *ekklēsia* of Matthew may as fittingly be rendered "the people of God" as "the church." In both the Qumran and the Christian cases a certainty of

election is testified to which the Jewish people also shared, be it all the circumcised and their womenfolk or merely the righteous among them, along with proselytes and Godfearers.

The gospel terms for a people of God formed by discipleship of Jesus are numerous: a flock (Mark 14,27 = Matt 26,31) which the shepherd frees from oppressive isolation (Matt 15,24; John 10,1-5; see Jer 23,1-8); the guests at a wedding (Mark 2,19 and parallels); God's planting (Matt 13,24) or building (Matt 16,18; see Hag 2,7. 9, "this house"); the city of God set on a hill (Matt 5,14; "Zion" in Isa 2,2-4; 25,6-8); members of a covenant sealed in blood (Mark 14,24 par.) which Luke (22,20) and Paul (1Cor 11,25) describe as "new."

No image of his followers as God's warriors, such as is found at Qumran, appears in Jesus' teachings. His disciples, having given up all to follow him (Mark 10,29f. par.), are the end-time family of whom God alone is the Father (Matt 23,9). Jesus is the master of the household, his followers the other members (Matt 10,25). In one extension of the idea, all in need or oppressed or desolate are called his least brothers (*'elachistōn*; Matt 25,40). Elsewhere, his followers are the children *(nēpioi)* of God's family (Matt 11,25) or a table-fellowship that anticipates the final banquet of salvation (Matt 8,11f).

It is impossible to know how the early followers of Jesus conceived of themselves unless one tries to get inside the world of eschatological Judaism. The Jews over their long history have had many ways to speak of themselves as elect, the recipients of the divine favor and at the same time of great testing (e.g., "dearer to me than all other peoples", Exod 19,5; "you shall be to me a . . . holy nation", v 6; "my people", Lev 26,12; "a people of the LORD", Num 27,17; "a people peculiarly his own", Deut 26,18; "a people sacred to the LORD", v 19; "his people", Ps 73,10; "I will be your God and you shall be my people", Jer 7,23; see Ezek 14,11. The most frequent usage is the oblique "my/your/his people"; it is always a "people of the LORD" in the Hebrew Bible because the divine name is specific; "people of God" seems to occur for the first time in Heb 4,9; see 11,25; 1Pet 2,10; see Wis 18,13, "the people was God's son").

Theoretically, believers in Jesus could call on all the imagery that preceded him to describe the reality of a relation with Israel's God. In fact, they were confined largely to the period of Jesus' brief public career and the time going backward to the Maccabean revolt and forward to the fall of Jerusalem. The imagery and working vocabulary of the Christian movement was that of apocalyptic Judaism. It is a commonplace to say that Jesus' followers expected consummation of the visible universe soon, and that the problem of second and third generation Christians was to account satisfactorily for his delayed coming. 2Peter discusses the problem in just these words, using the term "delay" (*bradytēta*, 3,9). Yet this latest of New Testament documents (ca. 135?) testifies to a time when Christian communities were no longer at ease with eschatological categories, just as Jewish communities under the influence of the up-surging academy at Javneh were not. A moment had passed in Jewish life. Neither the Jews under the influence of the rabbis—by far the greater part—nor those who followed Jesus as sole "rabbi" (also *didas-kalos* and *kathēgētēs;* see Matt 23,8-10) were able to recapture the urgent expectation of God's inbreaking. The difference was that the Jesus party continued to use this rhetoric throughout its history because it had come to birth during this moment and as part of this expectation.

It is not farfetched to make an analogy between the Qumran sect and the Christians, on the unlikely hypothesis that the former had accepted large numbers of Gentile proselytes and ultimately been replaced by them. The language of special choice, the vehement vocabulary of divine predilection would have continued undisturbed, with a clear distinction made between the chosen congregation and the faithless in Jerusalem who continued to practice debased temple worship. Thus, Acts 15,14 has James saying that Simon (Peter) has just told the apostles and presbyters "how God first concerned himself with taking from among the Gentiles a people to bear his name", while the Lord (Jesus) says to Paul in vision at Corinth that he should persevere, for, "There are many of my people in this city" (Acts 18,10). Those faithful on the new terms, in other words, receive the ancient designation of election "people", ethnicity apart.

We have to understand the original Jesus movement as an Israel of faith largely unconcerned with its ethnic composition if we are to understand it all (see Rom 1,16; 3,30). At times the word Israel will mean actual Jews in the New Testament but seldom those in opposition (thus "the Israel of God", Gal. 6,16—either synonymous with or contrasted with "all who follow this rule of life" i.e., the Jews and Gentiles of the church who are "created anew"; see Luke 1,68; John 1,31; Eph 2,12). At other times, the term "Jews" is employed for those of that stock who do not "believe," while "Israel" and "(true) Israelite" are reserved to those with potential right faith in God through Jesus Christ (see John 1,47.49; Rom 9,6; 11,1; but against this, see Rom 9,31; Heb 12,25). The latter people in its faith is heir to the promise, without regard to makeup as to "blood or the will of the flesh or the will of man" (John 1,13). This faith community comes to birth, like the Word itself, "from the will of God" (*ibid*).

Knowing what we do of Jewish thought on the remnant (*šearith*) that would cleave to the LORD faithfully through the terrible adversity of the exile, it is surprising to learn how little use the Christians made of the concept. Peoplehood for them, their status as a congregation of the LORD, was not a matter of birth or covenant circumcision (see Matt 3,9; see John 8,33. 39). It was a matter of faith, not simply the Pauline faith spelled out in Galatians and Romans, where it is primarily the corporate state of the justified (the righteous) as opposed to the corporate state of the non-justified (the unrighteous), but also conscious, individual response to the divine call. To be sure, there is a community of believers found in local churches but the communities are made up of those who come together in a response of faith. The gospel is preached to Jew first, then to Greek (Rom 1,16; 2,9). One may say, "to the Jew as a member of a covenanted people", since there is no other Jew. But, widescale as the invitation may be (i.e., to the Jewish people corporately), it is responded to individually. The respondents become members of a new body, a new people. In the earliest period, however, the concept was of a people Israel (Jewish by definition) adopting the new teaching and admitting to their company Gentiles who had the same faith in Jesus as the Christ.

Once only is the concept of the remnant invoked, where Paul speaks of there being a *leimma* "according to choice of grace" (Rom 11,5). He does so in a context of denying hotly that there has been any rejection by God of his people whom he foreknew (verse 2). Paul recalls Elijah as claiming on Carmel that he alone is faithful, against which boast the LORD cites the seven thousand remaining to himself who have not bent the knee to Baal (verse 4; see 1Kgs 19,18). Just as in the past, Paul argues, God chose the faithful whom he chose *freely*, so lately the "remnant" of his application of the idea—the Jews who believe in Christ—are chosen "by the grace of God, not because of their works; otherwise grace would not be grace" (verse 6). Grace for Paul is the divine initiative in freedom, as it was for other segments of the church that did not feature the term. Various as were the New Testament theologies of God's action in Christ, they were at one in holding that he chosen freely and was responded to equally freely. The fewness of the Jews who made the response was a theological problem to the New Testament writers. The surprising Gentile response was a problem of another kind. They reacted to it as their forebears had often done before, e.g., in the books of Ruth and Jonah, with praise for the mysteriousness of the divine choice. The Pauline explanation was that God chooses whom he will choose. He names a people who before were not "my people" to be "my people" (Rom 9,26; see Hos 2,25). "I am speaking about us whom he has called, not only from among the Jews, but from among the Gentiles" (Rom 9,24).

Much of the New Testament is devoted to the question, not of whether there is a people of God or whether the followers of Jesus are that people—its authors are convinced that both are the case—but how it can be that ethnic Jews are of that people in such poor strength; or that Jews and Gentiles are divinely intended to make up that people on equal footing, although the Jews will forever have been called first.

The solution to the first question provided by Matthew's gospel is fairly well known. There is the concluding commission of Jesus to preach the gospel to *panta ta 'ethnē*, all the *goyim*, after every avenue known to the evangelist has been explored. His account contains, he thinks, the record of missed opportunities by the people for whom the gospel of Jesus Christ was first divinely intended (Matt 21,43; 24,51; 27,25). Luke tells a story in two books in which Jerusalem is always the point of origin of the gospel with its pious poor (2,29-38), its "many priests" (Acts 6,7) who embraced the gospel, and its pride of place as the city of temple and law. Ultimately, the gospel must go out from Caesarea (Acts 27,2), across the sea to the Gentile capital Rome (28,28).

What Mark and Matthew do with "the scribes and Pharisees", and all four Evangelists in the passion accounts with the "high priests," John in the earlier part of his gospel uses the term "the Jews" to accomplish. It is hard to know who is included but it is clearly not everyone who is Jewish. John's *hoi Ioudaioi* are in most instances Jews other than the Jews marked by acceptance of Jesus on John's terms who populate his pages. Some have thought them Judaeans, others Jews in opposition to the Jesus party of John's day, still others Jewish believers in Jesus whose christology is not "high" enough for the evangelist. His people of God are those who love the light and not the darkness, who "hear" Jesus' words, who turn their backs on life in a *kosmos* set against God so as to possess the life of the new eon (*zoē aiōnios*, generally translated "eternal life.") To be a "Jew" in John, we may say, has everything to do with peoplehood—and nothing to do with it. Like the other evangelists, he finds himself rewriting the scriptures in the light of events, and redefining who it is that is called to be the people of God.

Clearly St. Paul attempted, in the early chapters of his epistle to the Romans, a relation of the two populations that made up the Christian community in that city, Jews and non-Jews. He marvels that God is the God, not of the Jews only, but of the Gentiles as well: "It is the same God who justifies the circumcised and the uncircumcised on the basis of faith" (Rom 3,30). He then asks if this view abolishes the law by means of faith and answers with a vehement negative: "Not at all! On the contrary we are confirming the law" (v 31). We quote him here without interrupting him to examine whether he is right or wrong. It should only be pointed out that at times in early Romans his Jews are Christian Jews (e.g. 7,1). Later, in chapters 9-11, he discourses on "my brothers . . . my kinsmen, the Israelites" for whose sake, in a rhetorical indirect voluntary, he might even wish to be separated from Christ. No exegesis of those chapters shall be attempted here, only a report of Paul's claim that, "not all who are from (or out of) Israel (are) Israel, not are all who are the seed of Abraham his children" (9,6). Whereas chapter 10 is full of assurance that the Israelites (v 1) are to be saved by the justice that comes with faith in Christ, chapter 11 seems to contain the acknowledgment of an unsearchable alternate plan of God (11,33-36) to save "his people" (11,1. 2) without reference to Jesus Christ, who is not mentioned in that chapter. In other words, the importance of Paul's thoughts on the Jews who do not follow Jesus, here and elsewhere, lies in what he does not know about God's design, not—as is generally assumed—what he knows.

The epistle to the Ephesians, which is an epistle only in form but in fact a treatise, was not originally addressed to Ephesus and is written by a disciple of Paul rather than Paul himself. It has perhaps never been taken sufficiently seriously by Christians. Ephesians claims that *the* mystery, the plan that God has revealed in Jesus Christ (see 1,9f.; 3,4. 9. 11) was his will to break down the barrier of hostility that had kept Jews and Gentiles apart, reconciling the two to God and making one humanity of them (2,14-18). Jews who do not believe in Jesus are rightly unhappy at the terms spelled out in this vision of unity, which are faith in Jesus as Lord. The document was not addressed to them, however, but to Christian Jews and Gentiles.

The Gentiles who have largely made up the church since A.D. 135 have not considered seriously the negation of the apostolic preaching which Christian faith can constitute, a new and higher wall between Gentiles and Jews. Many Christians have assumed that the entrance of Jews into the church is the one way to take Ephesians seriously, whereas the main theological problem of the epistle is obviously how Gentile nations can enter into a Jewish patrimony without creating total hostility. Jesus of Nazareth can have no part in such hostility, yet he is saddled with it as if he had been its author by his own design.

The problem is described here as "obvious" but it cannot be that if it has eluded Christians so successfully for nineteen centuries. Had they begun with a religious vision of human unity that was without precedent, then declaring believers in Jesus Christ to be "the people of God" made up of Scythians and non-Scythians, Nubians and non-Nubians, Greeks and barbarians would make all the sense in the world. Instead they saw themselves as an Israel made up of Jews and Gentile proselytes and Godfearers—not a "new Israel" or a "true Israel" but simply Israel —in full continuity with the only Israel there is—among whom ethnic Jews fell to near the zero point. This vision of the church as Israel enlarged can be called absurd or impossible, but it is in fact what came to pass. The Jewish tail stayed small and the Gentile dog grew large. Yet the Christian community had no other origins than these. Consequently, this tradition seeks understanding—and self-understanding—in designating itself biblically from earliest times the *laos* (the "people") that is the LORD's own. Its sole writings at the start were the Bible. It had not from the outset the self-designations "body" or "temple" or "vine". Matthew's *ekklēsia* (16,18; 18,17) which came after Paul's letters of the 50's was joined by a whole series of biblical antitypes, among them "bride," "holy city," and "new Jerusalem." The designation of the church as a "people" *(laos)*[3] came to the fore as early as the second century (Just *Dial* 70,5) with the additional phrases "his people" (*1 Clem* 59,4; *2 Clem* 2,3), "new people" (*Barn* 3,6; Clem Alex *Paed* 1,7), and "Lord's people" (*ibid., Strom* 7,16). Concurrently the Jewish people were being described as a *laos* (see *1 Clem* 55,6; *Barn* 8,1; Just *I Apol* 60,2), although sometimes as the "old people" (Clem *Paed* 1,7) or "first people" (Euseb *Marcell* 1,1). The word continued in use for the church before and after the development of faulty theories of "replacement" of the Jews by the church in the patristic period, beginning with Justin in his *Dialogue with Trypho*. In medieval and renaissance-reformation times the Matthean and Pauline term "church" prevailed, attended by the well-known struggles in the latter period—and ever since—as to the nature of this reality. While "people of God" continued to enjoy some favor, it normally meant to Christians the Jewish people of call and covenant as often as it meant themselves. As a common term for Christians it largely fell out of use. *"Populus Dei"* simply does not have a lively career in Western theology.[4]

The German-born abbot of Buckfast, Anscar Vonier, could write a popular treatment of the church in 1937 (after his longer *The Spirit and the Bride* of 1935), entitling it *The People of God*, and win approval for his poetic inventiveness. There he distinguished between the "church" as sacramental and cultic and the "people of God" as denoting God's total life in mankind. A. Oepke's *Das neue Volk Gottes* appeared in 1959 and Nils A. Dahl's *Das Volk Gottes* was published in German two years later. These books, like H. F. Hamilton's *The People of God*, 2 vols. (Oxford, 1912), explore the peoplehood of Israel in the Hebrew Bible and the Christian community as its New Testament inheritor. They do not explore the use of the term in postbiblical Christian history. The ecumenical movement within Protestantism was responsible in good part for the restoration of "people of God" to describe the whole Christian body, in its efforts to transcend some long-standing internal Christian differences. The reformers had set the tone by employing the term *congregatio*, rendered *Volk* and *peuple*, to avoid some of the associations of *ecclesia*.

The intent of modern ecumenists to avoid ecclesial rifts was clear, the return to early Christian usage admirable. Catholics seized on the term for an additional reason, namely its avoidance of the juridical aspects of the medieval development *corpus Christi mysticum*. Unfortunately a side effect—which the Protestant theological community and the Second Council of the Vatican seemed to disregard, if indeed they were aware of it—is that the newly favored term can be understood to say that the biblical people of God, the Jews, are no longer his people or that they simply *are not*, as a people. Worse still, in the light of Christian commitment to the whole human race, there is the exclusivist intimation that ancient Jews and modern Christians are God's people but that this is a title to which none of his other children can lay claim. In brief, the new enthusiasm for chosenness raises the specter of an exclusivism that accords ill with the conviction of God's universal love.

To read the document *Lumen Gentium* on the church of Vatican II (Nov. 21, 1964) is to be reinforced in the conviction that the resurrection of the term which serves as the title of Chapter II is an offense against long-term theological wisdom. What is fully comprehensible as first-century usage is far from that in the twentieth. Going directly from Jer 31,31-34 to 1Cor 11,25 and 1Pet 2,9-10 without a fairly extensive treatment of Jewish-Christian relations in the first century, as the document does, can be ecumenically insensitive. The gain in internal ecclesiology is offset by the loss in the Christian outlook on the Jews.[5]

This view is strengthened by a reading of the relatively enlightened Karl Rahner's two-page entry on "People of God" in *Sacramentum Mundi*, a theological encyclopedia in six volumes.[6] He writes:

> The community of believers in Jesus knows itself to be the new convenant founded on his blood, the new Israel in the *Pneuma* (Spirit), to whom the promises of the Fathers have been transferred. Hence it affirms that it is the real, true, and definitive people of God . . . the pneumatically united sum of all who are justified . . . The people of God includes all (and again in different ways) who in any way (at whatever degree) belong to the Church . . . One could also quite well envisage the possibility of calling humanity itself the people of God.

In the attempt at universalism, which can only be praised, the Jewish people from whom the promises have been "transferred" have all but been forgotten as a "people of God." But this is perilously like playing Hamlet without the Prince of Denmark.

Is the problem soluble? Can the phrase be used in any way that does not cause more alienation than it is calculated to create Christian solidarity? There are serious difficulties posed to the modern mind by any religious body that sees itself as the people of God in an exclusive sense. The difficulties are ancient but they are not insurmountable. Rahner is to be commended for proposing the notion of the human race as God's people, lest contemporaries with a global view think that believers must foreshorten the divine concern and see it centered on them in order to believe in it. Yet he does not avoid the opposite pitfall.

The chief point of this brief paper is to observe that the fathers of Vatican II have not distinguished themselves theologically or pastorally by solving an internal problem regarding the church or the churches while probably creating another with respect to Christian continuity with Israel. There is an important discontinuity as well, but it is not total. The very eagerness of the Christian bodies to employ the term "the people of God" to describe themselves only is an indication of how little alerted they are to their own coming to birth from a Jewish mother who continues in good health. The problem is therefore as much one of an understanding in depth of Christian origins as it is of "ecumenical relations with the Jews".

One winces each time the term is used in Christian self-attribution exclusively. It is so often thoughtlessly uttered—without any note of conscious exclusiveness. The development may prove in the long run a happy fault. It can only force Christians to an examination, at an early date, of their own state as called, and that of the Jews who are not concerned with Jesus as also called. It is not comfortable to belong to a church to which one is committed thoroughly that has not yet worked out a theory of its own relations with the womb that bore it and breasts that nurse it.

NOTES

1. J. Jeremias, *New Testament Theology. The Proclamation of Jesus* (New York: Scribner's, 1971) p 164.

2. 4Qp Ps 37,III:16. G. Vermes, *The Dead Sea Scrolls in English*, Baltimore: Penguin Books, 1962) p 245.

3. See G.W.H. Lampe, *A Patristic Greek Dictionary* (Oxford, 1961-69) s.v.

4. Yves Congar in his two volumes, *L'Ecclésiologie du Haut Moyen Age. Du Saint Grégoire le Grand à la désunion entre Byzance et Rome* (Paris: Cerf, 1968) and *L'Eglise de Saint Augustin à l'époque moderne* (*ibid.*, 1970) does not cite any theological

usage of the term "people of God" in that span of fifteen centuries. Jurdically, the church was seen as *populus christianus* or *congregatio fidelium* from the carolingian era onward, while "Gregory VII, Urban II and the gregorians" struggle for the freedom of the clerical order within this wider *christianitas* or *populus christianus* (*L'Eglise*, p 112f; see p 118, 129; *L'Ecclésiologie*, p 64f). In theological writing, however, the church was either *ecclesia* simply or "body," "mother," "bride," "city of God," *universitas fidelium* or *sobor* (Russian: assembly); in later times, *"congregatio fidelium"* (see *L'Ecclésiologie*, p 98-104). Tertullian spoke of the local church as composed of *ordo* (clergy) and *plebs* (people) while Cyprian referred to the whole as a *populus universalis* (see Robert F. Evans, *One and Holy. The Church in Latin Patristic Texts*. London: S.P.C.K., 1972 p 47, 55 and citations). Only in a liturgical context is the Western Church *populus tuus, plebs tua, familia tua*, but often with an adjective appended: *populus christianus, plebs fidelis* (see *L'Eglise*, p. 39, where works of liturgical history by V. Manz (1941), A. Schaut (1949), and P. Bruylants (1952) are cited). Congar repeats this documentation in "The Church: The People of God," *The Church and Mankind*, "Concilium", Vol. 1 (1965), p 22f. For the restoration of "people of God" he must refer to the work of D.M. Koster, *Ekklesiologie im Werden* (Paderborn, 1940) and L. Cerfaux, *La théologie de l'Eglise suivant saint Paul* (Paris, 1942).

    5. Yves Congar makes a case for the potentially revolutionary effect of the chapters of *Lumen Gentium* in the order: Mystery of the Church, People of God, Hierarchical Church, rather than the latter two reversed. He thinks that the term, People of God conveys the laity's primacy of importance and a dynamism of tendency toward a divinely purposed end, of which the rootedness of the Church in Israel's history is a part. *Op. cit.,* p 12f., 19ff.

    6. Vol. 4 (New York: Herder and Herder, 1969) p 4001f.

Prayer in Tradition

God as Father in the Proclamation and in the Prayer of Jesus*

DIETER ZELLER

Today the belief in God the Father is questioned in many ways. Psychology gives evidence how the image of Father-God is modeled after the individual's human father, sometimes it personifies what is lacking in his own father. There are even psychologists who explain the idea of a divine father as the product of an early childhood process of suppression and projection.[1] Sociology of Religion observes the interrelationships existing between societal organizations as family, clan, nation on the one hand and the idea of God on the other.[2] It fosters the suspicion that the authority of a Father-God serves to legitimize and support a certain patriarchal structure of society. Since the role of the father is subject to societal and historical vacillations, then, in light of social psychology which points to the contemporary "lack of the father"[3], it becomes difficult to assign to God his true status as father.

From this critical perspective, the fatherhood of God is an image which stems from either individual or collective imagination. However this image is destroyed, when it not only derives its meaning from certain psychological and sociological conditions, but also turns out to be on the whole a function of such conditions. In contrast P. Ricoeur[4] requires that one must leave behind the imaginary picture ("l'imaginaire") to arrive at the symbol. Then, the fatherhood of God comes not only to satisfy human needs and desires, but becomes an inevitable expression of border experiences which cannot be grasped in fixed terms but only in such metaphorical transfers of archetypal events between God and man. Exegesis can help to purify the metaphor of God as Father by studying its origins, how it relates to human experience and also how closely it is linked with human imagination.

---

*Translation from German by Mrs. Nora Quigley and the editors, with corrections by the author.

117

1. The Old Testament–Jewish Foundation

Popular opinion holds that Jesus is the founder of a new religion because he is said to have proclaimed God as Father for the first time in history. Thus, according to Schiller, can all people be brothers, for they are all children of the one benevolent Father residing above the firmament. History of religion dictates a two-fold revision of this opinion: 1. the designation of a deity as a father is a widespread phenomenon in ancient religions,[5] 2. the proclamation of God the Father by Jesus is rooted in Old Testament-Jewish foundations. Here, however, the fatherhood of God does not include all peoples but expresses a special relationship between Yahweh and his people Israel. Surely Israel recognized its God also as the Creator of the universe and the Source of all life. Because of this it would have been natural to call him Father, as the neighboring nations speak of their gods as "Father and Mother of the people", "Father of the country", "Father of heaven and earth".[6] But, for Israel, God's fatherhood begins with the historical act when Yahweh calls his son out of Egypt, as in Hos 11,1 (see Exod 4,22). In fact, it describes the covenantal relationship between God and Israel,[7] but it can be interchanged with other metaphors, such as that of a husband. From a statistical point of view it assumes no central place in the Israelite vocabulary denoting God.[8]

Yet, while it is rooted in history in such a way, it does not preclude the possibility of it also becoming an expression of mythological thought.[9] Examples of northwest Semitic tribal religions illustrate that the title "Father" often designates the kinship between the tribe and the deity and the role of a protector.[10] In this connection Moab calls itself the people of Chemosh; the Moabites are called his "sons" and "daughters" (Num 21,29; see Mal 2,11). Israel also addresses idols fashioned of stone and wood with "you are my father" and "you have given birth to me", when they hope for rescue (Jer 2,27). Only when their election as God's children was understood as unmerited gift, which at the same time points to obligation, do they not fail in using such an address to Yahweh (see Jer 3, 19; Deut 14, 1). Precisely in the Father-Son relationship they recognize their duty of obedience and fear of God (see Isa 1, 2-4; 30, 1.9; Jer 3, 14.22; Mal 1,6) but also Yahweh's undeserved mercy (see Jer 31, 9.20; Mal 3, 17; Ps 103, 13).

The same features in Judaism are attributed to God by using the title "Father". Here too, God is the Father of Israel and of righteous individuals because he has made them his people,[11] he loves them spontaneously[12] and educates them.[13] He struggles for his son,[14] cares for him and protects him.[15] This is why the Israelites—as already in the Old Testament (see Isa 63, 16; 64, 7)—may call to their Father when in peril.[16]

They use the stereotyped title "our Father" in the collective petitions for help,[17] for rain,[18] or for forgiveness.[19]

However, the fact that God creates and preserves the life of his people does not result in a natural relationship. Often we find next to the title "our Father" the additional one "our King."[20] The Father of Israel is raised above the concept of human fatherhood by adding "who is in heaven."[21] On the whole, the use of "Father" for God is relatively infrequent in pre-New Testament times; more common are the appellatives like "the Highest", "the Almighty", "the Eternal", "the Lord of heaven and earth".[22]

To be a son of God means an acknowledgment of God's authority. This is why the Rabbis often mention the will of the Father in heaven, as revealed in the Law.[23] R. Judah (circa 150 A.D.), in contradiction to R. Meir, emphasizes that the Israelites could be called children of God only if they behaved as such, that is, by being obedient.[24] In the Book of Jubilees, (which is closely related to the eschatological penitential movement of Qumran) but not with the Rabbis, one finds the prophetic thought (see Hos 2, 1-3) that this filial relationship is only realized to the fullest when God will turn the Israelites to himself in the end time and will create a new spirit for them (Jub 1,23ff). According to Ps Sol 17, 26f. the expected Messiah-King has the task of bringing together for God a holy people who are all sons of God.

At the time of Jesus the idea of God as Father was certainly alive in Judaism. It was grounded in the special election of Israel by God. Weighing against the danger that Israel might reserve "Father" for itself is the tendency toward a transcendental apprehension of God, whereby simultaneously the Law is taken seriously as an expression of God's will. Eventually, the filial relationship to God becomes the object of an apocalyptic hope for the future.

2. *God as Father in the Sapiential Admonitions of Jesus*

Does Jesus' proclamation of God as the Father offer a new teaching after all? A. von Harnack[25] believes that one could retrace the entire sermon of Jesus to these two lessons: "God as Father" and "the human soul so ennobled that it is able to unite with him". Here religion is supposed to rise above all particularistic and institutional boundaries. Recent authors[26] also maintain that Jesus is said to have freed the appellation "Father" for God from its association with the specific history of Israel and has attached a universal significance to it.

In order to examine this we confine ourselves to the reliable *logia* (sayings) of Jesus. The historical conclusions leading to this selection cannot be defended individually here. It becomes apparent that only in the argument of some sapiential admonitions[27] is God mentioned as the Father. It seems to me that not enough attention has been paid to this. In the form-critical view those arguments do not have the function of creating completely new insights. Their purpose is to make Jesus' demands comprehensible. This is why he appeals to what his listeners already know. Based upon general faith convictions, the admonitions shall become plausible. Let us examine in what context Jesus mentions God as the Father.

Life involves bodily needs and existential hardships. Jesus advises against anxieties (Matt 6, 25ff//Luke 12, 22ff) and argues from the carefree existence of the ravens and the wild flowers, who are nourished and clothed by God (Luke 12, 24.27f). Luke correctly ascribes this care of the Creator to *Theos*, while Matthew (6,26) mentions "your heavenly Father." Anyway, for Jesus' audience, God is not only the Creator, but the Father who knows what they need (Luke 12, 30b). Therefore, they have still fewer reasons for anxieties. Their intimate relationship with God, to whom Jesus refers as "your Father" seems to be constituted by their membership in God's people. For Jewish parallels also indicate that care for the sustenance of his children is one of the paternal duties of Israel's God.[28] This salvation-history background is evident in Luke 12,30a, a verse which, it is true, looks like an insertion. There "nations of the world" are mentioned as a contrast.

Similarly the argument is presented in Matt 10, 28-31//Luke 12, 4-7. Here, Jesus utilizes the example of the sparrows to demonstrate to the persecuted that they do not have to fear anything. Not even those insignificant birds perish apart from God's will. This is also mentioned in a rabbinic Apothegm.[29] While there the circumlocŭtion "Heaven" is used for God, Jesus employs "your Father"[30]. God's special protection however is not meant for all men here, but for his disciples in particular, whose lives are in danger because of their commitment to Jesus.

Furthermore, the father image appears in the context of prayer. The saying Matt 6,7f, which is perhaps Judaeo-Christian, in verse 8b echoes Luke 12,30b. Babbling in prayer is unnecessary because God is the Father of the suppliants and always knows what they need. Here again the pagans are adduced in a negative comparison. If this saying originated with Jesus, then it is clear that he appealed to the faith assumptions of his Jewish audience. He develops for them the idea of special closeness to "their Father in heaven" in the pericope encouraging them to pray (Matt 7, 7-11//Luke 11, 9-13). Thus he compares God's goodness with harsh human fathers, who can be softened by their children's entreaties. Similar analogies are used by the rabbis to elicit the confidence that the prayer will be accepted.[31] The image of "father" was familiar to Jesus since collective prayer so frequently addresses him. Here, he accepts this address literally and relates it to human experience by using a parable. He seizes upon the father instinct of his audience and actualizes what was already found in Israel's religious consciousness.

This appears similarly in the parable of the father and his two sons (Luke 15, 11-32). It is considered here even though there is no admonition form, and the father in the story is not explicitly identified with God. The astounding reaction of the father, which seems to exceed all proper norms, is to the audience an understandable human emotion. Jesus thereby develops the reality of God anew for them. He develops it in relation to what they know of him from the Old Testament. Especially, Hos 11, 1-9 and Jer 31, 18-20 demonstrate with the same imagery, that Yahweh possesses the heart of a father, that he is deeply concerned about the lives of his children and rejoices when they return to him.

Apparently, Jesus is aware that his audience knows of the mercy shown by their Father in heaven. Since it is an established fact that has been demonstrated again and again in the course of a long history he can formulate the demand: "You also be compassionate" (Luke 6, 36; see Matt 5, 48). Therewith he takes up a phrase already coined in the Targum.[32]

God's liberal indulgence extends to all his work; he causes the sun to rise on good men and evil and sends rain to fall on the righteous and the wicked alike. So it appears in Matt 5, 44f//Luke 6, 35 following the Jewish scriptural interpretation specifically on Ps 145, 9. Yet God's fatherly rule does not therefore extend to all mankind. First, Matthew's *tou patros hymōn* is probably not original.[33] Secondly, only those are called sons of God who imitate the Creator's kindness by loving their enemies in contrast to the ways of tax collectors and pagans (see Matt 5,46f, probably an addition). This corresponds to the rabbinic tradition, in which the Israelites can only be the children of God in a probationary manner. The promise in Matt 5,45a develops a wisdom tradition (see Sir 4,10) in an apocalyptic dimension. The gift of sonship is indicated for those who become worthy of an eschatological reward by an energetic *imitatio Dei*.

We can now summarize the results of our study of the admonitions, which are mostly preserved in the Logia source. The fact itself that God is their Father was known to Jesus' Jewish audience. Jesus reminds them of this in an immediate, arresting manner with vivid inductive examples. He does not restrict himself to foregone conclusions. Decisive for him are the practical consequences that must be taken from this relationship with the Father. This concerns the past, present and future of his hearers. Through a renewal of a filial relationship, they can overcome sin, pray confidently and become free from the anxieties of everyday existence and from fear of other men. Finally, they are asked to accept their neighbors unconditionally, including their enemies. Jesus also justifies his own ministry with the parable of the compassionate father in Luke 15, 11ff. By this he invites especially the Pharisees to acknowledge God's atonement for the sinners and to take them into the community[34] just as he himself does. Jesus' ministry in the name of this compassionate Father generates such opposition because he proclaims this familiar Father as the one who comes unexpectedly with his royal dominion. The memory of the past is realized in the sign of the future. It becomes evident in Jesus' behavior and his demands that the coming God is in many ways different from what his Jewish contemporaries pictured. Speaking in terms of "form criticism": the sapiential admonitions of Jesus are subordinated to his *Basileia*—proclamation.[35]

Both elements, the transmitted title of "Father" and Jesus' proclamation of God's Kingship are found together in the "Our Father", the prayer which Jesus in all probability recommended to his followers (Luke 11, 2-4).[36] Out of their filial communion with God they may dare to ask for the necessities of life but, most importantly, for the coming of his Kingdom. Since they receive God's forgiveness in the present time, the establishing of his reign can only mean salvation for them. In comparision with the contemporary "Eighteen Benedictions", it is evident that the petition for national restoration is omitted.[37] Furthermore, all other recurring appellations for God founded in salvation history are missing, unless they are concentrated in the simple *Pater*.[38] What else encourages the disciples of Jesus to use such an expression as "Father"?

3. God as Father in the Prayer of Jesus

Behind the address "Father" (Luke 11, 2) probably stands the Aramaic *"Abba"* which appears in Jesus' prayer at Gethsemane (Mark 14, 36). J. Jeremias[39] thinks that because "the personal address to God as 'my Father' cannot be shown in the literature of ancient Palestinian Judaism", and because "the address of 'Abba' to God is nowhere to be found in Jewish prayers," it seems that Jesus adopted *"Abba"* from everyday language of the time, and authorized his disciples to follow him in thus speaking to God, transmitting to them the "Our Father." "Therewith he invites them to share in his relationship to God." To test this frequently cited thesis[40], let us examine:

a) the tradition-history of "Abba"

In the Lord's Prayer, "Father" is primarily the way the *disciples* address God, unless this originated with the oldest Jewish-Christian community in Palestine.[41] According to this, the Matthean form "our Father" is probably more original: It conforms to the plural pronouns of the subsequent petitions. In the Mishna *"Abba"* can also represent "Our Father."[42] Therefore, we cannot conclude that Jesus alone was competent to use it, because of his unique sonship. The liturgical addresses *'abba', ho patēr* prove only that *"Abba"* was used in the bilingual communities of Palestine. That these were shouted ecstatically in the Spirit of the Son is primarily a theological assertion. This does not mean that they can be derived through tradition—history investigation from Jesus' liturgical usage.[43]

It is naturally quite difficult to ascertain how Jesus called on his Father in prayer because tradition tells us mainly about words addressed to human beings. Any word of prayer by Jesus is transmitted to us because it offered either a parenetic or an indirect Christological interest. The episode at Gethsemane (Mark 14, 32ff) demonstrates, for instance, how Jesus turns from seeming despair to an affirmation of God's will. This is written for the purpose of edification, most probably as a reflection of Jesus' humanity.[44] Since the "all-knowing narrator" stands above all matters, the question is superfluous whether the disciples might have heard the Master's prayer.[45] So, even here, we cannot show historically whether *"Abba"* is characteristic for Jesus.

The so-called prayer of thanksgiving (Matt 11, 25-27//Luke 10, 21f) can be attributed to Jesus, if at all, only in the first half (Matt 11, 25f).[46] Here we encounter again the address *patēr* or *ho patēr*, which might stand for *"Abba."* But except for v 27, one is unable to deduce from the content of this prayer that such an address can be attributed exclusively to Jesus. Like other prophets and the Teacher of Righteousness in Qumran, Jesus is initiated into God's counsel and enthusiastically proclaims it. But nowhere is it mentioned that he is so informed as Son. Yet does it not testify to a special boldness which ultimately is permitted only to the Son, that he calls God *"Abba"*? Let us clarify:

b) the semantics of "Abba"

The word has its origin in the language of children. Yet in pre-New Testament times it had been used by adults addressing their fathers or other honored personages. Only in certain connections do we find clearly that it means the first word children articulate.[47] Jeremias walks a tightrope when he tries to prove the unprecedented use of the word in the mouth of Jesus. On the one hand, it is not supposed to appear childish, as when it is rendered "Daddy" or "Papa." On the other hand, a familiarity must be contained within the phrase so that one becomes aware of the daring involved in addressing God as a child would his father "so simply, so intimately, so securely."[48] However why should such an address to God seem "disrespectful to Jewish sensibilities" if it also could be used for revered persons (see Matt 23, 9)? The context will show: In Matt 11, 25 the word "Father" is parallel to "Lord of heaven and earth." In Mark 14, 36 we can follow the translation of J. M. Oesterreicher "*Abba*, You all-powerful One!"[50] This does not seem to indicate a baby-like familiarity in the word "*Abba*". This word had nearly replaced the Hebraic-Aramaic "*Abhi*", and so Jesus had no other choice when he wanted to address God as "Father".[51] Still, Jeremias maintains that even this constituted an innovation. Therefore we present:

c) the history-of-religions findings

It is undisputed that the "Father" title for God appears in assertory texts, and that with the singular possessive pronoun, too.[52] In a few cases we even find the form "*Abba*" in Targ. Ps 89, 27 and Mal 2, 10; bTaʿanit 23b.[53] This last example comes from the first century A.D. It seems to me that Jeremias underrates this since Ḥanin Haneḥba need not consciously imitate baby-talk with the phrase "*Abba*, who can give rain." Now the question is whether there is really such a big step from speaking about God, the Father, to addressing him as Father.

In liturgical texts the Hebrew address "our Father" is quite common but the singular form appears only in later texts.[54] This could be explained by the fact that usually people prayed collectively, employing a "we" style.[55] For this reason one finds the address "Father" in the singular only in a few prayers which stem from Hellenistic Judaism.[56] However, Sir 23, 1.4 proves also that this manner of addressing God was also known in Palestine. Here we have only the Greek text, it is true, but there seems to be no reason to suppose with J. Jeremias[57] that the Hebrew original read "God of my father," since Sir 51, 10 mentions "*Abhi ʾattah:*" "You are my Father."

We conclude that, in none of the cases where the "*Abba*" can be ascribed to Jesus, does he speak to his Father exclusively. It is even doubtful whether use of this title in prayer is really so unique, that it bespeaks a unique Sonship-consciousness on the part of Jesus. Therefore one cannot imply from the linguistic phraseology that Jesus shared with his disciples his messianic relationship to God. The line of tradition is not followed here, where both the Davidic King and the expected Messiah are called "Son of God", a title which appears in the post-Easter confession of Christ who "according to the Spirit of holiness was designated as the Son of God when he was raised from the dead" (Rom

1, 4).[58] It is noteworthy that this tradition in the beginnings appears as unconnected with Jesus' speaking of the Father. With his audience Jesus shared the Father whom he disclosed anew. His own personal relationship to the Father is not represented outwardly in quite a new way, outside the given frame of ideas.[59] Jesus rather lives in this relationship as he points to the Father and indicates that such accessability to God is possible. The significance lies in how he does this. The Father, whom Jesus brings close to his listeners, remains the faithful God of Israel, who is linked with his people through their particular history. Yet, Jesus reinterprets God's nearness through the signs of the imminent Kingship *(Basileia)* of this same God. Thus he frees the image of God from national projections and renders God's concerning reality a matter of experience. This is especially manifested in practical consequences. The will of the Father is no longer fixedly laid down in the letter of the law. Jesus demands, especially in the name of the Father of Israel, a loving openness for the socially oppressed, which overcomes all religious appearances of group egotism.

NOTES

1. See special issue "Refus du père et paternité de Dieu" *LumVie* 20(1971) No. 104, the contributions of M. Gillet and J.-C. Sagne.

2. See e.g. G. Mensching, *Soziologie der Religion* (Bonn, 1947) p 65. For the O.T. compare P.A.H. de Boer, *Fatherhood and Motherhood in Israelite and Judean Piety* (Leiden 1974); he also points out (p 26ff) traces of a mother-oriented image of God in Israel. In contrast F. K. Mayr deplores a developing masculinity of the image of God in post-biblical times (see "Patriarchalisches Gottesverständnis?" *Th. Q.* 152(1972) p 224-255).

3. See A. Mitscherlich, *Auf dem Weg zur Vaterlosen Gesellschaft* (new edition, Munich, 1973) and the account of M. Rijk, "The Role of Father in Today's Culture", *Conc* 7(1971) p 304-314 (especially about the works of G. Mendel). See Tellenbach's introduction to the essays, which he also edited: *Das Vaterbild in Mythos und Geschichte* (Stuttgart, 1976) p 7ff.

4. *Hermeneutik und Psychoanalyse* (Munich, 1974) p 315-353; see also "Biblical Hermeneutics," *Semeia* 4(1975) p 27-148.

5. For the Indo-Germanic cultures, see G. Schrenk, *ThWNT V*, p 951ff; for the ancient oriental cultures, W. Marchel, *Abba, Père* (Rome: Pontifical Biblical Institute,[2] 1971) p 9-44.

6. See H. Ringgren, *ThWAT I*, p 3ff. When the concept of creation is used parallel to the title "father" it implies in the O.T. a beginning in Egypt (Deut 32, 6.15.18; Isa 43, 1.7.15; 44, 2; 45, 9-11; 64, 7; Mal 2, 10).

7. The speech about God-Father is not to be deduced from the covenant terminology, contra F. C. Fensham, "Father and Son as Terminology for Treaty and Covenant," H. Goedicke (editor), *Near Eastern Studies in honour of W. F. Albright* (Baltimore-London, 1971) p 121-135. He fails to show analogies for this

in an agreement between a king and his people. The theophoric names seem rather to imply that this phraseology originated in nomadic times. See S. Orrieux, "La paternité de Dieu dans l'Ancien Testament," *LumVie* 20(1971), Nr 104, p 59-74 at 63.

8. See Ringgren (see note 6) p 19, L. Perlitt, "Der Vater im Alten Testament," in Tellenbach (see note 3) p 50-101 at 98.

9. Contra E. Hübner, "Credo in Deum Patrem?" *EvTh* 23 (1963) p 646-672 at 655ff. and H. Bourgeois, "Le dieu père et théologie," *LumVie* 20(1971) Nr 104, p 104-138 at 105ff., 125ff. They believe that, though the image is taken from mythology, it eludes "ambiguité" because it is historicized.

10. See Ringgren (see note 6) p 7.

11. See Targum Onk Deut 32, 6 and Jerusalem Targum I Deut 32, 6 (Strack and Billerbeck I p 393); Midr Cant 2, 16 (102b) (S.B. I p 394).

12. Aboth 3, 14 (R. Akiba).

13. See Tob 13, 4f; Wis 11, 10; 12, 19-22; PsSol 18, 4 (with the subordinate idea of chastisement). NumR 17 (S.B. I p 394) enumerates five paternal duties of God, among which is the teaching of the Torah.

14. See 3Macc 7, 6.

15. See 1QH 9, 34-36; Mekhilta Exod 14, 19 (see G. F. Moore, *Judaism in the First Centuries of the Christian Era* Cambridge 1927, II p 203f.). See Wis 2, 18.

16. See Exod R. 46 (101b) (S.B. I p 393); bSota 9, 15 (p 394): Jerusalem Targum I Exod 1, 19 (p 396); R H 3, 8 and the third Kaddish-petition (p 395).

17. 3Macc 6, 2f. (see 5, 7); see *Ahabah Rabbah* (second Benediction before the *Shema^c*), the petition for Torah study with "our Father, our King"; J. Oesterreicher refers to the daily morning prayer of the community in "Abba. . . . .," J. J. Petuchowski and M. Brocke (ed) *The Lord's Prayer and the Jewish Liturgy* (London: Burns and Oates, 1978) p 132.

18. See already in the Old Testament Jer 3, 4; R. Akiba in bTa^can 25b (S.B. I p 394), out of which the Litany for New Year grew; see S. Lauer, "Awinu Malkenu," in Petuchowski op. cit. p 120-127.

19. See Apocr. Ezek frgm. 3; the 6th petition in the Eighteen Benedictions (Palestinian recension), which is an addition according to J. Jeremias, *Abba* (Göttingen 1966) p 30 note 59; prayers on the Day of Atonement are mentioned by Oesterreicher p 132. The Father in heaven is approachable in a penitential act according to a teaching in the name of R. Meir, Deut R 2 (198d) in a parable (S.B. II p 216); compare Pesiqta 165a (R. Isaac, third century) cited by Moore (op. cit.) II p 207. He cleanses from sins: so R. Akiba in Yoma 8, 9 (S.B. I p 395). Further examples are given in Jeremias p 24 note 33.

20. See Moore (op. cit.) II p 209f.

21. For the usage of the phrase, see Jeremias (note 19) p 20f. According to Moore (op. cit.) II p 205 it does not imply the "remoteness of God". Oesterreicher is closer to the truth (art. cit. p 128ff.) when he emphasizes that Judaism has never forgotten God's infinite nearness despite his infinite remoteness.

22. See W. Bousset/H. Gressmann, *Die Religion des Judentums im späthellenistischen Zeitalter* (Tübingen 1966) p 310ff. A definite aversion to the use of "Father" is observed in the Targum of the Prophets by G. Dalman, *The Words of Jesus* (Leipzig, 1898) p 156f., S.B. I p 394 and Jeremias (see note 19) p 21.

23. See Moore (see note 15) II p 205; see R. Elazar b. ʿAzaria in Sifra to Lev 20, 26 (S.B. I p 395); also Jeremias (see note 19) p 22 note 25, with examples of obedience to the heavenly Father.

24. B Kid 36a (see S.B. I p 371); also even earlier R. Akiba; BB 10a (p 371) and

later R. Judah b. Shalom, Deut R 7 (204c) (S.B. I p 371); also Exod R 46 (101c) (S.B. I p 393). In regard to the opinion of R. Meir that the Israelites even through sin do not lose their filial relationship to God, see the parallels mentioned by Moore (op. cit.) II, p 203, note 4. I do not agree with Jeremias (see note 19) p 23f. as to why the prophetic message which did demand obedience too should have changed here into "legalistic thought" or "be couched in the idea of merit".

25. See *Das Wesen des Christentums* (new edition, Munich-Hamburg 1964) p 49.

26. See H. W. Montefiore, "God as Father in the Synoptic Gospels," *NTS* 3(1956/57) 31-46; E. Lohse, *Outline of New Testament Theology* (Stuttgart 1974) p 36: Jesus is using the word "Father" in a new sense. "God's actions are no more confined to his relationship to Israel, but as Creator of the world he is the compassionate Father of all his creatures." Further opinions of this kind can be found in my "Habilitationschrift": *Die weisheitlichen Mahnsprüche bei den Synoptikern*" (Würzburg 1977) p 162 note 73.

27. For a form critical examination and a textual reconstruction, see my thesis.

28. See NumR 17 (S.B. I p 394); 1QH 9, 35f. Certainly in the analogy between feeding animals and nourishing humans who were created to serve God (Kid 4, 14; PsSol 5, 9ff.; see S.B. I p 436f), man as such is highlighted.

29. JShebi'ith 9, 38d, 22 (R. Simeon b. Yohai, about 150 A.D.; see S.B. I p 582f.).

30. If we can accept the Matt text. For an explanation see my thesis p 94 note 302.

31. Lev R 34 (132a) (R. Tanhuma, about 380 A.D., S.B. I p 459); see also Sifre Num 10, 29 para. 78. The phrase "God's family member" applies especially to the charismatic who prays; see Ta'anit 3, 8 and par. (S.B. IV p 109f). At this point he is compared to a son who ingratiates himself with his father. D. Flusser, *Jesus* (Hamburg, 1968) p 89f. has called renewed attention to this. In the Targum Isa 63, 16, it is said that the mercy of God for the Israelites is greater than that of a human father; see Jeremias (see note 19) p 24.

32. Jerusalem Targum I Lev 22, 28.

33. Even in case it is original, consider the possessive pronoun. The generous actions of God in v 45b do not prove him to be a father. P. Schruers, "La paternité divine dans Mt. V, 45 et VI, 26-32," in *EThL* 36(1960) p 593-624 at 610 is correct. Even when the ethical action is conditional to the gift of sonship, it still does not follow that everyone is so called: this contrasts with E. Grässer, "Jesus und das Heil Gottes," in G. Strecker (ed.) *Jesus Christus in Historie und Theologie* (Tübingen, 1975) p 167-184, at 177. He refers to Mark 3, 35, though the point there is the relationship with Jesus! The imagery in Mark 7, 27 puts in a sharp relief the Jewish self-understanding as the children of God. In the same way the parable of the two sons (Matt 21, 28-32) remains in a Jewish context even though two types of "children" are distinguished. Its attribution to Jesus is questionable according to H. Merkel, "Die Gleichnis von den 'ungleichen Söhnen' " (Matt 21, 28-32) *NTS* 20(1974) p 254-261.

34. P. Fiedler, *Jesus und die Sünder*, (Frankfurt-Bern, 1976) p 155ff. emphasizes that this follows the traditional belief in the unlimited readiness of God to forgive. See also R. Pesch, "Zur Exegese Gottes durch Jesus von Nazareth," *Jesus—Ort der Erfahrung Gottes* (Freiburg, 1976) p 140-189.

35. See my thesis p 169ff.

36. See A. Vögtle, "The Our Father—a Prayer for Jews and Christians?" *The Lord's Prayer and the Jewish Liturgy* (see note 17) p 93-117, at p 112 note 2. The name "Father" for God and his kingdom are also mentioned together in the

probably secondary ending of the Pericope about "no anxieties" (Matt 6, 33//Luke 12, 31) and again in the early Christian verse of consolation Luke 12, 32.

37. See K. G. Kuhn, *Achtzehngebet und Vaterunser und der Reim* (Tübingen, 1950).

38. G. Bornkamm, "Das Vaterbild im Neuen Testament" in Tellenbach (see note 3) pp 136-154, at 141.

39. *Abba* (see note 19) p 65; the following quotations p 33, 63; see also "The Our Father in the Light of Recent Research," *The Prayers of Jesus* (Naperville: Allenson, 1967) p 82-107 at p 97.

40. J. Oesterreicher offers critical reservations (see note 17) which I gratefully acknowledge.

41. S. Schulz, *Q. Die Spruchquelle der Evangelisten* (Zurich, 1972) p 87.

42. See G. Kittel, " ʾabba," in ThWNT I p 4-6 at 4f. Dalman (see note 22) p 157, in writing about the "Our Father" assumed an original ʾAbuna, i.e. the Galilean ʾAbunan, as beginning of the "Our Father."

43. In contrast to Jeremias (see note 19) p 63 note 56. E. Käseman is also cautious in *An die Römer* (Tübingen[3] 1974) p 219f.

44. Oesterreicher (p 121) thinks differently.

45. In contrast, T. W. Manson, *The Teaching of Jesus* (Cambridge[2] 1951) p 104 note 1 and Oesterreicher (p 122) emphasizes that the disciples fell asleep afterwards.

46. See F. Hahn, *The Titles of Jesus in Christology: their history in early Christianity* (New York: World Publishing, 1969) who thinks one can understand v 25f too only as Christian tradition. Furthermore, P. Hoffmann, *Studien zur Theologie der Logienquelle* (Münster, 1971) p 102ff rightly rejects the interpretation of v 27 by J. Jeremias.

47. See Jeremias (see note 19) p 60ff; Marchel (see note 5) p 107ff.

48. Jeremias (see note 19) p 63, who nevertheless corrects himself somewhat on p 64.

49. Oesterreicher also doubts this (p 123). See also H. Conzelmann, *Outline of the Theology of the New Testament* (New York, Harper and Row, 1969).

50. See *The Lord's Prayer and the Jewish Liturgy*, p. 125.

51. Jeremias himself admits this (see note 19) p 58; see also E. Haenchen, *Der Weg Jesu* (Berlin, 1966) p 493.

52. See Dalman (note 22) p 153f; Jeremias (note 19) p 25f; Marchel (note 5) p 90.

53. Other textually questionable places are isolated by J. Jeremias, "Characteristics of the *ipsissima vox Jesu*," in *Abba* (see note 19) p 145-152 at 146f and Marchel (see note 5) p 110f.

54. In the Seder Eliyyahu Rabba (tenth century); the *Abhi* is even attributed to R. Ṣadok (70 A.D.). See Jeremias (note 19) p 31; Marchel (note 5) p 91f.

55. See S.B. I p 410f; Moore (note 15) II p 208f.

56. Wis 14, 3; 3Macc 6, 3.8; Apocr Ezek frgm 3. In contrast to Jeremias (note 19) p 31, one should ask if it is so certain that these writings really reflect the usage of the Greek world.

57. In *Abba* (note 19) p 32, he refers to a late-Hebrew paraphrase.

58. Compare with this a more recent presentation by M. Hengel, *The Son of God* (Philadelphia: Fortress, 1975) 90ff. On the whole, referring to this problem, see A. Vögtle, "Der verkündigende und verkündigte Jesus 'Christus' ", in J. Sauer (ed), *Wer ist Jesus Christus?* (Freiburg, 1977) p 27-91.

59. I hope that even though I pursued a different path, I converge on J. M. Oesterreicher's position p 133f. He is convinced that Jesus' addressing God as ᵓ*Abba* is influenced by the spirit of Jewish prayer. This does not preclude for him the fact that Jesus gave this phrase his "personal impress and thus his particular meaning".

The Prayer of Jesus in Matthew*

ASHER FINKEL

Two forms of Jesus' Prayer (=JP) are transmitted in the Gospels, Matt 6,9-13 and Luke 11,2-4. This fact raises questions[1] as to the original composition of JP and as to the historical process of its dual transmission. The Lukan shorter version seems to be original, since liturgical texts tend to grow with time.[2] The Matthean longer version appears to have preserved the original wording and the Semitic poetic balance.[3] The liturgical development is credited to the oral transmission of JP in two separate churches[4], or even to the redactional work of Matthew expanding on Mark[5]. However, JP in either form was originally transmitted as "lectio brevior" to be used by his followers. The knowledge of JP and the privilege of using it were reserved for the full members of the church only.[6] No author would have dared to produce additional brief petitions or to make alterations in JP on his own.

The differences in the form and its intended usage must be first seen in light of composition criticism. The particular location in the Gospel, as governed by the structural presentation of the surrounding material, is to be examined in view of the redactional arrangement, given stresses, added comments and the specific terminology of the writer. Thus, the particular orientation, purpose and meaning of JP can be determined for each Gospel. The compositional evaluation must take into account the total tradition on prayer as it appears in Matthew and in Luke-Acts respectively.[7] This is to be considered in relation to the liturgical practice of the early church[8] and in view of Jewish prayer in the Temple and in the synagogue.[9] The results of this investigation are to be separated from the study of JP itself. Its meaning[10] can be only understood in

---

*This article is presented in honor and recognition of Msgr. Oesterreicher's relentless intercessory effort in behalf of the Jewish people and the state of Israel. His writings and lectures over the past years and his vision of Jewish-Christian scholarly cooperation in the development of a graduate program at Seton Hall University are lasting contributions to a period of understanding between Jews and Christians initiated in our time. Let his Hebrew name be the acknowledgement that he is a person whom "God has graced" (Yo-Ḥanan).

relation to other reliable teachings of Jesus and in the context of Jewish practice.

JP appears to have been transmitted prior to the composition of the Gospel in two ways. 1) JP like other teachings of Jesus, in particular the parables, were viewed as Scriptures to be interpreted.[11] The Gospel writers record not only JP but also its commentary in the form of a derived lesson (Matt 6,14.15) or in the form of juxtaposition to parables illustrating particular meaning (Luke 11,5-13). It would be incorrect to argue that the writer composed both JP and its commentary. 2) JP appears to govern the redactional arrangement of other sections in Matthew. This clearly demonstrates that his circle was already acquainted with its particular petitions. For Matthew is consciously employing them as a guide to the composition of his Gospel. The Lukan shorter form preserves with slight variations petitions identical to the Matthean text. It appears to be an early reliable Palestinian tradition, which Luke would not attempt to alter. Why then were two forms of JP transmitted as sacred texts, i.e. as Scriptures to be interpreted, during the Apostolic period? This article reexamines both the Matthean understanding of JP as reflected in his composition and the meaning of "Pater Noster" as a teaching of Jesus. It also distinguishes between the two forms as originally transmitted. However, the Lukan version in the context of his composition deserves a separate study.

Matthew presents JP of seven brief petitions in a section on the Jewish pietistic triad of almsgiving, prayer and fasting (6,1-18). This section which appears in the Sermon on the Mount as a redacted collection of Jesus' teachings,[12] is introduced with an admonition: "Beware of practicing your piety before men in order to be seen by them, for then you will have no reward from your Father who is in heaven." It then enumerates the acts of piety in three similarly structured paragraphs that reiterate the admonitory phrases. The three paragraphs speak of "when you give alms" (2-4), "when you pray" (5-6) and "when you fast" (16-18). They repeat the caution: "As the hypocrites . . . that they may be praised/seen by men. Amen, I say to you, that they have their reward." They offer the contrasting advice: "But when you give alms/ pray/fast . . . do so in secret and your Father who sees in secret will reward you." Matthew employs here the homiletic admonitory form, which usually refers to heavenly reward and punishment. It was a common theological appeal made by the rabbinic and Christian preachers as reprovers of the community. Thus, elsewhere in the Gospels Matthew concludes with similar admonitory forms.[13]

In this section the homiletic stress on reward and punishment brings into question the public Jewish pietistic acts which seek God's favor in time of distress. The community is summoned to give alms, to fast and to stand praying in the synagogues or in the town-square (Matt 6,5 the corners of *plateia* = *reḥobh*, M. Taʿanit 2,1). The public display of penitential acts is solicited by the religious teachers during a period of national calamity, especially at the time of drought affecting the agrarian society. The proscribed acts on a fast day as referred to in Matt 6,17 (no washing nor rubbing with oil) were occasioned by a period of drought extending into the mid-third month of Fall (M. Taʿanit 1,6). This was the practice before the Destruction to gather in the Temple or locally in the town-square and synagogue. It remained the practice for the latter after the Destruction. Two centuries later R. Elazar ben Pedath captures its meaning with a summary statement.[14] "Three things cancel out the harsh decree and they are prayer, almsgiving and repentance." He bases all three on God's response in a vision to Solomon following his prayer (2Chr 7,13-14). "When I shut up the heavens and there is no rain. . . and My people, who are called by My name humble themselves, pray (i.e. prayer) and seek My Face (i.e. the righteous act of charity, in view of Ps 17,15) and turn away from their wicked ways (i.e. repentance). Then I will hear from heaven." This addition in Chronicles to 2Kgs 9,2 indeed reflects the scribal understanding of the practice during the Second Temple period.

At such calamitous occasions, trumpets were sounded and the elders conducted the service (M. Taʿanit 2,1.2.5). In the Matthean section, they are the scribes and Pharisees who are called hypocrites (compare 6,1 with 5,20). Matthew did not develop this section in opposition to a Jamnian revised agenda of pietistic practice.[15] Matthew is preserving redactionally Jesus' response to public demonstration of piety in time of distress. This teaching relates to the common knowledge of public Jewish practice during and after the time of Jesus.[16] Thus, Jesus taught that your alms should be in secret, alluding to Prov 21,14: "Alms in secret avert anger." The stress is on averting evil judgment. Jesus taught also that the prayer should be in private, alluding to Isa 26,20: "Go my people, enter into your storeroom (LXX and Matt 6,5 : *tamieion*), shut your door . . . until the anger of the Lord has passed away." The stress is again on averting the evil judgment. Jesus taught that public fast should not become simply an act of bodily abstinence. He alluded to Isa 58,5, the admonitory lesson preached on such occasions.[17] "Is such the fast that I choose . . . to bow down the head like a rush and to spread sackcloth and ashes?" In contrast to these overt penitential actions, Isaiah depicts in the following verses the proper acts of righteousness. These are feeding the hungry, welcoming the oppressed stranger, clothing the naked (v 7) and visiting those who are in chains (including the sick, v 6). Matthew cites them in the scene of the Judgment Day, attributed to Jesus (25,42.43). In the performance of these altruistic actions, Matthew understands Jesus' demand for sincere pietistic expression as seeking closeness to God (Isa 58,2c; for Matt 25,40.45: an identity with Jesus). Thus, the admonitory introduction of Matt 6,1 refers to "practicing your piety (dikaiosynē=ṣedaqah)" in view of Isa 58,2: "As a people (goy; Matt 6,7 ethnikos, included the Jewish community) who practiced righteousness (ṣedaqah)." Matthew opens the section with an allusion to Isa 58,2 and he closes with a lesson on fasting, which echoes verse 5 of Isa 58. He reserves the reference to verses 6-7 for the last long discourse of his Gospel. For the reference is repeated redactionally (25,35-39.42-44) in the apocalytic teaching of Jesus on final reward and punishment.

JP is attached to the homiletic paragraph on prayer. This section provides the public Jewish practice in time of distress as background. For Matthew wishes to introduce the abbreviated JP in contrast to the longest liturgical service held on communal fast days. The public Jewish prayer included six petitions with respective Scriptural readings, following "Redeemer of Israel", in the daily Eighteen Benedictions.[18] The twenty-four petitions were recited in the Temple or locally in the town-square by religious officials. The additional petitions make also an appeal to God, "who hearkens to prayer". This formula, which echoes Ps 65,3, became the liturgical seal for public and private intercession. It is already reflected in the appeal which Solomon repeated to God in the First Temple that in time of distress, public prayer and private supplication will be heard in heaven (1Kgs 8,30.32.34.36.39.43). Similarly it is found in the Levitical prayer to God in the Second Temple during a period of national fast (Neh 9,27.28). In both cases it is an appeal to God's mercy. For it captures the ultimate expression of faith for the one who prays. It is heartfelt speech before God, whose Presence is addressed and whose mercy is sought.

Tefillah in biblical Hebrew means intercession,[19] to plead a case before the merciful Judge in heaven for the sake of the community. Thus, the Middle Section of the daily Tefillah consists of collective petitions for existential and eschatological needs. It converts the singular to the plural, in conformity with the "We" petitions, when citing Ps 119,153 for "Redeemer of Israel" and Jer 17,14 for "Healer of the Sick". This Middle Section concluded with an appeal: "Hearken, O Lord our God, to the voice of our prayers for you are merciful and compassionate. Blessed are you the Lord who hearkens to prayer" (the Palestinian recension). The private petitions of the High Priest, following the public reading on the Day of Atonement, conclude with: "Supplication and entreaty before you in behalf of your people Israel who need to be redeemed. Blessed is the Lord who hearkens to prayer" (MYoma 7.1; bYoma 70b and bSotah 41a). Both private and collective Tefillah have the same liturgical seal.

The Lengthy and Abbreviated Communal Prayers

During the Second Temple period in addition to the special communal fast days, there were daily gatherings in the synagogue or in the town-square for a public liturgical service.[20] Communal fast days were proclaimed by the religious teachers in time of distress only. Yet, every day of a particular week, the townpeople would also gather to witness a liturgical service conducted by the members of the Maʿamad. They were the religious lay delegates of the community on their way to the Temple to be present during the sacrificial and prayer service. They acted as the community's intercessors before God's Presence in the Temple. Thus they fasted during the week: "on Monday in behalf of sea voyagers; on Tuesday in behalf of those who travel in the desert (the caravans); on Wednesday in behalf of infants that croup may not attack them; on Thursday in behalf of pregnant women that should not miscarry and in behalf of nursing mothers that their children should not die" (jTaʿanit 4,4;68b and bTaʿanit 27b). Each day they read a selection from the Story of Creation, referring to God's providential care of his work on the particular day (MTaʿanit 4,2 and above, compare Sopherim 17,4). They offered the Tefillah in which the Middle Section concluded with the clause: "The Lord who hearkens to prayer."

Every day at the sacrificial service of the Temple, the Levitical choir chanted a given Psalm (MTamid 7,4; see the explanation of R. Aqiba in bRosh Hashanah 31a) and the priests offered the intercessory petition for God's acceptance of the service (bTaʿanit 27b). This petition ended with: "You alone shall we serve in awe," echoing Deut 6,13. This text is cited by Jesus in the Temptation Story, while Q preserves the liturgical phraseology "alone". It is also used by the Tannaim as Scriptural basis for the inclusion of prayer along with or without sacrifices in the service before God[21] (Sifre to Deut 11,13 in view of Midrash Hagadol to Deut 6,13). For it was the practice in the Second Temple to offer intercessory prayer and private supplications at the time of sacrifice (e.g. Luke 1,10). In response to prayer in the Temple the priestly petition for the service reads: "Accept in favor, O Lord our God, your people Israel and their prayers and may daily the (sacrificial) service of your people Israel be acceptable in favor before you." The prayer service of the synagogal Maʿamad and the priestly liturgy for the Daily Offering and the Festivals gave rise to the liturgical structure of the synagogue after the Destruction.[22] Their combined petitions were arranged and edited in Jamnia as the daily Eighteen Benedictions corresponding to the times of sacrifices in the pre-Destruction days. Their essential structure preserved the wording of the Second Temple period.[23] Jamnia reserved the Middle Section for the weekdays only and its liturgical seal, "who hearkens to prayer", for private supplication and fast days,[24] as it was the practice in pre-Destruction days. Three times daily the synagogal community offered Tefillah of the Ma‘amad and the priests as intercession for those who are in distress or are threatened by it.[25]

This is the historical background for public lengthy Jewish prayer known from the time of Jesus to the time of Matthew. The communal fast days fell on Mondays and Thursdays (MTa‘anit; 2,9); whereas the private fasts of the Ma‘amad lasted from Monday to Thursday. On both occasions the Tefillah was offered to the "Lord who hearkens to prayer." This relationship between fasting and public prayer is the background to the Didache's section[26] on fasting not on Monday and Thursday and on praying the abbreviated JP in the Matthew form with a communal doxology. Like Matthew, it views JP in light of public Jewish prayer in time of distress (fast days) and for those in distress (daily). Curiously, the Tiberian Amora Yoḥanan of the Third Century, who was acquainted with the Nazareans of Galilee, offers the reason for the Ma‘amad not fasting on Sunday: "So they will not say while we (the Christians) celebrate, they (the Jews) are fasting" (bTa‘anit 27[b] and Sopherim 17,4, ed Higger 300 n 22). For the tradition of the lay Ma‘amad and priestly watches were kept alive liturgically, and Yoḥanan produces an explanation elicited by the Jewish-Christian conflict. Only after the Bar Kochba period, the conflict with Jewish-Christians gave rise to the inclusion of "Nazareans" in the Jamnian malediction against *Minim*, the heretics of the Jewish community. The Genizah text of the later centuries adds *"Noṣerim"* to *"Minim"*, and the Patristic heretical lists preserve this distinction between *"Minim"* in pre-Bar Kochba days (Justin, Dialogue 80: *Genistai*) and *"Noṣerim"* of the Third Century (Epiphanius, Panarion 29.1, Compare Jerome, Epistle to Augustine; Commentary to Isa 2, 18; 49,7;52,4).

Matthew transmits JP as an abbreviated form of ecclesiastical intercession in time of distress. This is developed in the introductory comments to JP. "Do not use stammering *(batto-)* phrases as the Gentiles do, for they think that they will be heard for their many words" (6,7). This appears as the first explanation, pointing to the cacophonic litany of the crowds,[27] who repeat the cry: "Answer us", in time of distress. The stammering manner of collective shouts reflects disorder, lack of confidence or even scruple. Likewise the frenzied Gentile crowds in worship were seen by Jews and Christians in Syria. The Gentiles were participating in mystery cultic service with its mytho-dramatic forms of purgation and jubilation.[28] The abbreviated form of JP is offered in contrast. The Christian community is to pray in harmony and in order, displaying confidence and unity in their appeal to God. Matthew's particular stress on no hypocrisy but purity of the heart (5,8) and integrity (5,48) supports this observation. A contemporary pious teacher, Hanina ben Dosa,[29] noted for his efficacious intercession, related that only such prayer spoken in a non-stammering manner (*"shegurah bephyw"* in contrast to *"megamgem"*) is acceptable to God (MBerakhot 5,5 and the story in bBer 34[b]). Thus, R. Aqiba maintains that the Jamnian standardized Eighteen Benedictions can only be said if spoken in a nonstammering manner; otherwise an abbreviated form should be recited (MBer 4,3).

The second introductory comment to JP states: "For your Father knows what you require before you ask him" (6,8). The object-clause reads alliteratively in Aramaic: *"debhaʿithun qadam debhaʿithun."* Significantly, *"debhaʿithun"* can be translated as what "you require" or "you ask" as well as "you pray". For speech before God points to a faith in the Omniscient One, who searches the human heart and is cognizant of its needs. God alone knows the sincere act of repentance and prayer of the community in time of distress. Thus, the Palestinian Targum to Exod 2,25 renders "God knows" (the plight and the cry of Israel in bondage) as "The repentance that (Israel) did in secret, for no one knew of his fellow's (act of repentance), was known to him". (Compare Mekhilta to Exod 19,2). Matthew prefaces the second explanation to JP as Scriptural support for the efficacy of abbreviated prayer. He alludes to Isa 65,24a: "Before they call (Targum: pray) I will answer them (Targum: receive their prayer)." The later Christian homiletic work (2Clem 15) refers to the second half of this verse: "While they are yet speaking I will hear," as an exhortation to pray with confidence to God. He conflates it with Isa 58,9a: "I will say behold I am," the prospect of God's Presence at time of prayer and fasting (2Clem 15,4 thinks of Jesus' Presence; so Apostolic Constitutions 7.38: "The Lord be with you upon earth" in response to the entreaty of "You receive the prayers of your people", 7.37). Like Matthew, the homilist relates the proper performance of the pietistic triad of almsgiving, prayer and fasting (2Clem 16,4).

Matthew introduces JP with an allusion to Isa 65,24. This is significant in light of the rabbinic use of the Isaiah verse as a demonstration for the efficacy of brief prayer. "There is a prayer that even before one utters it, it is answered," citing Isa 65,24 (Deut Rabba 2,10 to 4,8; the reading of

Yalqut Simeoni to Isa 65,24; 509). It is compared with the brief intercession of Moses (Num 12,13) which averted God's judgment (Sifre ad
loc. and Midrash Prov 4;27b). The example of Moses became the practice
of the Righteous in formulating brief Tefillah (Mekhilta Simeon to Exod
15,25). It also prompted R. Eliezer of the First Century to question the
sincere intent of the one who abbreviated his prayer in public in order
"that they will say: He is a disciple of the Sages" (idem, omitted in
bBerakhot 34a). Similarly Jesus criticized those who pray in order to be
seen by men. For Jesus, like the Sages, as well as the Righteous and the
Prophets before them, also lived a life of intercessory prayer in healing
and in solitude (the Synoptic tradition). The prayers of Jesus preserved
in the Gospels reflect his use of brief forms. JP as transmitted in both
Gospels consists of brief intercessory petitions. However, the liturgical
intent for the followers is different. In Matthew JP is intended for the
community and in Luke for the apostles. The difference between the
communal prayer *(Tefillah=proseuchē)* and the private supplication
(Tahanun=deēsis) will be reflected in their respective forms. The
meaning and usage of "brief prayer" *(Tefillah Qeṣarah)* for the community and for the individuals must be first discussed.

The biblical orientation for *Tefillah Qeṣarah* is reflected in the Isaiah
verse (65,24). Prayer can be a continual human exercise in seeking
closeness to God's Presence.[30] God, however, is always ready to respond to sincere appeal in moments of despair. Total reliance on God's
mercy in the expression of humility and love is the sincere attitude of the
one who prays. He relates to God as a son or as a servant in doing his
will. The Prophets and the Psalmists,[31] who lived a life of prayer in
closeness with God, assumed such an attitude.[32] They related to God
affectively and they expressed theopathically their desire before him. At
the same time they stressed purity of the heart and the purity of action in
daily life. For they themselves were deeply affected by the needs and the
misdeeds of the community. They approached God in behalf of the
people as a defense attorney arguing his case before the heavenly
court.[33] In pathos of altruistic love they interceded for the salvation of
the community, which has rejected and even persecuted them.[34] The
Righteous or the Pious in the later period adopted the life style of the
Prophets and the Psalmists. They were known for their life of prayer and
efficacious intercession. This was the life style of John the Baptist and
James the brother of Jesus (Eusebius, Historia Eccl 2.23), who were
called the Righteous (Mk 6,20 and Eusebius ad loc. respectively.) Also
among the early rabbis, before and after the Destruction, there were the
Righteous or the Pious who lived a life of intercessory prayer. They are
mentioned in the Tefillah, the petition on the Righteous. The Christian

community was acquainted with the prayer life of the Baptist's disciples and the Pharisees (Lk 5,33). It promoted the same among their own members (Acts 1,14; 2,42; Col 5,2; 1Thess 5,16, 1Tim 2,1; Jam 4,13; 1Pet 4,7). It, therefore, treasured as efficacious prayer the particular brief petitions of Jesus. For Jesus, who was called *"ho dikaios"*[35] (Acts 3,14: Peter; 22,14: Ananias; Jam 5,6), remained in the mind of his Jewish believers even greater than all the Prophets.[36]

Two types of brief forms of Tefillah are described by R. Joshua the Levite, who was acquainted with the Temple liturgy.[37] He transmits a private brief supplication, which begins and ends with the phraseology of the last private petition of the High Priest on the Day of Atonement (MBerakhot 4,4). This intercessory form (which is also alluded to in Rom 9,1) is to be said on the road in the face of danger. In addition, R. Joshua speaks of the abbreviated form of the communal Eighteen Benedictions (ibid. 4,3). Both brief forms, for the community and the individual on the road, conclude with the seal, "who hearkens to prayer". Curiously, the Palestinian Talmud (Ber 4,4; 8a) preserves the reference to supplication in the end of the seal, corresponding to the opening phrase of the High Priest's petition. Different formulations of "Brief Prayer" are ascribed to the early Tannaim, who adopted and echoed the supplications of the Temple period.[38] This indicates the desire among the rabbis to preserve the private supplications as used efficaciously and taught by the different teachers. However, only two slightly different Palestinian versions of the communal "Abbreviated Prayer" are transmitted.[39] One version preserves the seals of the Eighteen Benedictions. The other version, which is called by its initial word, *"Habhinenu"*, is also transmitted by the early Babylonian academy of Samuel in a modified form of the Middle Section's petitions, which corresponds to the seals. This dual transmission reflects a history of the standard *"Tefillah Qeṣarah"*.

During the Second Temple period a longer form of public prayer and a corresponding abridgement were in use. The hymns of thanksgiving were chanted responsively on the Festivals,[40] as a longer form of Hallel (Pss 113-118). Correspondingly, a litanic abbreviation of a second shorter version[41] of Hallel (Ps 135) was recited in the Temple (Ps 136, called the Great Hallel). At the behest of the Levitical invitation[42]: "Give thanks to the Lord who (=ki) is good," the crowds repeated the refrain: "For his mercy endures forever." This commonly known liturgical appeal to God who is good prompts Jesus to respond that the appellative "good" is reserved for God alone (Mark 10, 18; Luke 18, 19).

Ben Sira too preserves an abbreviated form of Thanksgiving (appended to ch 51). It echoes the seals of praise and eschatological petitions of the Eighteen Benedictions and the seals of the High Priest's petitions.[43] In addition, Ben Sira transmits brief intercessory petitions in seeking God's Presence and his mercy (36, 12-19). It opens (36, 1) with the appeal, "Save us," and concludes (v 22) with: "You hearken to the prayer of your servant." This is an abbreviated communal Tefillah preserved by Ben Sira of the Second Century B.C.E. Thus, it also includes brief formulations, which echo the later edited Benediction following the Scriptural reading in the synagogue (vv 20,21, compare Sopherim 13,8. 10). Scriptural reading in public was introduced in the period of the Scribes (Neh 8,1-9,3) and it was continued during the Second Temple period (Acts 15,21). The practice was maintained after the Destruction with its particular Festival and Sabbath cycles.[44]

Another abbreviated form of the communal Tefillah appears in the First Letter of 2 Macc 1,24-29. It was recited by the priests, as the custom prevailed later, for the acceptance of the sacrifice (v 26). It closes with the brief phraseology of the eschatological petitions of the Eighteen Benedictions, and it opens with a list of God's appellatives as found in the first petitions of the Tefillah. Psalm 103 too opens with brief existential petitions of the Eighteen Benedictions. It enumerates God's merciful acts with a penitential appeal (vv 12b,13) to "remove our iniquities from us" and to "love those who revere him like a Father." "Father" becomes a significant popular address to God in intercession and repentance.[45] Ben Sira reserves the address for private supplication "to be delivered from evil" in time of distress (51,10). "Yea, I cried: You are my Father (Hebrew: ʾAbhi)." It echoes the collective lament of Deutero-Isaiah (63,16; 64,7): "For you are our Father (Hebrew: ʾAbhinu)." The Targum renders the address in light of the above cited Ps 103,13 reading ʾAbba. The meaning of Jesus' address "Father" will be discussed at the end.

The Palestinian and the Babylonian abbreviated versions of the communal Tefillah contain the Isaiah proof text (65,24). However, a different Scriptural insertion appears in connection with private brief supplication (jBerakhot 4,4; 8b: Tefillah of the Others). It cites Ps 28,6: "Blessed is the Lord for he hearkens to the voice of my supplication." The text refers to the brief petition in verse 9: "O save your people." This form was said by the High Priest as the concluding private petition and likewise transmitted as Tefillah Qeṣarah by the Levite R. Joshua. Thus, the later homilist suggests that this verse was the last intercessory Benediction recited by Moses before his death (Pesiqta de R. Kahana on Deut 33,1, ed Buber 198b).

The two different Scriptural proof texts as introduced later into the brief prayers[46] reflect the rabbinic distinction between the two forms. These relate to two different prayer settings, one for the community and the other for the individual. Luke employs in particular the term *"deēsis"* (supplication).[47] He preserves the Psalm text in the angel's reply to Zechariah's private supplication. "Your *deēsis* has been heard" (1,13). Matthew, however, alludes to the Isaiah verse in his introductory comment to JP. Thus the form of JP is presented in Luke to the disciples on the road (11,1-2); whereas JP in Matthew appears in the sermon addressed to the crowds as well as to the disciples (5,1;7,28).

Matthew in his introduction to JP is thinking implicitly of the Jewish model of lengthy prayers, while explicitly he refers to the Gentiles (also 6,32). He reveals a knowledge of the Jewish public service, which he subjects to Jesus' criticism. However, he does not fault their practice of offering abbreviated prayers. On one hand, the Matthean tradition promotes a mission to the Gentiles within a Jewish-Christian church (24,14;28,19). On the other hand, Matthew still preserves the contrast of Gentiles and the tax-collectors, i.e. the wicked of the community (5,46-47: read "Gentiles"; 18,17) with the people of God who are the lost sheep of Israel (10,6;15,24). This reflects a common biblical orientation for Matthew's circle and the Jewish community. The former adopts the liturgical and homiletic forms of the latter, while protesting the Scribal interpretation of the Pharisees. The early church indeed felt free to adopt the Jewish liturgy of the synagogue and the Temple, as evidence clearly shows.[48] In shifting from "hypocrites", i.e. the scribes and the Pharisees, to "Gentiles", Matthew suggests, as he explicitly states in 23,2, that their liturgical tradition should not be criticized but only their practice. A similar tendency appears in the Didache, which employs the Jewish prayer at mealtime christologically for the Eucharist while criticizing their practice.

Matthew in his first introductory comment also alludes to Isa 1,15b: "Even though you make many prayers, I will not listen." The first half of the verse is rendered in the Targum with reference to the priestly prayer in the Temple. For "I (God) will cause my Presence to be removed from you." This Prophetic indictment is addressed to the religious teachers and the priests, whose acts are compared to those of Sodom and Gomorrah (v 10; compare Matt 10,15;11,22.24). Matthew is thinking of his contemporary generation of Jews who witnessed the destruction of the Second Temple. The Jewish community has experienced the removal of God's Presence from the Temple.[49] The religious crisis was effected by "this (the present) evil generation", according to Matt 12,46. The cause offered in Isaiah is: "Your hands are full of blood". This is developed explicitly in Matt 23,29-39 with the historical reference to the actions of Zealots during the war with Rome.

Matthew presents JP with a lesson derived from the petition for Forgiveness (6,14-15). The same lesson is attached to another teaching of

Jesus, the parable of the unmerciful servant (18,23-43). The parable refers to remittance of debts, the Matthean phraseology in the petition for forgiveness. For "ḥobhyn" in Aramaic also means sins (Luke 11,4). The parable also preserves the penitent's appeal: "Lord, have patience with me and I will pay you all" (Matt 18,29). The first half of the petition refers to God's attribute of patience, as recorded in Exod 34,6. This text became the standard model for penitential address to God.[50] Thus, God responds in the parable: "You have mercy on your fellow servant as I have mercy on you." It echoes the prospect of God's grace in Exod 33, 19 with the meaning[51]: "I will have mercy on the one who shows mercy." This lesson is employed by early Jewish interpreters.[52] Similarly, God's act of grace as pronounced by the priests (Num 11,6), is also understood to mean: "He will give you (sympathetic) knowledge (da'ath) so that you will show mercy to one another" (Sifre Zuṭa, ad loc.). For the same is reflected in the arrangement of the petition for "da'ath" prior to the petitions for "Repentance" and "Forgiveness" in the daily Tefillah. Thus, R. Elazar ben ʿAzariah of Jamnia taught: "Transpersonal matters will be forgiven to you but not interpersonal matters until you reconcile your friend" (Sifra to Lev 15,30; the Palestinian Targum refers to penitential confession, which included the above petitions). The same teaching is advanced by Jesus fifty years earlier.

Matthew attached the lesson of forgiveness to JP in order to underscore the significance of purity of action in addition to purity of the heart (no hypocrisy) at the time of prayer. For prayer is an expression of *agapē* in a transpersonal relationship. It cannot be sincere unless *agapē* is likewise reflected in the interpersonal realm. This association between worship and ethics was taught emphatically by the Prophets. Yet many of the worshiping community did not conduct themselves accordingly, as indicated in Ben-Sira's exhortation (28,2). The second half of the penitent's petition in Matt 18,29 reflects the common practice of making payment to God in the form of sin or votive offering.[53] In protest Jesus taught, according to Matt 5,23-24: "First be reconciled to your brother and then come and offer your gift (=sacrifice)." The Jamnian teachers also saw the need to legislate the same rule in post-Destruction days (MYoma 8,9). Apparently Jesus, as Ben Sira before him and the Tannaim later, sought to discourage insincere acts of repentance by the people in the Temple and in the synagogue respectively.

Matthew too promotes this understanding for his Church in the curious arrangement of Jesus' teaching on prayer for those who persecute you under the commandment of "love your neighbor" (5,43-44).[54] One would expect that the example of altruistic love should be depicted in terms of interpersonal acts such as lending. For prayer is the service of the heart, the expression of love for God. It appears that Matthew is thinking of intercession as indicated in Pater Noster's shift to the collective in the last four petitions. Thus, no one can offer intercessory prayer unless he is free of ill feelings toward his fellowman. The test for purity of the heart before God can only be measured by the purity of action in the interpersonal realm. This becomes the Matthean lesson of perfection (5,48), which is juxtaposed to the section on communal prayer. JP can only be recited with a pure heart and in consequence of pure action: the lesson on forgiveness (6,14.15).

The Matthean stress on "beware of hypocrisy" highlights the proper usage of JP. Moreover, the Matthean form of JP preserves the acrostic: " ʾeSHMoR MiHoNePH" (I shall protect from hypocrisy). It was the practice to transmit liturgical texts acrostically as a mnemonic device.[55] Each initial letter of a substantive, i.e. the second word, in the petitions forms the acrostic. It begins with "Our Father" and avoids the last substantive which refers to "Evil" (see Appendix). In contrast to Luke, the Matthean form of JP is an intercession for the distressed community living in an evil-infested world. Therefore, it opens with a collective address to the Father, "who is in heaven" (so Isa 63,15: "Look down from heaven", v16: "You are our Father"). It includes a third petition, an expression of hope for the fulfillment of God's will on earth. It ends with a plea for deliverance from evil. For the earthly community seeks presently a release from the evil residing in the heart (Matt 15,19) which is implanted by the Satan in the world (13,39). This last appeal conforms to the acrostic theme of the Matthean JP, God's response (compare Ps 12,8 in view of 3). The community recites JP in Aramaic as reflected in the dual meaning of remit/forgive and debt/sin in the fifth petition. For the community in prayer is taught to offer its petitions in the vernacular (later in Greek). In response to their prayer, God's blessing as pronounced by the priests in Hebrew only (MSotah 7,2 in contrast to prayer, 7,1) governs the acrostic. "God will bless you and protect you" (Num 6,24). Matthew's circle preserved in the Hebrew acrostic the particular blessing of God's protection. For the priestly Benediction was also interpreted by the Essenes and the Rabbis with reference to protection from evil or demons (1QS 2,3; Targum, Sifre, Midrash Hagadol to Num 6,24).

The Matthean descriptive expression, "Father who is in heaven", is replaced by Luke with the "Most High" (6,35=Matt 5,45) and the "angels of God" (12,9-10=Matt 10,32-33). This suggests that the Matthean address, as found in Jewish liturgical sources (prayers, homilies and Targum),[56] was understood correctly in terms of God's transcendence. The providential Father exists duratively in a separate realm as the "Most High", whose Presence is enjoyed by the angelic *familia* in heaven. Like Israel, the Christian community is cognizant of the providential Presence in their history, while affirming a faith in the durative existence of the Wholly Other. In the expanded form of prayer on God's Holiness *(Qedushah)*, the Jewish community responsively declares God's holiness and his kingship, in connection with the angelic proclamation of Trishagion (Isa 6,3; compare Rev 4,8).[57] The community on earth joins the heavenly community in the collective experience of prayer, attesting to God's numinous Otherness and to his providential Presence. Yet, the community on earth is aware that although God's will is fulfilled by the heavenly *familia*, it has not yet become the universal human expression. Thus, Matthew transmits the petitions of God's holiness and his kingship in connection with: "Your will be done, as in heaven so on earth."

Matthew also compares God in the Temple, whose Presence is enjoyed by the earthly community, with God on his throne in heaven, whose Presence is enjoyed by the angelic hosts (23,21-22). In addition, he refers to this correspondence in connection with Apostolic and ecclesiastical authority: "Whatever you bind on earth shall be bound in heaven, and whatever you loose on earth will be loosed in heaven" (16,19; 18,18). This authority is given to the earthly community in legislative and liturgical matters, due to God's Presence in their midst (18,19-20).[58] Peter is designated by Jesus as the one to whom "my Father who is in heaven has revealed this (the messiahship of Jesus)" (16,17). This is the fulfillment of Jesus' Thanksgiving to God "who has revealed these to the babes" (11,25). Thus, Peter's christological affirmation: "You are the Messiah the Son of the Living God," became the basis for christological reformulation of Jewish liturgy.[59]

Matthew's JP ends with a plea for deliverance from evil. The community awaits the final event of universal redemption from evil residing in the human "heart of stone".[60] This prophetic prospect relates the elimination of evil in the heart with the act of God hallowing his name in the end-time (Ezek 36,23-27). Then God's will will be done on earth and his name will be acknowledged universally (Zech 14,9). Meanwhile the community must learn to live in the pursuance of this hope (universal mission) without demanding God's intervention (Matt 26,53 only). Only in the end-time will God send out his angelic hosts to save the worshiping community (the elect) from the final cataclysm (24,31). Thus, the four collective petitions of Matthew's JP relate to the existential needs of the worshiping community. It seeks daily bread, forgiveness of sins and deliverance from trial and from the evil residing in the world.

The Redaction of Matthew

The ecclesiastical JP of Matthew is indeed an epitome of Jesus' teachings in the sense that it coheres with his other sayings. This would indicate that the wording of the petitions was original to Jesus. However, it is necessary to preclude the possibility of redaction by Matthew. This can be demonstrated from the way Matthew redacts Q material as well as his own early tradition in three sections of the Gospel. In all three JP governs the arrangement of the material. In one place (4,3-10), Jesus' Scriptural replies to the Satan are governed by JP. It offers a *"Vorgeschichte"* for the Christian community in prayer at the time of trial. For it concludes with the Scriptural reference to serve God, which was interpreted to include communal prayer (the service of the heart). The other two places (6,25-34;23,9-33) relate the teachings of Jesus respectively as recommendation and as repudiation of contrasting religious practice. The former alludes to given petitions of JP, and it is introduced with a reference to serve God only (6,24). The latter arranges the "Woes" in the sequence of JP's petitions. These are prefaced with the reference to the liturgical address, "Father who is in heaven" (23,9).

a) Temptation Story (Q): Matthew arranges the three episodes differently than Luke. The latter offers the order of the last two in light of the Scriptural sequence cited by Jesus (Deut 6,13.16). Matthew deliberately reverses the order in conformity with JP's existential petitions. The first Scriptural reply of Jesus refers to "bread", the second to "trial" while the third introduces the denunciation: "Begone Satan!" Similarly Jesus silences Peter (Matt 16,23=Mark 8,33) who questions the messianic purpose of his master's ministry. In both cases, Jesus perceives the evil thoughts of the bearer and commands his departure. For Jesus has the authority, according to Matt 12,25-28, to perceive the evil thoughts of a person and to command the departure of the Satan. Thus, Peter's intention is questioned, "for your thoughts are not with God" and the Satan's temptation is rejected, "for . . . him (God) alone shall you serve." The latter is also the liturgical phraseology of Deut 6,13, recited by the priests in the Temple for the acceptance of the service. Jesus employs it as a repudiation of magical use of prayer associated with the worship of Satan. Likewise, the converts of the Christian community are asked to foresake in time of trial their former custom of using long and tedious magical formulas (Matt 6,7; examples in C. K. Barrett, *New Testament Background*, New York; Harper and Row, 1961 p 29-35). Instead, the worshiping community can only plead for deliverance from evil thoughts.

Luke does not mention "Begone Satan!" as he does not transmit the last petition. For his form of JP is intended for the apostles who share in

Jesus' victory over the world of evil, symbolized by the Fall of Satan (Luke 10,18). Significantly this introductory background to Lukan JP preserves the same Psalm text quoted by the Satan. Psalm 91 was recited as a Scriptural poem of exorcism (*Shir shel pegaʿim;* compare the Qumram Psalms ed Sanders, Col 27,10, mistranslated p 87); to repel the evil spirits and to invite God's protection (Midrash Ps 91,1; bShebhuʿoth 15b; jSabbath 6,2;8b). In Luke's Temptation Story, Jesus has conquered the Satan and the Psalm reference: "He will give his angels charge to protect you", has been realized. Thus, Luke does not need to mention in the conclusion: "And the angels ministered to him." The apostles who are sent to the seventy nations of the biblical world (10,1.17 in view of Gen 10: the seventy nations) receive authority to exorcise the demons. Jesus transfers this authority with a reference to the Psalm of exorcism (91,13.10.12b): "You will tread on (the lion and) the serpent, (the young lion) and the basilisk (Luke 10,9a:scorpion) . . . no evil shall befall you and no demon (Targum, Luke 10,9b: power of the enemy) . . . nor shall you stumble because of the evil inclination" (Targum, Luke 17,1.2). The signs accompany the apostles on the road for the Spirit of God is upon them (see the longer ending of Mark 16,17.18). Thus, Luke relates that Peter and John, who are filled with the Spirit to exorcise and to heal, can confidently say: "Is it right before God to listen to you rather than to listen to God?" (Acts 4,19). In apostolic life the prospects expressed in the two Matthean petitions (one closes the "You" petitions; the other the "We" petitions) have been actualized. They have been delivered from evil and their missionary life is a continual expression of doing God's will on earth.

As an apostolic JP, Luke included originally an appropriate petition, which was preserved by Marcion and in given manuscripts (162,170) as well as recorded by Gregory of Nyssa and Maximus the Confessor.[61] It reads: "Let the Holy Spirit come upon us and cleanse us". The distinctive reading of Codex Bezae anticipates the wording of this petition ("upon us let come"). For the petition for the Holy Spirit appeared in lieu of the petition for the Kingdom (except Marcion). Luke offers this petition obliquely in a section following the account of JP. It appears as a lesson on prayer (11,13). "How much more will heavenly Father give the Holy Spirit to those who ask him!" The lesson is inferred from the parable of a son asking his father for food. In a Galilean town, Greek and Aramaic words were common speech forms. A human father may hear his son making the sound *PTRʾ.* The form *"paṭira"* in Aramaic denotes flat bread but its Greek homonym *"petra"* means rock. The father will immediately perceive the intention of his small child and he will not be confused by the similarity of speech sounds.[62] The gift of the Holy Spirit is given to the apostles so they too can intuit the intentions of others and respond wisely (Luke 12,11.12). This gift was promised by Jesus to his disciples, according to Luke (24,49; Acts, 1,4.5.8). Its public manifestation in form of glossolalia was climaxed by Peter's preaching on the intended meaning of God's promise (Acts 2). Thus, the inclusion of the petition for the Holy Spirit is consonant with the guiding prayer for the apostles on the road. Jesus invites his disciples to call upon *Abba*, i.e. to share in Jesus' closeness to God (Rom 8,15.16; Gal 4,6.7). They already enjoy the Presence of God in doing his will. The Kingdom of God is within them (Luke 17,21, compare Matt 18,20) but attention is directed to the Spirit (compare John's Supper Discourse).

b) The Sermon on the Mount (Q): the section on communal prayer and pietistic acts is followed by a triad of sayings on storing heavenly treasures (6,19-21: through the act of charity, jPeʾah 1,1;15b); on sound eye (6,22-23: no covetousness, MAboth 2,9 in view of Aboth de R. Nathan II 30) and on serving one Master (6,24: repudiating Mammon). These teachings point to the proper religious orientation for the worshiping community. It is to become a community of "the poor in spirit" (5,5). To such a community in prayer the following section is addressed. It opens with a pericope on anxiety (6,25-31) and ends with lessons echoing the phraseology of JP. Verse 32 refers to the "heavenly Father". Verse 33 speaks of seeking (i.e. praying for) "his Kingdom" and "his righteousness". The latter is understood in the sense of "doing God's will" (3,15). Similarly Ps 40,9-10: "To do God's will" is "to announce righteousness before a vast assembly". Verse 43 refers to the petition for bread of "tomorrow . . . for today."

These liturgical lessons are given in contrast to the Gentiles' manner of praying. This obliquely suggests the way the Jewish community prays. It first begins the entreaty of the Middle Section with the existential petitions (*Daʿath*, Repentance, Forgiveness, Redemption, Healing and Blessing of the Seasons) and then it concludes with the eschatological petitions (Ingathering, Judgment, Defeat of Evil, Maintenance of the Righteous and the combined petition for Rebuilding Jerusalem and the Davidic Kingdom). According to Matthew, the uniqueness of JP lies in the order of the petitions. "First seek his Kingdom and his Righteousness and all these (the existential needs, beginning with 'Bread for tomorrow') be yours." This is the shift in JP from the eschatological petitions addressing "You", to the collective petitions for existential needs. The community orients itself eschatologically in prayer and lives accordingly. It lives in anticipation of the Parousia (Matt 10,23; 15,28; 24,42.44) while proclaiming the Kingdom (10,7) and doing God's will (7,21;12,50). It expresses *agapē* in providing the daily needs (24,45), in forgiving sins (18,22-35) and for some in not entering into trials (19,12). The first petition and the last petition are reflected in Matthew's exhortation for the members to pursue good works (5,16) and to avoid obstacles (18,7) respectively.[63]

c) Woes against the Scribes and the Pharisees (Q and Matt only): Matthean arrangement of the "Woes" is governed by all the petitions of JP. It addresses the hypocrites as in the Sermon's section on communal prayer. Thus, it opens (23,2-8) with a parallel indictment of their practice to be seen by men, enumerating in particular the pietistic acts. As interpreters and preachers of the Torah, the scribes sit on the *Kathedra* of Moses, the place of honor in the synagogue. They are greeted as rabbis (teachers) in the market place, where court sessions and public liturgical services were held. The Matthew introduces (v 9) the reference to JP's address to God. This address is reserved only for "one Father who is in heaven"[64]. Correspondingly, Matthew relates that there is only one leader for the Christian community,[65] namely Christ. This reflects the employment of a baptismal formula for non-Gentile members, which referred to Christ (Acts 8,16: Samaritans; 10,48: semi-proselytes; 19,5: Baptist's followers; 22,16: Paul). Paul employs the priestly Benediction as an epistolary salutation: "Grace to you and peace from God our Father and the Lord Jesus the Messiah" (Rom 1,7). For he too was familiar with the Matthean lesson of correspondence: "To us (there is) one God the Father . . . and one Lord Jesus Christ" (1Cor 8,6). For only he who was baptized to receive the Holy Spirit can say: 'Lord Jesus' (12,3). Eventually the formula evolved into a trinitarian form[66] for the baptism of the Gentile members (Matt 28,19). Thus, Matthew is thinking of the Jewish converts in offering criticism of the Pharisaic practice. The polemical discourse is governed by Pater Noster, the prayer taught to the baptized members.

Matthew continues with the lesson on service as a reflection of humility (23,11-12). He employs the principle of "imitatio Christi" (10,25a): to serve even as Jesus served unto death (20,27-28). The poor in spirit is praised (5,3) since he follows in the way of Jesus, the lowly in heart (11,28). "Whoever humbles himself like a child, he is the greatest in the Kingdom of Heaven" (18,4). For, "He who is the Small One (i.e. Jesus)[67] in the Kingdom of Heaven is greater than he (John)" (11,11). However, the stress on humility before God in the teaching of Jesus alludes to Isa 57,15. "Thus says the Highest (Targum: *Rama*)[68] who dwells in heaven (JP: Father who is in heaven) whose name is holy (JP: hallowed be thy name) who dwells (Targum, 1QIsa) in the highest (Targum: *barama*[68]) and holy (place) as well as with the contrite and the lowly in heart." God's name is hallowed among the lowly in heart. For his exaltation is found in the expression of humbleness (bMegillah 31a and Yelammedenu cited in Yalqut Makhir to Isa 57,15). Thus, Matthew repeats the lesson on service in connection with the example of Jesus' death as that of the humble Suffering Servant (20,27-28 in view of Isa 53,12c). For martyrdom (drinking the cup) is seen as an act of hallowing God's name.[69] Matthew, therefore, arranges the lesson on service following the saying on one leader in conformity with the sequence of the address and the first petition.

The list of seven "Woes", omitting v 14 (not found in BSDλΘ), follows the order of the last six petitions with the separation between two-beat stichs of the third petition. This is a significant arrangement in light of the proper delivery of JP's Aramaic stichs (see Appendix). The address plus the first three petitions make five two-beat stichs. These are followed by three five-beat stichs, which are strung together with the copulative *"ve (kai)."* The last stich is constructed as two petitions with the conjunction *"ella".* This poetic structure indicates how the community recited the "Pater Noster" in Aramaic. First, they intoned two-beat unstrung cries with a stress on the last beat in the middle three petitions: the appeal to you *(-akh).* This stress is already reflected in the opening cry: "our Father". At the same time, the worshipers are guided by the eschatological orientation of JP, which is expressed by "in heaven" in the first and last stichs. With the cry "as on earth", reflecting their existential situation, the community alternates to a *Qinah* (Lament) rhythm. They recite the last three stichs in a measured form (2+3; 3+2; 2+3), repeating the sound *"na-n"* (we). This signifies the collective appeal for existential needs. They end with a lament: "Deliver us from evil," the evil affecting the community on earth.

First "Woe" (23,13) reads: "You shut the Kingdom of Heaven . . . neither you enter *(eiselthein)* nor allow others to enter. "In contrast, the Christian's call is: "Your Kingdom come" (JP: *eltheto* and Kerygma 10,7: *engiken*).

Second "Woe" (23,15) reads: "You traverse sea and land to make a single proselyte." The Pharisaic proselytizing effort was seen as doing God's will on earth (Ps 40,9-10). In contrast, the spreading of the *Besorah* (good news) among the Gentiles is promoted in Matthew (24,14;26,13) without the imposition of a heavy yoke (11,30; Acts 15,10). Thus, "Your will be done."

Third "Woe" (23,16-22) ends with a lesson on correspondence, God's Presence in a punctual sense dwells on earth in the Temple. This corresponds to the durative existence of God in heaven. There God's Presence on the Throne is enjoyed continuously by the entire worshiping angelic community. This is a significant principle governing the teachings of Jesus on the Kingdom.[70] On one hand, the Kingdom is described as a future manifestation of God's durative Presence as it exists extratemporally in heaven. On the other hand, the Kingdom is proclaimed as a present reality, the punctual manifestation of God's Presence. The Christian community has become the new Temple on earth,[71] which seeks the joy of God's Presence for all in the appeal: "As in heaven so on earth."

Fourth "Woe" (23,23-24) points to the strict observance of tithing in the Pharisaic Levitical practice (15,20). Thus, the community prays with no reservation: "Give us our bread." Matthew may have also in mind the play on the word *MeHaR* (for tomorrow) in the petition (Gospel according to the Hebrews and Matt 6,34) and the transposed letters *HoMeR* (weightier matter) in the "Woe".

Fifth "Woe" (23,25-26) refers to the strict observance of the law of purity in the Pharisaic association. God's act of atonement is described metaphorically in the Bible as cleansing (Lev 16,30; Ezek 36,25 etc.). The "Woe" teaches that the external act of cleansing is ineffective as long as one is not cleansed internally. Matthew reads *"dakke"* (cleanse) in contrast to Lk 11,41 *"zakke"* (give alms).[72] For Matthew, cleansing means the elimination of extortion and rapacity, the evil ways affecting the interpersonal relationship. Likewise, the collective petition for Forgiveness is governed by the sincere act of reconciliation in the interpersonal realm.

Sixth "Woe" (23,27-28) depicts the Scribes and Pharisees metaphorically as sepulchers. They appear righteous but within they are full of hypocrisy and lawlessness. The Matthean denunciation of hypocrisy has become the test for righteous life in the Christian community. For the hypocritical intentions of the newcomers, the evil thoughts in the heart (Acts 5,4;8,22), were seen as "tempting the Spirit of God" (5,9). Thus the community prays: "Do not lead us into trial."

Seventh "Woe" (23,29-33) appears as an indictment against the last generation of the Scribes and Pharisees at the time of the destruction of the Second Temple. The fraternal war was intensified by the Idumeans at the call of the Zealots in year 67/68 (Josephus, Bellum 4.5). They were the followers of the Shammaitic Pharisees.[73] Their actions led to bloodshed in the city and the Temple. Zechariah the son of Berachiah was led to a mock trial and executed by the Zealots in the Temple (Bellum 4.5.4). This defiant act is explicitly mentioned by Matthew[74] in his sequel to the last "Woe" (23,34-35). The final "Woe", therefore, concludes with the admonition: "How shall you escape the judgment of Gehenna?" In contrast, the Christian community prays: "Deliver us from evil". "Evil" is a multifaceted word connoting also divine judgment. This was especially the case for the Jerusalem church, which at the behest of an oracle in response to prayer, departed from Jerusalem in the face of imminent catastrophe (Eusebius, Hist Eccl 3.5.3.).

Matthew has composed his Gospel in view of the apocalytic events that befell the Jewish people as witnessed by the Jerusalem church. He refers to the events in a closing apocalyptic statement: "Amen, I say to you *all these* will come upon *this* generation" (23,36 in view of 22,7). This comment introduces God's lament for the city and the desolated Temple,[75] as transmitted by Jesus (23,37-38=Luke 13,34-35). For Matthew, God's Presence has been removed from his people who committed bloodshed. The same reason is offered for the *Silluq* (Removal) from the generation of Menasseh prior to the destruction of the First Temple (2Kgs 21,12-15 in light of v 16. See Tosefta Yoma 1,10 and Cant Zuṭa 5, ed Buber 31). Thus God laments: "How often would I have gathered your children together as a hen gathers her brood under her wings." For God alone provides protection and care for his children in the City of Peace, as he did for the Mosaic generation in the Wilderness (Deut 32,10.12). God's lament ends in a promise: "You will not see me (the manifestation of God's Presence at time of pilgrimage to the Temple; Exod 23,17;34,23) until you say: "Blessed is he who comes in the name of the Lord" (the greeting of peace to the pilgrims; Ps 118,26;129,8). For God's Presence, an expression of his love, can only be experienced in the Temple by the pilgrims who relate in love and peace to the inhabitants.[76] However, at time of fraternal war causing the desolation of the Holy Place (Matt 24,15), the Christian community in Jerusalem is instructed to pray that their escape may not be in the winter. To which Matthew adds "nor on the Sabbath" (24,20). In light of the reference to a season, Sabbath connotes here the Sabbatical year, which occurred in 68/69 C.E.[77] It is possible to date the departure of the Jerusalem church to Pella in Summer 68. The opportunity for escape from Jerusalem was still available (Bellum 4.6.3). Until then the church, following the example of James the Righteous Intercessor (Eusebius, Hist Eccl 2.28), saw itself as a holy community in prayer averting the evil decree (3.5.3).[78]

Matthew has composed the Gospel in Syria a decade or so after the Fall of Jerusalem. His work reflects Scribal criticism and interpretation (13,52: new and old), which he most probably shared with the Jerusalem church, whose members were familiar with the teachings of the scribes[79] and the practice of the Pharisaic association. The indictment of the generation of the War and the criticism of the Shammaitic school[80] were transmitted to Matthew's circle by knowledgeable members of the

Jerusalem church who developed them along the lines of Jesus' teaching. Thus, Matthew's Sermon as well as the Epistle of James and the Didache emanate from a similar Jewish-Christian circle.

Matthew did not, however, compose his Gospel as a polemical response to the Jamnian academy established after 70. This can be refuted on two grounds. 1) Matthew's circle could not have direct access to the Academy's discussion unless the latter's members had joined his church or the Jerusalem church has restored intimate contacts with Jamnia. Both possibilities are ruled out for lack of evidence. The Jewish community in Diaspora only gradually became acquainted and then adopted the revised agenda of the Jamnian Academy. 2) The Jamnian community was not threatened by Christianity, as assumed in contemporary studies (see n.15). Moreover, the Tannaim have developed their interpretation in the Hillelitic manner, which did converge independently upon formulations similar to those taught by Jesus.[81]

Matthew has transmitted the Jesus tradition as developed in the Palestinian church. He composed his work as a result of the apocalyptic events affecting his generation at the time of the Destruction. Matthew sought to preserve what his circle accepted as the authentic meaning of Jesus' didactic and messianic ministry. In their view it was confirmed by the apocalyptic events of their day. Matthew transmits JP as brief intercessory petitions to be recited by the community in time of distress. As an ecclesiastical prayer, it eventually concluded with the Temple's doxological refrain[82] (1Chr 29,11): "For yours is the power and the glory for ever" (Did 8,2). In Christian practice "Pater Noster" was used three times daily in lieu of the Jewish Tefillah. For the early Christian community lived in an atmosphere of persecution and distress. JP was offered by the community as an affective expression of fellowship with the angelic *familia* in doing God's will and in seeking God's Presence collectively for the fulfillment of their needs.

The Meaning of Pater Noster

The significance of "Pater Noster" can be determined by the way it offers an epitomized form of petitions which embrace the totality of human relational attitudes. In accordance with the address to the Father, the first three petitions reflect a relationship between the person who prays and God. The transpersonal and eschatological attitude affects the person's existential petitions with reference to three human relationships. 1) The subpersonal relationship (the person and nature) gives rise to material possession and egoistic control. The fourth petition expresses temperance in living by Jesus' teaching on the removal of material anxieties (Matt 6,25-35). 2) The interpersonal relationship can breed ill feelings and all forms of human evil. The petition for Forgiveness comes to eliminate such tensions by the anticipatory human action of forgiveness. This conforms to Jesus' teaching on precautionary measures in interpersonal matters (5,21-48). 3) The intrapersonal relationship (the person and himself) becomes an internal struggle between the good and evil inclinations in overcoming trials. The petition on Temptation linked to the plea for deliverance from evil recognizes the complexity of personal growth which is in need of guidance from beyond the human order. This corresponds to the Matthean lesson derived from the parable of father and son. It states that only "your Father who is in heaven can give good (eliminating the evil) to them that ask (pray to) him" (7,11).

Jesus employs the address "*Abba*" (Father) in prayer. In Matthew's JP, the community members are instructed to lift their hearts collectively to "our Father". Yet in the private supplication of Jesus, the address is to " *ʾAbba*" only (Matt 26,39.42: " *ʾAbhi*"; Mark 14,36: " *ʾAbba*"=Luke 22, 42 and 23,34.46). This direct appeal to " *ʾAbba*" is reserved by Luke for the apostles on the road. They are instructed to pray a different form of JP in response to their request, noting that the disciples of John offer supplication as taught by their Master (11,1 in view of 5,33: "make *deēsis*"). In light of the original substitute second petition for the Holy Spirit, it reads: " *ʾAbba*, let your name be hallowed. Let your spirit of holiness come upon us and cleanse us. Your (Marcion) bread for tomorrow give us each day. And remit (=forgive: *shebhoq*) us our sins; for we also remit all who are indebted to us. And do not allow (*tishboq*, Marcion) us to be led into trial." This form preserves the Aramaic phrases, " *ʾAbba*" and "*Shebhoq*" with its dual meaning of remit (=forgive) and allow. It also maintains the balance in the last two petitions with "*ushebhoq*" and "*welaʾ tishboq*."

The acrostic formed by the initial letters of the Lukan JP refers to the Father's promise of pouring out the Spirit (Luke 24,49; Acts 1,5). *ʾǍbba* (Father), *Shemakh* (your name), *Qadisha* (holiness), *Mehar* (for tomorrow), *Hobhynan* (our sins) and *Nisyona* (trial) spell out acrostically *ʾeSHaQem Hen* (I will baptize them with grace). This eschatological promise is described in Joel 3,1: "I will pour out my Spirit" (Acts 2,17) and Zech 12,10: "I will pour out . . . a spirit of grace". The latter is a promise in response to supplication following the mourning period for the First Born, the Messiah.[83] This account offers the Prophetic background for the early Christian understanding of the events following the crucifixion. The acrostic in Hebrew recalls the priestly Benediction: "God will shine his Face upon you and give you grace" (Num 6,25). This response of God at the time of prayer in the Temple was interpreted by the Essenes and the rabbis with reference to the Holy

Spirit or illumination.[84] The Lukan stress on the reception of the Spirit and on the apostles' prophetic mission is the context for said form of JP.

Paul too indicates the significance of the address "*ʾAbba*" in prayer. He specifically mentions the address with reference to those who received the Spirit being able to cry "*ʾAbba*" (Gal 4,6;Rom 8,15). In light of intercessory prayer in his private life,[85] Paul repeats jointly or separately the priestly Benediction of God, "will give you grace" and "give you peace", in his epistolary greeting and farewell. For the gift of the Spirit has become a personal blessing for Paul (1Cor 2,13;7,25.40;15,8; 2Cor 1,11;12,1.8.9; Gal 1,15-16; 1Thess 1,4;4,8). Paul wishes to share with the community the joy of God's grace which has so affected his apostolic life. Paul seems to be acquainted with the private petition of the apostolic JP (Rom 5,5). "The love of God has been poured out in our hearts (in view of 5,1: the grace in which we stand) by *the Holy Spirit which was given to us.*"

Paul appears to be familiar as well with the ecclesiastical JP of Matthew. He depicts God's new covenant with the Christian community as: "I shall be unto them a Father and you shall be unto me sons and daughters" (2Cor 6,18). This covenantal formula is rooted in the liturgical experience of the community[86] in their appeal to "Our Father". Paul attaches the formula to Isa 52,11.12b, which is preceded by the *evangelion*: "The Kingdom of God has manifested" (v 7, Targum) and is followed by the hymn of the Suffering Servant (52,13-53,12). The deliberate choice of the Prophetic text in connection with the new covenantal formula is significant for it is juxtaposed to Lev 26,11-12. The latter refers to the formula for God's covenant with Israel. It is prefaced with the promise of God's Presence in the Temple (Sifra ad loc.). The Essene Temple Scroll 29,7-10 utilizes the Levitical text with reference to the earthly and heavenly Temples, an apocalyptic view shared by the Christians (Rev 21,22). Paul, however, calls the Christian community the Temple of the living God (2Cor 6,16; 1Cor 3,9.16). For God's Presence through Christ, in accordance with Pauline thought, now dwells among the believers in Jesus. Thus, Paul appeals to the Christian community to intercede in prayer for his deliverance from evil persons (2Thess 3,1.2; Rom 15,30-31).

Paul cites the concluding petition of Matthew's JP: "*rhyesthai apo ton ponērou.*" He attaches a particular meaning to the word "evil", since it is a multifaceted expression that lends to several interpretations. He similarly refers to said petition in connection with the ecclesiastical supplication or thanksgiving to the Father (1Cor 1,10-11; Col 1,12-13). It appears then that in citing the last petition, a particular form of JP is meant. Paul refers to the ecclesiastical JP. However, the Synoptic reference to pray that "you may not enter into trial" (Mark 14,38 parallels) is addressed to the disciples only. For it is the last petition of the Lukan apostolic JP. To the Thessalonians' prayer, Paul offers in response the opening priestly Benediction: "The Lord will protect you from evil" (2 Thess 3,3). This is the formula that governs the acrostic of Matthew's JP; while the priestly Benediction of God's grace is used in connection with Lukan JP (Rom 5,5).

Clement of Rome too indicates the significance of the communal appeal to " ʾ*Abba*" during a penitential service (1Clem 8,2.3). It opens with a citation of Ezek 33,11.12 similar to the conclusion of *Neᶜillah's* confessional service (bYoma 87b; see Amram's text in ᶜAbodath Israel ed Baer, 437). It concludes with an appeal, "to return with all your hearts and say: Father." This may refer either to the litanic cry:[87] "Answer us/Have mercy on us/Save us, Father" or to the recitation of "Pater Noster". Clement, a contemporary of Matthew, also refers to Isa 26,20: "Enter into your storeroom" (50,4=Matt 6,6) in his exhortation to pray for God's mercy. For only sincere penitential prayer, through the expression of altruistic love and humblemindedness (1Clem 13,2-4), can result in the forgiveness of sins. Clement,[88] who has preserved other ecclesiastical prayers, reflects lessons similar to Matthew while not quoting his Gospel. He probably was acquainted with the ecclesiastical JP, but he was reluctant to cite it.

Jesus employed the address "ʾ*Abba*" with reverential and relational meaning. This dual meaning must be seen first in light of its usage in Tefillah said in time of distress. It was the common Jewish practice on fast days during the penitential service for the people to cry the litany:[89] "Answer us, our Father, answer us". After the Destruction, R. Aqiba follows his teacher R. Eliezer's recitation of the twenty-four petitions on a fast day with the litanic appeal: "Our Father, our King; you are our Father!" (bTaᶜanit 25b; R. Ḥananʾel's text and see the litany in Amram Siddur). This form of address did not orginate with R. Aqiba. He simply used the spontaneous litanic form in lieu of the standard lengthy petitions. For the address to "our Father" was used in time of distress (Exod Rabba 46 to 34,1) as found in the Prophetic supplication (Isa 63,16; 64,7).

Before the Destruction, the humble grandson of Onias the Circle Maker (bTaᶜanit 23b; dated in light of jTaᶜanit 66d) is said to have heard the cry of school children in time of drought: "ʾ*Abba*, ʾ*Abba* give us rain!" He spontaneously offered an intercessory appeal: "Master of the Universe! Do for the sake of these (children) who can not distinguish between ʾ*Abba* who gives rains and ʾ*Abba* who does not give rain." This does not mean that the address "*Abba*" was used only in charismatic

Hasidean circles.[90] Rather, the children's use of ʾAbba elicited the spontaneous prayer of Onias' grandson. This reflects the type of religious instruction received in the schools prior to the Destruction.[91] The teachers would substitute ʾAbba, or similar expression, for God while reciting the Scriptures and prayers in deference to God's name. The children were instructed to pray in the style of the commoners,[92] utilizing brief petitions and subsitute terms for God. Onias' grandson was met by the children reciting the liturgical lesson taught by their teacher. In this instance, they recited the brief entreaty for rain ("Give rain"), which was used during the rainy season (M.Berakhot 5,2; Taʿanit 1,2). Since school children's recitation was seen as a divine omen,[93] their cry "ʾAbba" prompted the brief intercession. For Onias' grandson was also addressed in the community as "ʾAbba", an honorific title given to a philanthropic person.[94] He, therefore, employed the brief intercession: "Do for the sake of innocent school children" (see the litany in Amram's Siddur). He worded it as an appeal to ʾAbba who gives rain in sympathy with the innocent cry of the children.

Jesus employed reverential circumlocutions for God's name in his prayer and teachings.[95] According to Matt 5,34-35 and 23,21-22 Jesus instructs not to use related appellatives (Heaven, Earth, Jerusalem, Temple) in oath formulas in order "not to take God's name in vain" (Exod 20,9). "ʾAbba", therefore, is employed by Jesus in prayer when not citing Scriptures (so Mark 15,34=Matt 27,46; citing Ps 22) as a reverential address in God's Presence. It is not a unique speech form of Jesus, for it was used in public preaching and penitential prayer (see n.56). Thus, the homilist R. Isaac of the Third Century comments, in light of its usage, on Jer 3,19: "You should revere me as sons and call me your Father; for it says: "ʾAbhi (=Aramaic ʾAbba) you should call me" (Exod Rabba 32,5 to 23,20). However, ʾAbba in the prayer of Jesus does reflect the particular way he related to God. In Jewish life, an adult in reverence for his natural father did not call him by name. He instead used the address ʾAbba.[96] The Tannaitic midrash, which compares the reverence for God with the reverence for a human father (Sifra to Lev 19:3), is rooted in the common religious practice of not calling either by name. Jesus' ministry reflects a deep sense of loving service in the Presence of God. He follows the example of the Prophets who defended the honor of the Father as well as that of his son, Israel (Mekhilta to Exod 12,1; Aboth de Rabbi Nathan II 47). The Prophets were willing to face persecution by their people and even to sacrifice themselves in their behalf. Similarly Jesus was willing to face persecution and even to die for the sins of Israel. His closeness to God, who commissioned him to save the sinners among his people (Mark 2,17 parallels; Luke 19,10; Matt

1,21;15,24), is also reflected in his reverential humble attitude before God's Presence.

Once Jesus used the substitute form *ʾAbba* for God's name, he reserved this address exclusively for the heavenly Father. "Do not call any one on earth *ʾAbba*" (23,9). Similarly, he intructs not to use the term "good", the liturgical attribute of God, even for himself (Mark 10,18=Luke 18,19). Thus, Jesus enjoins both the community and the apostles to address God as *ʾAbba*, by not invoking his name but by linking the reverential address to the petition: "Hallowed be your name" (JP in Matt and in Luke). In a similar way, the Jewish liturgical setting of reading the Scriptures gave rise to the recitation of the *Qaddish* following the public preaching.[97] *Qaddish* is a reverential petition used in response to hearing God's name spoken during the Reading. It opens with: "Magnified and hallowed be your name" and closes with the communal response: "Let his great name be blessed from eternity to eternity." The refrain in Aramaic was used in the Temple as a doxological response upon hearing God's name pronounced by the High Priest.

The first meaning of the address *ʾAbba* comes to reflect on part of the person who prays a sense of reverence and humbleness before God's Presence. The second meaning reflects the particular relationship one seeks from God in prayer. It is significant that the address "our Father" is found only in penitential petitions and supplications of Jewish liturgy. As an example, the first three penitential petitions of the Middle Section are worded with an appeal to *"Abhinu"*. "Grace us, O our Father (with sympathetic) knowledge *(daʿath)* from you;" "Cause us to return, O our Father, unto your Torah;" "Forgive us, our Father, for we have sinned." The theological principle governing the liturgical address is that God's actions are viewed in a dual way,[98] in terms of judgment *(din)* and in terms of love *(raḥamim)*. The first form, as understood by the rabbis, is expressed biblically by the name *ʾElohim* (also means "judges") and the second by *YaHWeH* (which expresses his pathos duratively). In liturgy[99] the biblical address *YaHWeH, ʾElohim* was used in pre-Destruction time, corresponding to the reverential forms *ʾAbba, Melekh* (king) used as descriptive circumlocutions. The distressed community addresses YaHWeH as "our Father" in seeking his love and mercy to forgive their sins at time of judgment (see n.46). Jesus, like the Prophets of old, addressed *ʾAbba* in his prayer as an appeal to God's love at time of judgment.[100] Thus, both forms of JP make the appeal to *ʾAbba*. The community or the apostles intercede for Fatherly forgiveness of sins and for Fatherly protection in time of trial.

Jesus has taught his followers to use the address *ʾAbba* as a sincere expression of humility before God and as complete reliance on his love.

Corresponding to the human biological experience, the father engenders the human species while he remains apart during the period of gestation. God likewise causes and maintains the human reality, while he exists as a numinous Other in the history of human evolution. This imagery of God evokes in the heart of the one who prays a deep sense of creaturehood and humility before the Wholly Other. Yet at the same time, in addressing the Father as "You", one senses the nearness of the providential Presence. In sympathy with divine love, he opens his dialogue of prayer, a dialogue of human hope and divine promise. He petitions for existential needs that concern not only himself but mankind as well.

NOTES

1. For a review and discussion of the different scholarly questions, opinions and studies, see Jean Carmignac, *Recherches sur le Notre Père* (Paris: Letouzey 1969). He offers an artificial Hebrew translation of JP on p 396. The apparent Aramaisms in the fifth petition indicate that JP was not transmitted in Hebrew. For such prayers were recited also in the vernacular.

2. A. Baumstark, *Comparative Liturgy* (tr. London: Mowbray, 1958) establishes laws governing liturgical tendencies. J. Jeremias, *The Prayers of Jesus* (tr. Naperville: Allenson 1967) p 89 accepts conclusively the principle for the evolution of forms. See the valuable criticism of J. Heinemann, *Prayer in the Period of the Tannaim and Amoraim* (Heb. Jerusalem, 1966) p 131 especially with regard to Jewish liturgy and the principle of evolution. There are examples of Psalms that were transmitted as longer and as shorter recensions of the Temple Hallel.

3. See K. G. Kuhn, *Achtzehngebet und Vaterunser und der Reim* (Tübingen, 1950) and compare J. Jeremias, *Prayers,* p 90-92.

4. See F. H. Chase, *The Lord's Prayer in the Early Church* (Cambridge, 1898) and Gordon J. Bahr, "The Use of the Lord's Prayer in the Primitive Church," *JBL* 84 (1965) p 153-159. There is also disagreement on whether the two versions of JP relate to Q or are to be credited to M and L. J. Jeremias, *Prayers* p 88 distinguishes between the two in terms of the audience, Matthew to Jewish-Christians and Luke to Gentile-Christians.

5. M. D. Goulder, *Midrash and Lection in Matthew,* (London: SPCK 1974) p 296-300. He advanced the argument in *JTS* 14 (1963) p 32-45. Compare the attempt by S. van Tilborg, "A Form Criticism of the Lord's Prayer," *NovTest* 14 (1972) 94-105. W. D. Davies, *The Setting of the Sermon on the Mount* (Cambridge University Press, 1966) p 4f advances the thesis that Matt adapted the Lukan JP for his church. He further argues for an anti-Jamnian redaction. However, one cannot impose upon the results of redactional criticism a pre-understanding of the intent and meaning without submitting the Jewish sources to similar criticism. See J. Neusner's comments in *Greeks, Jews and Christians* (W. D. Davies Festschrift), Leiden: Brill 1977 p 89-111.

6. T. W. Manson, "The Lord's Prayer," *BJRL* 38 (1956) p 99-113; 436-448, offers a history of the liturgical usage of the Pater Noster.

7. For Luke, see Louis Monloubou, *La prière selon Saint Luc*, (Paris: Cerf 1976). J. Jermias does not examine the total liturgical background for each JP and thus his conclusion on the differences is *ex cathedra*. I hold the position that the two versions are indeed two different forms, an ecclesiastical JP in Matthew and an apostolic JP in Luke. I do not share the view that Jesus simply spoke it twice (so Origen). The disciples did not forget what they were taught but instead transmitted two prayers that contained similar petitions. The difficulty arose in the transmission which eventually brought the Lukan JP into conformity with the familiar communal Pater Noster.

8. See with caution F. Hahn, *The Worship of the Early Church* (tr. Philadelphia: Fortress 1976); Gerhard Delling, *Worship in the New Testament* (tr. Philadelphia: Westminster 1962) and J. Danièlou, *The Bible and the Liturgy* (Notre Dame University Press 1956). Compare the examples in A. Hamman (ed), *Early Christian Prayers* (tr. Chicago: Regnery, 1961).

9. On Jewish liturgy consult J. J. Petuchowski (ed). *Contributions to the Scientific Study of Jewish Liturgy* (New York: Ktav 1970); I. Elbogen, *Der jüdische Gottesdienst in seiner geschichtlichen Entwicklung* (rep. Hildesheim, 1962) and J. Heinemann, *Prayer in the Talmud: Forms and Patterns* (New York: de Gruyter 1977). See also *The Lord's Prayer and the Jewish Liturgy* ed M. Brocke, J. J. Petuchowski and W. Strolz (tr. New York: Seabury 1978), which reviews different facets of Jewish liturgy and JP. To this collection Msgr. Oesterreicher contributed a discussion of *ʾAbba* (p 119-136). For a recent examination, consult *Compendium Rerum Iudaicarum ad Novum Testamentum: The Jewish People in the First Century* ed S. Safrai and M. Stern (Philadelphia: Fortress 1976) II ch. 15-18.

10. See H. Schürmann, *Prayer with Christ* (tr. Montreal: Palm 1964) and consult the eschatological interpretation advanced by E. Lohmeyer, *Our Father: An Introduction to the Lord's Prayer* (tr. New York: Harper and Row 1965); J. Jeremias, *The Prayers of Jesus* (London: SCM 1967 ch. 3 appeared as *The Lord's Prayer*, Philadelphia: Fortress 1964) and Raymond E. Brown, *New Testament Essays* (Garden City: Doubleday 1968) p 275-320. Consult discriminately Strack and Billerbeck, *Kommentar zum Neuen Testament* I (Matt 6,1-17); IV. 1 Excurses 6-12 and contrast the evaluation in Israel Abrahams, *Studies in Pharisaism and the Gospels* (rep. New York, 1967).

11. This is a significant criterion for judging the original sayings of Jesus which was not employed by J. Jeremias. Unfortunately the latter's use of the questionable criterion of dissimilarity served N. Perrin in determining the reliable tradition in *Rediscovering the Teachings of Jesus* (New York: Harper and Row 1967). See A. Finkel, "Midrash and the Synoptic Gospels: An Introductory Abstract," *SBL* 1977 Seminar Papers ed. Paul J. Achtemeier (Missoula, Scholars Press). Consult the interpretive development in Robert L. Simpson, *The Interpretations of Prayer in the Early Church* (Philadelphia: Westminster 1965) ch. 2.

12. See W. D. Davies, *Sermon*. He is wrong in assuming (p 90) that the Jamnian Judaism is the true background for the Gospel. However, his thesis holds true for the later Syriac composition of *Didascalia Apostolorum* ed. R. Hugh Connolly (Oxford, 1929). It is a work written after the publication of the Mishnah *(Deuterosis)* which is explicitly criticized.

13. Matt 7,23, citing Ps 119,113 (Luke 13,27 cites Ps 6,9); Matt 16,27, citing Ps 62,13; Matt 8,12; 13,42.50; 22,13; 24,51; 25,30, alluding to Ps 112, 10; Matt 13,42; 25,46, referring to Dan 12,3 and 2 respectively. Similar forms in citing the

Scriptures appear in the homiletic perorations of Pesiqtas, Tanhumas and Rabboth.

14. JTaᶜanith, 2,1; 65ᵇ and Gen Rabba 44 (ed Theodor-Albeck p 434). It is proper to view the saying of Simeon the Just on the theocratic principles of Torah, Service and Acts of Love (Mishnah Aboth 1,2) as background to the redactional concern of Matt. It similarly governs the arrangement of three pericopes in Luke, which links the commissioning of the seven apostles with JP. Luke 10.25-28 quotes the recitation of *Shemaᶜ*, the liturgical service in the Temple (Mishnah Tamid 5,1). 10,29-37 depicts in a parable the works of love and 10,38-42 refers to hearing the word of Jesus, i.e. the Torah. However it is incorrect to argue for reinterpretation of the three-fold pillars by R. Johanan at Jamnia (so J. Goldin, PAAJR 27, 1958 and J. Neusner, *A Life of Yohanan ben Zakkai* Leiden: Brill second edition, 1970, ch. 7). During the Temple period the service included prayer as attested by the Temple liturgy and the acts of piety were even known to the proselyte Munbaz of Adiabene (Tosefta Peʾah 4, 18 and the definition in 19).

15. Against W. D. Davies, *Sermon.* Consult P. Schaefer, "Die sogenannte Synode von Jabne," *Judaica* (1975) p 54-64; 116-124 and A. Finkel, "Yavneh's Liturgy and Early Christianity" (to be published by the *Journal of Ecumenical Studies, 1980*).

16. See Compendium II ch. 17 and J. Heinemann, *Prayer,* ch. 5.

17. Compare the same lesson in Tosefta Taᶜanith 1,8 and jTalmud 2,1 (65a) and see the other types of admonition (Mishnah 2,1 and bTalmud 16a).

18. See Mishnah Taᶜanith 2,1-5; Tosefta 1,9-13; bTaᶜanith 16b, preserving the Temple liturgy for the fast which included the doxology. For the later poetic development in Geniza texts, see A. Marmorstein, "The Amidah of the Public Fast Days", *Contributions* (ed Petuchowski) p 449-454.

19. See Sheldon H. Blank, *Jeremiah: Man and Prophet,* (Cincinnati: Hebrew Union College 1961) p 234-239 on the terms *pagaᶜ* and *palal*. The presentation of a case in the court does affect the form of prayer, see J. Heinemann, *Prayer,* ch. 8. Thus, Luke 18,1-8 presents the parable on praying with reference to an appeal before the judge.

20. On the Maᶜamad and its influence on the synagogue institution, see Zeitlin, *PAAJR* 2 (1930-31) and compare the proposed setting for *"Alenu"* prayer in Heinemann, *Prayer,* p 174. For a handy reference on the traditions consult E. Levy, *Yesodoth Hatefillah* (Tel Aviv, 1961).

21. See M. Greenberg, "On the Refinement of the Conception of Prayer in Hebrew Scriptures," *Association for Jewish Studies Review* 1(1976) p 57-92.

22. See J. Heinemann, *Prayer,* ch. 9.

23. See L. Finkelstein, "The Development of the Amidah" *Contributions* (ed. Petuchowski) p 91-177. However one cannot argue for the original unified version, see J. Heinemann, *Prayer,* ch. 2.

24. So bAbodah Zarah 7b (Nahum the Median). Thus, the Middle Section, with its petitions for existential and eschatological needs, ends in "hearken to prayer", jBerakhoth 2,4; 4d. The same seal is used for the petition of private fast, ibid 72. For this reason the Middle Section is omitted on the Sabbath and Festivals; see J. Mann, *The Bible as Read and Preached in the Old Synagogue,* (New York: rep. Ktav 1971) II (ed I. Sonne) Heb Section p 110.

25. BSanhedrin 44b (R. Elazar). Compare J. Mann, *The Bible* I Heb Section p 294 (R. Johanan). On the significance of intercession by the individual or the community in time of distress, see Mekhilta to Exod 22,22.

26. Ch. 8. Contra J. Jeremias, *Prayers* p 84, that this impression is false. Lukan petition for the Holy Spirit is not only a baptismal prayer. This plea appears in the liturgy for ordination in *Hippolytus* ed G. Dix (Apostolic Constitutions, Book 8,5.18) as the appeal for forgiveness and deliverance from the snare of the Satan. The petitions of Pater Noster appear for the baptized (Book 8,8). For the Jewish liturgical and catechetical background to the Didache, see G. Alon, *Studies in Jewish History* (Heb Tel Aviv, 1957) I p 274-294.

27. On litany see F. Heiler, *Prayer* (tr New York; Oxford University Press, 1958) chs 2,3,11 and J. Heinemann, *Prayer*, ch. 6.

28. See F. Heiler, *Prayer*, ch. 3 and S. Angus, *The Mystery Religions* (rep. New York: Dover 1975).

29. See G. Vermes, *Jesus the Jew* (New York; MacMillan 1973) p 72-80; A Büchler, *Types of Jewish Palestinian Piety* (New York: Ktav rep.) and G. B. Sarfatti, "Pious Men, Men of Deed and the Early Prophets," *Tarbiz* 26 (1956-7) p 126-153.

30. R. Eliezer's dictum: "One who makes his Tefillah *Qebha^c*, his prayer is not supplication" (MBerakhoth 4,4). *Qebha^c* means at fixed times, so MBer. 4,1 and compare jBer 1,5 (3b). For the other meanings see bBer 29b and J. Petuchowski, *Understanding Jewish Prayer* (New York: Ktav 1972) ch. 1.

31. In the Prophets, see A.J. Heschel, *The Prophets* (New York, Harper and Row 1962); A. Neher, *The Prophetic Existence* (South Brunswick N.J., A.S.Barnes 1969) and Gerhard von Rad, *The Message of the Prophets* (New York, 1962). On the Psalmists, see H. Ringgren, *The Faith of the Psalmists* (London, 1963) and Leopold Sabourin, *The Psalms* (New York, Alba House 1970).

32. As servant before God, e.g. Jer 7,25; 44,4 and Ps 116,16 etc.; as son, a designation for Israel (Exod 4,22; Deut 14,1) and in particular the king (the Royal Psalms). A prophet was called "Son of *Adam* (Man)," Ezek 2,1 (Dan 8,17); for he depicts God in the semblance of Man, Ezek 1,26 (Dan 7,9). Thus, the Targum does not translate *"Adam"*. Contra G. Vermes, *Jesus*, ch.7 who cites the examples for *"Bar Nesha,"* an Aramaic circumlocution, which has nothing to do with the honorific title. The Righteous intercessor assumed the attitude of servant before God (Samuel the Small: bTa^canit 25b; Hanina ben Dosa: bBerakhot 34b) and as a son (Onias: bTa^canit 23a).

33. See n. 19. For the example of Moses, see Assumptio Mosis 11 and Exod Rabba 43 to 32,11 on Ps 106,23. The heavenly court appears in the vision of Micaiah (1Kgs 22,19) and the prologue to Job (2,1).

34. Mekhilta to Ex 1,1; Lev Rabba 10,2 ed Margolioth, p 197 and Yalqut Simeoni to Jonah 1,3 & 550. Thus, the only sin of Moses at the Waters of Contention (Num 20,10-13) is attributed by the Rabbis to his angry use of the affront: *"moros"* (idiot) per *"morim"*. See Midrash Hagadol to Num 20,10 and compare the strict teaching of Jesus in Matt 5,22.

35. The current studies on christology usually omit this significant designation. A future comparative study with early Jewish sources should include the meaning of *"Ṣaddiq's"* intercessory life and his effect on God's Presence, as well as the religious response to the *"silluq"* (death) of the Righteous. The "Righteous," or in a related religious context, the "Pious," do not belong simply to anti-ritual charismatic groups (so Vermes).

36. So the Synoptic depiction of Transfiguration. Jesus is proclaimed by the heavenly voice to be a prophet (Mk 9,7, parallels, citing Deut 18,15) and he appears alongside Moses and Elijah, the former and future great prophets of Israel. The tradition echoes the Jewish-Christian view, which is also preserved in the Gospel according to the Hebrews at Matt 3,16 (Jerome, Commentary to

Isaiah 11,2) and in the Gospel according to Thomas, logion 52, referring to 24 prophets as the 24 books of the Jewish canon (so Apocalypse Ezra 12,45).

37. Tosefta Sukkah 4,5 an acquaintance with the Temple service and liturgy; Sifre to Num 18,3: a member of the Levitical choir.

38. Tosefta Berakhot 3,7. Both R. Jose and R. Elazar ben Zadok preserve the brief formulas used on a fast day. Others preserve a brief formula for prayer at mealtime. See the notes of S. Lieberman, *Tosefta Kipheshutah* p 33,34. He also indicates the later Palestinian tradition on combining the two brief forms of Tefillah ascribed to R. Joshua.

39. One version appears in the explanation of the liturgical arrangement by R. Joshua ben Levi; jBerakhoth 2,4; 4d. Compare the text in M. Margolioth, *Hilkhoth Ereṣ Israel* (Jerusalem, 1973) p 144 bottom. The other version called "Habhinenu" appears in jBer 4,3, 8a. The later poetic version from the Genizah appears in J. Mann, "Genizah Fragments of the Palestinian Order of the Service" *Contributions* (ed Petuchowski) p 419-420. See also A.M. Haberman, *Tefilloth Me'en Shemoneh 'Esreh* (Berlin, 1933). The two versions are reflected in the two opinions of Rab and Samuel of the Babylonian academies (jBer 4,3; 8a). See also "Habhinenu" in *Encyclopedia Talmudith* ed Zevin (Tel Aviv, 1957) Vol 8 p 220-230.

40. The reading of Hallel on the festivals is mentioned in Mishnah Pesaḥim 5,7; 'Arakhin 2,3; b'Arakhin 10a. The manner of recitation is described in Tosefta Sotah 6,2.3; see Lieberman's notes p 668 and refer to I. Elbogen, "Studies in Jewish Liturgy" *Contributions* (ed Petuchowski) p 6-7.

41. *The Qumran Psalms* ed J. Sanders, cols 14,7-16.6, preserve the shorter form and the litanic abbreviation with a conclusion of Ps. 118,15.16.8.9. Its apparent use as in the Temple appears in the following Ps 145, called Hallel (bBerakhot 4b; bSabbath 118b), with the doxological refrain. Sopherim 18,25 designates Ps 135 for the first day of Passover and Ps 136 for the last day: the later Synagogue practice.

42. This is already reflected in 1Chr 16,41 (23,30); 2Chr 5,13; 7,3.6; 29,26-28: "Hymnos" of God (also called the Great Hallel in bPesahim 118a to Mishnah 10,7) accompanied by the flute.

43. See M.Z. Segal, *Sepher Ben Sira Hashalem* (Jerusalem, 1958) p 356-357.

44. On the distinction between the pre-Destruction septennial cycle and the post-Destruction triennial cycle, see A. Finkel, *The Pharisees and the Teacher of Nazareth* (Leiden: Brill 1974) p 143-149. J. Heinemann, "The Triennial Lectionary Cycle," *JJewishSt* 19 (1968) p 41-48, demonstrates from the liturgical poetry of Yannai in connection with the Sabbath lections that there was no fixed Palestinian cycle. However, all the texts follow more or less the triennial cycle. They mention "dew" in the Second Petition with the exception of Gen 44,18; Exod 12,29 (ed M. Zulay p 64, 89). Similarly the poetic texts that relate to the Festival cycle preserve "dew" for all with the exception of the first day of Passover (262) and the special Sabbath of Sheqalim (325), which belong to the rainy season. It is apparent that "dew" was mentioned throughout the year and "rain" was added for the winter. Thus, the Genizah Text of the Tefillah mentions "dew" in the second petition but refers to "rain" in the ninth petition (see Schechter, "Genizah Specimens" in *Contributions* ed. Petuchowski p 375-376). Yet Petuchowski in his introduction to *Contributions* p 21 accepts Heinemann's argument as overwhelming (sic!).

45. Relate Midrash to Ps 121,1 to Exod Rabba 46, 3 to 34,1 on Isa 64,16. The former describes the Judgment Day, as the time Israel lifts their eyes to their

Father in Heaven, saying: "You are our Father." The latter refers to the address, "Our Father", in time of distress with a parable on the nobleman's greeting to the Emperor's Assessor: *"Cheirie, Mari Abhi!"* God is likewise greeted as *Mari* or *Abhi*. Compare the popular use of *"Abhi"* by the sinner in the parable of the prodigal son (Luke 15,18. 21) as an address to God.

46. JBerakhoth 4,3;8a, for *"Habhinenu."* The same in the additional petition to "hearken to prayer" for private fast (see Abodath Israel, 98) in contrast to public fast, which is inserted at "Redeemer of Israel." For the latter, the included verse is Ps 107,6 or 28, the hymnic phrase for time of distress as used during the public prayer of the twenty-four petitions.

47. Luke 2,37 (widow) = 1Tim 5,5; Luke 5,33 (John's disciples and the Pharisees); 21,36 (the disciples) = Eph 6,18; 1Tim 2,1; Luke 22,32 (Jesus) = Heb 5,7. Luke in particular uses *"deēsis"* and *"deomai."*

48. See Eric Werner, *The Sacred Bridge* (New York: Columbia 1970). K. Kohler, "The Origin and Composition of the Eighteen Benedictions," *Contributions* (ed Petuchowski) p. 75-90 has indicated the relationship of Christian liturgy to Jewish prayer, as found in Apostolic Constitutions, Book VII ch 33-38. He mistakenly identified it with Essene prayer of the Sabbath. In reality, the text preserves a long version of the first three petitions of the Tefillah ending with brief formulations of the eschatological petitions (33-35). It continues in 37-38 with other references to the eschatological petitions and the final three petitions of the Tefillah as a long version. The Sabbath long petitions is given in ch 36. Thus, it offers a long version of the first and last three petitions as the frame for both daily prayer and the Sabbath liturgy.

49. A. Finkel, *The Evaluation of God's Presence and His Absence in History* (to be published by the Institute of Judaeo-Christian Studies at Seton Hall University). It is based on papers presented at the AAR consultation on "Theology of Catastrophe," Dec. 1977; Nov. 1978.

50. BRosh Hashanah 17b and see *Torah Shelemah* (ed M. Kasher) XXII p 58 notes. These "thirteen attributes" of mercy reappear partially in Prophetic and Psalm texts. Compare their significance in Rom 2,4; 1 Clement 53,4 and the midrash of Apoc. Ezra (IV Esdras) 5,132-138.

51. The implied reading of *"Yahon"* and *"Yerahem,"* so Midrash Prov. 11:27. Similarly the interpretation is rendered for Deut. 13:18 (Sifre and Tosefta Baba Qama 9,30). The other meaning of Exod 33,19, as cited in Rom 9,15, refers to theodicy, see *Torah Shelemah* XXII p 37.

52. Testament Zebulun 8,3; Pal Targum to Lev 22,27 prior to the condemnation by the Palestinian Amora R. Jose, jBerakhot 5,3; 9c and Sabbath 151b.

53. The Deuteronomic reference to payment of vows (23,22) is quoted by Matt 5,33 with reference to the practice of designating the offering in the name of God or His appellatives (Mishnah Zebhahim 4,6). *"Tashlumim"* (payment) is used rabbinically for bringing the required sacrifices (Sifra to Lev 23,41).

54. Jesus reads the commandment: "Show love (=do good; Luke 6,27.35) to your enemy (*Roʿakha* in lieu of the Masoretic *Reʿakha*) as (you wish others would do) to you (Matt 7,12; Luke 6,31). Jesus upheld the inalterability of the script (Matt 5,18) but allows for interpretive revocalization of the text. It aims at the Essene interpretive exclusion of the "Sons of Darkness" (including the Jews), 1QS 1,4. 10. It also responds to the Pharisaic exclusion of the Samaritans (the semi-proselytes), Sifra Lev 19,18 and b Baba Meṣiʿa 111b, according to Yalqut Simeoni reading to Lev 19,13; 408. The latter's interpretation is contrasted in Jesus' parable of the Good Samaritan (Luke 11,36.37).

55. See "Acrostics" by Nahum M. Sarna and Yehudah A. Klausner, *Ency-clopedia Judaica* I p 229-231. Aside from the alphabetical arrangement, there are thematic acrostics in Psalms: 2,1-10 *LeYaNaᵓY WeᵓiSHTW* (To Jannaeus and his wife, the nuptial occasion in Maccabean times); 11: *BeKHY* ("cry"); 14 (not the Elohist 53): *ᵓaYeH HaSHeM* ("Where is the Name = God?" : the Nabhal's question); 15: *MeHoLeL WeNoKHeL* (one who boasts and is deceitful); 26: *LeBH Kol SHoᵓaLaYᵓaᵓoR* (I curse the intention of all who seek me); 100:1-3 *HaᶜaBHoDaH* (the [Todah] Service); 110: *LeSHiMeᶜoN ᵓaMeN* (To Simeon Amen; at the time of installation of Simeon the Hasmonean in 140 B.C.E.; 1Macc 14,27). These acrostics reveal how the editors of the Psalms arranged the earlier hymns in light of their later usages.

56. See A. Marmorstein, *The Old Rabbinic Doctrine of God* (rep. New York, 1968) and E. E. Urbach, *The Sages* (Heb Jerusalem: 1969) ch. 4. J. Jeremias does not include in his study the reference to *"Abba"* in early rabbinic parables nor all the examples in the Palestinian Targums. (Both relate to Synagogue readings). He also failed (through his students) to check the manuscripts and the Midrashic anthologies preserving old sources (e.g. Midrash Hagadol), as well as *Selihoth* prayers.

57. See D. Flusser, "Sanktus und Gloria," *Festschrift for O. Michel* (Leiden: Brill 1963).

58. Compare Mishnah Aboth 3,6 (see J. Siever's article). Ps 82 was recited on Tuesday in the Temple. Verse 1 points to God's Presence in the *ᶜedah*, the gathering of at least ten for public prayer (Deut Rabba to 28,1 ed Lieberman p 108 in view of bBerakhot 21[b] on Num 14,27: *ᶜedah*). It also points to God's Presence among the judges, who are called "ēlohim" (Mekhilta to Exod 20,24). Jesus used the Psalm in defense of his ministry (John 10,34-38). The Gospel according to Thomas, logion 30 reads "where there are three gods," meaning the judges (compare *Didascalia* ed. Connolly p 93).

59. Curiously, a later Jewish Midrash refers to Peter's liturgical composition of *"Nishmath"* (text in Abodath Israel, p 206-208 notes). See Aggadatha de Simeon Kepha in *Beth Hamidrash* ed A. Jellinek V, VI. On the development, see J. Jungmann, *The Place of Christ in Liturgical Prayers* (tr. New York: Alba House 1965).

60. Contra W. D. Davies, *Torah in the Messianic Age* (JBL Monograph Series 7, 1952). See P. Schaefer, "Die Torah der messianischen Zeit," ZNW 65 (1974) p 24-42. In addition, all the references to a new Torah or to its abrogation are understood rabbinically in the context of Ezekiel's prospect (11,19; 36,26). Once the evil inclination is eliminated, given commandments become inapplicable. Compare the redefinition for all the commandments in 2Cor 3,3-6. Consult the refutation in *ᵓOzar Wikkuḥim* ed J. D. Eisenstein (rep. Israel, 1969) p 215,216, Yeshuᶜoth Meshiho by I. Abarbanel (Karlsruhe, 1828) and David Kimhi's com-ments to Isa 12,3; Jer 31,30.

61. Recently defended by R. Leaney, "The Lucan Text of the Lord's Prayer," *Nov Test* 1(1956) p 103-111.

62. On the Galilean dialect of Aramaic see Eduard Y. Kutscher, *Hebrew and Aramaic Studies* (Jerusalem, 1977). Compare G. Vermes, *Jesus*, p 52-54 and M. Black, *An Aramaic Approach to the Gospels and Acts* (Oxford: Clarendon, third edition 1967). The phenomenon of *Mischsprache* (Greek, Latin and Hebrew terms incorporated into Aramaic vernacular) in Galilee, as attested to in the Palestinian texts, was not fully explored by the above. The glossolalia indicates that the

Galileans, who were noted for their peculiar pronunciation (Mark 14,70 = Matt 26,73), could hear and understand different tongues (Acts 2,7-11). These are Persian, Aramaic, Greek, Latin and Arabic. In addition to the similar sound for flat bread and rock, the fish and the snake are also mentioned. They represent either the similar Greek forms *ichtys* and *echis* (Mekhilta to Exod 15,22) or the Greek *aphyē* (sardine) bHullin 66a, and the Hebrew *ʾephʿeh* (Isa 30,6) or the Galilean form *ʾawya* (Gen Rabba 26 to 6,4).

63. The Baraitha (bYoma 86a) depicts good works that elicit public praise for God as an act of endearing or sanctifying God's name, in view of Isa 49,3 (see Tanḥuma to 19,2 ed Buber p 72). The evil inclination is called obstacle (Isa 57,4; bSukkah 52b while God calls it evil, Gen 8,21). Its removal is related to Ezekiel's prospect (36,26); see Num Rabba to 10,2. The obstacle is defined as hypocrisy (Tosefta Yoma 4,12).

64. This phrase can be explained in light of the legend on the liturgical use of *Shemaʿ* in the synagogue. Jacob before his death has exhorted his twelve sons to "hear God of Israel who is your Father in heaven." It reads " *ʾel*" as God in lieu of the preposition "to" in Gen 49,2b (see Gen Rabba ad loc., ed Theodor-Albeck p 1252 notes). The twelve sons replied: "Hear O Israel—our (natural) father: the Lord is our God, the Lord is one" (Pal Targum to Deut 6,4).

65. *Kathēgētēs* is in Aramaic *Medabrana* (compare the salutation in bSanhedrin 14a). Matthew's stress on oneness with reference to God and Jesus is a repudiation of dualistic heresy and christological division, respectively. Compare Sifre to Deut 6,4 on undivided faith in one God and b.Sanhedrin 8a on no communal division on leadership.

66. See Harry A. Wolfson, *The Philosophy of the Church Fathers* (Cambridge: Harvard University Press, 1964) I ch 7.

67. See O. Cullmann, *The Christology of the New Testament* (tr. Philadelphia: Westminster, 1963) p 32 notes.

68. "Hosanna in the highest" is rendered in Aramaic *barrama* (Jerome, Letter to Damasus 20 on Matt 21,9). *Bar-Rama* connotes "the Son of the Highest" (compare Luke 1,32), which satisfies the parallel to "Hosanna the Son of David" in Matthew. The two christological appeals sandwich the liturgical salutation to the pilgrims (Ps 118,26) or later to members in the church, the new Temple. Compare the enactment of greeting in God's name, Mishnah Berakhot 9,5. Similar to it is the greeting of peace (Luke 10,5) in Christian life. Peace is an appellative for God.

69. Sifra to Lev 22:32; bSanhedrin 74a. The public service of hallowing God's name is also derived from the same verse, bMegillah 23b.

70. See N. Perrin, *The Kingdom of God in the Teaching of Jesus* (Philadelphia: Westminster 1963) which reviews and evaluates the contemporary discussion on the realized, proleptic and futuristic eschatology. The governing principle of correspondence in Apocalyptic thought and experience is not explored fully nor adequately employed in the discussion.

71. See Bertil Gärtner, *The Temple and the Community in Qumran and the New Testament* (Cambridge University Press 1965). His evaluation of the New Testament material is valuable. However, his comparative study with Qumran is inadequate. See Y. Yadin, *Temple Scroll* (Heb Jerusalem, 1977) I p 144 notes. Contra J. Neusner in *Judaica* 21 (1972) p 318 rep. *Early Rabbinic Judaism* (Leiden: Brill 1975) ch.2.

72. Already noticed by J. Wellhausen, see G. Dalman, *Die Worte Jesu* (rep. Darmstadt, 1965) p 50.

73. See J.N. Epstein, *Introduction to the Tannaitic Literature* (Heb Jerusalem, 1957) p 746 (Sifre Zuṭa).

74. On the rabbinic response, see L. Ginzberg, *Legends of the Jews* (Philadelphia; JPSA 1959) IV p 304 V p 396 and S. H. Blank, "The Death of Zechariah in Rabbinic Literature", *HUCA* 12/13(1937/38) p 327-346. Both relate the event to the death of the prophet in the First Temple. Yet the rabbis have interpreted the event as described by Josephus in relation to the past, a homiletic tendency affecting the description of catastrophic events. The Zealots' bloodshed that caused the removal of God's Presence in the Second Temple is described historically in Cant. Zuṭa to 8,14. See S. Liebermann, *Greek and Hellenism in Jewish Palestine* (Heb Jerusalem, 1962) p 138-146.

75. A rabbinic version of God's lament for his children is recorded in bBerakhot 3ª (R. Eliezer of the First Century). Compare Echa Rabba (ed Buber) 9,15. 25.

76. God's Presence is the expression of love, see Cant Rabba to 3,10 on *"appiryon"* as the Temple inlaid with love. Compare Pesiqta (ed M. Ish Shalom) p 22a. On the experience of *"homonoia"* see E.E. Urbach, *Sages*, ch. 3; 43. Thus, God's relationship to the pilgrims is described as a "Father who dwells among his children" (Exod Rabba 34, to 25,10.8 and Midrash Hagadol, ad loc.).

77. The Temple was destroyed in Summer of 70, a post-Sabbatical year (Seder Olam Rabba 30). Consult B. Z. Wacholder, *Essays in Jewish Chronology and Chronography.* (New York: Ktav 1976), who fixes the date as 69/70.

78. Eusebius preserves the religious view of the church: "When holy men desert the city, the judgment of God will overtake them (in the city)," in view of Abraham's appeal to God, Gen. 18,24-32 (Gen Rabba to 18,32; Pirke de R. Eliezer 25). In addition, Eusebius offers a later Christian view on the punishment: "For all their crimes against Christ and his apostles". He ends with a malediction: "Let all the generation of the wicked be utterly blotted out from among men". Compare the wording of the Jewish malediction in the Tefillah, as it appeared in Eusebius time: "Let the Nazareans and the *minim* (= the doers of evil, other recensions) . . . be utterly blotted out from the book of life".

79. A significant example is the midrash of the Scribe on *Shemaᶜ* (Mark 12,33-34). The scribe interprets love for God and the neighbor as greater than sacrifices, citing Hos 6,6. Ḥesed expresses love for neighbor and *daᶜath* love for God. Matthew employs Hos 6,6 as Scriptural support for the teaching of Jesus on table-fellowship with the sinners (9,13) and healing on the Sabbath (12,7). Hos 6,6 was likewise used by R. Joḥanan of Jamnia (Aboth de R. Nathan I 4; II 8). This was not a revolutionary discovery (sic!) as claimed by J. Goldin, which misled J. Neusner, *Yoḥanan*, p 193. The common liturgical lesson of the pre-Destruction scribe was already known to Mark. Compare Pal Targum to Gen 35,8 and Deut 34,6, enumerating the acts of piety in *imitatio Dei* (see Pirke de R. Eliezer 12). Contra J. Neusner, *Development of a Legend* (Leiden: Brill 1970) p 114.

80. A. Finkel, *The Pharisees*, p 134-143. This would clearly show that Matthew's detailed knowledge of the Pharisaic practice was prior to the Hilleitic revision of the Halakhah at Jamnia. Compare the recent studies of E. Levine, "The Sabbath Controversy According to Matthew" (arguing for a pre-70 setting of the Omer controversy) and J. Neusner, "First Cleanse the Inside" (pointing to the Shammaitic practice) in *N.T.S.* 22 (1976). The latter does not acknowledge

my work. In his conclusion, he is not able to explain this phenomenon satisfactorily; contra his thesis in *Rabbinic Traditions about the Pharisees* (Leiden, 1971).

81. The example of healing on the Sabbath (Mekhilta to 31,12) and the stress on love for the person, the Hillelitic teaching (Aboth 1,12). Thus, transpersonal commandment is set aside by interpersonal commandment in a conflict situation (so the criticism of the priestly practice pre-70, Tosefta Yoma 1,12). Jesus similarly debates with the Pharisees of his day: 1) Saving a life on the Sabbath (Mark 3,4 parallels); 2) Acts of piety cannot be set aside due to pollution caused by a seemingly dead person (Luke 10, 30-35: the priest and the Levite cross over to the other side); 3) Support for parents cannot be cancelled by declaring the food items sacred (Mark 7,9-13 = Matt 15,3-9: "You transgress the (interpersonal) commandment of God for the sake of your tradition" (on making vows in transpersonal matters). Jesus himself is not a Hillelite but he appears to interpret the Scriptures in their spirit. His messianic consciousness cannot be simply determined by a particular religious personality.

82. On the doxology see E. Werner, *Bridge*, ch 9; J. Heinemann, *Prayer*, p 85-85.

83. The text is cited by John 19,37 (the Scriptural sign for Jesus' messianic death) and by Matt 24,30, the sign for the coming of the Son of Man (so Rev 1,7). Thus, both aspects of Jesus' advent are interpreted by this Prophetic verse. The text was likewise used by the later rabbinic apocalypticists with reference to the dead Messiah, the Son of Joseph (bSukkah 52a). The "grace" referred to in the verse is connected with the priestly Benediction on God's grace, i.e. the reintroduction of prophecy (printed Tanhuma to Num 6,25).

84. See 1QS 2,3: "eternal *da'ath*"; 1QSb 2,24: "the Holy Spirit (= 1,5: "*da'ath* of the Holy") and Sifre to Num 6,25: "Light of the Presence (= the Face)", i.e. illumination (*zyw*). Most significantly, the transmission of the lections recited by the Levites in the Temple at the Sabbath additional sacrificial service is governed by an acrostic (bRosh Hashana 31a; jMegillah 3,8; 74a; Sopherim 12,7). The initial letters of Deut 31,1. 7. 19. 36 form *HaZYW LeKHa*, i.e. ("God's) illumination unto you (singular)."

85. See Gordon P. Wiles, *Paul's Intercessory Prayers* (Cambridge University Press 1974).

86. Originally the covenantal formula: "I am unto you . . . and you are unto me. . . ," expresses a nuptial declaration (Hos 2, 20 in view of 2,4, see Elephantine marriage certificate, ed Kraeling 2,3,4). The Prophets depict matrimonially the relationship between God and Israel (e.g. Ezek 16; see A. Neher, op. cit., part III,2). For the earthly community, the nuptial union with God was experienced liturgically and ritualistically in the Temple. Thus, Canticles (the songs of the lover and his beloved) were interpreted allegorically in the first Centuries (so Cant Rabba; Pesiqta Rabbati 5; Pesiqta de R. Kahana 1, compare Origen's Commentary). The homilist preserves the covenantal formula as an expression of God's declaration (Exod Rabba to 25,8): "You are my sheep/vineyard/sons and I an your Shepherd/Keeper/Father," or as the community's response (Cant Rabba to 2,16): "He is unto me a God/ a Father/ a Shepherd/ a Keeper and I am unto Him a nation/ a son/ sheep/ vineyard". Thus, the liturgical recitation of *Shema*ᶜ is offered as an example of this covenantal experience (idem and Sifre to Deut 33,26). See also K. Hruby's article.

87. The litanic cry *eleison* is preserved in early Christian liturgy. Correspondingly the litanic appeals to Jesus are transmitted in the Gospels as "save"

(Matt 8,25; 14,30; 21,9. 15) "help" (15,25) "have mercy" (Mark 10,47-48 parallels).

88. The prayers appear in chs 24, 27, 29, 53, 59, 60, 64. Clement preserves lessons on the proper orientation in prayer similar to Matt: on repentance 8; on righteousness 9; on humble-mindedness 13, 17, 56; on peacefulness 15; on purity and integrity 21, 23; on reconciliation 48; on prayer 50 and on deliverance from evil 51.

89. The litanies are preserved alphabetically in Amram's Siddur with the appeal to "our Father." The repeated cries appear as "*Hosanna*" (the liturgy for Tabernacle Festival); "Answer us" (prayer for the fast day); "Do for the sake" and "our Father, our King" (as above).

90. Contra D. Flusser, *Jesus* (tr New York 1969) p 95 and G. Vermes, *Jesus*, ch 8, 4. J. Jeremias, *Prayer*, p 35-48 distinguishes between "our Father" and "my Father" of *²Abba*. This is nothing but a distinction between the collective address and the substitute form for God's name, as used by individuals.

91. On religious education in the schools, see S. Krauss, *Talmudische Archaeologie* (rep Hildesheim, 1966) III, 12 and *Compendium*, II ch. 19.

92. The prayer of the commoners is brief without even referring to God (Tosefta Berakhot 4,45; see S. Liebermann's notes). However, the substitute terms of "*Rahmana*" (Merciful One) or "*Mara*" (Master) and "*Hamaqom*" (the Place) were also used (bBer. 40b).

93. See the examples in A. Finkel, *The Pharisees*, p 110. The particular significance attached to child's recitation is mentioned by Matt 21,15-16, citing Ps 8,2 (read *Yisarta* = you are praised in song, in view of 1Chr 15,22). The Tannaim employ this verse to illustrate the innocent children's recitation of the Song at the Sea as a perception of God's Presence (Tosefta Sotah 6, 4.5 and Mekhilta to Exod 5,1).

94. So Onias' cousin, Ḥilqiyah, is called *²Abba* (bMakkoth 24a) and see Y. Heilprin, *Seder Hadoroth* (rep. Jerusalem, 1956) on Onias' grandson who was called the meek. *²Abba* denotes patron or communal administrator. Compare Matt 23,9 on the use of the honorific title *Abba* in the community (examples in Strack and Billerbeck, *Kommentar* I p 918).

95. See J. Jeremias, *New Testament Theology* (tr. New York: Scribners 1971) p 9-14, 179 and compare the liturgical use in Martin McNamara, *Targum and Testament* (Grand Rapids: Eerdmans 1968) ch 9, 12. See A. Marmorstein, *Rabbinic Doctrine*, on the pronunciation of the Tetragrammaton.

96. BKiddushin 31b. See Gerald Blidstein, *Honor Thy Father and Mother* (New York: Ktav 1976).

97. See David de Sola Pool. *The Kaddish* (New York 3rd ed, 1964) and J. Heinemann, *Prayer*, p 163f.

98. See S. Schechter, *Aspects of Rabbinic Theology* (rep. New York: Schocken 1961) ch 2. M. Kadushin, *The Rabbinic Mind* (New York: Bloch, third edition 1972) ch 4, 2. E.E. Urbach, *Sages*, ch 15,4.

99. The employment of YHWH, ELOHIM in prayer is discussed and used as a criterion for judgment of pre-Destruction forms of prayer. See L. Finkelstein, "Development of Amidah" *Contributions* (ed. Petuchowski). J. Heinemann, *Prayer*, p 120 indicates that JP addresses God as Father as well as King in the petition for the Kingdom, as both conceptions appear in Jewish liturgy. However, he also maintains that "Pater Noster" is a private prayer, since it does not contain the name in the address nor a praise formulation. Jesus indeed offers his

private brief prayer for the community to pray. Since Jesus made it available, according to Matthew's redaction, for the time of distress. It addresses "You" as the petition for rain in Jewish practice. There is no evidence, however, for the time of Jesus that individuals prayed the Eighteen Benedictions, but there is evidence that these were recited publicly in a briefer version. Furthermore, the private petitions of the teachers became a part of the communal liturgy.

100. Pesiqta de R. Kahana 4, 36b, bSukkah 14a; Midrash Tannaim to Deut 3,24.

APPENDIX: MATTHEW'S ECCLESIASTICAL PRAYER OF JESUS

ACROSTIC			THE ARAMAIC FORM	
ʾe	ADDRESS:		*ʾaBHuNaN'	De*BHiSHMa'YYa*
			Our Father	who is in heaven
SH	ESCHATOLOGICAL			
	PETITIONS:	I	YiTHQaDDaSH'	SHe M*aKH*'
			Hallowed be	Thy name.
Mo		II	TeTHe ʾ'	MaLKHuTH*aKH*'
			Let come	Thy kingdom.
R		IIIa	YiTH ʿaBHeD'	Reʿ uTH*aKH*'
			Done be	Thy will,
.		IIIb	Ke*BHiSHMa'YY*a	Weʿ aL- ʾaR ʿa'
			as in heaven	so on earth.
Mi	EXISTENTIAL			
	PETITIONS:	IV	LaHM*aN*' MeHaR' ¹: HaBH' *LaN*' YoMaNa'	
			Our bread for tomorrow give us today.	
Ho		V	USHeBHoQ' *LaN*' HoBHY*NaN*':	
			KeDHiSHeBHaQ*aN*' LeHaYYaBHY*NaN*'	
			And remit² us our debts³	
			as we remit² our debtors³.	
Ne		VI	*WeLa* ʾ- Te ʿaLi*NaN*' LeNiSYoNa'	
			And not cause us to enter⁴ into trial.	
PH		VII	ʾella ʾ' PaSSiN*aN*' ⁵ MeBi'SHaʾ	
			But deliver us from evil.	

1. *EPIOUSIOU* captures the meaning of tomorrow, *MeHaR (epi ienai)* and of speedily, *MaHeR (epi einai)*. Galilean dialect does not distinguish between the gutturals. *MaHeR* is used in Jewish petitions, a reflection of the desperate need of the community.

2. *SHeBHoQ* connotes both remit and forgive, indicating Aramaism.

3. *HoBHaʾ* means both debt (Matt) and sin (Luke), indicating Aramaism.

4. The Aramaic captures both meanings in Greek: *eisenenkēs* (lead) and *eiselthēte* (enter), Mark 15,38.

5. *Rhyesthai* translates *NaSaL* in LXX. So Matt 27,43, citing Ps 22,9 (see Targum).

NOTE: The beats are stressed and the same expression is underlined. Division of the meter is indicated by a colon. An asterisk points to the initial letter of the acrostic.

"Where Two or Three . . ." : The Rabbinic Concept of *Shekhinah* and Matthew 18,20*

JOSEPH SIEVERS

I. The origins of the term *Shekhinah*

Rabbinic literature commonly expresses the idea of the presence of God by the term *Shekhinah*. It is an abstract feminine noun derived from the verb *shakhan* which means to dwell, rest, repose, abide. This verb and its derivatives are frequently used in the Old Testament with reference to God and to his sanctuary.[1] *Shekhinah*, however, never occurs in the Hebrew Bible or, as far as I have been able to determine, in the Dead Sea Scrolls. Thus, when scholars have searched for the origin of the concept, they have relied almost exclusively on the rabbinic texts themselves. While this method is legitimate, it leads to meager results, for the term is not well attested before the generation of Rabbi Akiba in the early second century.

Some rabbinic references to *Shekhinah* may be earlier than that, but they are found in texts which have undergone changes until considerably later. Therefore, they cannot be used as reliable guides. One example is the reference to the "abode *(Shekhinah)* of his might in the loftiest heights" in the *Aleinu* prayer which in its earliest form goes back to Temple times and is now part of the daily service.[2] Another prayer, an addition to the Eighteen Benedictions attributed to the *ḥasidim ha-rishonim* ("pious men of old"), is preserved in the ninth century (or later)

---

*The idea of the present article was first conceived in 1969 while I was studying the Mishnah with Professor Kurt Schubert in Vienna. I sensed then that a comparative study of the concept of divine presence might have important implications for Jewish-Christian dialogue. It is with great pleasure that I dedicate this article to Msgr. Oesterreicher who has perhaps done more than anyone else to promote this dialogue.
I gratefully acknowledge helpful suggestions from Professors S.J.D. Cohen, A.M. Goldberg, T. Hartmann, and J.T. Townsend, as well as from the editors.

Midrash on Psalms: "Merciful (Lord), in your great compassion return your *Shekhinah* to Zion and restore the Temple service to Jerusalem."[3] If we knew that the *hasidim ha-rishonim* were connected with the *Asidaioi* of the early second century, this prayer could be considered a reference to the desecration of the Temple by Antiochus IV (167 BC). But unfortunately we know too little about this group of "pious men of old" to ascertain the historical setting reflected here. Much less can we be sure about the original wording of the prayer.[4]

The references to the *Shekhinah* in Targum Onkelos as well as in the various recensions of the Palestinian Targum are numerous. Although the Targumim contain much earlier material, they were not redacted in final form before the third century. Therefore, they are of little help in establishing the origin of the term *Shekhinah*.[5].

A more fruitful search for the origins of the concept of *Shekhinah* may be carried on outside rabbinic literature. Second Maccabees, written in Greek and completed before 63 BC, may give us a clue. While reporting events of 161 BC, it includes a prayer of Jerusalem priests for the purity of the "Temple of your indwelling" *(naon tēs sēs skēnōseōs)*.[6] *Skēnōsis*, an abstract feminine noun, finds its closest Hebrew parallel in meaning as well as in form in *Shekhinah*.[7]

Although he was not referring to this specific passage, Goldberg suggested that the designation of the Temple as "House of God's dwelling" may have been at the origin of the term *Shekhinah*.[8]

Second Maccabees appears to corroborate that conjecture by showing us an early stage of the development which led to the meaning "God's presence," or "God" (who is present in the Temple), instead of simply a "dwelling." It is no longer possible to determine when this development was completed, but a date some time before the destruction of the Second Temple (70 AD) is most plausible.[9] The meaning of *Shekhinah*, however, did not remain confined to the divine presence in the sanctuary, as we shall see.

II. *Shekhinah* and Torah

In rabbinic literature *Shekhinah* came to signify all modes of God's presence in past, present, and eschatological future. In other words, it became a synonym for God whenever and wherever his nearness was implied. This fact, however, did not eliminate the distinction and even tension between different forms of divine presence.[10] Here we concentrate on those situations for which the rabbis thought the presence of the *Shekhinah* possible among three or even two people.

A passage in the *Mekhilta*, a relatively early midrash on Exodus,[11] shows us the connection between God's presence in the Temple and among people outside the Temple. It interprets Exod 20,24, "In every place where I cause my name to be mentioned I will come to you and bless you," as follows:

> Where I reveal myself to you, that is, in the Temple. Hence they said: The Tetragrammaton is not to be pronounced outside of the Temple.[12]—R. Eliezer b. Jacob says: If you come to my house I will come to your house, but if you do not come to my house I will not come to your house. The place my heart loveth, thither my feet lead me.—In connection with this passage the sages said: Wherever ten persons assemble in a synagogue the *Shekhinah* is with them, as it is said: "God standeth in the congregation of God" (Ps 82,1). And how do we know that he is also with three people holding court? It says: "In the midst of the judges he judgeth" (ibid.). And how do we know that he is also with two? It is said: "Then they that feared the Lord spoke one with another," etc. (Mal 3,16). And how do we know that he is even with one? It is said: "In every place where I cause My name to be mentioned I will come unto thee and bless thee."[13]

This Midrash presents anonymously two opposing opinions: one restricts God's presence to the Temple, the other affirms it also for other places. The saying of R. Eliezer b. Jacob stands apart from them and tells us nothing about the setting of the two traditions.[14] It is, however, an indication that the redactor understood the problem to be God's presence or absence, not where the Tetragrammaton may be pronounced. We should note that the proof text for the *Shekhinah's* presence among ten in the synagogue or "three people holding court," that is, those who judge, is taken from a psalm that was part of every Tuesday's liturgy in the Temple (*mTamid* 7,4). This observation does not allow us to date the origin of this idea or to consider identical God's presence inside and outside the Temple, but it weakens Goldberg's thesis that there was no connection between the ideas of the *Shekhinah* in the Temple and in the community.[15]

The presence of the *Shekhinah* among three or more judges is a recurrent theme in rabbinic literature. It is assumed in criminal and civil cases as well as during their deliberations concerning the fixing of the calendar.[16]

The *Mekhilta* attaches no conditions other than fear of the Lord and remembrance of his name to the presence of the *Shekhinah* with one or two persons. In this it differs from most other traditions which consider preoccupation with Torah as the main requisite. Several sayings in the

Mishnah tractate *Abot* illustrate this. They include the only two occurrences of the term *Shekhinah* in the entire Mishnah.[17] The first and best
known saying is attributed to Rabbi Hananiah ben Teradyon:

> If two sit together and the words between them are not of
> Torah, then that is a session of scorners, as it is said, *Nor hath
> sat in the seat of the scornful.*[18] But if two sit together and the
> words between them are of Torah, then the *Shekhinah* is in their
> midst, as it is said, *Then they that feared the Lord spoke one with
> another; and the Lord hearkened, and heard, and a book of remem-
> brance was written before him, for them that feared the Lord and that
> thought upon his name* (Mal 3,16).[19]

Rabbi Hananiah ben Teradyon was a contemporary of Rabbi Akiba.
According to the Talmud he died a martyr's death in the persecution of
Hadrian (c. 135 AD). His exceptional emphasis on study and observance
of Torah is highlighted by the story that he was burned alive wrapped in
a Torah scroll.[20] The above saying is fitting for such a man in a time of
persecution. In its present form, including the reference to Torah, it may
be original with Hananiah. The idea of the *Shekhinah* with two people,
however, is a concept that can be traced to the first century.[21] The
relation of this tradition to the above-quoted *Mekhilta* passage is not
clear. But it is reasonable to suppose that the belief in the *Shekhinah's*
presence among at least ten people existed earlier.

A parallel to Rabbi Hananiah's saying is attributed to his contemporary Rabbi Halafta of Sepphoris in *Abot de Rabbi Natan*. He speaks of the
presence of the *Shekhinah* with any "two or three who sit together in the
marketplace and the words between them are of Torah."[22] Similarly, in
Abot Rabbi Simeon bar Yohai (c. 100-170) is quoted as saying: "When
three eat at one table and do speak words of Torah there, it is as though
they have eaten from the table of God."[23] *Abot* continues with a variety
of sayings concerning the importance of Torah in one's life. Included is a
dictum of Rabbi Halafta of Kefar Hananiah (late second century) main-
taining that the *Shekhinah* is with those who occupy themselves with
Torah, be they ten, five, three, two or only one.[24]

In this context "Torah" should not be understood too narrowly as
only the Pentateuch or as the Written and Oral Law in any strictly
defined sense. In rabbinic literature the term is used in a variety of
meanings, often including all the living halakhic traditions and their
applications in life. A text dealing with the question of the *Shekhinah*
among judges states that "also court proceedings are Torah," and one
rabbi maintained that even the everyday talk of people in the Holy Land
is Torah.[25] At least one modern homiletic commentary explains that the

saying of Rabbi Ḥananiah ben Teradyon implies an "obligation to apply and reflect the 'words of Torah,' its values, its norms and laws, in our everyday social and business world."[26]

In rabbinic thought occupation with Torah is not merely an intellectual enterprise, but a sharing in God's own activity.[27] It is because of this that Torah is considered a way to experience his nearness, the *Shekhinah*.

An area where the presence of the *Shekhinah* with two people is particularly stressed is married life. God is considered the third partner. A saying attributed to Rabbi Akiba reads as follows: "When husband and wife are worthy, the *Shekhinah* abides with them; when they are not worthy fire consumes them." This saying is not simply a play on words, not just a pun, but it really seems to express the possibility of God's nearness to the married partners.[28]

This and numerous other instances show the ethical implications of the presence of the *Shekhinah*. People must be worthy of it. Sinful behavior, such as murder, adultery, idolatry, and slander, causes the departure of the *Shekhinah*.[29] On the other hand, "whoever is meek will ultimately cause the *Shekhinah* to dwell with man on earth."[30]

III. The context of Matt 18,20

Whereas it is not clear how widespread the concept of *Shekhinah* was in the first century AD, the Gospels of Matthew and John appear to attest to its use.

Time and again scholars have pointed out that a most striking parallel to the saying of Hananiah b. Teradyon that we quoted above, is found in Matt 18,20: "For where two or three are gathered in my name, there am I in their midst." This verse forms part of a chapter of instructions for the early Christian community.

In its present context it stands between the teachings concerning reconciliation (v 15-17) and forgiveness (v 21-22). It is preceded by the promise that the prayer of two people offered in unison will be answered (v 19) and by the bestowal of the power to bind and to loose (v 18). Verses 19-20 are clearly set off from their context by the introductory formulas in vv 19 and 21, and by their form and contents. They constitute two originally independent sayings, although v 20 is redactionally linked to v 19 by the conjunction "for" (*gar*).[31]

There have been several recent in-depth studies of Matt 18 in general[32] and 18,20 in particular.[33] Therefore, instead of attempting a complete exegesis, I shall address myself to the question of what light rabbinic texts throw on v 20 and vice versa. So far, little has been done to try to explain the nature of this relationship. One of the reasons for this

certainly lies in the difficulty of relating a gospel passage dating from the
first century to rabbinic sayings redacted over a century later. Sandmel
rightly warns of "parallelomania."[34] And yet, a careful attempt at
comparison of parallel features can be made.

m. Abot 3:2	*Abot de Rabbi Nathan* B Ch. 34, p. 74	Matt 18,20
		For
If two	If two or three	where two or three
sit together	sit together in the marketplace	are gathered
and the words between them	and the words between them	
are of Torah	are of Torah	in my name
then the *Shekhinah* is	then the *Shekhinah* is revealed	there am I
in their midst.	to them.	in their midst.

On the surface the differences are quite obvious: Matthew has "my
name" instead of "words of Torah," and refers to Jesus instead of the
Shekhinah. These divergences, however, are more understandable when
we recognize that we are dealing with a "parallel with a fixed difference".[35] Almost consistently the gospels attribute to Jesus what rabbinic
texts say about God and the Torah. If we further consider that the
passages under consideration are distinct theological statements and not
general ethical norms, the parallelism becomes even more interesting.

Since the parallels are so close, there is reasonable probability that
some literary relationship exists. It is not to be excluded *a priori* that
some rabbis knew Matthew's Gospel or similar Christian traditions and
adopted some of them for their own use. It is, however, not likely that
the theological development of a concept as important as *Shekhinah* was a
direct response to Christianity. Thus, most scholars readily admit that
Matt 18,20 is based on a Jewish tradition and not vice versa.[36]

IV. Analysis of Matthew 18,20

Two or three: the quorum for a special form of presence may simply be
left vague or it may be an echo of the "two or three witnesses"
mentioned in v 16b. There are, however, other possibilities. The concept

of the *Shekhinah* between three judges may have been at work in this formulation. This cannot be proven, but because of the previous verses concerning Church proceedings in the case of a person's misconduct, it should not be dismissed lightly. In fact, a connection with Ps 82,1 and its rabbinic interpretation becomes even more plausible in a parallel apocryphal saying "Where there are three (gods), they are gods."[37] It is unclear whether there is any direct relationship between the *two or three* in Matt 18,20 and in *Abot de R. Natan B* quoted above.

Are gathered (eisin . . . synēgmenoi): It has frequently been suggested, now again by Englezakis,[38] that Matt 18,20 refers to liturgical gatherings only. This, however, goes counter to the evidence: (a) In the NT the verb *synagein* is rarely used for liturgical assemblies. In Matthew, where it occurs most frequently (24 times), it never has such connotations. (b) V 20 speaks in a more general way than v 19 and does not specify a particular setting. (c) Even v 19 is not strictly limited to liturgical prayer. (d) Vv 15-18 deal with disciplinary, not liturgical matters. (e) 1Cor 5,4, which in several respects resembles Matt 18,20, speaks of an assembly for disciplinary action, not liturgical celebration (see Col 3,17). (f) *m. Abot* 3,2b and similar rabbinic texts do not presuppose a liturgical setting or any *formal* gathering.[39]

In my name (eis to emon onoma): It has frequently been indicated that this phrase translates the Hebrew/Aramaic *lishmi*[40]. This can be rendered "for my sake." One should compare a saying attributed to Rabbi Yohanan the Sandal-maker (mid-second century): "Every assembly which is for the sake of Heaven *(leshem shamayim)* will in the end endure; but one which is not for the sake of Heaven will not endure in the end" *(m. Abot* 4,11; see 5,17). Heaven is here, as frequently in rabbinic and NT texts, a synonym for God. We should note that several biblical texts which the rabbis connected with *Shekhinah* speak of God's name. Mal 3,16, the prooftext for the *Shekhinah* between two, speaks of those who "think of his name" (see Exod 20,24).

It is unclear whether in the Jewish tradition underlying Matt 18,20 there was a reference to the Torah or to God. In several passages in the synoptic gospels Jesus takes the place of Torah.[41] This fact, however, has to be seen in conjunction with Matt 5,17: "Think not that I have come to abolish the law and the prophets. I have come not to abolish them but to fulfill them."

There am I: This statement is the most radical departure from Jewish tradition. Some authors consider it in polemical antithesis to the rabbinic concept of God's presence.[42] It appears, however, that Matthew's source does not intend to replace but to explain that idea: the *Shekhinah* is manifested in Jesus. This impression is reinforced by the present context which speaks of reconciliation, prayer, and forgiveness, rather than of polemics.

It obviously cannot be proven that the underlying Jewish tradition actually used the term *Shekhinah*. The likelihood, however, is rather great. We are dealing with a motif of presence which can easily be traced to OT notions (e.g., Exod 20,24). But v 20 is modeled on rabbinic formulations which in this context use *Shekhinah*. An allusion to the concept of *Shekhinah* itself may probably be found in the prologue of John's Gospel (1,14), and perhaps also in Rev 21,3.[43]

In their midst: Neither the rabbinic texts nor the NT presuppose a visible presence. In the rabbinic texts the *Shekhinah* is sometimes imagined as standing or hovering above the people.[44] Trilling compares this presence of Jesus "in their midst" to the *Shekhinah* in the Temple. He emphasizes its static nature and cultic connotations.[45] But Goldberg has shown that although the *Shekhinah* is sometimes connected with a place, e.g., the Temple, it is at other times associated with people or events regardless of location.[46]

Besides the similarities in wording, v 20 closely resembles *m Abot* 3:2b in structure too. Whereas Matt 18,15-19 contains a sequence of conditional sentences (*ean* plus aorist subjunctive is used 9 times), v 20 uses the indicative present. In contrast with v 15-19, it is not directed to a specific audience, but has the form of a general statement, with the dependent clause in the third person. This is apparently not a redactional development but is another indication that v20 is—at least in part—based on a separate source.[47]

If, as our findings suggest, a Jewish saying underlies Matt 18,20, the concept of God's presence with two or three persons must have existed at least some time before the redaction of Matthew's gospel. Furthermore, if we can find a *terminus post quem* for the Jewish tradition, this applies to Matt 18,20 as well. In this regard, however, our sources yield no precise data and we can only list the possibilities.

On one hand, it is possible that the concept of the *Shekhinah* with ten or less people existed already during the Second Temple period, although we have no verification for this.[48] In this case we have no way of dating the origin of Matt 18,20. There is, however, substantial agreement that its present formulation presupposes the Easter event.[49]

On the other hand, it has frequently been suggested that the broadened understanding of *Shekhinah* may be explained most plausibly as a response to the crisis caused by the destruction of the Temple: The *Shekhinah* is no longer in the Temple, but under certain conditions its presence can still be experienced, even by two or three people.[50] If this was so, Matt 18,20 attests to the continuing links between Matthew's source and rabbinic Judaism as it developed in Jamnia (Yabneh) after the destruction of the Temple. In this case it also reflects a continuing profound experience of the Lord's presence in the Christian community.[51]

V. Conclusion

The theme of God's presence among people runs through much of the rabbinic tradition as well as through the NT in general and the Gospel of Matthew in particular. Neither tradition denies that God can be with a single individual, but both attach special meaning to his presence with a group, however small it may be. The origins of the term *Shekhinah* lie in the Temple. Its adaptation to other situations has in part a liturgical basis (Ps 82). At least very soon after the destruction of the Temple it was felt that the *Shekhinah* was not bound to a particular place, that it could be found anywhere, not only in liturgical settings, if certain conditions were met. It seems that it is in this sense that Matthew's source adopted it. While common prayer is a principal occasion in which "two or three" can experience Jesus' presence, the only condition is that they are together in his name.

The rabbis call God's presence *Shekhinah,* a circumlocution that affirms his nearness without denying his otherness. The Christian recognizes this presence in (and through) Jesus. Can one compare these two expressions without sounding blasphemous to the Jew and watered-down to the Christian? Can Jews and Christians meet "for the sake of Heaven," in the name of God, and in his presence?

On the Christian side the recent Vatican Guidelines for Implementing the Conciliar Declaration *Nostra Aetate* encourage "a common meeting in the presence of God . . . in whatever circumstances as shall prove possible and mutually acceptable."[52] On the other hand, Martin Buber affirms that "where two or three are truly together, they are together in the name of God."[53] Ultimately, especially for Jews, the question is not only theological, but also historical. How can nineteen hundred years of separation, conflict, persecution, and indifference be overcome? Can Jews and Christians truly be together again?

NOTES

1. E.g., Exod 25,8.9; 29,45; Num 5,3; Ps 74,2. For the pervasive theme of God's presence see S. Terrien, *The Elusive Presence. Toward a New Biblical Theology* (New York: Harper and Row, 1978).

2. J. Heinemann [*Prayer in the Talmud* (Berlin/New York: De Gruyter, 1977) p 273] considers the reference to the *Shekhinah* to be part of the oldest stratum of the prayer. This is possible, but his arguments are not convincing.

3. *Midrash Tehillim* 17, ed S. Buber (Vilna: Romm, 1891) p 127. English translation: W. G. Braude, *The Midrash on Psalms* (New Haven: Yale, 1959) I p 208. See P. Birnbaum, *Daily Prayer Book* (New York: Hebrew Publishing 1949) p 91-92. Concerning the Passover Haggadah see A. M. Goldberg, *Untersuchungen über die Vorstellung von der Schekhinah in der frühen rabbinischen Literatur* (Berlin/New York: De Gruyter, 1969) p 435.

4. See J. Maier, *Geschichte der jüdischen Religion* (Berlin/New York: De Gruyter, 1972) p 134. E. Bickerman, "The Civic Prayer for Jerusalem," *HTR* 55(1962) p 164.

5. A Diez Macho [*Neofiti I* (Madrid: Consejo Superior de Investigaciones Cientíﬁcas, 1970) vol. 2, p 55* n. 4] admits additions to Neofiti under the influence of Onkelos. See also A. M. Goldberg, "Die spezifische Verwendung des Terminus Schekhina im Targum Onkelos," *Judaica* 19(1963) p 43-61.

6. 2Macc 14,35. The parallel passage in 1Macc 7,37-38 contains a different prayer. It is impossible to determine which one is more original. Both texts reflect the particular interests of the authors of the larger works: 1Macc emphasizes defeat of Israel's enemies at the hands of the Hasmoneans, 2Macc stresses the sanctity of the Temple. See Ezek 37,25(LXX).

7. See Goldberg, *Untersuchungen* p 439.

8. *Untersuchungen* p 441.

9. *Ibid.* p 440-442.

10. *Ibid.*, p 471-530, 457. See also 1Kgs 8,12-13.27.

11. Perhaps of the fourth century, but B. Z. Wacholder ["The date of the Mekilta de-Rabbi Ishmael," *HUCA* 39(1968) 142] dates it as late as the eighth century.

12. This is in reference to the priestly blessing (Num 6,24-26). The divine name contained in it three times was to be pronounced in the Temple, but *Adonai* was substituted for it in the synagogues (*mSotah* 7,6).

13. *Mekilta de Rabbi Ishmael* (Baḥodesh, Jethro Chap. 11), ed & transl. by J. Z. Lauterbach (3 vols; Philadelphia: JPS 1933-35, repr. 1976), II p 287. A Christian parallel to the divine presence with one person is found in the apocryphal Gospel of Thomas, 30. See B. Englezakis, "*Thomas*, Logion 30," *NTS* 25(1979) p 262, 265.

14. There are two Tannaim by this name. One flourished in the late first, the other in the mid-second century. See Goldberg, *Untersuchungen*, p 387, but consult p 501.

15. *Untersuchungen* p 500.

16. *Ibid.* p 376-386.

17. M Abot 3,2b(3), 6. Concerning *mSanh.* 6,5 see Urbach, *The Sages*, p 702 n 17.

18. The entire passage is meant here: "Blessed is the man who . . . meditates on (*or* reads) his Torah day and night" (Ps 1,1-2).

19. *MAbot* 3,2b(3). Translation by J. Goldin, *The Living Talmud: The Wisdom of the Fathers* (New York: New American Library, 1957) p. 120-121.

20. *BAbodah Zarah* 18a; also *Sifre Deut* 32,4, paragr. 307.

21. See below p 176 Consult C. H. Dodd, *New Testament Studies* (Manchester: Manchester Univ., 3rd ed, 1967) p 61.

22. *Abot de R. Natan B* 34, ed Schechter, p 74. English translation: A. J. Saldarini, *The Fathers According to Rabbi Nathan (Abot de Rabbi Nathan) Version B: A Translation and Commentary* (SJLA 11; Leiden: Brill, 1975).

23. *MAbot* 3,3(6). See the requirement of common prayer when three men eat together (*mBer* 7,1). Both passages underscore the sacred character of every meal.

24. *MAbot* 3,6(9). The prooftexts are the same as for the above quoted *Mekhilta* passage. The reference to Torah here fits the prooftexts less well than the reference to synagogue (for 10) and court (for 3) in the *Mekhilta*, which contains a more cohesive and probably more original tradition. See Goldberg, *Untersuchungen* p 387.

25. *BBer* 6a; *Lev Rab* 34.7 (A late Midrash, perhaps seventh-ninth century). See S. Schechter, *Aspects of Rabbinic Theology* (new ed.; New York: Schocken, 1961) p 125-126, 134-137.

26. I. M. Bunim, *Ethics from Sinai* (2nd ed.; New York: Feldheim, 1964) 1.235.

27. L. Finkelstein, in Schechter, *Aspects* p. XX.

28. *B Sotah* 17a. Husband (Hebrew consonants *alef, yod, shin*) and wife (*alef, shin, he*) minus God (*yod, he*) equals fire (*alef, shin*). Urbach, *Sages* p 43. Contrast Goldberg, *Untersuchungen* p 419.

29. *Sifre Deut* 23,10, paragr. 254; Goldberg, *Untersuchungen* p 142-160, esp. 147-148.

30. *Mekilta*, Baḥodesh, Jethro, Chap. 9; Lauterbach II p 273.

31. G. Rossé, *Gesù in mezzo. Matteo 18,20 nell'esegesi contemporanea* (Rome: Città Nuova, 1972) p 114, 137-138. J. Caba, *La oración de petición. Estudio exegético sobre los evangelios sinópticos y los escritos joaneos* (AnBib 62; Rome: Biblical Institute Press, 1974) p 199-200, 213-214.

32. W. Trilling, *Hausordnung Gottes. Eine Auslegung von Matthäus 18* (Düsseldorf: Patmos, 1960); id. *Das wahre Israel. Studien zur Theologie des Matthäusevangeliums* (Munich: Kösel, 3rd ed., 1964). W. Pesch, *Matthäus der Seelsorger. Das neue Verständnis der Evangelien dargestellt am Beispiel von Matthäus 18* (Stuttgart: KBW, 1966). W. G. Thompson, *Matthew's Advice to a Divided Community: Mt 17,22-18,35* (Rome: Biblical Institute, 1970).

33. In addition to the works by G. Rossé and J. Caba there are J. M. Povilus, *La presenza di Gesù tra i suoi nella teologia di oggi* (Rome: Città Nuova, 1977) and, with particular emphasis on patristic exegesis, C. Lubich, *"Jesus in the Midst"* (New York: New City, 1976); see now also B. Englezakis, *"Thomas, Logion 30,"* NTS 25(1979) p 262-272.

34. *JBL* 81(1962) p 1-13.

35. M. Smith, *Tannaitic Parallels to the Gospels* (Philadelphia: SBL, 1951, reprint Missoula: Scholars Press, 1978) p 152.

36. E.g., R. Bultmann, *The History of the Synoptic Tradition* (New York: Harper & Row, 1963) p 142; C. H. Dodd, *New Testament Studies* p 58-62; Trilling, *Das wahre Israel* p 41-42. Contrast B. T. Viviano, *Study as Worship: Aboth and the New Testament* (Leiden: Brill, 1978) p 70. The only arguments adduced in favor of Matthean priority are (a) that Matthew predates all rabbinic authorities quoted with *Abot* 3,2b, 6 and (b) that the quorum required makes sense in Matt 18,20 (consult v 16b), but not in *Abot*. But (a) applies to many tannaitic parallels to the gospels and does not take into account the disagreements in attribution and the

anonymity of the *Mekhilta* tradition. (b) fails to recognize the rabbis' interpretation of scriptural prooftexts. B. Englezakis [*NTS* 25 (1979) p 264] denies any connection between the origin of Matt 18,20 and the *Abot* sayings simply on the grounds that "they are later than Matthew."

37. Pap. Oxyrhynch. I^r. 2-3. See text and variant readings in Englezakis, *NTS* 25(1979) p 262, consult 266.

38. *Ibid.* p 264.

39. Rossé, *Gesù in mezzo* p 132-134; H. Frankemölle, *Jahwebund und Kirche Christi* (NTAbh NF 10; Münster: Aschendorff, 1974) p 35. Contrast Caba, *Oración* p 218. J. D. M. Derrett (" 'Where two or three are convened in my name . . .': a sad misunderstanding," *Exp Tim* 91 [December 1979] p 83-86) unduly narrows the meaning of Matt 18,20 to the settlement of disputes between church members.

40. E.g., H. Bietenhard, "Onoma," *TDNT* 5(1967) p 274-276.

41. M. Smith, *Tannaitic Parallels* p 156.

42. W. Grundmann proposed this in a deplorable publication (*Christentum und Judentum*, Leipzig: Wigand, 1940, p 76); more moderate G. Bornkamm, "The Authority to 'Bind' and 'Loose' in the Church in Matthew's Gospel: The Problem of Sources in Matthew's Gospel," *Perspective* 11(1970) p 41.

43. See L. Bouyer, "La Shekinah: Dieu avec nous," *Bib Vie chr* 20(1957) p 19; R. E. Brown, *The Gospel According to John I-XII* (AB 29; Garden City, N. Y.: Doubleday, 1966) p 33-34; J. Abelson, *The Immanence of God in Rabbinical Literature* (London: Macmillan, 1912) p 80-81. Contrast Terrien, *Elusive Presence* p 419-420. For the emphasis on divine presence in Matthew see 1,23; 10,40; 25,40. 45; 28,20.

44. Goldberg, *Untersuchungen* p 448.

45. *Das wahre Israel* p 41.

46. *Untersuchungen* p 388, 453-454; consult M. Kadushin [*The Rabbinic Mind* (3rd ed.; New York: Bloch, 1972) p 227] about "normal mysticism." See also Rossé, *Gesù in mezzo* p 135-136.

47. Contrast Rossé p 146, but see p 131 n 151.

48. So Goldberg, *Untersuchungen* p 500.

49. R. Bultmann, *History of the Synoptic Tradition* p 149; Pesch, *Matthäus der Seelsorger* p 37; Caba, *Oración* p 218. See now, however, Englezakis, *NTS* 25(1979) p 263.

50. Goldberg, *Untersuchungen* p 443; Urbach, *Sages* p 43; A. Marmorstein, *The Old Rabbinic Doctrine of God* (London: Oxford Univ. P., 1927) p 104.

51. One should compare here Luke 24,13-35.

52. "Guidelines and Suggestions for Implementing the Conciliar Declaration *Nostra Aetate*" by the Vatican Commission for Religious Relations with the Jews. Reprinted in H. Croner (ed), *Stepping Stones to Further Jewish-Christian Relations. An unabridged collection of Christian Documents* (London/New York: Stimulus Books, 1977) p 12.

53. *Eclipse of God* (New York: Harper & Row, 1952) p 9.

The Proclamation of the Unity of God as Actualization of the Kingdom*

KURT HRUBY

It is generally agreed that the synagogue liturgy has evolved from two basic elements: the *Shema˓ Yisrael*[1] and the benedictions which surround it on one hand and, on the other, the public reading of the Torah.[2]

The rabbinic tradition considers Deut. 6,7 ("you shall teach (these words) diligently to your children and you shall talk of them when you sit in your house, and when you walk by the way, and when you lie down and when you rise") as the wording of a divine commandment and hence that it is necessary to recite the *Shema˓* twice a day, morning and evening.[3]

At the beginning of chapter two of the Mishna *Berakhot* (2,2) the question is raised in order to know why Deut 6, 4-9 precedes 11, 13-21 in the recitation. Here is the answer given by Rabbi Joshua ben Korḥa, a master of the second century:

> "So that the one who (recites the *Shema˓*) first of all accepts the
> ˓ol malkhut shamayim (the yoke of God's domination), then the
> ˓ol ha-miṣwot (the yoke of the commandments)".[4]

Therefore what is the exact meaning of the expression "to accept the yoke of God's domination?"[5] In itself, the acknowledgment of the domination of God distinguishes the religious man in the biblical sense of the word, that is the one who recognizes God as Creator and Provider, from the non-religious man, who denies either the creation of the world by God or else the permanent care of the Creator for his work (or both at the same time). This permanent divine solicitude for the world which he has called into existence is expressed in the first benediction which, in the morning prayer, precedes the recitation of the *Shema˓. Meḥadesh bekhol yom tamid ma˓asseh be-reʾshit:*[6] "Each day God

---

*Translation from the French by Mrs. Claude Seyler and the editors.

renews the work of creation", which is to say, strictly speaking, that creation is not an act posited by God once and for all but rather a continuous process under the permanent guidance of God. "To accept God's domination" is therefore, first of all, on the part of the believer, the actualization of this belief within the framework of the central prayer of the Jewish liturgy.

Objectively speaking, this domination of God is certainly a fact which exists, independently of man's acknowledgment. However, God's plan of salvation is precisely his dealing with humanity. The active and positive acknowledgment of this fact on the part of man is nonetheless necessary, for all creation is oriented towards mankind. Without this acknowledgment by man, an essential element, so to speak, would be lacking in the fulness of this domination of God. The rabbinic tradition expresses this idea in the form of a Midrash:7

> Before our father Abraham came into the world, God was, so to say, but the King of heaven, as it is said (Gen 24,7): "The Lord, the God of heaven, who has taken me from my father's house and from the land of my birth". But after our father Abraham came into the world, he made him the God of heaven and earth, as it is said (Gen 24,3): "I make you swear by the Lord, the God of heaven and by the God of the earth."

Since one should consider this acknowledgment of God's domination on the basis of the plan of salvation in its entirety, it is evident that in what concerns Israel, this act, far from being a purely theoretical general affirmation, entails a very precise aspect: Israel being the privileged instrument of God's plan with humanity, this is the people who, thanks to the Covenant, are committed to particular obligations towards God. This is why the acknowledgment of God's domination is intrinsically linked, for Israel, *to the Sinai Revelation and to the gift of the Torah*. Being the authentic expression of God's will, the Torah is also the charter containing the laws and precise rules through which God exercises his domination over the world. Obviously, the final objective always remains the full acknowledgment of God's sovereignty by all men without exception. However, this sovereignty is inserted into the framework of a history which necessarily contains stages. During the period marked by Israel's formal acknowledgment of God's royal character, in accordance with the Covenant, God assumes a particular title: "the King of Israel". This does not infringe upon his absolute domination over the other nations. Nevertheless, it does not appear yet in its full light as long as other peoples do not in turn acknowledge it.

It seems necessary at this point to emphasize this aspect in order to avoid any interpretation which describes this sovereignity of God as a purely eschatological fact. The "Kingdom of God" *is* an eschatological fact, in the sense that it is only in the *eschaton*, in the time of fulfillment, that it will appear in all its radiance, but it is at the same time an *actual reality* to the degree in which God's sovereignty is already and from now on fully recognized by Israel. In this respect, Israel anticipates a state of things which, for the other nations, is still situated in the future. It is in that sense that Solomon Schechter[8] very pertinently distinguishes three aspects in the Kingdom of God: 1. the invisible Kingdom, such as it exists since the creation of the world; 2. the universal visible Kingdom, such as it realizes itself in function of the Covenant with Israel and; 3. the Kingdom fully manifested in eschatological times.

Such a global vision of the "Kingdom of God" conforms to the vision both in Scripture and in ancient rabbinic tradition. It constitutes as well the response to a reproach formulated by authors such as Max Kadushin[9] who states that certain Jewish theologians have interpreted the concept of the Kingdom of God as though it dealt with a purely eschatological fact. Kadushin believes that these authors were influenced far too much by Christian theology. Without wanting to go into details, it seems, under the circumstances, to be a question of a somewhat summary and hasty judgment of the Christian concept. Here the "Kingdom" becomes an eschatological reality precisely in relation to the coming of Jesus. This does not prevent it from being a permanent and actual reality for the one who has "accepted" it by adherence to the Gospel,[10] even if it remains true that the plenitude of the Kingdom will appear only at the Parousia. The difference between the traditional Jewish vision and the Christian concept rests rather in the nature of this plenitude which, for the Jewish masters, is by all evidence a phenomenon belonging to this world and not to the "world to come", as Kadushin notes so well.[11]

The full acceptance and, consequently, the full acknowledgment of God's domination by Israel is therefore in direct relation with the Revelation of the Torah. By declaring from the beginning (Exod 24,7): "All that which the Lord has spoken, we will do, and we will listen", the people expresses its unbounded confidence in the God of the Covenant and in his word.[12] Since the highest point of reference is the Torah, and the essential element of the Torah is constituted by the *miṣwot* (God's commandments), we can distinguish between ῾ol malkhut shamayim and ῾ol ha-miṣwot. The one does not go without the other, in accordance with the integral meaning of the Revelation. It is in accepting the Torah with all that it contains[13] that Israel "takes upon itself the yoke of God's domination". This acknowledgment and acceptance henceforth are translated exclusively by fidelity to the dictates of the Torah.

The Midrash in turn points out to this intrinsic link between *ʿol malkhut shamayim* and *ʿol ha-miṣwot:*[14]

"You shall not have other gods before me" (Exod 20,3). Why is that said? Because it is written (ib. 2): "I am the Lord your God." (Here is) a parable: A flesh and blood king came into a province. His servants said to him: Have decrees published for them (the inhabitants of that region)! He said to them: No; it is (only) when they have accepted my reign that I shall publish decrees concerning them, for if they do not accept my reign, neither will they accept my decrees. God said likewise to Israel: "I am the Lord your God! You shall not have other gods before me!" He said to them: It is I whose reign you have accepted in Egypt.[15] They answered him: Yes; God continued: Just as you have accepted my reign, accept my decrees! "You shall not have other gods before me." - Rabbi Simon b. Yohai said: It is what is written further on (Lev 18,2): "I am the Lord your God!" It is I whose domination you have accepted at Sinai. They answered him: Yes, indeed! You have received my domination, receive (as well) my decrees!

In a somewhat different manner, the same reality is expressed in another passage of the Mekhilta.[16]

"I am the Lord your God!" (Exod 20,2). Why were the Ten Commandments not stated at the beginning of the Torah? (The masters) have explained it by a parable. To what can this be compared? To someone who entered into a city. He said then to the inhabitants: I want to reign over you! They answered him: Have you done some good deed for which you should reign over us? What did he do? He built for them the (enclosing) wall, brought water (into the city) and fought battles for them. (Then) he said to them: I shall reign over you! They answered him: Yes, indeed! God did likewise: He brought Israel out of Egypt, divided the (red) sea for them, made manna rain down for them, made the well fill up, had quails sent to them, and led the war with Amalek for them. (Then) he said to them: I want to reign over you! They answered him: Yes, indeed! Rabbi Judah *(ha-Nassi)* said: This proclaims the praise of Israel for when they were at Mount Sinai in order to receive the Torah, they were all unanimous in accepting God's domination joyfully. And not only that: they were vouching for each other.

With regard to the acknowledgment of God's domination by Israel which took place, according to the Midrash, at the Red Sea, the rabbinic tradition has an identical reflection to that which we have noted in the case of Abraham.[17]

> Then Moses and the children of Israel chanted in honor of the Lord the following canticle" (Exod 15,1). This is what the Scripture writes (Ps 93,2): "Your throne was established from the beginning,[18] from everlasting it is you, Lord." Rabbi Berechiah says in the name of Rabbi Abbahu: Even though you were from all eternity, your throne was not established and you have not become known in the world before your children sang a canticle. . .

The Sinai experience is an essentially collective one, engaging the people totally and for all generations.[19] However, the path to which the people commit themselves consequently through history in constant conformity to God's will expressed in the Torah does not imply automatic, blind response. Such a vision of things is fundamentally contrary to the liberty of man ceaselessly opting for or against the "royal way" (Deut 11,26-28):

> Behold, I set before you this day a blessing and a curse: The blessing, if you obey the commandments of the Lord your God that I command you this day, and the curse, if you do not obey the commandments of the Lord your God, but turn aside from the way which I command you this day, to go after other gods which you have not known.

For that reason, the ratification of this acceptance of God's domination must occur with each generation. The Midrash indicates this demand by saying for example that during the time of Joshua, son of Nun, the Israelites have accepted God's domination with love and in the time of Samuel the Prophet with fear,[20] love and reverential fear being the two characteristic attitudes of man facing the sovereign domination of God which is exercised in the world.

However, the permanent acknowledgment of God's domination was a collective act of the Jewish people, where the collective exists only as a sum of responsible individuals in the same unique destiny. That is why this acknowledgment is incumbent upon the individual and must be affirmed daily in the recitation of the *Shema*ᶜ, morning and evening. Considered from this angle, the recitation of the *Shema*ᶜ appears as the individual's solemn confirmation, of the collective commitment undertaken by the people at the time of the Sinai Revelation, and as a declaration of solidarity with this commitment throughout the generations. In this manner, there exists an intrinsic link between the acknowledgment of the domination of God and the obligation to observe the commandments of the Torah. Everything has its root in the Torah, outside of which the affirmation to recognize the sovereignty of God almost seems to be a gratuitous act because it is not followed by immediate application in life.

In conformity with the given practice, we have spoken about "recitation" of the *Shema^c*, an expression which risks a measure of misunderstanding. The Hebrew term *Qeri᾿ah* signifies the "reading" of the *Shema^c* and may appear to stress that it is not so much a question of a liturgical formula *as the reading of a passage from the Sacred Scriptures*. In order to set forth the value of *qabbalat 'ol malkhut shamayim* inherent in the first verse of the *Shema^c*, the masters have stipulated that one inserts between that verse and the rest of the text, the formula which formerly in the Temple was said by the people as an antiphonal confirmation of the prayers and liturgical actions. *Barukh shem kevod malkhuto le-'olam wa'ed* ("Blessed be the glorious name of his Kingdom forever.") This was proclaimed especially at the hearing of the Tetragrammaton.[21]

Because of the importance of the *Shema^c* as a concrete expression of Israel's acceptance of the content of the Sinai Covenant and, thus, of God's sovereign domination over the whole of life, the Midrash puts it in relation with the gift of the Torah:[22]

> Which (part of the *Shema^c*) expresses (the acceptance of) the domination of God? (The words): "Hear, O Israel. . ." When did Israel deserve the right to recite the *Shema^c*? R. Pinhas b. Hama said at the time of the Sinai revelation: You find that it is by this word *(Shema^c)* that God began to speak at Sinai.[23] He said to them: "Hear, O Israel, I am the Lord your God." They all responded with "the Lord our God, the Lord is one." And Moses answered: "Blessed be forever the glorious name of his Kingdom!"

To have the value of commitment, the reading of the *Shema^c*, made within the framework of prayer, demands a *Kawwanah*, a special intention and concentration and therefore a conscious awareness concerning the pledge that one contracts in this manner. This important question is already taken up in the Talmud (Ber 13b) wherein the masters discuss the problem of knowing if this *Kawwanah* is required for the whole of the *Shema^c* or only for the first verse. They finally decide that it suffices if one says the first verse with all the attention required. It is indicated by the person who lengthens the last syllable of *᾿eḥad* ("one") and covers the eyes with the hand in order to avoid all distraction at this moment of intense concentration. Here is what the Talmud says about it (ib.):

The masters have taught (in a Baraita):[24] "Hear, O Israel, the Lord, our God, is the only Lord" (Deut 6,4). Up to this part it is necessary to recite (the *Shema*ᶜ) with a heartfelt devotion *(kawwanat ha-lev):* the saying of R. Meir. Rabba says: The Halakhah is in accordance with R. Meir. Somkhos (Symmachus, a disciple of R. Meir) says: whoever lengthens the word *ʾeḥad* shall have his days and years prolonged. Rab Ashi (the early editor of Babylonian Talmud) adds the comment: In particular, one must not slur the *ḥet*. R. Jeremiah was seated in front of Rabbi Hiyya and he saw that the latter was prolonging (the word *ʾeḥad*) a long time. He said to him: If you have accepted the kingship (of God) above, below and in the four cardinal points of heaven, it is not necessary (to prolong) any further. The masters have taught (in a Baraita): "Hear, O Israel. . ." it is the *Shema*ᶜ of R. Judah *ha-Nassi*. Rab says to Rab Hiyya: I have not seen Rabbi (Judah) to have taken upon himself the kingship of God.[25] He replied to him: . . . It is while he was passing his hands over his face that he accepted the yoke of God's kingship.[26]

In a way, the acceptance of God's sovereignty and the commitment to observe the commandments of the Torah as expressed by the *Shema*ᶜ are the prototype of all Jewish prayer. Central to it is the *berakhah* ("blessing") which expresses the permanent praise of God. In this respect, tradition transmits two significant teachings:[27] R. Johanan[28] said: A benediction where one does not (mention) the domination of God[29] is not a (true) benediction. The other teaching of R. Johanan:[30] Whoever wants to assume wholly the domination of God must first take care of his (natural) needs, wash his hands and put on the phylacteries. Then he must say the *Shema*ᶜ and the Tefillah: this is the complete acknowledgment of the domination of God.

The eschatological aspect of the domination of God

It is undeniable that the acceptance of God's sovereignty expressed and actualized permanently by Israel in the *Shema*ᶜ also takes on an eschatological aspect. Israel anticipates an act which, in the end time, will be fulfilled by the whole of mankind. Israel, by virtue of the Covenant with God and the people's acceptance of concrete obligations which flow from the Torah, will actually be the witness and the prototype. It is in this sense that the plenitude of the "Kingdom" will not appear to the eyes of all the living except at the end of time. Already Targumic tradition interprets a certain number of biblical passages, as for example Isa 52,7: "Your God reigns," by: "Here is the Kingdom of your God manifested."[31]

However, one should not see this eschatological Kingdom a realization which would be situated beyond earthly reality. In rabbinic tradition, it is always a question of a fulfillment and a plenitude whose context is this earth: a world which will be at that moment "filled with the knowledge of God," and a state of perfection which will be reached in messianic times. For this reason, the plenitude of the Kingdom coincides with the messianic realization in the rabbinic thought. One of the essential functions of the Messiah will be precisely to promote universally this knowledge of God, the indispensable condition for all men to submit deliberately and spontaneously to God's domination. Then he will be recognized by all as the sovereign King of the universe. This is conveyed by the prophetic words (Zech 14,9): "The Lord shall be King over all the earth. On that day, the Lord will be one, and his name one."

What in reality prevents the Kingdom from blossoming totally is the fact that the domination of God is not recognized but is even contested by the other nations. Even greater is the merit of the pagan who, without having benefited from wonders and mighty deeds that God through history has done on behalf of Israel, arrives at the knowledge of the true God and submits himself to his domination. The Midrash relates as follows on this matter:[32]

> Resh Laqish said: "The proselyte who becomes Jewish is more loved (by God) than the Israelites standing at Mount Sinai: If they had not perceived the voices, the lightning bolts, the mountain tremors and the sound of the *Shofar*, they would not have accepted the Torah. But this one (the proselyte) comes without having seen anything concerning all of that, surrenders himself to God and accepts the yoke of the Kingdom of heaven . . ."

Israel, with regard to the Kingdom—so to say along with Franz Rosenzweig[33]—"has already arrived at the term." The succession of the years is for Israel "but an awaiting, at most a progression but not a growth, for that would signify that fulfillment is still inaccessible to him in time, which would amount to negation of his eternity. Now eternity consists precisely in this (fact) that between the actual moment and fulfillment, time no longer has any place, for in the 'today' the wholeness of the future may be seized." The other nations, however, are still "on the road" towards the Kingdom. On this road, Israel must be their guide by its permanent submission to the demands of the Kingdom. At the same time the people which, twice a day, reaffirms its commitment in relation to the Kingdom by its recitation of the *Shema*ᶜ, offers to God its fervent prayers so that all mankind may reach a spiritual level allowing it to accept in its turn "the yoke of the Kingdom", as it is stated in the prayer of ᶜ*Alenu* which tradition attributes to Rab:[34] . . . "to put right the universe by the domination of the Almighty. . . All shall accept your reign, and soon you shall exercise the domination over them forever."

This ardent awaiting and this unshakable trust that one day all humanity without restriction will recognize in its turn the sovereign domination of God with all that this implies as commitment is at the center of Jewish life. It has found its most beautiful expression in the prayer of *Rosh ha-Shanah:*[35]

> Our God and God of our fathers! reign over the entire world in your glory and be exalted above all the earth in your splendor and manifest yourself in the splendor of your strength to all the inhabitants of your world. (Then) every creature shall recognize that it is you who has created it and every being shall understand that you have shaped it. And everything which has breath shall say: "The Lord the God of Israel is King, and his Kingdom rules over all."

It is when this level will be reached, that progress and materialization shall coalesce in the true *eschaton*, in the union of all men under the sole domination of God.

NOTES

1. The *Shema*ᶜ is composed of the following passages: Deut 6,4-9, 11,13-21; Num 15,37-41.

2. See I. Elbogen, *Der Jüdische Gottesdienst in seiner geschichtlichen Entwicklung* (3rd ed., Frankfurt 1931) p. 15 and 16 ff.

3. The first chapters of the treatise *Berakhot* of the Mishna are dedicated to this question.

4. Deut 6,4-9 contains the confession of the unity of God and the commandment to love the Lord above all things while Deut 11,13-21 is concerned with reward and punishment as related to the fulfillment of the commandments of the Torah.

5. We take for granted that the exact sense of the often analyzed notion of *Malkhut shamayim* is known. In our context, the best manner to translate this term seems to be "royal domination of God". We imply "royal" as being evident and omit it in order not to burden the terminology needlessly.

6. S. Baer, *Seder ᶜAvodat Yisrael* (new edition, Berlin, 1937) p. 76.

7. *Sifrei to Deut* 32,10 313 (p 334b) ed. Friedmann.

8. *Some aspects of Rabbinic Theology* (2nd edit., New York, 1936) p 65ff.

9. *The Theology of Seder Eliahu* (New York, 1952) p 58ff.

10. Jesus announces at the same time the imminent coming of the Kingdom (consult Matt 4,17 and Mark 1,14: "The time is fulfilled and the Kingdom of God is near") and the presence of the Kingdom in those who, henceforth, possess the required conditions of receptivity (see Luke 17,21: "The Kingdom of God is in the midst of you").

11. *Op. cit., ib.*

12. Rabbinic tradition comes back at innumerable occasions to this aspect, which is considered as the basic element of the merits of Israel in the acceptance of the Torah. See, for example, bShab 88a: Rabbi Simlai states: At the time when the Israelites said at first "we will do" then "we will listen" (Exod 24,7), sixty myriads of serving angels braided two crowns for each Israelite, one because of "we will do", the other because of "we will listen . . ." Rabbi Elazar (ben Azariah) states: At the time when the Israelites were first saying "we will do" then "we will listen," a celestial voice was heard, exclaiming: Who has divulged to my children the secret used by the serving angels. As it is written (Ps 103,20): "Bless the Lord, O you his angels, you mighty ones who do his word, listening to the voice of his word." first the act, then the listening.

> Rabbi Hama b. Hanina states: It is written (Cant 2,3): "As the apple-tree among the trees of an orchard . . ." Why does one compare Israel to an apple tree? It means: even as the apple-tree produces its fruit (i.e., its flowers) before the leaves, so did the Israelites say "we will do" before saying "we will listen".

13. This means both the written Torah and the oral Torah. The two are absolutely inseparable in rabbinic thought.

14. *Mekhilta* to Exod; *Ba-Ḥodesh* chap 6, ed Horovitz-Rabin, p 222-223.

15. Tradition takes into account Exod 15,2 and 18 as the expression of the Israelites' concrete and deliberate acceptance of the domination of God. See also *Sifra* to Lev. 18,6, *Aḥare mot*, chap 13, Weiss edition, p 85a.

16. *Ba-Ḥodesh*, chap 5, p 219.

17. Exod R 23,1 to Exod 15,1.

18. The Midrash reads this verse as follows: "Your throne set since then . . .," putting it in relation to Israel's affirmation of the domination of God at the moment of the crossing of the Red Sea (Exod 15,1 begins "since then".)

19. Printed *TanhumaYitro*, 11: "This Covenant and this oath with those who are present today with us before the Lord, our God" (Deut 29,14f.)" "With those" refers to those who have already been created. "Are present" refers to those who live presently in the world. "And with those who are not here" (29,15): those who shall be created and do not yet exist. "With us today" (29,15): these are the souls who will be created in the future . . .

20. *Seder Eliyahu R.*, ed M. Ish-Shalom, p 86.

21. MYoma 3,8.

22. Deut R 2,22 to 6,4.

23. In Deuteronomy, the Decalogue begins with: "Hear, O Israel. . ." (5,1). This Midrash reflects how the *Shema*ᶜ was recited.

24. A Baraita is a tradition going back to the masters of the Mishna that is introduced into the talmudic discussion.

25. Rabbi Judah was continuing his exposé when the moment came to say the *Shema*ᶜ.

26. It arises from the continuation of the text that under these conditions, Rabbi Judah was satisfied by simply saying the first verse of the *Shema*ᶜ.

27. BBer 12a; jBer 9,1 (12d).

28. Bar Nappaha was a Palentinian master who died in 279. In the Jerusalem Talmud, this saying is transmitted in the name of Rab (Abba Areka), founder of the academy of Sura in Babylonia. He died in 247.

29. Upon saying: "Be blessed, Lord, our God, King of the Universe."

30. BBer 14b.

31. Targum: ʾitgaliat malkhuta deʿElohayikh.

32. TanhumaBuber, *Lekh lekha*, p 32a.

33. *Der Stern der Erlösung* (3rd edition, Heidelberg, 1954) p 86-87.

34. See note 29. The ʿAlenu served originally—and still serves—as introduction to the *Malkhuyyot*, to the solemn proclamation of God's Kingship at *Rosh-ha-shanah*. For long centuries, it is recited at the end of each synagogue service. See *Seder ʿAvodat Yisrael*, p 397-98.

35. *Seder ʿAvodat Yisrael*, p 393.

Service of the Heart:
Liturgical Aspects of Synagogue Worship*

ARNOLD GOLDBERG

This study attempts to clarify how far and in what way the synagogue prayer service, as it was shaped by the rabbis during the centuries after the destruction of the Temple, is liturgy. The question arises from the relationship between synagogue worship and the exilic period when worship in the Temple had become impossible. There are obvious difficulties in determining whether synagogue worship should be defined as liturgy or not from the viewpoint of history of religion and theology.[1] An attempt is made to establish a viewpoint and criteria which will resolve this question concerning liturgy in synagogue worship by presenting certain definitions which may prove productive for history of theology and religion. It is necessary to determine methodically from liturgical data how far these correspond to a concept of liturgy in Jewish understanding. This is not simple because there is no formal Jewish definition of liturgy which could serve as a guideline. Only the orientation in *halakhah*, the legislation of religious rules for prayer, is binding. However, it does not tell us to what point worship is considered as liturgy. There is also custom, *minhag*, which legitimizes traditions of worship evolving in individual communities. Furthermore, there are the interpretations of the rabbis appearing in the early rabbinic sermons which explain the content of such worship and its value. These reflect important religious realities but they are not binding. Finally, one can inquire into the formulated and commonly practiced prayers.

The question cannot be answered by comparisons. Certainly, a Christian definition of liturgy cannot be used as a criterion for Jewish liturgy and a religious phenomenological interpretation can establish only superficial parallels. Yet the historical parallels between Jewish and

*Translation from the German by Mrs. Nora Quigley and the editors. This study is dedicated to Msgr. John M. Oesterreicher on the occasion of his 75th birthday.

195

Christian worship lead us to the core of the problem. After the destruction of the Temple, the Church (historically) carried on a form of worship which perhaps only much later and first only in the East is called *liturgy*, a term corresponding exclusively to the Greek designation for Jewish Temple worship. This was possible, not only because the Christian community left worship in Jerusalem behind as incomplete, but because the worship of the Christian community was mandated, and as such it was accepted on faith. Historically the Church, like the synagogue, continued Israel's practices of worship after the destruction of the Temple. However, there was a basically different understanding of this worship, not only in its content (the Church introduced and continued sacrificial worship) but also because of its special designation. The Christian church understands this worship as instituted by Christ, precisely as the liturgy which corresponds to the *'abodah*, the service of the Temple. Historically the community of Israel probably continued the synagogue worship of the pre-Christian era, without establishing it as liturgy, *'abodah*. If the worship of the community of Israel demonstrates liturgical characteristics, inasmuch as it is, or at least can be, a service before God, then one may ask: In what do these characteristics of liturgy consist, how they are possible, where do they originate?

I. *Rupture and Continuity*

The destruction of the second Temple brings a definite break in the history of Jewish worship. There was a preparation for this rupture because, according to the Pharisees, the second Temple was imperfect just as the deliverance from the Babylonian exile was an imperfect redemption.[2] However, the worship instituted by God had taken place there in perfect validity. Alongside the Temple there were already synagogues in the Land of Israel as well as in the Diaspora. We know hardly anything about their practices but undoubtedly there was a service of the Word, consisting in prayers and probably also public readings of Scripture and preaching. From 60 B.C. until 72-73 A.D. there was a Jewish temple at Leontopolis in Egypt which was tolerated somehow. In the Land of Israel we find the worship of the *ma'amadot* which was legitimately connected with the Temple. From each district priests, Levites and laymen were sent to the Temple in Jerusalem as representatives for the given district. At the same time services were conducted in the province which corresponded to the sacrificial worship and the priestly blessing was given.[3] Little is known about these worship services but there is much in favor of the idea that synagogue worship after the destruction of the Temple derives from this cult of the *maʿamadot.*[4] No matter how one explains the origin of synagogue worship,[5] the community of Israel had the possibility, just as the Church did, of explaining that synagogue cult is a legitimate continuation of Temple cult, establishing it as divine worship.

> At first glance the possibilities for this seem limited. The historical circumstances must be considered. After the destruction of the Temple the Pharisaic strain of Judaism prevailed over the Sadducees, the Essenes and whatever else existed. It was certainly a critical situation but also conducive to substantial changes. A central organization which could have instituted a liturgy was lacking. There was no longer any possibility of revelation, the rabbis rejected any charismatic spontaneity[6] and the academy at Jabneh, which reorganized the Jewish community after the destruction of the Temple, was probably not able to accomplish more than it did in fact, that is, organize and mandate the prayer service.

This discussion about the possibility of establishing a liturgy is purely hypothetical. It means only to point out alternatives. According to the opinion of the rabbis, there was neither any possibility nor reason to provide a substitute for Temple worship. At the time, the termination of Temple service was not considered to be final; rather, one counted on the possibility of its re-establishment, as the Bar Kochba revolt indicates. The concern of the rabbis was much more to prevent any possible alternatives to this worship. They explained that the holiness of the place of the Temple remained,[7] even though they could have denied this since the Temple had been destroyed. Thus they decided against any sacrificial cult outside of the Temple. If they had denied that the holiness of the place endured, then something similar to the "worship on the high places" might have been permitted, as occurred before the centralization of the cult (the sacrifices in the period of the Judges). Those alternatives did exist and it seems that especially the paschal sacrifice was offered outside of the Temple.[8] Certainly there were good theological and also pragmatic reasons for refusing to allow the continuation of the Temple cult. The continuation of a specific service before God anywhere would have put forth the position that the dispersion was so intended by God. At the same time, it would have suggested the possibility of normal existence without a center of cult in Jerusalem, which is God's dwelling place. The rebuilding of Jerusalem would have been unimportant at the least, if not useless. The development in Judaism would have been not unlike that in Christianity. Instead the exile was decreed, not only Israel's exile but also as God's exile, because with the Temple in Jerusalem God had lost his dwelling place in the midst of Israel. To be sure, it was said that the *Shekhinah*, God as he was present in the Temple, would never leave the place of the destroyed Temple. There was no return of God to heaven but in a way the *Shekhinah* was destined to have a place of exile in the ruined Temple.[9]

The Temple cult could and should not be continued in any way until the time when it would be established again in its perfection; for the majority this would be the work of an awaited Messiah. Consequently this also meant that the cult could not be transferred to the synagogue. Here the rabbis were strict, more or less successfully. They forbade the imitation of sanctuary vessels and their use in the synagogues. It is no longer possible to know to what extent some parts of the Temple liturgy were adapted to synagogue worship. Prayer services and hymns of the Temple are almost completely forgotten and it seems as if they were deliberately cast into oblivion.[10] The only cultic act of the synagogue service, the only priestly function, still in use is the priestly blessing. Similar to the case of the *ma'amadot*, it is imparted only on special occasions, and never became a prerequisite for synagogue worship. Temple service was suspended and set aside for the time being as well as all rites connected with it. In synagogue worship it could be introduced only as a memory and in the prayer for its speedy restoration. The prayer was directed to its restoration, so it was not possible at the moment. Liturgy in the sense of a concrete holy service before God, as it was instituted by God for the Temple, came to an end; it had to cease if it was to be restored.

Synagogue and its worship, the daily prayers of individuals and of the community, really do not continue a component of Temple worship even if that had been possible, but it constitutes a practice of praying, which already existed historically before the destruction of the Temple and, in the opinion of the rabbis, had been commanded already in the Torah, even though it was difficult to find such a prescribed prayer in the Torah.[11] But the obligation to pray has no relevance in the liturgy. Prayers were established by God, were practised already by the Patriarchs, according to the tradition, put in order by the Elders of the Great Assembly after the Exile. So here is the establishment and continuity of the prayer service, but precisely this leads prayer service away from the Temple liturgy. The historical continuity of this prayer regulation factually verifies the suspension of the liturgical service of the Temple, although this was not mentioned outright. There simply is no historical connection between the two ways of worship. One continues, the other is suspended. However, the Temple service was projected, as it were, in a temporal line of expectation in the daily service of the synagogue. The community prays for the speedy restoration of the Temple. The Temple, which during the time it stood was the earthly center of liturgical thought, is shifted to a mostly eschatological line of expectation. In this way the service loses its earthly center of focus, even though the suppliants face toward Jerusalem when praying. The place of the Temple toward which the people turn their faces is no longer a place of service but a place of hope for a (mostly eschatological) restoration.[12] The prayer service is thus unmediated by sacred place or liturgical acts. (The commonly used wording, which here speaks of "spiritualization," is incorrect.) Undoubtedly, this immediacy is something tremendous, but it is the grandeur of a commonly shared need of God and man because the exile brings precisely the absence of a specific liturgical center and its restoration is the content of many prayers.

II. *Compensation*

The synagogue service is not a substitute but a service with an order of its own. Usually the immediacy of this service is taken more as a reminder of loss than as valuable in itself. The desire to compensate for the missing means and also for the missing center was probably always quite strong and, what according to the theological and liturgical viewpoint was correct, seemed to be a deficiency in daily religious life. For the community, the synagogue had to become the House of God and the synagogue service cult. And so, in spite of much resistance, there was an inevitable transferal of ideas. The synagogue became the *miqdash me'at,* the minor, little sanctuary.[13] The Torah shrine which contained the Sacred Scriptures, the venerated Torah scrolls, became a holy place in the synagogue, indicated by a perpetual light.[14] The synagogue service, in itself simply a prayer service, acquired a few cultic characteristics: cultic garb of the suppliants (prayer shawl), common recitation of prayers, the installation of a prayer leader whose task was to order the prayers but who held a cultic function as "delegate of the community" a role he really should not have had.[15] The carrying, the unfolding and rolling up of the Torah scroll all developed into legitimate and ordered forms of the prayer service.

Indeed the synagogue could never become a sacred place, but one circumstance contributed to making it such. The designation as house of prayer gave it a degree of *qedushah,* of holiness, which found its expression in the reverence with which it was regarded and in the rule that it should not be sold.[16] The accessories (Torah shrine, garments, etc.) were sacred. They were intended only for worship and, up to a point, supposed to be made with this purpose in mind. But, in reality, sacral holiness pertains neither to the synagogue nor to its accessories. They are not the house and the appurtenances of a Temple; they are not consecrated and no priest has anything to do with them. The synagogue is holy not by virtue of consecration but by virtue of a designation (dedication). The ritual implements of synagogue as well as of private use are what they are by virtue of dedication and origin. From the beginning of their production, by virtue of intention, of *kawwanah*, they are made to be used for ritual purpose.[17]

As activity, the worship of the synagogue is not a "service before God". What is being done is commanded, or is a custom *(minhag)* and as such it is revered yet it is not a sacred action which fulfills what God commanded as worship. Certainly these things compensate for a cult; the need for a sacred place, words and actions seems to be inherent in human beings. But they do not substitute for anything and they do not constitute a cultic service in its own order. Prayer service does require an order, but not a cultic liturgical order.

III. Interpretation

Compensation cannot occur through installation, for instance, by declaring: "This is . . ." Indeed, a commandment is fulfilled in the synagogue worship, the command to pray at certain times and at a certain manner. However, it is not possible to transfer this *de jure* to a commandment which establishes cult or liturgy as the command to build a sanctuary and offer sacrifices. Prayer remains always just that, as a command or a duty accomplished. Yet the possibility of interpretation in general and analogizing in particular always exists. So it is said that prayers were prescribed corresponding to the morning and afternoon sacrifices.[18] This correspondence has first a practical ground, allowing the choice of the times for prayer to be derived from the times for sacrifice. But this might be applied at any time, prayer and sacrifice combining especially as values; prayer is like a sacrifice, agreeable to God. It is to be performed in like spirit. Prayer does not substitute for sacrifice but does compensate for it, inasmuch as it satisfies a need—a need of God no less than of human beings.

In principle, the means for compensation is interpretation. The prayer service does not derive its liturgical character or value from what is prayed or how, in order to compensate for the lack of a concrete liturgy, but rather from the interpretation. This involves the explanation that this or that corresponds, the times of prayer to those of sacrifice. Here time is the *tertium comparationis* which is common to both prayer and sacrifice. How important the time—the *right* time—is requires only the evidence of phenomenology of religion. Prayer at certain hours of the day contains a definite liturgical aspect which is more than mere comparison, and which is not only compensation. Prayer does not thereby become liturgy, but it shares very definite times with the latter.

Points in common can also be established by certain values. In a midrash to Deut 11,13 it is said: "Serve the Lord with all your heart." That is prayer. But does it not mean sacrificial service? (For this alone is called "service".) But is there a service of the heart (it can take place only in the sanctuary)? What, then, does Scripture teach when it says "with all your heart"? (What kind of service can take place in the heart?) That is prayer (Sifre Deut, para.41).

The formal and informal characteristics of this midrash are too complicated to explain here. It indicates that Daniel called his prayer a service (Dan 6,11.21) and it mentions the psalm (141,2) which compares prayer to the incense sacrifice. I would like to refer only to the logical *tertium comparationis* "heart." The service needs the heart and so does prayer; they even have the heart in common (in the same way as time). To put it more concretely: God is there, the heart is there, but sacrifices have become impossible. Then it is prayer which unites God and the heart. Therefore it too can be called a service, but it is a service of another order. With the designation "service" a liturgical dimension is established.

The means of interpretation should not be less appreciated. In the time when revelation is not possible it is the way to gain knowledge. But interpretation can only establish new aspects; it can and must not have the binding force of a mandate.

IV. *God in the Community (Shekhinah)*

The presence of God *(Shekhinah)* does not pertain to the place of the Temple, which was sanctified through selection, but to the place in the midst of the people.[19] Nothing can substitute for the sacred place of the *Shekhinah;* the visible sacred center disappeared with the destruction of the Temple. But not so the presence of God in Israel. God, the *Shekhinah,* shares the exile of his people, and the exile of the *Shekhinah* implies that it no longer has a place and cannot reveal itself any more. But it is there, God is present, with the one at prayer, with the judges in judgment and in the praying community.

For the liturgical aspects of divine worship the presence of the *Shekhinah* in the community is of greatest importance. Here it must be stated first that the praying community has no historical, factual or even ideal relationship to the cult community of the Temple. The ideal cult community of the Temple is all Israel, for it maintains the cult as a community, for which the service in the Temple is offered. But the praying community of the synagogue is a community of prayer service which, historically and ideally, already existed before and alongside Temple worship. (Only the praying community of the *ma'amadot* had a factual relationship to the Temple through the sending of delegates to Jerusalem.)

> The praying community is not institutionalized. The religious bodies who provide the necessities for synagogue worship are legal and *not* liturgical communities. As a suppliant each Israel-ite is a member of the "community of Israel" because he prays as an Israelite. From a specific viewpoint (see below), the community of Israel also constitutes a liturgical community, but it exists, so to speak, only in faith and is neither constituted or institutionalized. Since the downfall of the high priests (and perhaps also the Sanhedrin) no constituted Israel exists any more; there are neither sacred or juridic institutions in which all Israel is represented.

The praying community is constituted *ad hoc,* that is, for the purpose of common worship. This *ad hoc* community probably comes into being by the sole statement that a quorum of ten Israelites is present (a *minyan* or the old *'edah*[20]). Thus the community originates through tacit agree-ment and in the same way disperses after worship. The ten men are necessary for a proper service to be celebrated. The rule is grounded especially on the premise that "everything which is done in holiness" requires a community of ten. This "in holiness" of the prayer service corresponds especially to the recitation of the *qaddish* prayer and the communal *qedushah,* the *Trishagion,* and to reading from the Torah on certain weekdays and feastdays.

The *Shekhinah* is present in this community. The Talmud[21] attempts to differentiate. To what point is the praying community different from the council of judges or from individuals at prayer, with whom the *Shekhinah* is also present? The answer is given: When ten go into the synagogue God precedes them and awaits them there.

The *Shekhinah* in the praying community can be a reality of faith or also (and at the same time) a value. First, the Talmud is concerned with the value: God is waiting for the ten Israelites to gather at a certain place in order to pray. The communities should choose a place in which to pray regularly; there God will be among them, and thus they prepare a place for God. This preparation of a place for God, who no longer has a place, unites the prayer community, that is, those who gather regularly, with the place of the synagogue. No doubt there have been attempts to prepare a place in the synagogue for the *Shekhinah* also.[22] Furthermore there were attempts to relate the idea of the presence of the *Shekhinah* with the recitation of the *Shema*ᶜ (Deut 6,4) in a special way. When the Israelites sit in the synagogue and recite the *Shema*ᶜ, the *Shekhinah* hovers over them;[23] because of each praise whereby Israel praises God, he lets his *Shekhinah* rest upon them (according to Ps 22,4). In this way the singing and praising worshipers prepare a throne for God in their midst. In any case, these are values which are given to prayer especially in the community, values indeed which can pertain to the reality of faith in, or to the mystical experience of, God's presence.

However, the concept of the presence of the *Shekhinah* in the community has no relation to the presence of the *Shekhinah* in the Temple. To be sure, any concept of the *Shekhinah* which is linked with the synagogue compensates for the loss of the presence of God in a place[24] but, as far as I see, it does not have any relationship to worship. To be sure, the presence of the *Shekhinah* in Israel now in exile is this manner of presence. There is also the possibility to prepare a place for God in exile, showing that not only is Israel not abandoned by God, but that God is not abandoned by Israel. But this experience does not enter into worship itself. Of course, it is impossible to determine experiences precisely, but the synagogue service does not touch upon the presence of the *Shekhinah*, and moreover gives no possibility for this. The presence is real but it is primarily spiritual and commemorated and experienced. One cannot turn toward the *Shekhinah*; the worshiper turned his face toward the Temple, to the Holy of Holies where the *Shekhinah* was. He still turns in that direction and the seventeenth of the Eighteen Benedictions concludes: "Who restores his *Shekhinah* to Zion." There is no connection between the place of the Temple and the *Shekhinah* of the praying community, and also none between prayer and the presence of the *Shekhinah* in the community. Certainly, the presence of God and prayer belong together, but not the presence of the *Shekhinah* with a definite prayer.

The priestly blessing might be mentioned here as a possible exception. In some midrashim to Cant 2,4 it is said that God (the *Shekhinah*) hastens from one community to another in order to bless them and to stand behind the outspread fingers of the priest as if behind a latticework.[25] In this one priestly act of worship there remains a trace of the concept of God's presence with the priest who blesses, less an aspect of liturgy than a liturgical remnant.

Otherwise it seems that the concept of the presence of the *Shekhinah* in the praying community does not establish any liturgical dimension. The destruction of the Temple leads here to a (new?) direct relationship between man and God. The walls of the Holy of Holies no longer stand between God's presence and Israel at prayer. But this God is present only to the hearts of those who offer service here; he is present and no more to the specific service which does not perceive his unmediated presence, for it should not be perceived because it must not replace the service in the Temple.

V. *Harmony with the Heavenly Liturgy (Qedushah)*

The destruction of the Temple also places the praying community directly "before God in heaven". While the Temple stood "the face was turned toward the Holy of Holies and the heart toward the Father in heaven". We do not know what the latter phrase meant. Certainly, however, one portrayed the throne of God and a heavenly Temple (at least in a spatial dimension, as it were) corresponding to the earthly Temple. Surely one knew of a heavenly liturgy which corresponded to a human one, indicated already in Isaiah's vision (6,1ff). The Temple was indeed the place at which God's heaven coincides with God's earthly dwelling place among human beings.[26] That spatial center being destroyed, heaven was opened directly, not only over Jerusalem but over every praying community. We do not know how much the praying community took into Exile with it from the Temple cult, inasmuch as it was seen in analogy to the heavenly liturgy. It is possible that a direct, historical filiation exists.[27] But it is certain that under the influence of "*merkabah* mysticism" (an esoteric discipline concerned with heaven and the divine throne-chariot) heaven became wide open. The pragmatic objective of these mystics was to bring initiates, either in spirit or in body, before God's throne in heaven.[28] This had already taken place in apocalyptic.

> In the writings of these mystics, which certainly were used partly for propaganda purposes, not unlike many apocalypses,[29] the path of the initiates through heaven is described, as well as the chants sung before the throne of God and the worship which takes place there. In contrast to the scribe who gains his knowledge through the Scriptures and ultimately can only say "I think", the initiate could say "I saw", "I heard". The *merkabah* mystics attempted in a way to overcome the exile and, as in prophecy, to experience the will of God through vision and hearing. The Temple has almost disappeared in the writings of these mystics, and so should it be, since heaven is completely open.[30]

The message brought from heaven by the mystics says that the *qedushah*, the *Trishagion* of Israel, as it is recited and chanted in the synagogue service of all small communities, is more precious before God than the *qedushah* of his heavenly choirs. The angels are silent until Israel has intoned its "holy." Thus Israel not only joins in the liturgy of the angels, but rather the angels participate in the prayer of Israel. Israel is more important before God than the heavenly court; it is closer to God.

We cannot evaluate in detail the influence of *merkabah* mysticism on divine worship. Certainly it was quite considerable, in any case so that one must attribute the strongest liturgical characteristics in the synagogue service to this *merkabah* mysticism.[31] But even here it does not come to formal institution of definite acts. *Merkabah* mysticism was not widely accepted but in virtue of their vision and hearing the mystics could say: When Israel prays, something takes place in heaven. Israel stands concretely, and not only in theory, in the presence of the glorious and powerful God who is enthroned above the cherubim in heaven. This is surely a mystery, which the initiates disclose to the worshiping people. Somehow it was strong enough to remain in orthodox Judaism until the present.

The "before God" of the *qedushah* is totally different from the presence of the *Shekhinah* in the community. Here was really a means and a liturgical communion which united all the communities and the hosts of heaven. In practice it even became an outward action. When the community recites the *qedushah* it rises with feet together and, standing on tip-toe, imitates the flight of the praising seraphim.[32] The *qedushah* is a sacred action through recitation; it can only be proclaimed in a community of at least ten men.

But the *qedushah* presents only an aspect of liturgy. It does not become the center of synagogue worship such as the Eucharist in the Christian liturgy. This is clear already by its place in the sequence of prayers. It is prepared by the *yoṣer* prayer in the additions to the benedictions of the "Hear, Israel" which contain a special *qedushah*. Here hymns are offered praising God as the Creator of the world who each day renews the work of creation. At this point the curtain is drawn aside, as it were, and the angelic liturgy is described in a few words. In the third of the Eighteen Benedictions Israel itself first joins in the *qedushah*. There is no connection in the order of prayer between these two points: the *qedushah* in the *yoṣer* and the *qedushah* in the *shmoneh ʿesreh*. The prayers were not composed with the viewpoint that the *qedushah* or the description of heaven in the *yoṣer* are in any way central. Only later, and depending on the attitude of the community were they elevated to prominent positions. Then they could become focal points; thus in the prayers of feast days, they were accompanied by solemn hymns and chants.

The synagogue service as a whole cannot be set in parallel with the heavenly liturgy. Only at one point does it offer an aspect, here a view in the ordinary meaning of the word, which enables the one at prayer to catch sight of God's throne imaginatively and places him in the community before this throne. At least as a possibility, this moment is a liturgical reality and presence. It is not substitution, not memory nor anticipation of a future event. To be sure, the person praying must return immediately into his own life just as the pilgrim had to leave the Temple again and again. The temporal perspective, the past and above all the future, is suspended only for the moment and is changed into a spatial sacred perspective. The historical "once" indeed can be present as memorial, but the eschatological "once" becomes as insignificant as the Temple taken as center. Graphically speaking, it is like a slash through the cosmos which touches the time line only at one point between "before" and "after". It is an event that as such can never become history. If the person praying could rise up to a place before the throne, where already the souls of the righteous Israel are gathered, then he could reach his eschatological goal, which no longer lies in the time line.

This new, liturgical world view corresponds to the relatively recent presentation in Israel of heaven as the "abode of souls". At first this seems to contradict the eschatological expectation of a resurrection of the body and a historical, end-of-time restoration of Israel and the world. Theologically this contradiction was so resolved that the after life or the expectation of heaven is the possibility of the present, which finally meets the projected line of historical and eschatological expectation (restoration of the Temple as the center of the revealed presence of God) at its end point.

VI. *Qaddish*

The expectation in time is found in another prayer which must be recited in holiness, the *qaddish*. It is a prayer for the sanctification of the divine name and the coming of God's kingdom. Its popular meaning (tradition attributed special power to it, and the bereaved recite it as a prayer for the dead[33]) has little to do with its liturgical significance and its contents.

It concludes the order of prayers concerned with the immediate and eschatological future. The Babylonian Talmud (Berakhot 3b) tells a story about the prophet Elijah who appeared to R. Jose bar Ḥalafta at the entrance to the ruins of Jerusalem and said: Whenever Israel goes into the synagogues and schools and there (in the *qaddish*) answers: "May his great Name be blessed," the Holy One, blessed be he, shakes his head and says: "Blessed be the king who is thus praised in his house (that is, in the Temple). But what is there for the father who had to banish his sons? And woe to the sons who had to be banished from their father's table."

First and especially in light of the aspect indicated above, the *qaddish* is very unliturgical. Interpreted in such a way, it indicates the absent liturgical center as exile. Thus it is probably the most direct of prayers and blessings. There is no analogue for it in the Temple service, and none in heavenly worship. It is a prayer unknown to the angels, and they envy men for knowing it.[34] In its immediacy it unites God and the human being more than any liturgy could. God suffers the exile no less than Israel does; both want to end the exile in order to establish God's kingship in its perfection. This kingship is not only internal, but also clearly external: God can reveal himself in his glory and the human being can be before God in a Temple which orients toward the consummation of creation.[35] This kingship is always theophany too, indeed that theophany which with the revelation of God at creation took a beginning in time. As a prayer for the redemptive consummation it departs from the exile's lack of mediation in time and points to a liturgical center, located in Jerusalem, but not the restoration of the old Temple (although the prayer comes from its destruction) but rather the consummation of creation. In this new liturgical center, which is prayed for, immediacy (which is a value) is not to be taken away, but its negative condition, the exile, is to be removed. An eschatological, liturgical mediation should be established as a face-to-face encounter, as perfect knowledge of God, which also shines through the exile. Or this may be seen hierarchically as a center which is God himself, and to which the human being stands closest as *ṣaddiq*, as righteous and holy one, even closer than the angels created in holiness.[36]

The expectation in time is not set into a remote future; the *qaddish* uses the words "in your days, during your lifetime", but in spite of this proximity there is a time line. Thus, in the meaning of the word, the *qaddish* unfolds a liturgical aspect pointing toward the future. Formally, the *qaddish* does not come from the *qedushah* but in their situation they both arise at the same point, also from the same person at prayer. The *qedushah* discloses a heavenly presence of God in the here and now. The *qaddish* reveals a presence in time as "once", or in the hope for the future as "soon". The *qaddish* points out the exile situation of the *qedushah*, which in the absence of mediation is not visible.

VII. *Interpretation and Intention*

The prayer service repeatedly shows liturgical aspects, but (at least as far as the rabbis are concerned) it is not *ʿabodah*, service, therefore not a liturgy but rather a worship of the heart. The absence of a liturgical center and mediation was accepted. By way of compensation, of course, many attempts were made to fill the gaps, which is understandable. But compensation does not belong directly to the essence of synagogue worship; rather it corresponds to general human, religious need. Lack of mediation was accepted more as a "worship of the heart". This service is not liturgy but it contains liturgical aspects, whether it is through interpretation of Scripture, or through the immediacy of mystical vision, whereby in the last analysis the vision is only interpreted. As far as I can see, such an interpretation can never pertain to a liturgy. The consciousness that this synagogue service is a service of another order from Temple worship cannot be weakened. And yet the liturgical aspects are firm. The worship of the heart is not an "as if". It is what it is, not by virtue of interpretation (this cannot substitute for the lack of constitution), but by virtue of intention, by virtue of *kawwanah*, in the ordering of the senses, of the heart. Through the intention in a precise understanding, to pray in this self-understanding, the liturgical aspects become efficacious and they are realized. Intention is in fact a matter of the heart and makes worship come from the heart. Intention is something genuine. It does not change the prayer service into liturgy but it bestows on it liturgical aspects. It gives the prayer service, so to speak, something of liturgical life. With its immediacy, it cuts through the absence of a center, the lack of liturgical action, the missing signs, the lost substance.

Kawwanah, intention, belongs in any prayer; only through intention is life breathed into rigid, literary formulae.[37] But not all intentions can disclose liturgical aspects. We are concerned here with the special *kawwanah* which desires to make prayer into a service before God, in a liturgical sense. The meaning is given through interpretation, the direction through *kawwanah*. The *kawwanah* of the Qabbalists evolved to technique, and shows how strongly the *kawwanah* influenced by interpretation gives a definite liturgical direction to prayer. Each prayer is to be recited with a definite *kawwanah*. In this way each prayer, especially in the Lurianic Qabbalah, had a definite function; it brought about something, not only the granting of the prayer, but also the restoration of the disturbed world order, the *tiqqun*.[38]

One should not be tempted to think that the intention, which effects the liturgical aspects, enabling one to have a liturgical outlook or liturgical insights, can be considered as interiorization.[39] The contrasting concepts external-internal should not be used in liturgical reflections. Liturgy is revelation in its essence, revelation of God in theophany, revelation of man in service. This takes place in concrete action, in gesture and in word. They spring from the internal, yet the purpose is to be able to approach each other in an external encounter, to become a concrete presence. Internalization is never liturgical, it can only be mystical and is a withdrawal, a retreat of God from his creation, if that were possible, and a retreat of man from his creaturehood. By contrast, liturgy is a face-to-face encounter, at least in the Jewish and probably in the Christian understanding. It is not oriented towards the hereafter as a perfect and therefore shapeless internal reality, but toward a fulfillment, a knowledge in the liturgical sense. Where and whenever this concreteness arises, liturgical aspects are revealed in the prayer service of the synagogue.

NOTES

1. My reflections are stimulated directly by Jakob J. Petuchowski's book *Understanding Jewish Prayer* (New York 1972 p 26-34). That Petuchowski refers to Romano Guardini in order to qualify the synagogue worship as liturgy seems to me in contradiction to liturgical data. See also my review in *ZRGG* 26 (1974), p.177-178. However, further reflections indicated to me that the possibility of affirming or denying the liturgical character of synagogue worship is a peculiarity of this worship itself.

2. See A. Goldberg, *Die Vorstellung von der Schekhinah in der frühen rabbinischen Literatur* (Berlin 1969) p 490ff, henceforth abbreviated to *"Schekhinah."*

3. See 1Chr 24;mTa'anit 4,2.

4. See M. Rosenmann, *Der Ursprung der Synagoge und ihre allmähliche Entwicklung* (Berlin 1907) p 27ff.

5. See the various hypotheses of K. Hruby, *Die Synagoge, geschichtliche Entwicklung einer Institution* (Zürich 1971) p 19ff, and the very detailed description of the evidence by M. Hengel, "Proseuchē und Synagoge," *Tradition und Glaube*. Festschrift für Karl Georg Kuhn (ed Gert Jeremias) (Göttingen: Vanderhoeck & Ruprecht 1971) p 157-183.

6. See A. Büchler, *Types of Jewish Palestinian Piety* (London 1922) p 8-67; A. Goldberg, "Der Heilige und die Heiligen," *Frankfurter Judaistische Beiträge (FJB)* 4(1976) p 21ff.

7. See A. Goldberg, "Die Heiligkeit des Ortes in der frühen rabbinischen Theologie," *FJB* 4(1976) p 26-31.

8. See bMegillah 10b; mEduyyot 8,6. A. Guttmann, "The End of the Jewish Sacrificial Cult," *HUCA* 38(1967) p 137-148.

9. A. Goldberg, *Schekhina*, p 176ff.

10. Historical evidence of an orientation of synagogue worship to cult in the Temple or a continuity in liturgical texts proves, considering the facts, that this continuity can be verified only through archeology and not through theological tradition. Moreover, one should not understand such a persistence as continuity.

11. See for instance bBerakhot 21a; Moses Maimonides, *Hilkhot Tefillah* 1,1 and *Kesef Mishneh* in the same place.

12. See A. Goldberg, "Die Heiligkeit des Ortes . . ." (note 7).

13. According to Ezekiel 11,16; bMeg 29a, there is mention of the synagogues and schools in Babylonia. More important is Targum Jonathan at Ezekiel 11,16: "I gave them synagogues, which take second(place) next to my Temple." It seems worthy of note that this interpretation, as far as I can determine, is found in early rabbinical literature only at these two places.

14. See the literature of J. Mayer, *Geschichte der Jüdischen Religion* (Berlin 1972) p 114.

15. See F. Böhl, "Zur Fürbittfunktion des Vorbeters," *FJB 2*, (1974) p 53-64.

16. See mMegilla 3,1-3; bMegilla 26b-27a, see also the commentaries of K. Hruby, *Die Synagoge*, p 72ff.

17. See for instance Moses Maimonides, *Hilkhot Tefillin* 1,11ff.

18. BBerakhot 26a, however, see also the formulation jBerakhot 4,1.

19. See A. Goldberg, *Schekhinah*, p 474.

20. I. Elbogen, *Der jüdische Gottesdienst in seiner geschichtlichen Entwicklung*,[3] 1931, p 493.

21. BBerakhot 6a, see also A. Goldberg, *Schekhinah*, p 500ff.

22. See A. Goldberg, *Schekhinah*, p 503ff.

23. See Bereshit Rabba 48,27 (Theodor p 482); A. Goldberg, *Schekhinah*, p 390f.

24. The most tangible presentation was linked with the synagogues of *Shafweyatiw*, bMegillah 29a; bNiddah 13a. See also A. Goldberg, *Schekhinah*, p 503.

25. See Shir Rabba 2,9; Bamidbar Rabba 11, para 2; Pesiqta Rabbati 15, p 72a, especially the commentary by Friedmann here. Also bHagigah 16a: One should not look at priests who, standing in the Temple, lift up their hands to bestow the priestly blessings (Rashi: because the *Shekhinah* is above their uplifted hands). Although this prohibition was valid only during the time when the Temple stood, it remained in force.

26. See J. Maier, *Vom Kultus zur Gnosis, Bundeslade, Gottesthron und Märkaba* (Salzburg 1964); H. Bietenhard, *Die himmlische Welt im Christentum und im Spätjudentum* (Tübingen 1951).

27. It is possible that the community at Qumran already knew of a community of angels and men in liturgy; P. Schäfer, *Rivalität zwischen Engeln und Menschen* (Berlin 1975) p 36ff.

28. See G. Scholem, *Jewish Gnosticism, Merkaba Mysticism and Talmudic Tradition*[2] (New York 1965).

29. See A. Goldberg, "Einige Bemerkungen zu den Quellen und redaktionellen Einheiten der grossen Hekhalot," *FJB 1* (1973) p 45ff.

30. J. Maier, *Vom Kultus zur Gnosis*, defends the thesis that *merkabah* mysticism resulted from the priestly esotericism and that the liturgical material transmitted here, especially the angelic liturgy, belonged originally to the Temple liturgy.

This seems to be correct. But it is worth noting that the priestly tradition of these writings was lost completely. The initiate is not a priest and does not see himself in any relationship to the Temple.

31. See Ph. Bloch, "Die *ywrdy mrkbh*, die Mystiker der Gaonenzeit und ihr Einfluss auf die Liturgie," *MGWJ* 37(1893) p 18-25; 69-74; 257-266; 305-311. I. Grünwald, "Piyute Jannai wesifrut Yorde hamerkabah," *Tarbiz* 36(1966-67) p 257-277. A. Altmann, "Shire qedusha besifrut hahekhalot haqeduma," *Melilah* 2 (1945-46) p 1-24.

32. See the commentaries and instructions to the prayer books.

33. See D. De Sola Pool, *The Qaddish* (Leipzig, 1909).

34. BSotah 33a

35. As it says in the *qaddish*: "Magnified and sanctified be his great Name in the world which he created according to his will. May he establish his kingdom soon."

36. This is because the *ṣaddiq* stands closer to God than the ministering angel; see P. Schäfer, *Rivalität*, p 192-200; A. Goldberg, "Der Heilige und die Heiligen," *FJB* 4 (1976) p 14f.

37. See J. Petuchowski, *Understanding Jewish Prayer*, p 3-16.

38. See G. Scholem, *Die jüdische Mystik und ihre Hauptströmungen*, 1957, p 302ff. Here a functional analogy exists between prayer and sacrifice in the understanding of scholars of religion.

39. This is the title of an essay by H.G. Enelow: "*Qawwanah*, The Struggle for Inwardness in Judaism," *Studies in Jewish Literature in Honor of Professor Kaufmann Kohler* (Berlin 1913) p 82-107.

Observations on the Concept and the Early Forms of Aḳedah-Spirituality *

CLEMENS THOMA

In recent times much has been written about the Aḳedah in late antiquity, namely the historical influence of Gen 22, 1-19 on inter-testamental, New Testament and rabbinic periods.[1] Especially in the last fifty years an animated discussion has taken place in Jewish circles about the significance of the "binding" (ʿqd) of Isaac (see Gen 22,9).[2] For Christian researchers, the manuscript of the Palestinian Targum Codex Neophiti 1 (CN 1),[3] which was discovered in 1957 in the Vatican Library, has been stimulating.

1. *Description of Aḳedah-spirituality*

The narrative found in Gen 22 had not only a significant religious and spiritual development in late Old Testament times and afterwards, but above all, it affected the history of piety. Many people, finding them-selves in difficult situations, were able to sustain themselves on the strength of this account about Abraham who, confidently obeying the God who was "testing" him (Gen 22,1), was prepared to slaughter his only and beloved son, and about Isaac who was willing to be offered as a sacrifice. This expression of obedience by Abraham and submission by Isaac constitute an example worthy of imitation. The story motivated people to accept obediently and submissively in their lives what seemed incomprehensible, unendurable and contradictory and to reflect upon it. The determination to imitate the persons and their deeds recorded in biblical revelation, applying them to personal circumstances can be

---

*As a figure of faith and salvation Abraham has for many years occupied a central position in the scholarly works and personal devotion of John Oesterreicher. This is why an examination of the early Aḳedah-piety seems to be a fitting tribute at the occasion of his 75th birthday on February 2, 1979.
Translation from the German by Mrs. Nora Quigley and the editors.

considered as an expression of piety or spirituality. Piety is a general concept. Spirituality, understood as appropriation by the Spirit, points to the specific type of piety. Spirituality is an internal, intellectual, appropriation, the application of revelation for the individual soul and life situation effected by a confident submission to God.[4]

A rabbinic explanation of Akedah-spirituality can be found, for instance, in the Codex Neophiti 1 to Gen 22,14: "Abraham worshipped and prayed in the name of the Word of the Lord and said: I beseech by the mercy that is before you, O Lord. All things are manifest and known before you: that there was no division in my heart the first time that you said to me to sacrifice my son Isaac, to make him dust and ashes before you, but that I immediately arose early in the morning and diligently put your Word into practice with gladness and fulfilled your decree. Now, when his sons are in the hour of affliction, remember *(dkr)* the *ʿaqedah* (binding) of their father Isaac and listen to the voice of their supplication and hear them deliver *(šyzb)* them from all tribulation. . . ."[5]

Abraham himself wishes that Isaac's submission should be imitated and adapted spiritually. This is to be accomplished in moments of distress. Here the theological key word is *zkr/zkrwn/dkr/anamnesis/memoria*/remembrance. But the above Targum quotation would be misinterpreted if it imagined that the remembrance of Isaac's submission could generate a powerful current from Isaac to the oppressed person. Rather, "remembrance" is meant to be an appeal to God that he might listen to and rescue the oppressed person just as he once showed mercy to Abraham, obedient in the darkness of faith and to Isaac on the altar. Thus, Akedah-spirituality is a prayer motif pleasing to God on the part of an oppressed person and not a magical practice. The inner core of this prayer is praise of God, who once revealed himself as the merciful redeemer, and whom one trusts will respond to present needs.

Akedah-spirituality presupposes that Abraham and Isaac, as two persons, form a perfect human-religious unity. In connection with the biblical account, which emphasizes the intimate relationship between father and son (Gen 22,6-8), it is said in the Midrash: " 'And the two of them set out together' (Gen 22,8)—the one to bind and the other to be bound, the one to kill, the other to be killed" (Gen R 56,4). In Akedah-spirituality both the submissive Isaac and the obedient Abraham are placed in the lime-light. The inner unity of father and son always shines through. Philo of Alexandria begins his paraphrased account of Gen 22 with the following statement: "But his greatest action which deserves reporting must not be passed over in silence. For I might also say that all the other actions which won the favour of God are surpassed by this." (Abr 167).[6] In Philo's eyes it is Abraham, not Isaac, who accomplishes this action which is most pleasing to God. Philo continues thus: "Here we have the most affectionate of fathers himself beginning the sacrificial rite as priest with the very best of sons for victim. Perhaps too, following the law of burnt offering, he would have dismembered his son and offered him limb by limb. Thus we see that he did not incline partly to the boy and partly to piety, but devoted his whole soul through and through to holiness *(hosioteti, 1ᵉqidduš)* and disregarded the claims of their common blood." (Abr 198 p.97). Philo is not interested in contrasting Abraham's action with Isaac's. Like all the Targums and Midrashim, he emphasizes the unity of intention and action demonstrated in the Akedah by father and son (see Abr 172). It is generally accepted then that the adherent of Akedah-spiritually imitates Abraham in a special way when he is threatened with the loss or removal by force of something beloved and dear to him. In contrast, when someone finds himself as a sacrifice on the altar, when rejected, ill or close to death, then Isaac comes into the center of focus. Ultimately the person concerned with Akedah-spirituality concentrates his inner sensibilities neither on Abraham nor on Isaac, nor on the two of them together, but on the God of Abraham, Isaac and other great witnesses of faithful obedience and submission. It appears, then, that it is impossible to find an Akedah-spirituality that is not influenced by Abraham and Isaac.

2. *Ineffectiveness of Akedah-spirituality during the persecution under Antiochos IV Epiphanes (175-163 B.C.)?*

Today no one will deny that individual traditions in the Targum and Midrash concerning the Akedah go back to pre-Christian times.[7] As demonstrated in the Book of Jubilees (ca. 100 B.C.) the Akedah was even then linked to the Feast of Passover (Jub 17, 15-18.19).[8] The Book of Jubilees is the most important pre-Christian literary evidence that enables us to assign an early date to certain targumic traditions, according to which the creation of the world, the Akedah, the Exodus from Egypt, redemption at the end of time, together formed the secrets of the Passover celebration (see CN 1 to Exod 12, 42). In the history of motifs, there seems to be no problem in locating the Akedah-spirituality in the second to first centuries before Christ.

The central problem, however, is that we have hardly any evidence of Akedah-spirituality in the time of the Seleucid persecution of the Jews under Antiochos IV Epiphanes (175-163 B.C.) or shortly thereafter, when the Akedah motif would have brought great encouragement and consolation. One would have expected to find some trace of Akedah-spirituality in the Book of Daniel and in the first two Books of Maccabees where the Seleucid persecutions are clearly described. However, neither Abraham nor Isaac are mentioned in the Book of Daniel. In the first Book of the Maccabees the Akedah is referred to only once: "Was not Abraham found faithful *(pistos)* when tested *(en peirasmo)*? And it was reckoned to him as righteousness" (2,52). In form then, this is a commonly used, abbreviated connection of citations from Gen 22 and Gen 15,6. This connection can also be found in the New Testament (Gal 3,6-18). But for us the context of 1Macc 2,52 is more important. Mattathias, a nationalist and religious leader of the Hasmonaean rebels, says these words shortly before his death in order to encourage his sons to continue the rebellion against the Seleucids and also to inspire the Jewish sympathizers for this cause. Comparing this verse with Sir 44, 20 and Judith 8, 26 one can deduce that Gen 22 was not designated by the key word "binding" (from Gen 22,9) at the time of the Maccabees; rather more pertinent is the key word "temptation," "testing" *(peirasmos, nsh,* from Gen 22,1). Viewed in connection with the Hasmonaean family the story of Abraham and Isaac in Gen 22 is used as an example to further the national and religious revolution. Mattathias was not interested in the sacred value or religious application of the story. He used it explicitly to dispel any doubts his sons and followers might have had about a victorious rebellion. Here one can speak of Akedah-spirituality only incidentally. Also in the second Book of Maccabees the Akedah is at most touched upon only indirectly. There is a prayer: "May God do good to you and may he remember his Covenant with Abraham and Isaac and Jacob, his faithful servants." (2Macc 1,2). This sentence comes from the Palestinian tradition of communal prayer, so it is stamped with a spiritual overtone. The verse appears again in a more elaborate form in the second century A.D. in the final redaction of the 18 Benedictions (first blessing) and in the early rabbinic penitential liturgy (mTaʿanit 2,4). However, it does not refer clearly to Akedah-spirituality.[9]

One could probably find adequate reasons to explain this absence of Akedah-spirituality in the first two Books of Maccabees as accidental. One can hardly expect to find information about people's spiritual life in history books! However, anyone who studies Maccabean times will become perplexed when he compares the martyr stories in chapter 6 and 7 of 2Maccabees with those of 4 Maccabees. The latter takes up the story of the martyrdom of the teacher Eleazar (2Macc 6, 18-31) and that of the seven "Maccabean" brothers with their mother (2Macc 7), telling them in relation to a Jewish tailoring of the Stoic ideal (4Macc 4-18). In 4Maccabees the martyrs are mentioned several times as being the children of Abraham (4Macc 6,22; 7,19; 9,21; 15,28 etc.). The preparation for martyrdom by the seven "Maccabean" sons is motivated by the Akedah. The mother exclaims: "Remember that for the sake of God you have come into the world, and have enjoyed life, and that therefore you owe it to God to endure all pain for his sake; for whom also our father Abraham made haste to sacrifice his son Isaac, the ancestor of our nation, and Isaac, seeing his father's hand lifting the knife against him, did not shrink." (4Macc 16, 18-20;[10] see also 4Macc 7, 11-14; 13,12). In 2Macc 6-7—this significant *Vorlage* of 4 Maccabees—there is no mention of Abraham or the Akedah. At the latest, by 50 B.C. 2Maccabees existed in the form known today.[11] This difference between the Second and Fourth Books of Maccabees must be emphasized especially because only about a century elapsed between the final redaction of both books and because the martyrdom stories are found in both.

Theological-historical explanations for the absence of Akedah-spirituality in 2Macc 6-7 and for its presence in 4 Maccabees are easily found. First, the Jewish victims of the Seleucid persecutions were not saved at the last moment before death, as Isaac was. They lost their lives. Secondly, the process of theological awareness had not developed so much in the second and first centuries B.C. that Abraham's faithful obedience and Isaac's submissiveness were seen as a perfect expression of martyrdom. This latter image emerges only with the passage of time. Philo of Alexandria says: "And so the boy was saved, since God returned the gift of him and used the offering which piety rendered to him to repay the offerer. For Abraham the action, though not followed by the intended ending, was complete and perfect, and the record of it as such stands graven not only in the sacred books, but in the minds of the readers (Abr 177 p 89). In the subsequent period, Abraham and Isaac became more and more the prototype and model of martyrs—especially in Pseudo-Philo, Liber Ant 32, 1-4; in 4Macc; Mekhilta to Ex 12,13 (ed Horovitz 24f), the New Testament and rabbinic writings. But even these allusions in the history of theology are not quite satisfactory. Was there really no Akedah-spirituality evident at the time of Seleucid persecution? It must have existed in some form; otherwise it would be inconceivable that so many Jews could have persevered with such fidelity through a time of affliction and threat against their very lives!

3. *Spirituality of faithful obedience and devotion without reference to Abraham and Isaac.*

The study of Akedah-spirituality at the time of the Seleucid persecution of the Jews from the viewpoint of motif-history can only reap an incomplete and scanty harvest. It should focus on the spiritual content and meaning of the Akedah-spirituality and not be curtailed by the absence of certain submotifs. Then one can discover rich expressions of this spirituality during that time of oppression to the threat of life and limb. The spiritual attitude indicated by the Akedah was quite evident among the Jewish faithful who lived under Seleucid dominion in this time of religious persecution. When their loyalty to the God of Israel was tested to the utmost, they manifested faithful obedience and devotion. They did not see special importance in explicit reference to Abraham and Isaac.

The most beautiful story which expresses Akedah-spirituality in its highest form is in Dan 3, 1-30. It is the legend of the three young men who were thrown into the fiery furnace. This story, which may have originated in earlier times, was included in the Book of Daniel, which was written during the Seleucid persecution of the Jews, between 168 and 164 B.C. It offered an example to the oppressed, confused and despondent Jews. Three young and highly gifted Jewish men fall victim to a court intrigue. They are accused of rejecting the laws of Nebuchadnezzar's empire, which in the Book of Daniel portrays the Seleucid kingdom under Antiochos IV Epiphanes (175-163 B.C.). Nebuchadnezzar threatens to burn the young men in a fiery furnace if they persist in their refusal to worship his golden statue. He adds to this threat the malicious statement: "And who is the god who could deliver (šyzb) out of my hands?" (Dan 3, 15c; see above quoted CN 1 to Gen 22, 14). The young men were not intimidated. Their acknowledgment of the God of Israel is neither tainted with arrogance nor does it allow for the least shadow of doubt. It is a testimony that expresses complete submission and total trust: "If it be so, our God, whom we serve, is able to deliver us (šyzb) from the burning fiery furnace and he will deliver (šyzb) us out of your hand, O King. But if not, be it known to you, O King, that we will not serve your gods or worship the golden image you have set up" (Dan 3, 17f.). And so the story takes its relentless course. The three men are thrown into the furnace which is heated to seven times its normal temperature but through divine intervention they are not burned but miraculously saved. The king himself sees this miracle occur in the oven: "Did we not cast three men bound into the fire? . . . But I see four men loose walking in the midst of the fire and they are not hurt; and the appearance of the fourth is like a son of the gods" (Dan 3, 24f). After inviting the men to step out of the furnace the king praises the God of Israel in the language used by the Jewish people during their worship: "Blessed be the God of Shadrach, Meshach and Abednego, who has sent his angel and delivered (šyzb) his servants who trusted in him, and set at naught the king's command, and yielded up their bodies rather than serve and worship any god except their own God" (Dan 3, 28). Finally the king decrees that everyone in his kingdom shall worship the God of the three men. The men are given high positions in the government of his kingdom.

This legend has several levels of meaning: salvific, historical and spiritual.[12] The fate of the three young men and their miraculous deliverance from the furnace (Dan 3, 1-23) symbolizes faithfully obedient and devout Jewry which is being tested and purified in its fidelity to and trust in the God of Israel during a time when it must reject conformity to the attitude of many foreign peoples. At the end of this period of harsh trials the time of salvation dawns in which the Jews should be unoppressed and happy. Then the non-Jews will praise the God of Israel as the Jews have done from antiquity (v 24-30). However, this interpretative level of *salvation history* is only incidental to the legend. On the other hand, the application to contemporary history deeply touched the Jewish listeners and readers at the time of the Seleucid persecution. The legend contains an urgent admonition against syncretistic attempts at appeasement under the pressures of Seleucid authority and their Jewish accomplices. It emphasizes unconditional loyalty to the God of Israel in the midst of confusion and oppression. The *spiritual* aspect of the legend is equally clear. Withstanding persecution can be brought about only by an unconditional obedience to God and by an equally devout submission to his will. A further aspect of the spiritual level in the story is the key word: $\check{s}yzb$ = to rescue. God can deliver from any distress, so hope must never be abandoned. The temporary affliction is a test which points to deliverance. *How* God will save remains his sovereign right.

The story of the trial of the three young men in the furnace preserves the content of Akedah-spirituality. In both instances, the emphasis is on faithful obedience and devotion in extreme affliction. In both, the merciful, redeeming God of Israel stands behind a situation which, from the human viewpoint, is meaningless and desperate. A salvation history symbolism permeates both narratives.[13]

Instead of three men in the furnace there could be just two: Abraham and Isaac! One can verify that the situation is similarly interchangeable from the history of literature. In Pseudo-Philo (first century A.D.) we find a legend about Abraham in which enemies throw him into a furnace:

"Taking him, they built a furnace and started a fire, and into the furnace they threw fire-burnt stones. Then prince Jectan, weakened by the heat, took Abram and put him in the fiery furnace with the bricks. However, God produced a great earthquake, and the swirling fire leapt from the furnace with flames and sparks, devouring all who stood around the furnace. The number of those burned that day was 83,500. But Abram did not experience the slightest injury in the fire. And Abram came out of the furnace, and the fiery furnace fell apart. Abram was saved and he went to the eleven men who were hidden in the mountains and told them all that had happened to him. They came down from the mountains with him, rejoicing in the Name of the Lord, and no one who met them that day frightened them" (Liber Ant VI, 16-18).

It was evident to the author of Fourth Maccabees that the three young men, Abraham and Isaac, and the seven "Maccabean" martyrs with their mother form an unbroken unity. He ascribes, for example, to the Maccabean martyrs the following words of encouragement: 'Let us die like brothers, O brethren, for the Law. Let us imitate the three children at the Assyrian court who despised this same ordeal of the furnace. Let us not turn cravens before the proof of righteousness. . . .' And another recalling the past, 'Remember of what stock you are, and at whose fatherly hands Isaac for righteousness' sake yielded himself to be a sacrifice.' And each and all of them together, looking at each other brightly and very boldly, said: 'With a whole heart we consecrate ourselves unto God who gave us our souls, and let us lend our bodies to the keeping of the Law. . . . Let us then arm ourselves with divine Reason's mastery of the passions. After this our passion, Abraham, Isaac and Jacob shall receive us, and our forefathers shall praise us.' " (4Macc 13, 9-17 Charles II, p 679).

When it was a matter of realizing the spirituality of faithful obedience and devotion during great affliction, it did not matter whether this was linked to a furnace story with the three young men, with the Maccabaean family of martyrs, or with Abraham. The legend of the fiery furnace preserved in Pseudo-Philo and connected with Abraham corresponds to similar stories during the time of the Seleucid persecution (Dan 3) and about the time of Christ (4Macc). These legends are also interpreted in the same spiritual way as the narrative in Gen 22. The story of Abraham, who was willing to sacrifice his only beloved son, is therefore only one of the many expressions to emphasize an obedient and devout attitude of life in severe affliction.

There is a direct line leading from Dan 3 to Dan 6. The legend of Daniel in the lion's den and his miraculous deliverance demonstrates the same spiritual, time-conditioned, and salvation history background as that of the three young men in the furnace. The story of the lion's den breathes the same trusting obedience of faith and devotion. Here too the main theme of the narrative involves a testing and delivering God (see

Dan 6, 21-24). Moreover, an angel of the Lord appears as the messenger of the merciful redeeming God (Dan 6, 23) just as in Gen 22, 11f and in Dan 3, 25.28. In Fourth Maccabees this connection between Daniel in the lion's den and the Maccabean martyrs is noted (16, 3f).

This posture of faithful obedience (or faithfulness to the Law which, in the last analysis, means the same thing) and devotion was, in the time of the Maccabees, the most decisive and fiercely defended religious attitude in Judaism. This is borne out not only by the contemporary interpretations of Gen 22 and by the legends of the three young men in the furnace and Daniel in the lion's den. A whole series of narratives which either originated during the Maccabean period or became significant at that time contain this spirituality. To these, for instance, belong the Book of Esther (especially in its Greek form), the Book of Judith (see especially Judith 8, 11-36), the story of the chaste Susanna (Dan 13, 1-64) and the legend of Heliodorus (2Macc 3). From these and other stories a short and direct path leads to Jesus Christ who sacrificed himself obediently as the Son of Abraham and as a Jewish martyr in order to do his Father's will (see Mark 14, 32-42 par).

NOTES

1. The latest, most comprehensive and, for me, available research has been done by Robert J. Daly, "The Soteriological Significance of the Sacrifice of Isaac" *CBQ* 39 (1977) p 45-75. See P. R. Davies and B. D. Chilton, "The Aqedah: a revised tradition history," *CBQ* 40 (1978) p 514-546.

2. In the early fifties, Shalom Spiegel steered the Jewish researchers most emphatically toward the theme of Akedah, especially with this essay: "Meʾaggadot haʿaqedah, The Legend of Isaac's Slaying and Resurrection," *A. Marx, Jubilee Vol.* (New York, 1950, translated by Judah Goldin, *The Last Trial,* New York: Schocken 1969). Further points of investigation are mentioned, for instance, by R. J. Daly.

3. Discoverer and editor is Alejandro Diez Macho *Neophiti 1,* Targum Palestinense MS de la Bibliotheca Vaticana, 4 volumes, Madrid/Barcelona 1968-1974.

4. Compare with Clemens Thoma, *Christliche Theologie des Judentums,* Aschaffenburg: Paul Pattloch 1978 p 144-152. An English translation will be published by Paulist Press.

5. Diez Macho op. cit. (note 3 p 552 English translation). Similarly, CN 1 to Lev 22,27 and Gen R 56, 10 to Gen 22, 14.

6. De Abrahamo 167, quoted from F. H. Colson *Philo* VI (Loeb Classics) p 85.

7. An especially thorough examination of the literary and oral pre-history of Akedah-theology and Akedah-piety found in the Targum and Midrash was made by Roger LeDéaut, *La Nuit Pascale,* Essai sur la signification de la Pâque juive à partir du Targum d'Exode 12,42 (Rome: Pontifical Biblical Institute, 1963). The book by LeDéaut is the first wide-ranging examination of the interpretation-history of Gen 22 and Exod 12, 42 in connection with the discovery of CN 1.

8. Compare with J. van Goudoever, *Biblical Calendars* (Leiden: Brill 1961) esp. p 68.

9. To 2Macc 1, 2-4a as part of a Palestinian communal prayer, compare Y. F. Baer, *Israel among the Nations* (Jerusalem 1955) p 122ff.

10. R. H. Charles (ed) *A. P. O. T.* II p 682.

11. See Christian Habicht, 2 Makkabaerbuch, *Jüdische Schriften aus hellenistisch-römischer Zeit*, Vol. 1 (Gütersloh 1976) p 167-285, esp. p 169-185. The seventh chapter seems to be the last inserted into Second Maccabees.

12. In the latest commentaries on the Book of Daniel the third chapter is touched upon only briefly. In contrast, it is evident that the church fathers and rabbinic Judaism knew how to draw a great deal from the story of the three men in the furnace. They appreciated the exemplary character of the narrative. Modern historical-critical research often has the disadvantage of failing to observe the various levels of meaning inherent in non-historical legends.

13. For the salvation-history meaning of Dan 3 by the Rabbis, see (among others) bSan 92b-93a; for the salvation-history meaning in Gen 22 see (among others) Gen R 56, 2 to Gen 22, 5.

Theology and Poetry in the Liturgy of the Synagogue

JAKOB J. PETUCHOWSKI

Theology, by definition, is the rational discourse about God, and, by extension, the rational discourse about religious matters in general. Man is a rational—though not *only* a rational—creature, and, as such, he is ever striving to verbalize, to rationalize, and to systematize. If God is the highest of which man can conceive, it follows that man not only tends to rationalize and systematize his conceptions of God, but also that he is prone to view his rational discourse about God as the highest form of rational discourse.

Thus it was that, for many centuries, theology could rule man's intellectual endeavors as the Queen of the Sciences. Only in more recent generations did the sciences rebel against their "handmaiden" status and become queens in their own right—queens, moreover, who would not infrequently challenge the "established conclusions" and absolute certainties of their erstwhile mistress, theology.

Theologians may have reacted to the demotion of their discipline with good or ill grace, but, by and large, they were in no doubt about the fact that theology was, at any rate, *one* of the sciences, even if she was no longer *prima inter pares,* let alone the "queen" of all human intellectual enterprises.

Admittedly, the philosophic garb in which theology appeared, and the metaphysical weapons with which she defended herself, changed from time to time—even as the various philosophical systems with which theology periodically aligned herself were subject to the changing intellectual fashions among men. There have been Platonic theologians and Aristotelian theologians, Neo-Platonic theologians and Idealistic theologians, just as, at the present time, we have Existentialist theolo-

Material for this essay has been drawn from several chapters of the author's book *Theology and Poetry:* Studies in the Medieval Poetry, (Boston: Routledge & Kegan Paul 1978). The publisher has granted permission to use it.

gians as well as theologians who accept the limitations placed on them by Logical Positivism.

However, in all of those alliances, theologians have not seldom lost sight of the fact that theology is an *interpretative* discipline, rather than itself a primary source of religious knowledge. As the late Samuel S. Cohon has put it: "Theology is to religion what grammar is to speech."[1] Experience, says Cohon, must not be identified with its interpretation.[2]

Yet if theology is rational discourse *about* a primary experience, rather than that experience itself, we are faced by the problem whether rational discourse can really do full justice to the primary experience. What if the experience transcends the capacity of rational language? What if it involves aspects of the human personality which lie beneath the level of consciousness? What, finally, if, by its definition, the very subject matter of theology eludes the human grasp?

In that case, we would have to admit that, far from dealing with clearly definable data as the physical sciences do, or with the type of analytical mental constructs which form the subject matter of metaphysics, theology is compelled to rely on *intimations*. When we speak of something *of* which we only have hints and intimations, we can speak of it likewise only *in* hints and intimations. We can allude to it, and we can suggest it; but we can hardly formulate it in propositions which will pass muster before the bar of logical rigor. We had, therefore, best express it in the images and nuances of poetry.

It has actually been suggested by Walter Kaufmann that the theologian should regard himself as dealing with poetry, rather than with science and metaphysics.[3] Although Kaufman holds that "religion is poetry, but not 'mere' poetry," and, as such, he is able to appreciate religion, his words are nevertheless those of a severe critic of the whole theological enterprise as it has thus far been conducted. They have, therefore, had little perceptible impact upon the professional theologians. Yet, to suggest the link between theology and poetry does not necessarily always mean that the work of the theologian is not being appreciated.

Approaching the subject from quite a different perspective, the late Henry Slonimsky has argued that "whatever in philosophy is capable of translation or transformation into poetry is alone vital and valuable; and . . . whatever has originally been conceived as myth is alone real and effective, for it is something capable of being believed and therefore loved."[4] It is interesting to note in this connection that Slonimsky was writing as a philosopher, rather than as a theologian—which, perhaps, makes his evaluation of myth and poetry even more striking.

There is no reason why the theologian, too, could not admit—while making no apologies for the fact that there *are* times and situations when rational discourse about God and religion is both wholesome and inescapable—that the data with which theology is working are data derived from the realm of poetry and myth. Nor is there any reason for him to deny that only those elements of his theological system which can be translated and transformed into poetry will retain their value and their vitality.

This, in fact, is what has always happened in Judaism. By the side of its technical theological tractates, Judaism has had its prayerbook—next to the Pentateuch, the Prophets and the Psalms, practically the only "theological" *vade mecum* which many Jews, throughout the centuries, have had at their immediate disposal. And the language of prayer is, of necessity, the language of poetry.

Theological systems may come and go; but the theology which is translatable into liturgy remains. Maimonides' need to square his Judaism with his Aristotelianism may be a need which, at any rate, in those specific terms, is no longer felt. But the poetic recasting of Maimonides' theological propositions, the hymn, *Yigdal*, is still a part of Jewish worship today. The peculiar theology of the German Jewish Pietists of the twelfth and thirteenth centuries, with its near-Gnostic distinction between the Hidden God and the Glory of God accessible to man, is a theology shared by few, if any, modern Jews. But the *Shir Hakabhod*, to which that theology gave birth, continues to be sung in the synagogue. Here are a few stanzas of it:

אֲסַפְּרָה כְבוֹדְךָ וְלֹא רְאִיתִיךָ, אֲדַמְּךָ אֲכַנְּךָ וְלֹא יְדַעְתִּיךָ.

Your glory I shall tell, though I have never seen you.
I know not what you are, but image can describe you.

טַלְלֵי אוֹרוֹת רֹאשׁוֹ נִמְלָא, וּקְוֻצּוֹתָיו רְסִיסֵי לָיְלָה.

His head replete with saving dew of light,
His curls still wet with dewdrops of the night.

כֶּתֶם טָהוֹר פָּז דְּמוּת רֹאשׁוֹ, וְחַק עַל מֵצַח כְּבוֹד שֵׁם קָדְשׁוֹ.

The image of his head appears like fine pure gold;
Engraved upon his brow, his holy name is told.

מַחְלְפוֹת רֹאשׁוֹ כְּבִימֵי בְחֻרוֹת, קְוֻצּוֹתָיו תַּלְתַּלִּים שְׁחוֹרוֹת.

His head of plaited hair like that of youthful time;
His locks flow in black curls as they do in one's prime.

בִּרְכָתִי תַעֲלֶה לְרֹאשׁ מַשְׁבִּיר, מְחוֹלֵל וּמוֹלִיד צַדִּיק כַּבִּיר.

My blessing, may it now ascend to God who all sustains,
Creator, Father, Righteous One, Almighty he remains.[5]

The medieval German Jewish Pietists subscribed to as radical a "negative theology" as did Maimonides. But that was with reference to God himself. When it came to the Glory of God, their anthropomorphic exuberance seemed to know no bounds.

If poetry is the medium through which "normative" theology ("normative" at least for its time and place) best expresses itself, then poetry becomes a still more fitting medium for the expression of theological views which, even if they are not fully heretical, nevertheless represent a challenge to what has become normative and conventional. We are, of course, not speaking of the kind of heresy which is a downright denial of fundamental religious principles, but of the kind of "argument with God" which is one, though by no means the sole, posture typical of the Jew's relation to the Deity. We mean the challenge hurled at God—in prayer.

Statements and arguments which, in prose, would immediately be branded as "heretical," have become, once they were couched in poetic form, ingredients of the liturgy, and continue to be rehearsed—often with more devotion than comprehension—by multitudes of the unsuspecting pious who would be utterly shocked to discover the true intent of their authors.

Take, for example, a liturgical Passover poem by the Spanish Jewish poet-philosopher, Judah Halevi (born before 1075, died in 1141). On the face of it, the poem is a thanksgiving hymn, commemorating the passing through the Sea of Reeds. But it is also an argument against God, a very daring one, at that, claiming that, on account of their faithful observance of the rituals of fringes and circumcision, the Jews *deserve* their redemption from the current exile. This represents quite a contrast to the usual medieval submission to exile and persecution because "we were exiled on account of our sins." Here are a few stanzas of Judah Halevi's poem:

My banners you will raise again	דְּגָלַי כֵּן תָּרִים.
Over the people that remain.	עַל הַנִּשְׁאָרִים.
You'll gather those dispersed in scorn	וּתְלַקֵּט נִפְזָרִים.
Like one who gathers sheaves of corn.	כִּמְלַקֵּט שִׁבֳּלִים.
Your cov'nant's sign they proudly bear,	הַבָּאִים עִמָּךְ.
As with you the old pact they share;	בִּבְרִית חוֹתָמָךְ.
And, from their mother's womb still fresh,	וּמִבֶּטֶן לְשִׁמָךְ.
Your signet's cut into their flesh.	הֵמָּה נְמוֹלִים.
Their tokens you may show to all	הַרְאֵה אוֹתוֹתָם.
Whose eyes upon your people fall.	לְכָל רוֹאֵי אוֹתָם.
To their garb's corners, four to match,	וְעַל כַּנְפֵי כְסוּתָם.
They faithfully the cords attach.	יַעֲשׂוּ גְדִילִים.

Inscribed is this at whose behest?	לְמִי זֹאת נִרְשֶׁמֶת.
Discern now; have the truth confessed:	הַכֶּר נָא דְבַר אֱמֶת.
Who may the signet's owner be?	לְמִי הַחֹתֶמֶת.
And who can claim the cords from me?	וּלְמִי הַפְּתִילִים.

Then marry her as once before,	וְשׁוּב שֵׁנִית לְקַדְּשָׁהּ.
Not to divorce her as of yore.	וְאַל תּוֹסִיף לְגָרְשָׁהּ.
And let arise her sun's bright light,	וְהַעֲלֵה אוֹר שִׁמְשָׁהּ.
Putting her shadows to the flight.[6]	וְנָסוּ הַצְּלָלִים.

What makes this poem so particularly daring is the fact that, for the ritual fringes and for circumcision, Halevi uses some unusual circumlocutions. In fact, he borrows his terminology from the thirty-eighth chapter of Genesis. There, the story is told of how Judah failed to keep his promise to his daughter-in-law, Tamar. She thereupon disguised herself as a harlot, and had Judah lie with her. Judah, unable to pay immediately for the favors of the night, leaves a pledge: his cord, his signet, and his staff. When Judah sent a messenger to redeem the pledge, the "harlot" could no longer be found. After some months, the patriarch is told that his daughter-in-law is with child. He summons her, accuses her of infidelity, and condemns her to be burnt. At that point, Tamar produces the staff, the signet and the cord, and informs Judah that the owner of those items is the father of her unborn child. Whereupon Judah, recalling his broken promise, confesses: "She is more righteous than I." By using the vocabulary of Genesis 38, and Tamar's challenge to Judah, Halevi has cast Israel in the role of Tamar, and God in the role of Judah. The implication here is that Israel has a rightful claim on God.

Again, Isaac bar Shalom, a German Jewish poet who was a contemporary of the persecutions of the year 1147, hurls this challenge at God:

אֵין כָּמוֹךְ בָּאִלְּמִים.
דּוֹמֵם וְשׁוֹתֵק לְמַעֲגִימִים.
צָרֵינוּ רַבִּים קָמִים.
בְּהִוָּסְדָם יַחַד לְנַדְּפֵנוּ.
אַיֵּה מַלְכְּכֶם חֵרְפוּנוּ.
לֹא שְׁכַחֲנוּ וְלֹא שִׁקַּרְנוּ.
אַל דֳּמִי לָךְ!

There is none like you among the dumb,
Keeping silence and being still in the face of those who aggrieve us.

Our foes are many; they rise up against us,
As they take counsel together to revile us.
"Where is your King?," they taunt us.
But we have not forgotten you nor deceived you. Do not keep
  silence![7]

While the refrain of this poem is a quotation from Psalm 83,22, and while its daring opening line has talmudic precedent,[8] the combination of the two, together with the detailed description of the destruction of a Jewish community, inserted in the standard prayer which praises God for the liberation from Egyptian bondage, represents one of the most daring and "unorthodox" additions to the traditional liturgy.

It does happen, of course, that, on occasion, the gap between the poet's concern and the "normative" theology of the moment becomes apparent; and then we find purists like Maimonides fulminating against "the truly ignorant poets or such as think that what they speak is poetry," and castigating those poets for composing "vituperative utterances against what is above".[9]

Yet, on the whole, the protests of Maimonides and those who thought like him have been of no avail. Liturgical poems expressing the unconventional and the idiosyncratic continued to share the same prayerbook pages with formulations of the generally accepted and conventional notions of Jewish theology. The conventional and the unconventional shared the same pages of the prayerbook as they had always shared the same pages of the Talmud and of the Midrash—where no uniformity of theological positions was ever enforced nor ecclesiastical control of religious feelings intended. Indeed, novel and startling as some of the ideas expressed by the medieval poets may have been in contrast to what, by the poets' time, had become crystallized as *the* "normative" theology, few, if any, of those ideas were altogether without precedent within the vast reaches of Rabbinic literature.

Two thousand and sixty pages in Israel Davidson's monumental *Thesaurus of Mediaeval Hebrew Poetry*[10] are almost exclusively devoted to a mere bibliographical listing of the medieval synagogal poems, the *piyyutim*. Of course, no single community ever included all of the available poems in its worship services. Indeed, it is clearly one of the dividing lines between one liturgical rite and another that some *piyyutim* are recited and that others are excluded.

Today, by and large, and not excluding many an Orthodox Jewish community, interest in the *piyyutim* has shifted from the synagogue to the classroom and the scholar's study. On the whole, *piyyutim* tend to be more significant as historical documents of an earlier piety than as vehicles of contemporary religious expression. Thus removed from the house of prayer and from nineteenth-century battles about their abolition or retention, the *piyyutim* have begun to be appreciated for the light they can shed on the development of the Hebrew language, on various forms of the triennial cycle of Pentateuchal readings, on historical events, on the relationship of various Jewries to their environments, on the evolution of Jewish liturgy, and on the diversity of theological views sanctioned by Judaism's pluralistic tradition.

While, on occasion, a modern Jewish worshiper may voice the desire for a liturgy which would give expression to a uniform theological position, usually of a non-orthodox kind, it is ironical that the orthodox liturgical tradition stands forth as the classical representative of theological pluralism. It could not have been otherwise. A liturgical compendium which is the product of centuries and millennia, rather than the work of a single man or of a specially appointed committee, must of necessity reflect the manifold changes in religious mood and theological consensus which the vagaries of a long and eventful history have wrought among the Jewish faith-community. Thus it could happen that poems expressing unconventional theological positions became embedded within a framework of standard liturgical formulae speaking in quite different accents.

But this peculiarity of Jewish worship has been in evidence from the very beginning, going back to biblical prayer itself. There is a certain dialectic in classical Jewish prayer, an awareness of tension, of pulls in opposite directions. There is an assertion of the "yet," and of the "even so."

According to 1Kings 8,27-28, Solomon, after he had built the Temple, prayed:

> But will God in very truth dwell on earth?
> Behold, heaven and the heaven of heavens cannot contain you;
> How much less this house that I have built!
> *Yet* have regard unto the prayer of your servant,
> And to his supplication, O Lord my God,
> To hearken unto the cry and unto the prayer
> Which your servant prays before you this day.

Psalm 8 begins by invoking the majesty of God as revealed in his creation; and, in verses 4 to 6, continues with:

> When I behold your heavens, the work of your fingers,
> The moon and the stars that you have set in place,
> What is man that you are mindful of him,
> Mortal man that you take note of him?

Yet you have made him little less than divine,
And adorned him with glory and majesty.

And the well-known *Kaddish* prayer presents a veritable thesaurus of praises of God—in full awareness of man's inability to praise God adequately:

Blessed and praised,
Glorified and exalted,
Extolled and honored,
Magnified and lauded
Be the name of the Holy One, praised be he—
Although he transcends all the blessings and hymns,
Praises and consolations,
Which can be uttered in the world.

It is, then, in this tradition that the author of the *Shir Hakabhod* can say:

אֲסַפְּרָה כְבוֹדְךָ וְלֹא רְאִיתִיךָ, אֲדַמְּךָ אֲכַנְּךָ וְלֹא יְדַעְתִּיךָ.

Your glory I shall tell, though I have never seen you.
I know not what you are, but image can describe you.

On a more daring level, Isaac bar Shalom not only declares, "There is none like you among the dumb!", but he meant his gruesome description of the destruction of a medieval Jewish community to be inserted in that part of the liturgy where God is celebrated as Israel's Redeemer. The prayerbook proclaims:

True it is that you are the Lord our God and the God of our
    fathers,
Our King, our fathers' King,
Our Redeemer, our fathers' Redeemer,
Our Maker, the Rock of our salvation,
Our Deliverer and our Rescuer,
Your name is from eternity;
There is no God beside you.[11]

But just before the prayerbook goes on to say:

You have been the help of our fathers from of old,
A Shield and a Savior to their children after them,
In every single generation,[12]

Isaac bar Shalom cries out: "There is none like you among the dumb!", and tells his tale of woe.

Something of that kind of contrapuntal effect was attempted in a Conservative prayerbook, recently published in the United States. In the *Kaddish*, the doxology *par excellence*, which concludes the martyrology of the Additional Service of the Day of Atonement, each phrase is coupled with the name of a place notorious for the pogroms and for the genocide committed there:

Yithgaddal	— Kishinev,
Veyithqaddash	— Warsaw,
Shemeh rabba	— Auschwitz,
etc.[13]	

Here we have affirmation of faith which suffering cannot destroy, and, at the same time, a piety profound enough to allow for accusations hurled against God. Isaac bar Shalom no doubt attempted something very similar in the twelfth century.

Such contrapuntal effects and such juxtapositions of opposites all presuppose a considerable intellectual effort on the part of the worshipper. Thought is required as well as devotion, analysis and synthesis in addition to enthusiastic faith.

As long as they were still understood, the synagogal poems catered to that intellectual component of the Jewish worship experience. The charge often brought against the *piyyutim* in the nineteenth century, that they are difficult to comprehend, and that much biblical and Rabbinic learning was required for their proper understanding, is a charge to which their authors would certainly have pleaded guilty—and with pride. The modern worshipper and even many a modern student may wish to denigrate and to dismiss those poems as "riddles." But it was Eleazar Hakallir, one of the major founders of that art, who joyfully and intentionally *introduced* the *piyyutim* as such. He begins his poetic treatment of the Prayer for Dew on the first day of Passover by saying:

בְּדֵעְתּוֹ אַבִּיעָה חִידוֹת, בְּעַם זוּ בְּזוּ בְּטַל לְהַחֲדוֹת.

With God's approval, I shall utter riddles (*ḥiddoth!*)
To make happy this people in this service
With the prayer for dew.[14]

Perhaps, unlike his ancestors, the modern Jew goes to his synagogue primarily—if not exclusively—for the purpose of edification. He relegates the aesthetic and intellectual joys of "problem solving" to the crossword puzzle in his daily newspaper. The medieval synagogue was more comprehensive. It made "problem solving" and other intellectual "games" a part of the total worship experience. Many of the *piyyutim*,

232 STANDING BEFORE GOD

the theologies recited and sung as poetry, remain as eloquent witnesses of this—products of mind and heart, of thought and of faith.

NOTES

1. Samuel S. Cohon, *Jewish Theology* (Assen, 1971) p 2.
2. Ibid., p 1.
3. Walter Kaufmann, *Critique of Religion and Philosophy* (New York, 1958) p 163-173.
4. Henry Slonimsky, *Essays* (Chicago, 1967) p. 62.
5. Hebrew text in Philip Birnbaum, ed, *Daily Prayer Book.* New York, 1949, p 415-419. My translation.
6. Hebrew text in *Sabbath and Festival Prayer Book* (New York: The Rabbinical Assembly of America and The United Synagogue of America, 1947) p 184. My translation.
7. Hebrew text in *Siddur Otzar Hatephilloth* (Vilna, 1914) Vol. II, p 256. My translation.
8. Cf. bGittin 56b.
9. Moses Maimonides, *Guide of the Perplexed* (tr. Shlomo Pines, Chicago, 1963) p 137-143.
10. Israel Davidson, *Thesaurus of Mediaeval Hebrew Poetry* (2nd edition. New York, 1970) 4 volumes.
11. Hebrew text in Birnbaum, op. cit., p 347. My translation.
12. Ibid.
13. *Mahzor for Rosh Hashanah and Yom Kippur* (ed Jules Harlow. New York: The Rabbinical Assembly, 1972) p 566.
14. Hebrew text in Birnbaum, op. cit., p 633. My translation.

The Church of Jerusalem and the Christian Calendar

RICHARD MORTON NARDONE

Of the various church calendars used throughout the Christian world, those of the Roman and Byzantine churches are particularly important in the history of Christian worship. These calendars were themselves influenced by that of the mother church of Jerusalem, first during the apostolic age and later during the Byzantine period. After the destruction of Jerusalem in the two Jewish Wars (A.D. 66-70 and 132-135), the Judaeo-Christian bishops of Jerusalem were replaced by Gentiles and the church itself became a Gentile community.[1] For two hundred years it survived in obscurity, overshadowed by the great churches of Antioch, Rome, and Alexandria, and even the nearby church of Caesarea. It was restored to greatness after the triumph of Christianity in the fourth century, when pilgrims came from all over the world to visit the splendid shrines built over the Christian holy places. The Council of Nicaea in 325 recognized the historical importance of the city, and in 451 the Council of Chalcedon gave the bishop of Jerusalem patriarchal rights over all Palestine.[2] The Christian ascendancy ended with the Arab conquest in 638, except for the twelfth-century Latin kingdom (1099-1187).

The two oldest elements in the Christian calendar, the Sunday eucharist and the Easter festival, date from the apostolic age. It is a reasonable assumption that the Jerusalem church, from the very beginning, celebrated the Sunday eucharist in memory of the death and resurrection of Jesus and in anticipation of his coming in glory. The New Testament is not very informative, but we are told that St. Paul took part in the "breaking of bread" on the first day of the week when he visited the Christians at Troas, in the province of Asia (Acts 20,7). There are a few other references to the breaking of bread (Acts 2,42) or Lord's supper (1Cor 11,20), and St. Paul mentions a collection for the Jerusalem

233

church "on the first day of every week" (1Cor 16,2). Sunday therefore came to be known as "the Lord's day" (Rev 1,10).

The Christians celebrated the eucharist on Sunday because, as all the Gospels carefully note, it was the day of the Lord's resurrection.[3] Jungmann points out that the evangelists "otherwise never indicate the day of the week on which an event took place (unless they are calling attention to a dispute about the Sabbath)".[4] We are told in the *Didache:* "On the Lord's day come together, break bread, and hold eucharist" (xiv). It is sometimes called the eighth day, to signify that a new age has begun.[5] The First Apology of Justin Martyr, addressed to pagans, used the common term Sunday, and gave two reasons for the celebration of the eucharist on that day: it was the day when God created the universe and when Jesus rose from the dead (*Apol.* 67).

What connection, if any, does the Christian Sunday have with the Jewish Sabbath? Christian worship certainly has its roots in Judaism.[6] But there is no evidence of any attempt, prior to the fourth century, to transfer the Sabbath rest from the seventh day of the week to the first day. The Jewish Sabbath was either abandoned along with the other Jewish holy days, or else it continued to be observed in addition to the Sunday eucharist.[7] Tertullian mentions rather scornfully that even the pagans were beginning to imitate the Jews by making Saturday a day of leisure.[8] But judging from the anti-Jewish polemic of the early Christian writers, it seems likely that most Gentile Christians made a point of *not* resting from work on the Sabbath, assuming that they had any choice in the matter. The observance of the Sabbath finally became a peculiarity of the Judaeo-Christians and the Ebionites. According to Eusebius, the latter "observed the Sabbath and the whole Jewish system; yet on the Lord's day they celebrated rites similar to our own in memory of the Saviour's resurrection."[9]

But if there was no *direct* connection between the Jewish Sabbath and the Christian Sunday, the very fact that Christian worship was organized on a weekly basis shows the influence of the weekly Sabbath. The seven-day week was distinctively Jewish. It was introduced in the Roman world at the beginning of the Christian era, partly by the Jews of the diaspora and partly by the astrologers who assigned to each day its governing planet: Sun, Moon, Mars, Mercury, Jupiter, Venus, and Saturn.[10] The Christian church had no use for astrology, and not much use for the Sabbath, but the weekly eucharist betrayed its Jewish roots. Inevitably the Christian Lord's day became a day of rest as well as a day of worship. In the year 321 Constantine ordered the closing of the law courts and places of business on "the venerable day of the Sun," but permitted farmers to do whatever work was necessary.[11] The laws seemed to be concerned more with Sun-worship than Christian worship, but the distinction was probably not yet clear to Constantine.[12] The fourth-century Synod of Laodicea decreed that "Christians must not judaize by resting on the Sabbath, but must work on that day, rather honoring the Lord's day and, if they can, resting then as Christians" (canon 29). Thus the early church paid its tribute to Judaism, however unwillingly, by transferring the Sabbath rest to the Lord's day.

Evidently the church could not simply ignore the Sabbath; to this day the seventh day of the week is still officially called the Sabbath in the Catholic Church. But the observance of the Sabbath evolved in different ways in the Latin and Greek churches. In the Latin West the Sabbath became a fast day in imitation of the fast on Holy Saturday, the vigil of Easter. Tertullian is the earliest witness to the custom, at the beginning of the third century.[13] The Sabbath fast proved burdensome, however, since Fridays were also fast days, and is no longer observed. In the Greek church the Sabbath became a kind of second Sunday: fasting was forbidden on the Sabbath, as on Sunday, and during Lent the eucharist was permitted only on those two days. In the East the Sabbath was dedicated to the memory of the faithful departed, while in the West it was dedicated to the Virgin Mary.

It could be objected that the observance of Sundays, holy days, and fast days involved a return to ritualism, although these observances seem to be as old as Christianity itself. It is true, nevertheless, that the massive borrowing of Jewish liturgical traditions occurred in the second and third centuries.[14] There is nothing particularly paradoxical about this: the primitive Judaeo-Christian church had no need to borrow from Judaism, since it was itself Jewish. But when Gentile Christianity separated from Judaism, it had to organize its own distinctive forms of worship, and in doing so drew on the liturgical tradition of Israel.

The second element in the primitive Christian calendar was the annual Easter festival, the Christian Passover *(Pascha)*. It was probably celebrated by the apostolic church in Jerusalem, but there seems to be no mention of it in the New Testament. St. Paul was thinking of the Christian life in general when he wrote that: "Christ, our paschal lamb, has been sacrificed. Let us therefore celebrate the festival, not with the old leaven, the leaven of malice and evil, but with the unleavened bread of sincerity and truth" (1Cor 5,7). It seems likely that the Judaeo-Christian community continued to celebrate the Jewish Passover, with the Lord's supper as their paschal meal. After the destruction of the temple and the separation of Christianity from Judaism, it became a distinctively Christian festival, but was still called the *Pascha*.[15]

When the Easter controversy broke out a hundred years later, the

Christians in the province of Asia were still celebrating the feast on the same day as the Jews; they claimed that they had received this tradition from the Jerusalem church, specifically from Philip the evangelist and John the apostle.[16] The Roman church had also adopted the feast, but kept it on the following Sunday. Evidently the feast in Asia was primarily a memorial of the death of Christ, while the Roman feast celebrated the Resurrection. There had been some difficulty about this in the year 155, when Polycarp, the bishop of Smyrna, visited Rome to discuss some minor differences with Pope Anicetus. It is possible that the feast had not yet been adopted in Rome, and was only introduced under Soter, the successor to Anicetus. Pope Victor, the bishop of Rome from 189 to 199, required all the churches to follow the Roman custom and threatened to excommunicate the churches of Asia when Polycrates, the bishop of Ephesus, refused to comply. The bishops of Palestine, however, assured Victor that they were already in agreement with Rome. They added, "We may point out to you that in Alexandria they keep the feast on the same day as we do, for we send letters to them and they to us, to ensure that we keep the holy day in harmony and at the same time."[17]

Given the traditional conservatism of the Roman church, it is highly probable that the rest of the Christian world was already celebrating Easter, either on the Jewish Passover or on the following Sunday, before Rome adopted it. Rome naturally preferred a Sunday celebration, since every Sunday was a memorial of the Resurrection; the custom of the churches of Asia must have seemed strange and alien. In fact the only real difference between Easter Sunday and any other Sunday was the preparatory fast, and that is precisely what our sources mention. Irenaeus, the bishop of Lyons, told Victor: "The dispute is not only about the day, but also about the actual character of the fast. Some think that they ought to fast for one day, some for two, others for still more."[18] Originally, the only question was whether the churches of Asia should celebrate a feast on the Jewish Passover; Pope Anicetus did not approve. As Irenaeus put it: Polycarp could not persuade Anicetus to keep the Passover, and Anicetus could not persuade Polycarp *not* to keep it. But when Victor became bishop of Rome, Easter Sunday was observed with a preparatory fast of one or two days, or even longer. Only the churches of Asia ended their fast on the Jewish Passover, which could fall on any day of the week. That meant that in most years they would not be fasting with the rest of the Christian world. And according to Eusebius, "it was improper to end the fast on any day other than that of our Saviour's resurrection."[19] It was the conflict in fast days that caused the controversy.

A few years later, about A.D. 200, Tertullian proposed Easter Sunday or Pentecost Sunday as the most suitable day for baptism: "However, every day is the Lord's. Every hour, every time is suitable for baptism."[20] The association of baptism with Easter would profoundly affect the Paschal liturgy of Rome, but there is no reason to think of it as primitive. Hippolytus of Rome, about A.D. 215, gave a detailed description of the baptismal rites: the candidates fasted on Friday and Saturday, kept a vigil on Saturday night, and were baptized early on Sunday morning. But there does not seem to be any reference to Easter, despite the titles added by Gregory Dix in his translation.[21] Hippolytus does mention Easter further on in his treatise, but in connection with fasting, not baptism. Before Easter there should be a fast of two days, or one day for the sick and pregnant women, who may take bread and water if necessary.[22] This agrees exactly with the emphasis on fasting in the Easter controversy.

The date of Easter was originally determined by the date of the Jewish Passover, but the Jews did not achieve uniformity in their religious calendar until the fourth century. During the early Christian period the Jewish communities in the diaspora sometimes kept the Passover on different dates. The Christian churches therefore tried to work out their own Paschal calendars. Hippolytus of Rome devised a Paschal calendar beginning with the year 222; it was not accurate. In 314 the Council of Arles decreed that Easter should be celebrated on the same date throughout the world and, "as is customary", the bishop of Rome should notify the other churches.[23] Evidently the decree was not effective, and so in 325 the Council of Nicaea again called for uniformity, based on the Roman and Alexandrian dates. Unfortunately, Rome and Alexandria did not always agree in their calculations. Constantine's letter to the bishops on the subject was violently anti-Jewish: "We desire, dearest brethren, to separate ourselves from the detestable company of the Jews, for it is truly shameful for us to hear them boast that without their direction we could not keep the feast."[24] He claimed that uniformity already existed among the churches of the West, South, North, and "some of those of the East". He named Asia, Pontus, and Cilicia among the conforming churches, but not Syria and Palestine.

The churches of Syria and Palestine officially ratified the Nicene decree at the Council of Antioch in 341, and ordered excommunication for anyone who celebrated the Paschal feast on the same day as the Jews.[25] Rome and Alexandria tried, without much success, to settle their differences over the Paschal computations. Uniformity was finally achieved in the sixth century, except in the Celtic fringe, where a different usage persisted into the ninth century. The introduction of the

Gregorian calendar in the sixteenth century divided the churches once again, a problem still not resolved.

For three centuries the Christian calendar consisted of nothing more than the Sunday eucharist, with a special Pentecost season of fifty days from Easter Sunday to Pentecost Sunday. Tertullian wrote, around A.D. 200, "We do not permit fasting or kneeling in worship on the Lord's day. We rejoice in the same privilege from Easter to Pentecost."[26] In 325 the Council of Nicaea (canon 20) ordered all churches to enforce the rule against kneeling on Sundays and during the Easter season. The fifth canon of Nicaea mentions, for the first time, a Lenten season of forty days; it did not necessarily mean forty days of fasting. In 339 the church of Egypt had not yet adopted the Lenten fast when Athanasius, the exiled bishop of Alexandria, sent a Paschal Letter from Rome to Bishop Serapion: "You should proclaim the fast of forty days to the brethren and persuade them to fast lest, while all the world is fasting, we who are in Egypt should be derided as the only people who do not fast."[27]

In addition, the churches observed the anniversaries of their local martyrs on fixed days of the year, according to the Roman civil calendar. These anniversaries were kept at least from the second century, when the *Martyrdom of Polycarp* listed St. Polycarp as the twelfth martyr of the church of Smyrna, gave the date of his death (February 23), and announced that services would be held on "the birthday of his martyrdom".[28] The Roman church, as usual, was more conservative; the cult of martyrs there seems to date from the mid-third century. Even the anniversaries of St. Peter and St. Paul were not recorded, and the reason for their feast on June 29 is somewhat conjectural.[29] The famous Roman calendar of the fourth century had 24 entries, including a memorial of the birth of Christ on December 25.[30] The martyrs listed were all Roman, except the African saints Perpetua and Felicity, and Cyprian of Carthage. Obviously only a few names were preserved out of the vast numbers of Christians martyred in Rome during the centuries of persecution. But the cult of martyrs required not only the name of the martyr, but also the date of death and the place of burial.

The little church of Jerusalem had only a few martyrs, but it had a much greater claim to glory: the tomb of Christ himself. Eusebius, the bishop of Caesarea in Palestine, described how Constantine and his mother, St. Helena, ordered the building of a great shrine over the Holy Sepulchre, and other churches on the Mount of Olives and in Bethlehem.[31] At the Holy Sepulchre there were actually two churches: a basilica known as the Martyrium, and behind it a circular church over the tomb itself, known as the *Anastasis*. Calvary, the place of the

Crucifixion, was in an open court between the two buildings. The shrine was dedicated in the year 335.

Sometime around the year 400 a pilgrim to the Holy Land, probably a Spanish nun, wrote a description of the Jerusalem liturgy known as the *Pilgrimage of Etheria.*[32] According to Etheria, the Dedication of the Holy Sepulchre was celebrated as a major feast day, on a par with the great feasts of Easter and Epiphany.[33] Each of these festivals was celebrated for eight days in imitation of the dedication of the temple by Hezekiah and by Judas Maccabeus (2Chr 29,17; 1Macc 4,56). The observance of a dedication feast became customary for all Christian churches, and in homage to the mother church, the feast of the Dedication of the Holy Sepulchre was added to the Byzantine calendar, on September 13. It was not added to the Roman calendar, and in fact it was only in the eleventh century that the Roman church began to celebrate the dedication of its own great basilicas.

When Etheria visited Jerusalem, the dedication feast also commemorated the Finding of the Holy Cross.[34] Fifty years earlier, Cyril, the bishop of Jerusalem, had mentioned the discovery of the Cross of Christ during the reign of Constantine.[35] Etheria saw the relics of the Cross displayed on Good Friday, when they were exposed for the veneration of the faithful.[36] Stories were already in circulation that the Cross had been discovered by St. Helena under miraculous circumstances.[37] Eusebius, however, in his *Life of Constantine*, wrote a detailed description of the building and dedication of the Holy Sepulchre without any mention of the finding of the Cross. The Western feast of the Finding of the Holy Cross, on May 3, removed from the Roman calendar in 1960, was based on the legend of St. Helena.

The feast of the Holy Cross on September 14 was added to all the Christian calendars. It reached the West in the seventh century, but there it was associated with a more recent event, the recovery of the Cross by the Emperor Heraclius. The Persians had captured Jerusalem in 614, destroyed the church of the Holy Sepulchre, and carried off the relics of the Cross. Heraclius invaded Persia, recovered the Cross, and returned it to Jerusalem in 629. The church of the Holy Sepulchre was destroyed a second time by Caliph Hakim in 1009. Restoration began immediately after the capture of Jerusalem by the Crusaders in 1099 and was completed fifty years later, on July 15, 1149. The Franciscans, who were given custody of the Latin shrines in the Holy Land, added the feast of the rededication to their own calendar.

The feast of the Apparition of the Sign of the Cross, added to the Byzantine calendar on May 7, commemorates a phenomenon described by Cyril of Jerusalem. In a letter to the Emperor Constantius he reported that a huge luminous cross had appeared in the sky over Jerusalem, extending from Golgotha to the Mount of Olives. It was seen at about nine in the morning, and remained visible for several hours. Cyril chose to interpret it as an omen of victory for Constantius in his war with the usurper Magnentius.[38]

It was probably Cyril of Jerusalem who organized the Jerusalem liturgy during his long term of office (c. 350-387).[39] Taking full advantage of the Christian shrines in and around Jerusalem and Bethlehem, he introduced a new historical emphasis in place of the older eschatological type of worship. The whole drama of the birth and death and resurrection of Jesus was reenacted at the very places where these events had originally occurred. But what particularly impressed visitors like Etheria was the selection of psalms, hymns, and scripture readings appropriate to the feast day. Elsewhere, apparently, special readings were used only on Easter Sunday, but soon the whole Christian world was imitating the Jerusalem rites.[40]

Etheria's Jerusalem journal began with a description of the regular daily services in the church of the *Anastasis*.[41] They began at two in the morning with a vigil service attended by monks and nuns from the local monasteries and devout laity. At daybreak the bishop and his clergy arrived for Morning Prayer. The office of Sext was sung at midday, and None at three o'clock, followed by Vespers at four. The office of Terce at nine in the morning was sung only during Lent. On Sundays, at the end of the vigil service the bishop read the gospel of the Resurrection, while censers were brought in for the burning of incense. At daybreak the Sunday eucharist was celebrated in the basilica. There was nothing unusual about it ("fiunt omnia secundum consuetudinem qua et ubique fit die dominica"), except that all the priests present were invited to preach in turn, followed by the bishop's sermon. Afterward everyone except the catechumens went to the church of the *Anastasis* for the thanksgiving ("aguntur gratiae Deo"). Was this a thanksgiving after mass or was it the eucharist itself?[42] In the latter view only the liturgy of the word took place in the basilica. But on Pentecost Sunday it seems that the "offering," i.e., the eucharist, was made in the basilica and this was the normal procedure ("offertur iuxta consuetudinem qua dominica die consuevit fieri").[43]

The church year, as described by Etheria, began with the feast of the Epiphany on January 6.[44] At Jerusalem and Bethlehem the Epiphany was primarily, if not exclusively, a feast of the birth of Christ. It was celebrated with the same solemnity as Easter, and like Easter the festival lasted for eight days. It apparently came from Egypt where, as early as the second century, the Gnostic Christians commemorated the baptism of Jesus at the time of the winter solstice.[45] The Jerusalem church added, on February 14, its own feast of *Hypapante* to commemorate the presentation of Christ in the temple forty days after his birth (Luke 2,22).

Under Constantine the Roman feast of the birth of Christ on December 25 replaced, or at least supplemented, the pagan feast of the Unconquered Sun. Since the Roman church was not much given to innovations, the impetus may have come from Constantine himself.[46] He combined the worship of the sun and of Christ by making Sunday a weekly holiday, and in the same way the great annual feast of the sun could now be legitimately celebrated by Christians. In the East, where the Epiphany was already established, the adoption of Christmas made the Epiphany a feast of the baptism of Christ, as it probably had been originally. During the last quarter of the fourth century the Christmas feast was introduced in Constantinople and Antioch, but Egypt held out until the fifth century. By the sixth century even Jerusalem fell into line; today only the Armenian Church still celebrates Christmas on January 6.

Duchesne thought that the Annunciation on March 25 might have determined the date of Christmas on December 25, rather than vice versa.[47] It was an attractive theory, since it would have brought Christmas into closer relation with the Paschal cycle and freed it from any association with the pagan sun worship. There is, in fact, evidence that as early as the second century some Christians thought that Christ had *died* on March 25.[48] But it was only after the introduction of the Christmas feast that it became the date of the Annunciation. The medieval martyrologies usually listed March 25 as the date of the crucifixion and conception of Christ, and also the creation of the world. Even the modern Roman Martyrology lists March 25 as the feast of the Good Thief who was crucified with Jesus.

Although Jerusalem was the last church to accept the Roman feast of Christmas, it was from Jerusalem that the Roman church borrowed the principal rites surrounding its observance.[49] In the first place, the Epiphany was adopted at Rome as a second Christmas feast, a commemoration of the Magi's visit (Matt 2,1-12). The baptism of Christ, which was the principal theme of the Epiphany in the other Eastern churches, was given only a minor emphasis in the Roman liturgy. Secondly, the Epiphany rites in Palestine were copied in the Christmas rites of the Roman church. In Palestine the bishop of Jerusalem attended the vigil service in the church of the Nativity in Bethlehem, and then returned in procession to Jerusalem for the morning mass in the basilica. In Rome the pope went to St. Mary Major, symbolizing Bethlehem, for the midnight mass, and then went in procession to St. Peter's, symbolizing Jerusalem, for the mass of the day. It may be sheer coincidence that a dawn mass was later (sixth century) added at the *titulus Anastasiae,* a church dedicated either to the Resurrection or to the memory of its foundress.[50]

The feast of the Presentation of Christ in the Temple, celebrated in Jerusalem on February 14, forty days after the Epiphany, was adopted in the other Eastern churches on February 2, forty days after Christmas. It was celebrated in Rome under Pope Sergius I (687-701). Sergius also observed, on March 25, the feast of the Annunciation, which may be connected with the church of the Annunciation in Nazareth. The fifth-century church was built on the site of a Judaeo-Christian "synagogue-church".[51] From Palestine the feast was introduced in Ephesus about the year 500.[52] Previously the Annunciation, or Incarnation, was commemorated during Advent because of the rule against feast days in Lent. The commemoration in Rome was on the first of the Advent Ember Days, in Milan on the last Sunday of Advent, and in Spain on December 18.[53] But in 692 the Council *in Trullo* (canon 52) allowed the feast to be celebrated on March 25 as the only exception to the Lenten rule.

Since the late fourth century the feast of Christmas has been followed by several important saints' days. Originally, as we have seen, the veneration of saints was restricted to the local martyrs, and normally the martyr's name, date of death, and place of burial had to be known.[54] It was simply an anniversary service conducted at the tomb. Before the end of the fourth century, however, a more liberal policy allowed the veneration of saints who were neither local nor martyrs. It then became possible to honor the great saints of the New Testament, even though their anniversaries, and even their tombs, were unknown. The days following Easter would have been suitable for their memorials, and in fact Easter Week was used for that purpose in the church of Mesopotamia.[55] But the Greek and Roman churches preferred to keep all the feasts of the saints on fixed days of the civil calendar. Since Easter was a movable feast, the alternative choice was the octave of Christmas.

Stephen the First Martyr naturally came first, on December 26, although the Eastern churches later gave that honor to the Virgin Mary. The choice of Stephen shows that sainthood was still associated with martyrdom. The next two days were originally assigned to the chief apostles: Peter and Paul, and John and James. These festivals were certainly being celebrated in the year 379, when they were mentioned by Gregory of Nyssa.[56] According to Gregory Dix, they probably originated in Jerusalem, where they could be considered feasts of local saints.[57] But since Christmas was not celebrated in Jerusalem, the place of origin should be Antioch. In Jerusalem it might have been awkward to institute the feast of a local martyr, such as Stephen, when even his tomb was unknown. In the year 415, when the new feasts were being celebrated in Jerusalem, the priest Lucian claimed the discovery of Stephen's remains.[58] The relics were later enshrined in a basilica built by the Empress Eudocia outside the Damascus Gate. The Finding of St. Stephen is commemorated in the Byzantine calendar on August 2; the Roman feast, on August 3, was suppressed in 1960.

The Eastern feast of Sts. Peter and Paul on December 27 or 28 was changed to the Roman date (June 29) by the end of the fifth century. Jerusalem, however, was still keeping the old date in the seventh century.[59] As for John and James, there was some confusion about their identity in the early calendars.[60] John the Apostle or John the Baptist? James the Apostle or James the Lord's brother? (We may pass over the even more complicated question of whether John the Apostle was the same person as John the Evangelist, or whether James the Lord's brother was the same person as James the Less). It is generally assumed that John and James are the sons of Zebedee, but in that case we would expect to find them listed as James and John, as they are in the New Testament.[61] In the Byzantine calendar they are given separate feast days: James on April 30 and John on September 26. James the Lord's brother is commemorated on the Sunday after Christmas and on October 23, and James the Less on October 9. At Rome only John the Apostle was commemorated on December 27; the Roman church had no other feasts of the apostles, except Peter and Paul, until the sixth century. The Calendar of Carthage listed John the Baptist and James the Apostle on December 27, but a Gallican calendar has John the Apostle and James the Lord's brother.[62] To add to the confusion, in modern times the notice in the Syrian Martyrology ("John and James the Apostles in Jerusalem") gave rise to the theory that John had died a martyr's death in Jerusalem.[63]

The feast of the Holy Innocents (Matt 2,16) was instituted somewhat later, in the fifth century. It was celebrated in the West on December 28 and in the East on the following day. It was only a minor feast day in the Roman church until 1568, when it was given the same rank as the preceding days.

Etheria's journal, after describing the festivals of the Epiphany and the Presentation, continues with the "Paschal days" in Jerusalem, that is, the seasons of Lent and Easter. Etheria was used to the Western custom of fasting on all the weekdays of Lent, including Saturdays. But in Jerusalem there was no fasting on Saturdays or Sundays (except Holy Saturday), and therefore Lent began eight weeks before Easter so that there could be forty days of fasting. The manner of fasting was left up to the individual. Some heroic souls ate nothing at all from Monday to Friday, some ate only once or twice, and some had a meal every evening. The usual daily offices were sung in the church of the *Anastasis*, with an additional office of Terce at nine in the morning.

During the Great Week, as it was called, the services in Jerusalem were held at the appropriate sites. On the Saturday before Palm Sunday, after the morning eucharist, everyone went to Bethany two miles outside the city. They visited the two churches there, marking the place where Martha and Mary went out to meet Jesus and the place where Lazarus was buried (John 11,1-45). The story of the raising of Lazarus was read, and then the beginning of the next chapter: "Six days before the Passover Jesus came to Bethany, etc. " (John 12,1-11). In the Byzantine rite this is still called the Saturday of Lazarus and the same pericope is read. In the Roman rite, however, it was formerly read during the fourth week of Lent and is now assigned to the Fifth Sunday of Lent (in a three-year cycle).

On Palm Sunday the eucharist was celebrated in the morning as usual, but in the afternoon special services were held at the churches on the Mount of Olives. Then the bishop was escorted back to the city in a procession with palm branches. The Palm Sunday procession was imitated in the other Eastern churches, reaching the West in the eighth and ninth centuries, and was finally accepted in Rome. In the West, however, the procession was held before the morning mass instead of after it. At Rome the palms were first blessed at St. Mary Major and then the procession went to the Lateran Basilica for the mass of the day.[64]

On the following Tuesday night services were held on the Mount of Olives, at the place where Jesus gave the discourse that immediately precedes the Passion narrative (Matt 24 and 25). The Gospel was read by the bishop himself. On Wednesday night, in the church of the *Anastasis*, the reading of the Passion was begun with the story of the betrayal of Jesus by Judas Iscariot: "There is such a moaning and groaning of all the people that no one can help being moved to tears."[65] In the Byzantine rite the same passages from the Gospel of Matthew are still read on these days of Holy Week.

On Thursday afternoon, according to Etheria, the eucharist was celebrated in the basilica. The bishop then offered a mass in the church of Golgotha, where all received communion. It seems that there was a church or chapel "behind the Cross" on the south side of the basilica, used for mass only on this day of the year. It also appears from Etheria's account that on other days not everyone who attended mass received communion. On the Saturdays in Lent, for example, she observed that "all who wish to do so receive communion on that day in the *Anastasis*."[66] But why was the eucharist, on the night of the Last Supper, celebrated at Golgotha and not at the Cenacle? The choice of Golgotha is obvious enough: the eucharistic sacrifice was closely linked with the sacrifice of the Cross. On the other hand, in Etheria's time the place now known as the Cenacle (dining room) was simply called Zion. The church there marked the site of the "upper room" where the apostles received the Holy Spirit on the first Pentecost (Acts 1,13). It was venerated as the mother of all Christian churches, and services were held there at Pentecost and on other occasions. It is reasonable to suppose that the Last Supper was held in the same "upper room" (Mark 14,15; Luke 22,12), but originally that was not the focus of attention. Later traditions made it the place where the Virgin Mary died and where King David was buried.[67]

On Thursday night an extraordinary vigil service was held at the churches on the Mount of Olives, beginning at sunset and ending at sunrise on Friday. The last part of the vigil took place at Gethsemane, where the story of the arrest of Jesus was read and the lamentations of the people "may be heard perhaps as far as the city."[68] On Friday morning they went to the Zion church to pray at the column where Jesus was scourged, and then to the church of Golgotha to venerate the relics of the Cross. From noon to three o'clock the services continued in the open courtyard, ending with the account of the death of Jesus in St. John's Gospel. Vespers followed in the basilica, and then the story of the burial of Jesus was read at the tomb in the church of the *Anastasis*. The office of the Burial of Christ in the Byzantine rite is a development of the Jerusalem liturgy.

There was no vigil service on Friday night; by then many of the worshippers must have been exhausted. But the church of the *Anastasis* was kept open through the night, and Etheria reported that a great crowd remained in the church, singing hymns and antiphons until morning. On Saturday the usual offices of Terce and Sext were celebrated, but there were no afternoon services. Etheria described the Easter Vigil as basically similar to what she was used to in the West, except that the bishop led the newly baptized (the *infantes)* from the baptistry to the church of the *Anastasis,* and then to the basilica where the congregation was waiting. After the Easter mass they all went to the *Anastasis,* the Gospel of the Resurrection was read, and the bishop offered a second mass, said quickly, "for the sake of the people" ("et denuo ibi offeret episcopus; sed totum ad momentum fit propter populum, ne diutius tardetur").[69] In the evening, after Vespers, there was a procession to the Zion Church, the site of the upper room where Jesus appeared to his disciples after his resurrection (John 20,19-25). The appropriate text from the Gospel was read, with hymns and prayers.

Except for the Easter Vigil, the Roman church at the beginning of the fifth century had nothing comparable to these elaborate Holy Week ceremonies. The St. Matthew Passion was read on the Sunday before Easter, and for all practical purposes that took care of Holy Week. On the usual station days, Wednesday and Friday, there was a service of readings and prayers. The only special service, therefore, was the Easter Vigil and even that was a very simple affair: readings and prayers, followed by baptisms and the Easter mass.[70] The lighting and blessing of the paschal candle was already customary in the other Western churches, including the churches of Italy, but at Rome, according to Baumstark, the blessing of the paschal candle was still unknown in the ninth century.[71] The Mass of the Lord's Supper on Holy Thursday was one of the earliest additions to the Roman *ordo* of Holy Week; it had already been introduced in the African church by the late fourth century.[72] The ancient readings for the Easter Vigil (Hosea 6 and Exodus 12) were transferred to Good Friday, and were replaced by the long series of readings from the Old Testament in the Jerusalem liturgy.[73] By the seventh or eighth century the adoration of the Cross took place on Good Friday in imitation of the Jerusalem rite, and communion from the reserved sacrament was permitted, at first in the parish churches and finally in the papal liturgy itself.[74] The adoration of the Cross may have come to Rome by way of Constantinople, where it was observed in the seventh century, but it has since disappeared from the Byzantine rite, or rather it has been transferred to the Third Sunday in Lent.[75]

During the eight weeks of Lent, according to Etheria's journal, the bishop of Jerusalem gave catechetical instructions to the candidates for baptism.[76] They were given in the basilica every morning from six to nine o'clock, except during Holy Week, when there was no time for them. During Easter Week further instructions were given to the newly baptized concerning the Christian mysteries (sacraments). They were given in the church of the *Anastasis* after the morning liturgy, and the faithful (but no outsiders) were allowed to attend. The bishop also conducted a prayer service every day of Easter Week on the Mount of Olives, followed by Vespers in the *Anastasis*. If Etheria was in Jerusalem around the year 400, the bishop would have been John II (387-417), the successor of St. Cyril. It is possible that John was the author of the *Mystagogical Catecheses*, usually attributed to Cyril, or he may have used Cyril's lectures in his own instructions.[77]

On the Sunday after Easter an evening service was held in the Zion

Church to commemorate the appearance of the risen Christ to Thomas the Apostle (John 20,26-31). The reading from the Gospel was a continuation of the passage read there on the evening of Easter Sunday (John 20,19-25). The Ascension of Christ was commemorated at the very end of the Easter season, on Pentecost Sunday, but on the fortieth day after Easter the liturgy was celebrated at the church of the Nativity in Bethlehem.[78] The choice of Bethlehem can probably be explained in the light of Cyril's Lenten instruction: "He descended from heaven to Bethlehem, but he ascended to heaven from the Mount of Olives.[79] The same thought appears in the Byzantine liturgy, at Vespers for the feast of the Ascension: "We who live on earth glorify your coming down to us and your rising away from us."

On Pentecost Sunday, after an early mass in the basilica, the congregation went directly to the Zion Church, where the Holy Spirit descended upon the apostles at the third hour of the day (Acts 2,15). The bishop offered mass there ("offertur et ibi"), and in the afternoon went to the Mount of Olives to celebrate the Ascension of Christ. The day ended with a candlelight procession from the Mount of Olives to the basilica and the church of the *Anastasis,* and finally to the Zion Church. Evidently it seemed proper to end the Easter festival by recalling the Ascension of Christ together with the Descent of the Holy Spirit, but there was already a festival of some kind on the fortieth day after Easter (see Acts 1,3), and inevitably this became the principal memorial of the Ascension. The same idea of Pentecost as the completion or summing up of the whole mystery of salvation appears in a slightly different form in the Byzantine rite, where it has become a festival of the Holy Trinity. In the West the feast of the Holy Trinity was assigned to the Sunday after Pentecost; at Rome, where "feasts of ideas" were not particularly popular, it was not accepted until 1334, centuries after its adoption in northern Europe.

The last pages of Etheria's journal are missing; they probably contained a description of the Jerusalem saints' days. It appears from other sources that the biblical saints, including those of the Old Testament, figured prominently in the Jerusalem calendar. The early Roman calendar did not include any biblical saints except Peter and Paul, who were venerated as local martyrs. But the Jerusalem Church could claim all the saints of the Bible as *local* saints, even if their date of death or place of burial had been forgotten. The dedication of a church in honor of the saint could provide a date for the feast, if the date of death was unknown. As for the saints' relics, they were discovered so conveniently that one may suspect that the demand sometimes created the supply. We have already seen that the most important saints—Stephen, Peter and Paul, and John and James—were commemorated during Christmas week. At Jerusalem December 25 was originally the feast of King David and James the Lord's Brother.[80] It was transferred to December 26 when the Christmas feast was adopted, displacing the following feasts by one day. In the Byzantine calendar, however, it was assigned to the Sunday after Christmas, with an additional feast of St. James on October 23. The Roman church never admitted King David to the calendar, but he is commemorated in the Roman Martyrology on December 29. James the Lord's Brother was generally identified in the West with James the Apostle, the son of Alphaeus, who was commemorated on May 1.

Both King David and James the Lord's Brother were important saints in the Jerusalem church. According to the New Testament, Jesus "was descended from David according to the flesh" (Rom 1,3). St. Peter, in his first sermon, said that David's tomb "is with us to this day" (Acts 2,29). When the Crusaders rebuilt the Zion Church, later known as the Cenacle, they erected a cenotaph which the Jews now venerate as the "Tomb of David". James the Lord's Brother became the head of the Jerusalem church after Peter's departure (Acts 12,17), and was regarded as the first bishop of Jerusalem. His martyrdom was recorded by Flavius Josephus, the Jewish historian, and by Hegesippus, the Judaeo-Christian writer.[81]

Besides King David, the Byzantine calendar also commemorates all the prophets of the Old Testament and, in addition, Moses, Joshua, Samuel, Elijah, Elisha, and Job. The feast of the Holy Maccabees (August 1) was celebrated in all Christian churches, even in Rome, where all the other saints of the Old Testament were excluded from the calendar and relegated to a simple listing in the martyrology. Evidently the Christian imagination was stirred by the story of the seven young Jewish brothers martyred under King Antiochus IV, with their mother and the scribe Eleazar (2 Maccabees 6 and 7). At a time when sainthood was still associated with martyrdom, these Jewish martyrs were honored more than Moses or David or the other prophets.[82] Only Elijah, the greatest of the prophets, could rival their importance, at least in the Eastern churches. He was also venerated by the Latin hermits who lived on Mount Carmel in the twelfth century. The Carmelites later settled in the West, where they added the feast of Elijah to the calendar of their order (July 20). The Carmelite calendar, which was based on the Latin rite calendar of Jerusalem, also included a feast of the Patriarchs Abraham, Isaac, and Jacob (October 6); the Tombs of the Patriarchs at Hebron were venerated by Christians, Jews, and Moslems.[83]

Of the New Testament saints, the cult of John the Baptist led to the discovery of his reputed relics at Sebaste (Samaria) in Palestine in the fourth century; the feast of his martyrdom on August 29 may be connected with the dedication of the church of St. John (now a mosque). The Birthday of John the Baptist on June 24 apparently originated in the West and became the principal feast of St. John in the East as well. The date was based on the notice in the Gospel that John was born six months before the birth of Jesus (Luke 1,26). The cult of the Virgin Mary antedated the Council of Ephesus (431), which was held in the basilica of St. Mary, but the definition of her divine maternity was obviously important in the development of Marian feasts. The oldest calendars had no special feast in her honor, but in Spain at least the feast of the Annunciation (December 18) was known as the *Dies Sanctae Mariae*. [84] In the Byzantine calendar the Deposition of the Robe of Mary in Constantinople (July 2) goes back to the year 469, and shows the need for relics of some sort, even if they were only items of clothing. In the sixth century the Syrian and Gallican churches had a feast of St. Mary in mid-January, which may be the oldest memorial of the Mother of God. [85] The association of Mary with Christmas led to a special commemoration in her honor on December 26 in the Byzantine calendar and January 1 in the Roman calendar.

The Dormition or Assumption of Mary on August 15 and the Birthday of Mary on September 8 are probably the dedication dates of churches in Palestine. [86] According to the Eastern tradition the Probatic Church in Jerusalem, at the pool of Bethesda, was the site of her birth. The church was built in the early fifth century and rebuilt by the Crusaders, who called it St. Anne's; it was recovered by the Catholic Church in 1856. The Zion Church, or Cenacle, was the site of Mary's "dormition." For that reason the Crusader church was known as St. Mary's on Mount Zion. The modern Benedictine Abbey of the Dormition was built on the adjoining property, since the Moslems had taken over the Cenacle. The tomb of Mary was located in Gethsemane, where a church was built in the fourth century and replaced by a larger basilica under Patriarch Juvenal (422-458). Only the crypt remains; its ownership passed from the Franciscans to the Greek Orthodox Church in 1757.

These and other feasts of Mary were accepted readily in the East, but there was some resistance in the West because of certain apocryphal elements associated with them. By the seventh century, however, both the Birthday and the Dormition of Mary were celebrated in Rome, and from Rome they passed to the other churches of the West. In the fourteenth century the papal curia at Avignon adopted the feast of the Presentation of Mary in the Temple (November 21). The date is apparently the dedication day of New St. Mary's Church, built by the Emperor Justinian at the south end of the temple mount (now the

Al-Aqsa Mosque). The feast was suppressed by Pope Pius V in 1568, but restored in 1585. The feast of the Visitation of Mary (July 2, now on May 31) was also adopted at Rome in the fourteenth century; the modern Franciscan church of the Visitation at Ein Karem, near Jerusalem, replaces the Byzantine and Crusader shrines. July 2, the original date of the feast, was the first day after the Octave of St. John the Baptist.

According to the second-century *Protoevangelium*, the parents of Mary were Joachim and Anna. In the sixth century churches were built in honor of St. Anne in Jerusalem and Constantinople. She was commemorated in the Byzantine calendar on July 25, and her Conception of Mary on December 9. There is also a memorial of Joachim and Anne together on September 9. It was not until 1584 that their names were added to the Roman calendar, where they are now commemorated on July 26 (since July 25 if the feast of St. James the Apostle). The cult of St. Joseph was very late in developing, even in the East. In fact there is still no feast of St. Joseph in the Byzantine calendar, except for a general memorial, with King David and James of Jerusalem, on the Sunday after Christmas. In the West his name was added to the Roman calendar in 1479, and in 1621 his feast (March 19) became one of the major holy days.

The other New Testament saints made their way into the church calendars in a very haphazard fashion, still not complete as far as the Roman calendar is concerned. Still missing are several saints honored in the Eastern churches: Zechariah, the father of John the Baptist; Simeon and Anna the Prophetess; Longinus, the name given to the centurion who presided at the crucifixion of Jesus; Cornelius the Centurion, the first Gentile Christian; Philip the Deacon and the other "deacons" of the Jerusalem church; Ananias, who baptized St. Paul; Silas (or Silvanus), the companion of St. Paul; Philemon and Onesimus, Andronicus and Junias, and Dionysius the Areopagite. Peter and Paul, and John were the only apostles commemorated in Rome before the sixth century, when Andrew (November 30) and Philip and James (May 1) were added. Most of the other apostles and evangelists were given feast days in the ninth century, but Mark, Matthias, and Barnabas had to wait until the eleventh century. Mary Magdalene and Martha of Bethany were added even later, and although Mary Magdalene is no longer identified with Mary of Bethany, the latter has not yet been admitted to the Roman calendar. Timothy, the disciple of St. Paul, has been commemorated in the West since the thirteenth century, but Titus, Paul's other disciple, was not given a feast day until 1854.

The post-biblical saints of Palestine are well represented in the Byzantine calendar, but only a few of them were listed in the Roman calendar and even fewer survived the reform of 1969. There are now only three saints representing the Holy Land: St. George, Cyril of Jerusalem, and John of Damascus, who became a monk at Mar Saba in Palestine. St. George was honored at Rome from the seventh century, but Cyril of Jerusalem and John of Damascus received feast days as recently as 1882 and 1890, respectively. No longer listed in the Roman calendar are: Simeon, the second bishop of Jerusalem; Hilarion, the first Christian monk in Palestine; and Sabas, the founder of the famous monastery of Mar Saba.

In the Byzantine liturgy the feast of St. George the Great Martyr is one of the major feasts in the calendar of saints, and there is an additional feast, on November 3, of the dedication of the church of St. George at Lydda. Other prominent saints in the calendar are Euthymius, Sabas, and Theodosius, the founders of the monastic life in the Holy Land. There are also memorials of the martyrs of Palestine, and of St. Sophronius, the patriarch of Jerusalem, who surrendered the city to the Moslems in the year 638. But most of the Palestinian saints were monks. Several monks of Mar Saba contributed hymns to the Byzantine liturgy and, through John Mason Neale, to the Anglican hymnals: John of Damascus, his nephew Stephen of Mar Saba, Cosmas the Poet, Andrew of Crete, and Joseph the Hymnographer.[87] Perhaps we should also include among the Palestinian saints the pious Roman emigrés who settled in the Holy Land in the late fourth century. St. Jerome, for example, is listed in the *Elenchus Geographicus* of the new Roman Calendar as a saint of "Yugoslavia," but in fact he lived in Bethlehem for more than thirty years (386-420), and died there.[88]

Finally, a note about the feast of the Transfiguration of Christ (August 6). According to the synoptic Gospels, Jesus led the apostles Peter, James, and John up a high mountain, and in the presence of Moses and Elijah was transfigured before them.[89] Cyril of Jerusalem, in his Lenten Lectures, speaks of Mount Tabor in Galilee as the traditional site of the Transfiguration.[90] The feast was celebrated in the East from the fourth or fifth century; it is one of the twelve Great Feasts in the Byzantine rite. The date is usually explained as the dedication day of the fourth-century church on Mount Tabor, but there is an alternative theory that August 6 was chosen as the fortieth day before the feast of the Holy Cross (September 14).[91] According to tradition the Transfiguration took place forty days before the crucifixion of Jesus, but in order to give it a fixed date it was celebrated forty days before the feast of the Holy Cross. It was adopted by some Western churches during the Middle Ages, but it was not added to the Roman calendar until 1457, to commemorate a Christian victory over the Turks at Belgrade. It was only a minor feast in the Roman rite until 1914, when it was raised to the rank of a feast of the second class. The Roman liturgy still retains the older practice of reading the Gospel of the Transfiguration on the Second Sunday in Lent; in the Lutheran liturgy it is read on the Last Sunday after Epiphany. The mention of "booths" in the Gospel of the Transfiguration suggests some connection with the feast of Tabernacles or Booths, one of the three great temple feasts of Israel. It has, in fact, been proposed that the Dedication of the Holy Sepulchre, celebrated in Jerusalem on September 14, was the Christian counterpart of the feast of Tabernacles.[92] In her description of the eight-day festival, Etheria compared it to the dedication of the Jerusalem Temple by Solomon, during the feast of Tabernacles (2Chr 5,3).[93] In the West, however, September 14 was celebrated only as the feast of the Holy Cross.

NOTES

1. Eusebius, *Hist. Eccl.* 4.5; 5.12.
2. Nicaea, canon 7; Chalcedon, Session VII.
3. Matthew 28,1; Mark 16,2; Luke 24,1; John 20,1.
4. J. A. Jungmann, *The Early Liturgy* (Notre Dame, Ind. 1959) p 19.
5. Letter of Barnabas, 15.9. See Jean Danielou, *The Bible and the Liturgy* (Notre Dame, Ind. 1956) p 262-86.
6. See W. O. E. Oesterley, *The Jewish Background of the Christian Liturgy* (Oxford, 1925); Eric Werner, *The Sacred Bridge* (London & New York, 1959); Ferdinand Hahn, *The Worship of the Early Church* (Philadelphia, 1973).
7. Danielou, *Bible and Liturgy* p 222-41.
8. Tertullian, *Apology*, 16.
9. Eusebius, *Hist. Eccl.* 3.27.
10. N. M. Denis-Boulet, *The Christian Calendar* (New York, 1960) p 32-34.
11. Cod. Theod., II.8.1; Cod. Just., III.12.3. See J. Stevenson, *A New Eusebius* (London, 1974) p 333-34.
12. See A.H.M. Jones, *Constantine and the Conversion of Europe* (Penguin Books, 1962) p 103.
13. Tertullian, *De Jejunio*, 14.
14. See Hahn, *Worship* p 100-02.
15. See Maurice Goguel, *The Primitive Church* (London, 1963) p 408.
16. Eusebius, *Hist. Eccl.* 5.24.
17. *Ibid.* 5.25.
18. *Ibid.* 5.24.
19. *Ibid.* 5.23.
20. Tertullian, *De Baptismo*, 19.
21. Gregory Dix, *The Apostolic Tradition* (London, 1968) p 30-43.
22. *Ibid.* p 55-57.
23. Council of Arles, canon 1.
24. Eusebius, *Vita Const.* 3.18. See A.H.M. Jones, *Constantine* p 160-62.
25. Council of Antioch, canon 1.
26. Tertullian, *De Corona*, 3.
27. Athanasius, Paschal Letter XII.
28. *Martyrium Polycarpi*, 18-19.

29. See Daniel Wm. O'Connor, *Peter in Rome* (New York & London, 1969) p 126-34.

30. See H. Leclercq, "Kalendaria," in *D.A.C.L.* 8/1, 635.

31. Eusebius, *Vita Const.* 3.25-45.

32. *Peregrinatio Aetheriae.* Latin-French ed., Hélène Pétré, *Sources Chrétiennes* (Paris, 1948); Latin ed., Aet. Franceschini et R. Weber, *Corpus Christianorum, Series Latina,* Vol. 175 (Turnholti, 1965); Latin-English ed. of chapts. 24-49 in L. Duchesne, *Christian Worship* (London, 1919) p 492-523, 541-72.

33. *Ibid.* chapt. 49.

34. *Ibid.* chapt. 48.

35. Cyril of Jerusalem, Letter to Constantius, 3; Lenten Lectures 4.10, 10.19, 13.4.

36. Etheria, chapt. 37.

37. Ambrose, *De Obitu Theodosii,* 40-48; Paulinus, Ep. 31.4.

38. Letter to Constantius, 5.

39. See Gregory Dix, *The Shape of the Liturgy* (Westminster, 1945) p 350-53.

40. *Ibid.,* p 334.

41. Etheria, chapts. 24-25.

42. According to Gregory Dix (*Shape of the Liturgy* p 437-38), only the liturgy of the word took place in the basilica, while the eucharist proper was celebrated in the church of the Anastasis. Hélène Pétré (*Ethérie,* p 199, note 4) shows, on the contrary, that the *oblatio,* the eucharist proper, followed immediately after the liturgy of the word in the basilica, and that the service in the Anastasis was a thanksgiving *after* mass.

43. Etheria, chapt. 43.

44. *Ibid.,* chapt. 25.

45. See Anton Baumstark, *Comparative Liturgy* (Westminster, Md., 1958) p 153; Oscar Cullmann, "The Origin of Christmas," in *The Early Church* (London, abridged ed., 1966) p 21-36.

46. Jungmann, *Early Liturgy* p 148.

47. Duchesne, *Christian Worship* p 261-65.

48. According to Tertullian, Christ died "in the month of March at the time of the Passover, on the eighth day before the Kalends of April," i.e., on March 25 (*Adv. Judaeos,* 8).

49. See Baumstark, *Comparative Liturgy,* p. 154; Duchesne, *Christian Worship* p 265.

50. St. Anastasia, a martyr of Sirmium, is commemorated in the Byzantine calendar on December 22. The *titulus Anastasiae* in Rome was probably named after the foundress of the church, but as in similar cases, she was later venerated as a "Roman martyr".

51. See Bellarmino Bagatti, *The Church from the Circumcision* (Jerusalem, 1971) p 122-28.

52. Duchesne, *Christian Worship* p 576.

53. See Archdale King, *Liturgies of the Primatial Sees* (Milwaukee, Wis., 1957), p 374-75 (Milan), 548-50 (Spain).

54. See P. Jounel, "Le Culte des Saints" in *L'Eglise en Prière,* ed A.G. Martimort (Tournai, 1961) p 766-85.

55. Baumstark, *Comparative Liturgy* p 183-85.

56. Gregory of Nyssa, *In laudem Basilii* (PG 46, 789). He does not mention the precise dates, but says that they were commemorated between Christmas and the anniversary of St. Basil on January 1.

57. Gregory Dix, *Shape of the Liturgy* p 377-78.

58. *Epistula Luciani* (PL 41, 807-16).

59. Duchesne, *Christian Worship* p 268, notes 1 and 2. The seventh-century date for Peter and Paul was December 28.

60. See Hermanus Schmidt, *Introductio in Liturgiam Occidentalem* (Rome, 1960) p 663.

61. They are listed as John and James in the Syrian, Carthaginian, Gallican, and Hieronymian calendars.

62. See H. Leclercq, "Kalendaria," *D.A.C.L.*, 8/1, 645, 661.

63. See A. Wikenhauser, *New Testament Introduction* (New York, 1958) p 288-89.

64. Baumstark, *Comparative Liturgy* p 148-50.

65. Etheria, chapt. 34.

66. *Ibid.*, chapt. 27.

67. The upper room of the Last Supper is called *anágaion* in Mark and Luke; the upper room where the disciples met after the Resurrection is called *hyperóon* in Acts. Both words are translated as *coenaculum* in the Latin Vulgate, and seem to be synonymous.

68. Etheria, chapt. 36.

69. *Ibid.* chapt. 38.

70. See Jungmann, *Early Liturgy* p 261-64.

71. Baumstark, *Comparative Liturgy* p 146.

72. Duchesne, *Christian Worship* p 247-48.

73. See Gregory Dix, *Shape of the Liturgy* p 339, 440.

74. Duchesne, *Christian Worship* p 248-49.

75. Baumstark, *Comparative Liturgy* p 142-44.

76. Etheria, chapt. 45-47.

77. See A. A. Stephenson, "The Mystagogical Lectures" in *The Works of Saint Cyril of Jerusalem*, Fathers of the Church, Vol. 64 (Washington, D.C., 1970) p 143-49.

78. Etheria, chapt. 42.

79. Cyril of Jerusalem, Lenten Lecture 14.23.

80. Baumstark, *Comparative Liturgy*, p 184.

81. Josephus, *Antiquities*, 20.9; Hegesippus in Eusebius, *Eccl. Hist.*, 2.23.

82. The memorial of the Maccabees was removed from the Roman calendar in 1969.

83. See Archdale King, *Liturgies of the Religious Orders* (Milwaukee, 1955) p 249. The feast of the three Patriarchs was removed from the Carmelite calendar in 1930.

84. Archdale King, *Liturgies of the Primatial Sees* p 548.

85. Duchesne, *Christian Worship* p 269; Baumstark, *Comparative Liturgy* p 186.

86. Baumstark, *Comparative Liturgy* p 188-89.

87. See Theodore Edward Dowling, *The Orthodox Greek Patriarchate of Jerusalem* (London, 1913) p 102-06.

88. *Calendarium Romanum* (Typis Polyglottis Vaticanis, 1969) p 151.

89. Matthew 17,1-13; Mark 9,2-13; Luke 9,28-36.

90. Cyril of Jerusalem, Lenten Lecture 12.16.

91. J. van Goudoever, *Biblical Calendars* (Leiden, 1961), p 206-09.

92. *Ibid.*, p 210-14.

93. Etheria, chapt. 48.

Reflections

The Unique One:
The Uniqueness of God according to Deutero-Isaiah*

WALTER STROLZ

These biblical reflections concern Deutero-Isaiah, the great, anonymous prophet of the Babylonian exile. The time of his appearance among the deported Israelites can be determined quite accurately. His prophetic activities fall within the time between the destruction of Jerusalem in 587 B.C. and the collapse of the Babylonian empire in 539 B.C. Credit must be given to Old Testament scholarship which, by intensive research in recent decades, established the historical background and the occasion for the message of Deutero-Isaiah as it developed the prophetic movement in Israel. These exegetical efforts point to the central meaning of the prophet's preaching which relates Yahweh's self-revelation as unique and incomparable in the majestic unity of his Divinity over creation and history. The historical and theological studies on Deutero-Isaiah have shaped the conscious faith of Christians only slightly and, with reference to these prophetic words, have failed to develop a universal view. The reason for this cannot be examined here. It is sufficient to emphasize that Jesus' message remains strictly linked with this belief in the only God. Jesus never deviates from this claim of biblical revelation, but confirms it with the eschatological promise of the coming kingdom of God, an expectation which subjects time and history to a manifestation not achieved by human beings.

I

An attempt to explain how faith in the uniqueness of God complies with Deutero-Isaiah's thought is a risky undertaking. As we face the

---

*Translation from the German by Mrs. Nora Quigley and the editors.

question of what the prophetic message about the unique and incomparable God, directed to Israel in exile more than 2500 years ago, says to us, we must consider the historical situation in which this message was proclaimed. This retrospection is nothing more than an invitation to reflect on the durability of the word of God. What is man, who is a perishable being destined for death from the moment of his birth, when compared to the word of the unique One, which endures forever (Isa 40,8)? How can the faith of past historical experiences bring light to our own situation? On what is the continuity of this tradition of comforting, discerning, supporting, and guiding word of revelation founded? What does it mean to hope in view of Deutero-Isaiah's message? What makes the divine word once proclaimed in a different situation still a guiding light for people today (Isa 55,13) who live in a new epoch of history?

After 500 B.C., Deutero-Isaiah directs his prophetic word of salvation to the people of Israel who, in the communal lamentations of the Babylonian exile, feel that Yahweh seems to have abandoned them. Their deeply rooted faith in God's guidance of Israel's history seems to be shaken. One must consider the effects that the destruction of Jerusalem in 587 B.C. had on them. Until that time the Israelites rejoiced because they lived in the promised land. The Jerusalem tradition of faith proclaimed Yahweh's redemptive acts which manifest his presence in the world. Now they face a situation similar to that of their forefathers in Egypt. They are ruled by an alien power and exiled in a strange country. The concrete implication of this experience, endangering and even destroying the existential faith of the deported Israelites has been expressed by the Old Testament scholar O. H. Steck:

> Israel has lost its Land to the Neo-Babylonians. Thus, Yahweh has annulled the salvific act wherein the Land was promised. The kingdom is laid low and with it the promise made to David. Zion is ravished and with it the place where for centuries the people of Jerusalem experienced the protection of Yahweh, present there and governing the world. One thinks what it means theologically: with one stroke this catastrophe which descended on Judah and Jerusalem overturned all accepted beliefs in salvation for Israel. The people are propelled into a vacuum devoid of salvation, which puts the existence of Israel and even that of Yahweh in doubt. What has become of this Yahweh who has withdrawn his promise of salvation? The assurance of the entire theology developed in Exile, that this catastrophic situation manifests Yahweh's judgment is only one side of the picture. The darker reverse side produces the bitter consequence which theologically challenges any new and saving situation. Trust in Yahweh is fundamentally destroyed. Thus, the problems emerge, whether ever again Yahweh will

renew his salvation for Israel after having withdrawn these promises or will he even be able to do so? Has the year 587 B.C. demonstrated that not he but the gods of the victorious Babylonians hold sway over the affairs of the world? How will the trust in a new promise of salvation, as proclaimed by Deutero-Isaiah, stand?[1]

Deutero-Isaiah, who was called and empowered to be a prophet during the Babylonian exile and who deeply sympathized with the doubting and hopeless Israelites, contrasts the crisis of their faith in Yahweh with the message of Yahweh's majestic uniqueness. This unique One is the incomparable Lord of creation and history, whose rule is unsurpassed and who cannot be deposed by anyone. In the powerful introduction of Deutero-Isaiah's proclamation of God's words, the incomparability of Yahweh is repeated three times. It appears to those exiled as a word which distinguishes between all creatures and the unfathomable transcendence of God who, in his divine mystery, is also near to mankind when his voice is heeded. This word of Yahweh as the unique and incomparable Being, is real and concrete, that is, it cannot be derivative. It cannot be deduced from a previous generally established principle. As a prophetic word, it is critical of history and points to the future. This message in Deutero-Isaiah gives a first impression of being argumentative, accusing, judging, and annulling as well as liberating, inspiring, and encouraging. Whatever happens in the realm of gods and under the rule of earthly powers is not final and conclusive because all that is human remains under the sign of nothingness, as questioned by the past. With reference to Israel can these gods and idols endure? Whether they open Israel's future by bringing about the return to their homeland or whether the time has come for their demise, no one will mention them any more. All of this has to be taken into account when we read in Deutero-Isaiah (40,13-15):

Who has directed the Spirit of the Lord,
or as his counsellor has instructed him?
Whom did he consult for his enlightenment,
and taught him the path of justice,
and taught him knowledge
and showed him the way of understanding?
Behold the nations are like a drop from a bucket
and are accounted as the dust on the scales.

The claim of uniqueness by the God of Israel is already formulated with the daring question found in the prologue of the message about the Babylonian idols (Isa 40,18):

To whom then will you liken God,
or what likeness compare with him?

It is answered by God's creative powers and praise of his lordship over history. The radical scepticism concerning any other claim about the Divinity invests the faith of Israel in this highly critical phase of their history with unprecedented tension. As the unique and incomparable One, God is the creator of heaven and earth. He has spread out the heavens like the roof of a tent so that man can live beneath it. He is the one who has called forth the visible world, supporting and preserving it. Thereby he enables mankind to realize a historical existence on this soil, this gift of nature. People who make an image of God and worship that which they themselves fabricated compare God with created things, whether this expresses their mythical relationship with nature or through a speculative philosophy demonstrating God's existence or from a nihilistic viewpoint idolizing nothingness. According to biblical prophecy God cannot be compared to anything. This results in an unimaginable challenge which liberates the person in thought and belief.[2] The proclamation of God's uniqueness leads man to the task of differentiating between spirits, thus embarking on a task that remains as long as he lives. The historical experience resulting from faith in the only God has both critical and unifying characteristics. It is critical because it exposes the enthronement of the absolute through human beings as idol worship. It can be ideological making an absolute of an idea, a given conception of history, a single interpretative principle for the evolutionary process. Also it can be the dogmatic authoritative demand of a church which addresses those who believe differently in order to subjugate them. Forgetting God's uniqueness or no longer knowing it within the experience of faith is detrimental to human dignity and liberty. Openness to non-scientific interpretations of existence and the creative initiative of individuals may be suppressed by peer pressure or by totalitarian power politics. Whenever the decisive insight into the basic, multifaceted nature of human existence and of non-human creation is no longer maintained, the latitude for free self-realization will vanish. Solidarity is initiated by belief in the uniqueness of God and his universal, unlimited lordship over creation and history. The earth was entrusted to human beings as their dwelling place. It will remain a viable environment only as long as we observe the already established order in nature that comes from creation. Human habitation in this world depends entirely on the evolutionary laws of nature as created. At creation it received the blessing of continuing fecundity.

God in his uniqueness allows various possibilities within a historical time span from the beginning to an irrevocable end. However, Yahweh does not remain an unalterable, completely atemporal eternity; rather he governs history by guiding it from the darkest beginnings until the remotest future, always remaining one and the same (Isa 43,13). The self-identification of Yahweh, which expresses a knowledge of time and history having nothing in common with Western metaphysics, reads as follows (Isa 41,4):

> I, the Lord, the first
> and with the last, I am he.

The unheard boldness of this statement of faith welds Israel's destiny together with mankind and non-human creation, inseparable in their differentiation. According to Deutero-Isaiah the exiled Israelites bear witness to the majestic unity and incomparability of God. The prophetic word of the divine commissioning of Israel is expressed in Isaiah 43,10-11:

> You are my witnesses, says the Lord,
> and my servants whom I have chosen,
> that you may know and believe me
> and understand that I am he.
> Before me no God was formed
> nor shall there be any after me.
> I, I am the Lord
> and besides me there is no saviour.

II

The freedom and sovereignty of God's action in the history of the chosen people reaches its peak in the oracle about Cyrus. In a completely unthinkable, scandalizing move God selects a pagan king to be the "anointed" and uses him as the instrument which initiates Israel's deliverance and return with the aim of rebuilding Jerusalem and the Temple. The implications of this choice outside of Israel's royalty and outside of its faith surpasses by far its historical situation, as important as this will become to the survival of Israel in its Land. This call of God raising up a foreigner for Israel's salvation emphasizes that Israel's fate is not dependent on its political power or weakness. The exercise of political power can be taken away and Israel can be scattered to the four winds, but in spite of this, it remains the chosen people. According to Deutero-Isaiah, Yahweh has created Israel for his glory (Isa 43,21) and he will never forget this (Isa 44,21). Cyrus, who worships idols and does not know the only God, enters into Israel's history of redemption and thereby offers to the faithful the opportunity for a monotheistic recognition of God, which breaks through what appears possible within the context of earlier tradition. This calling of the Persian king Cyrus manifests two truths: the mystery of God's presence in history and his majestic transcendence kindling a new hope for the Israelites in the midst of distress and persecution; the radical creativity of Yahweh's initiative for the redemption of his people. The commissioning of Cyrus concludes with Yahweh's powerful self-revelation (Isa 45,5-7):

> I am the LORD, and there is no other,
> besides me there is no God,
> I gird you, though you do not know me,
> that men may know from the rising of the sun,
> and from its setting, there is none besides me;
> I am the LORD, and there is no other.
> I form the light and create darkness,
> I make weal and create woe,
> I am the LORD, who do all these things.

Through prophetic speech, Yahweh announces the omnipotence of his divine rule. He manifests himself as the unique One even over the primeval opposites of light and darkness, good and evil. These created forms give way before this word of revelation concerning God's lofty transcendence. Evil does not stand with good as an equal power as it does in the myth of ancient Persian dualism, nor is darkness an independent being contrasting with light, but God as the unique One formed both in their strict exclusivity. Such a radical notion of God's uniqueness, which subjects all that is and was to the sovereignty of its creative presence transcends both hearing and seeing. The far too human attempt of justifying or exonerating God in the face of evil falls to dust. The idea of "permitting evil," which one finds in Christian theology, seems equally unacceptable. The question about the origin of evil becomes even more obscure in view of Deutero-Isaiah that God himself creates evil and woe. Only in two other biblical texts are such statements made and intended for human ears: in the "Song of Moses" (Deut 32,39) and in the Book of Job (12,16-25). Should one hold his ground or acknowledge that such realities are beyond human comprehension, and therefore keep silent?

Let us not forget that this saving word of Yahweh's uniqueness and omnipotence comes to assist and enlighten the Israelites during their exile in Babylon. It is to be understood primarily as a word of encouragement. The threatening idols and political powers surrounding Israel are not invincible. They were created like all earthly things and therefore are not eternal. They know that the conflict among themselves is not to be traced back to primeval principles of good and evil that secretly guide events. According to Deutero-Isaiah the human being must trust in God's Word as the word of the unique and incomparable One, and so on earth, among the vicissitudes of history, participate in the work of discerning good from evil. These things are possible only because they are created. If God's divinity consists in sovereignty over good and evil, salvation and woe, and if no one else can attain this creative power, then it is imperative that man, faithfully hearing the words of revelation, be responsible as a free, discerning being in the struggle against the tyrannical pretensions of power which appear in every age. This prophetic demand corresponds to Jesus' answer in the hour of temptation, recorded in the New Testament, the continuation of Israel's history of faith. Jesus rejects the offer of power and wealth by the Evil One in return for adoration. He quotes the words of Deuteronomy:

> It is written, you shall worship the Lord your
> God and him only shall you serve (Matt 4,11).

From the text, which speaks of the all-inclusive uniqueness of God, it is obvious that evil has superhuman dimensions. With regard to its effects and especially in its origins it cannot be understood in a purely human context. This is already demonstrated in the story of creation with the myth of the snake tempting the human being. But in Deutero-Isaiah evil is attributed to God himself ultimately because he is the One who created good and evil, salvation and woe. In view of this divine self-description, does the human being stand before a God who is evil? So disturbing, even frightening is Yahweh's word through the prophet's mouth, that it seems not merely to introduce an issue of theodicy. It is pertinent to the justification of faith to ask the meaning of this unprecedented general statement. Any reduction of evil to man's doing becomes untenable in the light of these words. In any case, God's divinity does not exclude it. How could anything exist outside of his sovereignty or independent of him who is Creator and Lord? As God's creature, the human being possesses nothing that has not been given to him. Every human inconsistency and everything evil emanating from the human heart opposed to God is possible only within creation already given beforehand. Ontologically, the power of evil is always linked to this prior and enduring gift, and through it the faithfulness and forbearance of the Creator is manifested. Therefore evil is never "pure" from a self-sustaining power but it is conditioned by the unsurpassed good existing at the beginning of creation. The power of evil directed against God is doomed from the very outset. The text speaks of God's sovereign power of discernment; as discerner he stands over the discerned. Also, goodness is not necessary, but is an unmerited, free gift of the Creator. When Yahweh proclaims himself as the Creator of light and darkness, salvation and woe, he confirms his uniqueness and with this total exclusivity his incomparability, as in an unfathomable way he rules over all creation as the Creator.

Such an explanation of Isaiah 45,7 does not remove the puzzle from us who experience the continuous existence of evil which produces fear and anguish, restlessness and bewilderment. Man remains responsible for his actions even though he alone does not bear the guilt for evil which existed from the beginning of human history as implied in the myth of the serpent in the biblical account of primeval history. Evil relates to God in so far as it is within the sphere of creation. Therefore, evil is completely subject to God. Mortal man must place his hope on this faith-consciousness so that he will not be put to shame (Isa 49,23) and acknowledge that it is Yahweh "who made all these." In spite of the intolerable paradox in the prophetic text, Isaiah 45,7 remains a message of hope to humanity which is destined to struggle against evil throughout its existence. "God saw all he had made, and indeed it was very good" (Gen 1,31). This declaration in the creation account does not gainsay the subsequent deluge, but it does make possible the renewal of God's blessing for Noah for all ages of the world. In the same way, the unknown prophet of the Babylonian exile confirms that the Creator is Lord over history.

III

The message of Deutero-Isaiah ends in the call to repentance. Those who despair, who worship idols, who allow themselves to drift dejectedly, who have nothing to say to those who search, who bow down to the powers that be, who remain silent when they should speak, who are undecided when the time calls for decision—all of these must turn toward God who is all-forgiving. With this call to repentance the God of Israel demonstrates once more that he is a God who opens the future and respects man's freedom. Ernst Bloch remarks correctly that in the Bible "every call to return is hypothetical, that is, with the assumption of personal conversion on the premise of personal choice and its alternative."[3] In Deutero-Isaiah the call for return is followed with an uplifting and strengthening word from the incomparable God in whom the indivisible unity of creation and history rests (Isa 55,8-11):

For my thoughts are not your thoughts
neither are my ways your ways, says the LORD.
For as the heavens are higher than the earth,
so are my ways higher than your ways
and my thoughts than your thoughts.
For as the rain and sun come down from heaven,
and return not thither but water the earth,
making it spring forth and sprout,
giving seed to the sower and bread to the eater.
So shall my word be that goes forth from my mouth:
it shall not return to me empty
but accomplish that which I purpose
and prosper the thing for which I sent it.

This prophetic saying unveils the mystery of God's majestic sovereignty. As the heavens stretch above the earth and no human scale can measure their width and height, so God's thoughts and plans stand in perfection above the ways of man (Rom 11,33). This divine uniqueness and incomparability draws human beings to glory as they experience it in faith. As it contradicts all the idols of history, this message makes human beings open and free to receive God's life-giving word in creation and history. In Deutero-Isaiah nature itself, with its assurance of an ever-renewing order, becomes the comparison for God's loyalty. The scientific or technical concourse with nature cannot reverse this relationship with creation. It can only displace it so that future habitation of the earth becomes questionable and the irresponsible excesses of global exploitation endanger its very existence. The imagery of the prophet's message sets confidence in nature in relation to the word of God, to the unalterable consciousness of faith, which was given to mankind as a living promise. This promise does not deceive and is as constant as the Creator's blessing on the natural world. This powerful word of God in the language of man guaranteed a new beginning for Israel whenever it found itself in a desperate and seemingly hopeless situation (Isa 45,15; 51,8). Faith in the helping and saving word of the unique One, again attested in the New Testament (1Cor 8,4-6; 1Thess 1,9), is something other than a definite assurance of salvation. Today we must understand the truth of God's uniqueness as stated in Deutero-Isaiah in an extended context. We dismantle theological and ecclesiastical security systems in order to sharpen our focus for the continuing struggle with powers and forces inside and outside of Judaism and Christianity. When God's promised faithfulness (Isa 54,10) in the all-embracing unity of creation and history responds to man's trust, then is God's word proven to be fulfilling, discerning and unifying. The God of

Abraham, Isaac and Jacob does not desire to be God without human beings! World history is and remains the arena for the sanctification of his name.

In a hymnic fragment written in his later life (Der Vatikan), Hölderlin bears witness to an experience of God which seems like an echo sounding across the centuries to remind us of the message of Deutero-Isaiah concerning God's incomparability:

> Gott rein und mit Unterscheidung
> Bewahren, das ist uns vertrauet,
> Damit nicht, weil an diesem
> Viel hängt, über der Büssung, über einem Fehler
> Des Zeichens
> Gottes Gericht entstehet.[4]

NOTES

1. See O. H. Steck, "Deuterojesaja als theologischer Denker," in *Kerygma und Dogma*, 15 (1969) p 285.

2. Here I would like to mention two poems by Jehuda Halevi (1080-1145): "The Incomparable" and "No One Else." They demonstrate magnificently the liberating effect of Deutero-Isaiah's two basic statements concerning faith in the uniqueness of the one God. See F. Rosenzweig, *Jehuda Halevi: Zweiundneunzig Hymnen und Gedichte*, second edition, Berlin O. J., p 23-24.

3. See E. Bloch, *Atheismus im Christentum* (Zur Religion des Exodus und des Reichs), Frankfurt 1968, p 138-139.

4. See Hölderlin, *Sämtliche Werke*, Grosse Stuttgarter Ausgabe, Band 2, Gedichte nach 1800, p 252.

Prayer, Proof, and Anselm's *Proslogion*

EDWARD A. SYNAN

When Anselm, first the Prior and then the Abbot of Bec, composed his *Proslogion* in 1077-1078[1] he produced a remarkably durable instance of "the scandal of the history of Philosophy". Observers of that history, to say nothing of contributors to it—we might think, for instance, of Descartes[2]—have felt scandalized by the spectacle of wrangling philosophers, as acerbic as they are verbose, whose dialectic never comes to rest in a conclusion on which all can agree. This short work by Anselm, more precisely, the argument presented in a series of its Chapters (II, III, and IV), has divided philosophers and theologians from his day to our own; no end is in sight.

Denial of probative value to Anselm's argument for the reality of God by Aquinas or by Kant has enriched us with philosophical insights that are precious in their own right, but to the point that such dissent assumes a world-view other than that of Anselm, it is less than satisfactory.

The same must be said of those who have spoken in favor of the argument, for not every reader sympathetic to Anselm has agreed with him *tout court*. As John Duns Scotus expressed it, the argument needs to be "colored"[3] and with Karl Barth[4] or Charles Hartshorne[5] this tradition of "touching up" Anselm's dialectic goes very far indeed.

For as long as critics permit themselves the freedom of evaluating the argument in a setting other than that given by its author, the controversies must remain interminable in principle. My intention is not to comment on commentaries, but rather, by noting what has not been noted, to suggest another approach to the enigmas of the *Proslogion*. This approach, it may be hoped, would have seemed familiar to the Prior and Abbot of Bec.

Anselm's famous argument stems from his reflection that his monks might find excessively complex the dialectic he had given them in his *Monologion*, a demonstration of divine Reality with no appeal to Scrip-

267

ture. He therefore obliged them with the single[6] *Proslogion* argument, equally innocent of appeals to biblical authority. In fact the argument does not rest upon the Bible; in its fashion the whole *Proslogion* is an instance of unalloyed rationality. Still, despite Anselm's rigor in renouncing support from the Sacred Scriptures, the Bible is present to his dialectic in modes other than that of "authority." Anselm prayed for at least limited success—*quantum scis expedire*—in the traditional Augustinian enterprise: to understand what had been believed. It will be seen how biblical this ambition and its limitation are. Furthermore, the points of belief that he aspired to understand are two: that God is *as* faith believes him to be *(quia es sicut credimus)* and that God is also *what* faith believes him to be *(et hoc es quod credimus).* It is Anselm's reasoning on the first of these points, on what is habitually dubbed the question of the "existence" of God,[7] that has made the *Proslogion* and its author famous.

At the heart of his reasoning is the formula Anselm proposed as an expression of what faith holds God to be: "something than which nothing greater can be thought," *aliquid quo nihil maius cogitari possit.* What preoccupied this believer was how he might show that God, thus characterized, must be understood to be in reality:

> Lord, you grant understanding to faith; therefore grant to me that I may understand, as much as you know to be expedient, that you are as we believe and that you are what we believe. And indeed, we believe you to be something than which nothing greater can be thought. Therefore, since "the fool has said in his heart: 'God is not,' " can it be the case that no such nature is?[8]

With this preliminary statement of his concern in place, Anselm distinguished between an existentially neutral understanding of *what* something might be and the understanding *that* something exists in reality.[9] Even the fool has the first sort of understanding with respect to God in that he understands the meaning of the formula "something than which nothing greater can be thought"; precisely because he is a fool, however, he does not possess the second:

> But certainly this same fool, when he hears this that I am saying, "something than which nothing greater can be thought", understands what he hears, and what he understands is in his intellect, even though he may not understand it to be. For, that a thing be in an intellect is one case, but to understand a thing to be is quite another. When a painter thinks over in advance what he is going to make, he has it in his intellect, to be sure,

but what he as yet has not made he does not understand to be. Now, however, when he has painted it, he both has it in intellect and what he now has made, he understands to be. Even the fool, therefore, is convinced that there is at least in intellect "something than which nothing greater can be thought" because he understands this when he hears it and whatever is understood is in the intellect.[10]

Thus far Anselm has no reason to think that the fool would quarrel with him. That "than which nothing greater can be thought" is in the fool's intellect as a designation of the God to whom the fool refused being in reality. According to Anselm, God thus designated cannot be understood coherently as non-existent. The fool may claim to have done so, but in this claim he stands convicted of identifying contradictories: "that than which a greater *cannot* be thought" is for the fool identical with "that than which a greater *can* be thought":

And surely "that than which a greater cannot be thought" cannot be in intellect alone. For if it were in intellect alone, it can be thought to be in reality as well—which is greater. If, therefore, "that than which a greater cannot be thought" is in intellect alone, then exactly "that than which a greater cannot be thought" is "that than which a greater can be thought". But surely this cannot be. Beyond doubt, therefore, something than which a greater cannot be thought exists, both in intellect and in reality.[11]

An otherwise unknown monk of Marmoutier named Gaunilo responded promptly with a respectful, but searching, analysis and refutation of this argument. Gaunilo's acuteness did not armor him against a misreading of Anselm's point, nor did his courtesy prevent his expressing, for the first time in the long history of this argument, the dismay that is generally felt by common-sensical readers when they first encounter Anselm's *tour de force*. By an *a pari* argument Gaunilo stipulated a putative island, "more excellent than all other lands" (and surely a real island is more excellent than a merely imaginary one!); he then observed:

If, I say, this man should wish to establish for me through these words that this island truly is and that it ought no longer to be doubted, either I should believe that he was jesting, or I know not whom I ought to regard as the more foolish: myself (supposing that I should concede this to him) or him (if he should suppose that he had established with any certainty the being— *essentia*—of this island).[12]

In an exhibition of courtesy difficult to duplicate in the history of intellectual controversy, Anselm guaranteed Gaunilo's reputation when he directed that Gaunilo's disclaimers and his own response to them be copied in future along with the *Proslogion* text.[13] His directions are still honored in our printed editions. Gaunilo thus heads the file of those who have struggled in public with this argument. On the negative side (to name only the most eminent) are Aquinas,[14] Locke,[15] and Kant;[16] on the other side we can align Alexander of Hales,[17] Bonaventure,[18] Descartes,[19] Leibniz,[20] and Hegel.[21] Both streams have representatives among our contemporaries.[22] What labelling can make sense of this dissent? "Nominalist" versus "realist," "tough-minded" versus "tender-minded," "empiricist" versus "rationalist"—to mention these labels is to realize that they must be jettisoned. Anselm, to be sure, may have thought of himself as a "realist" when he thundered against the "nominalist" Roscelin, but the extravagant nominalism ascribed to Roscelin attracted no known followers. Can either Gaunilo or Anselm be termed "tender-minded"? As between Kant and Hegel the nominalist-realist dichotomy hardly applies and William James, to whom we owe the terms "tough-minded", "tender-minded," would not have objected to our counting them both alarmingly "tender-minded",[23] yet they were at odds on the late versions of the *Proslogion* argument that were familiar to them. The doctors are grievously divided; we are free to weigh the puzzle.

SCRIPTURA SOLA

Even though Anselm faithfully renounced scriptural authority in both the *Monologion* and the *Proslogion* meditations on divine Being, no reader of his can safely forget that as a Benedictine monk Anselm was dedicated to the "work of God," the *opus dei*, in the form of a daily chanting of the divine Office. In Anselm's time (and until yesterday) that Office was constituted of texts from the Latin "Vulgate" Bible, of homilies, commentaries, and other ecclesiastical writings, all of which are permeated with the vocabulary and the conceptual schemes of that version of the Scriptures. If we never think without words, Anselm's thought was couched in biblical words. Three notions of the highest importance for the intelligibility of what he intended to do in the *Proslogion* are patently scriptural.

The first of these biblical notions is that only a posture of prayer can be acceptable for a rational creature. Like all creatures, men and angels are ineluctably in the presence of the Holy One upon whom they depend but, unlike irrational beings, men and angels are conscious of this fact and ought to respond by prayer. Our total dependence upon the Divine for our being and activity, including thought, transcends any marshalling of proof-texts; it is implicit or explicit on every page of Scripture. Apart from the prayer that is the *Proslogion*,[24] Anselm produced an extensive dossier of formal prayers and meditations which assume and put into words our radical dependence upon the Creator.[25] What sets the *Proslogion* apart from this collection in a thematic way is that, although addressed directly to the God of biblical faith, the *Proslogion* purports to give a logically rigorous understanding of the necessary Being ascribed to God by the believer and of why it is logically necessary to ascribe to God those attributes assigned to him by Christian, biblical, faith.[26]

Should this setting within faith not be conceded, Anselm must be convicted of question-begging as crass as it is improbable in one of his logical expertise[27] for he asked divine aid in the very enterprise of demonstrating the necessary truth of the sentence: "God is" on the ground that the assertion: "God is not" does not meet the criteria for rationality. He escapes this charge if and only if we allow legitimacy to the project of attempting to understand the inner necessity of an assertion on which faith has not wavered. Anselm did not begin with a problem as to how a perhaps non-existent "god" might be demonstrated to be and to be what Christians believe about their God. He was exercised rather to show that the fool who denies God's reality is for that reason truly a fool, but it was no part of his intention to provide a proof of the ultimate Object of faith prior to that faith and from a standpoint outside faith. In words of his that echo Augustine:

> I do not seek to understand in order that I might believe, but I believe in order to understand. For this also I believe: Unless I shall have believed, I could not understand.[28]

At the same time, he was persuaded that, once having attained the *Proslogion* understanding, a future failure in faith must leave intact a rationally secure conviction that God is:

> I give you thanks, good Lord, because what by your gift I formerly believed thanks to your illumination I now understand in such a way that, if I should be unwilling to believe you to be, I could not fail to understand you to be.[29]

A second conception inseparable from Anselm's reasoning is that of the biblical fool. The Abbot of Bec rarely provided statistically impressive evidence of what inspired his thought. Every reader must be struck by the continual presence of Augustinian and Boethian materials, yet a glance at the Index of direct citations, Volume VI of the critical edition, names only five works by Boethius and two by Augustine.[30] Hence, the relatively rare occurrences of directly cited biblical pericopes that contain one of the several terms used by Scripture for "fool" ought not to deceive us. What counts is that Anselm's use of the opening verse of Psalm 13 (14) and of Psalm 52 (53), "The fool has said in his heart: 'God is not' " makes it clear that Anselm thought of the fool as does the Bible, namely, as of one who is both intellectually and morally perverse.

No passage in the Hebrew Scriptures makes this more explicit than does the episode of the churlish Nabal, husband of Abigail, recounted in the First Book of Samuel (25,2-42). When David asked courteously for supplies to support his men in the wilderness, Nabal outraged the traditions of desert hospitality by refusing. Now "nabal" is one of the words for "fool" in Hebrew and it is the one used in the two Psalms that inspired Anselm. In the Vulgate *nbl* is translated in those two psalms by *insipiens*, whereas in 1 Samuel, *nbl* is transliterated as the proper name Nabal (25,3 *bis*, 9. 10. 14. 19. 25. 26. 34. 36. 39 *ter*); where the word is used in that account as a common noun (25,25), the Vulgate *stultus* translates it: *secundum nomen suum stultus est*. "Nabal-fool" was well named. What he was in reality answered precisely to the name by which he was called and the foolishness that justified so woeful a name was as wicked as it was irrational. His wickedness in breaking the law of hospitality is patent and the unwisdom of that crime is hardly less so. For Nabal was struck dead after a drunken rout and his wife passed willingly into the harem of David whose overtures Nabal had despised; he is the paradigm case of the scriptural fool. In the outspoken way of wives, Abigail explained everything to David:

> Pay no heed, my Lord King, to this iniquitous man Nabal for, in accord with his name, he is a fool and foolishness is his companion. . . (1Sam 25,25).

Biblical language is always deliberate in assigning names. Reverent reluctance to name the Holy One (Exod 20,7), the use of the very term "Name," *ha-Shem*, as one surrogate for the Tetragrammaton of Exod 3,14, Adam's ("man's"—Gen 1,26) naming the beasts so knowledgeably that the names he gave them "are their names still" (Gen 2,19), the popular etymology of the remark that he named the companion God had given him "woman," *ishshah*, because she had been taken from "man," *ish* (Gen 2,23), her alternative name "Eve," *hawah* from *ḥayah,* "to live," because she is the mother of all our race (Gen 3,20) and the changes of name with changes of mission for Abram (Gen 17,5) and Jacob (Gen 32,27. 28), for Simon (Matt 16,17. 18) and Saul (Acts 13,9)—all these reveal the value that the Hebrew Scriptures and their Christian continuation give to names.

This Hebrew conception of the fool with his twofold perversity accounts for the crescendo of fault and penalty embedded in Matthew's report of the sermon on the mount by Jesus:

> If anyone is angry with his brother he shall be liable to judgment; who says to his brother *"raca!"* shall be liable to the Sanhedrin; who says "fool!" shall be liable to hellfire (Matt 5,22).

Our modern uneasiness with these penalties for what pass with us as trifling verbal improprieties means no more than that we do not share the respect for names that marks Hebrew tradition; at the same time, it is one more link in the chain that binds the Christian to the Hebrew covenant. When we recall what reality is named by "fool" in the hearing of ears attuned to biblical idiom, penalty and fault seem far less disproportionate. Perhaps it is not necessary to remark that the fool whose foolishness entails atheism is worse, from a biblical perspective, than that of the clumsy and churlish Nabal. To echo the turn of phrase Anselm used, the denial of divine Being is an instance of foolishness "than which a greater cannot be conceived".[31] That this was Anselm's opinion accounts for his opening line in reply to Gaunilo:

> The author of these objections is by no means a fool, but a Catholic speaking "in behalf of the fool"; enough, I think, that I respond to the Catholic.[32]

The man who merited the name "fool" by saying that God is not must be wrong in what he says. In Anselmian terms, he stands convicted of a failure against rectitude in the order of enunciation: The fact is not what he alleges it to be. In those terms too, he must be wrong in the order of morals, for to speak is to act and false speaking is acting without rectitude. Thus did Anselm give a rational account of the biblical usage according to which any and all sins count as lies[33] and Satan is named the "father of lies" (John 8,44).

Third, Anselm was faithful to a scriptural insight when he added to his prayer that he might "understand" the reservation: "as much as you know to be expedient".[34] For Adam and Eve, to become "like gods, knowing both good and evil" (Gen 3,5) had been far from expedient. Moses feared to look upon the Holy One (Exod 3,6) even though the Lord was to speak to him "as a man to his friend" (Exod 33,11) and so much did his skin shine after speaking with the Lord that he found it necessary to veil his face lest by reflected Glory he dazzle the eyes of the people (Exod 34,29-35). Here again the Christian Scriptures maintain a Hebrew biblical theme: The Holy One dwells "in inaccessible light" (1Tim 6,16), a text not far from Anselm's mind as he elaborated the *Proslogion*. [35] The Ever-present is as unseen as if absent;[36] the burgeoning infinity of the Divine over-powered the contracting tininess of Anselm: *nimia mihi est*, "it is too much for me!"[37] Not only his creaturely limits disabled him in that blinding Presence, but, worse yet, was the darkening by sin, both his own and that in which he had been conceived: "not only have I fallen . . . I fell before my mother conceived me."[38] Twice Anselm evoked Isaiah: "Never have they heard, nor taken into their ears, no eye has seen any god apart from you, taking the part of those who wait for him" (Isa 64,4) and the echo of Isaiah in Paul: "Things beyond our seeing, things beyond our hearing, things beyond our imagining, all prepared by God for those who love him" (1Cor 2,9).[39] Trapped in the paradox of a Light without which his soul is blind, yet a Light that blinds if seen,[40] Anselm could rely only on God in order to know God; hence his opening prayer, hence his claim that, not only to understand any truth about God, but to understand anything at all, he must see in the Light and the Truth that is God.[41]

Without implying that Anselm made a covert appeal to faith in contriving his argument, we are constrained to acknowledge that this logician was also a man of faith. He set his argument within a prayer and set his sights upon a scripturally limited understanding; most of all, he found in the analysis of the way a biblical fool "thinks" what he counted a rational insight into the truth that God must be and must be what faith hold him to be.

Not all discussions of the *Proslogion* by logicians, nor even those by theologians, will persuade us that their authors have been sensitive to what reality the term "fool" named under the pen of Abbot Anselm, that they have caught the sense in which his essay is a prayer, or that they have given full value to Anselm's biblically grounded consciousness of human limitations before the divine transcendence. Against his credal background Anselm's *Proslogion* argument was intended to achieve an understanding that might anticipate to a limited degree the vision that will mark the world to come, where faith and hope will fade into irrelevance (1Cor 13,8-13).

RATIO SOLA

A *Festschrift* presented on his 75th birthday to the scholar responsible for the critical edition of Anselm's works, the late F. S. Schmitt, O.S.B., carries the felicitous title: *Sola ratione,* "By Reason Alone,"[42] a title that might be thought to contradict Anselm's scriptural mind-set. An estimate worthy of Anselm, however, must be wide enough to encompass both his all-pervasive faith and his creative use of reason. For Anselm possessed a philosophical mind of the first order and, as we have noted, he twice deployed his rational resources in order to penetrate in some small measure the most awesome of Mysteries. It is easy to feel across the centuries what pressure the monks of Bec had put upon him for, like Anselm, they thirsted to understand what they strongly believed. Twice they challenged him to strike the water of understanding from the rock of reason; Gaunilo and Anselm were not the only born logicians in the eleventh century cloisters of Gaul!

In the long antiphony of dissent and assent, it is the rational aspect of the *Proslogion* enigma that has been scrutinized explicitly. From the early thirteenth century onward, the mediaeval estimates were made by Masters of the Sacred Page, that is, by university theologians who shared Anselm's familiarity with the Bible. As young instructors, they all had been apprenticed as "bachelors of the Bible" and later, as regent masters in theology, they counted the exposition of Scripture a primary and most characteristic duty. To them the biblical setting of this avowedly rational argument may have seemed too obvious to require comment. Secular philosophers who succeeded them in this discussion, from Descartes forward, would make it a point of honor to put faith and Bible "in brackets" as they cultivated their love of wisdom. By the paradox Aristotle has noted,[43] their opposition on faith put mediaeval theologians and secular philosophers into the same genus; from their opposed premisses they reached the same conclusion, namely, that only the logical status of the *Proslogion* reasoning demands evaluation. Their estimates proceed apart from the religious, even devotional, context in which Anselm had embedded his "single argument". To have attempted, in contradiction to their procedure, some remarks on the biblical context does not, of course, abrogate my duty of adverting to its text and of venturing some precisions on the logic of Anselm's reasoning.

It must be conceded by all hands that Anselm was acutely aware of the distinction between what men accept on faith and what they accept because they understand it. Our contemporaries are fond of translating this into a distinction between "theology" and "philosophy". Even on the plane of terminology this translation can be misleading. We ought to remember that, two generations after Anselm had written, Abelard was to outrage some eminent personalities by employing the term "theology" to designate speculation that involves biblical faith as well as reason.[44] Throughout the lifetime of Anselm the term "theology" retained the questionable air it wears in Augustine: The word smacks of heathen discourse about "gods" who are not the God of Abraham, Isaac, Jacob, Jesus, and the *Proslogion*. Anselm's dialectic in that work proceeded for a moment under a title that stems from one of the two readings to which Augustine had thought Isaiah 7,9 susceptible:

> Again, this saying of that same prophet Isaiah, "Unless you shall have believed, you shall not understand", has a second interpretation: "Unless you shall have believed, you shall not hold out". Which of these ought to be followed is a matter of uncertainty, unless copies in the original language be read. Still, to those who read knowledgeably *(scienter)*, something important is conveyed by each of them.[45]

Thus Augustine around the year 397; when he came to write his great work *On the Trinity* seventeen years later, the first of these two readings (Hebraists would insist he chose wrong) had become a proof-text for his basic methodology:

> Faith seeks, intellect finds; this is the reason that the prophet says: "Unless you shall have believed, you shall not understand".[46]

In the spirit of this methodology, the first title Anselm gave to the book we know as the *Proslogion* was "An Example of Meditation on the Intelligible Structure of Faith," a title replaced by *Fides quaerens intellectum* and then by *Alloquium* and *Proslogion*—Latin and Greek equivalents for "a speaking to" the Holy One in contrast with the interior dialogue of the soul with herself that is the *Monologion*. Understanding, with its connotation of repose in an achieved goal, was for Anselm's masters, Augustine and Boethius, to be attained either by an intuitive grasp of self-evident truths or by the exercise of discursive reasoning.[47] Both paths are followed in the *Proslogion* argument: As an argument it entails discursive reasoning, but the ground of that reasoning is a set of intuitively certain truths.

The most basic philosophical position to which Anselm granted axiomatic status is the principle of non-contradiction. To have identified "that than which a greater can be thought" with "that than which a greater cannot be thought" was the blunder of the fool. Anselm's "this cannot be" may wear an off-handed air, but the remark is apodictic evidence that he put the principle of non-contradiction at the center of his reasoning. Since he nowhere discusses its validity, we are authorized to say that he accepted the principle as did Aristotle himself, whose discussion of its indemonstrable quality Anselm cannot have known directly,[48] as beyond debate.

Hardly less fundamental is Anselm's confidence that what is known about reality, created or Uncreated, can be expressed in sentences and that those sentences impose names, at times with truth, but at times without truth. Anselm perceived dialectic as, before all else, the correct use of names. Here the Aristotle of the *Categories* and the *On Interpretation* was his ultimate master and Boethius stood at the Stagirite's elbow.[49] Their "correspondence" theory of truth was universally accepted by mediaeval thinkers and, above all, it was accepted by both sides in the perennial quarrel on universals. Thanks to this association of correspondence theory and the debate on universal names—"fire" or "water," for instance—it is possible to specify how Anselm saw the problem of using names in general, including the Name of "God". Thus the Abbot of Bec did not hesitate to use the worst pejorative at his disposal for the offensive dialectic of Roscelin: As a dialectician, Roscelin was "heretical". The fault that earned Roscelin this vituperation was, quite simply, that he was willing to use terms for realities to which they do not correspond. As Anselm read him, Roscelin so despised words that he thought it a small matter whether they were used correctly or not. Only Church usage, in Roscelin's view, prevents our speaking of three Gods![50] In a long article on the *Proslogion* argument in which he took account of Karl Barth's *Fides quarens intellectum*, Etienne Gilson made the shrewd observation that Anselm's complaint against the Psalmist's fool is that the fool "thinks as does Roscelin: He is a nominalist".[51] In an Anselmian perspective, to apply the Name "God" to a merely mental being is to misuse that Name. The authentic dialectician applies to each reality, *res*, the correct name, *nomen*; he must be unwilling to tolerate the capricious application of an incorrect name to any reality, even to those short of the Divine. A variant reading with a wide manuscript base, although excluded from the text of the critical edition, is given in the apparatus; if not from the pen of Anselm, this pericope is totally in his spirit:

> For indeed, no one understanding that which fire and water are can think that fire is water, from the point of view of the realities, although he could do so from the point of view of the words . . .[52]

Perhaps this is a gloss by some nameless reader but the line remains no more than an expansion of Anselm's assertion:

> A reality is thought differently when the word that signifies it is what is thought than when what is understood is the very item which the reality is.[53]

The responsibility of the dialectician who assigns the Name "God" outdistances immeasurably the responsibility of the philosopher of nature who manipulates the names "fire" and "water". Furthermore, divine Reality imposes a unique burden on us because to use the Name "God" correctly means using that Name for a Reality of which we can have no positive understanding.

Yet another insight that Anselm held to be a ground of discursive reasoning rather than a conclusion reached by reasoning is the hierarchical structure of all that is real. He had said in the *Monologion* (and did not unsay it in the *Proslogion)* that the cosmos within which correct reasoning proceeds is one in which the good is subordinated to the better in orderly series.[54] He thought this so obvious and so essential to the very possibility of understanding our world that the man who would deny it is, on that account, to be denied the name of "man", that is, such a one is shown by that fact alone to be deficient in the rationality that specifies our race:

> Anyone who would call into doubt the fact that a horse is by nature better than a log, and that a man is of more worth than is a horse, is forthwith to be denied the name of "man".[55]

Against this background, God is held to be above, and therefore outside, the series of limited goods, the series in which the lesser has its debts to the greater, the series in which the lower participates in the excellence of the higher. God is in debt to nothing and to on one;[56] he is by his substance what creatures are by graduated participation.[57] In the lexicon of "good and better", of "lower and higher", of "great and greater", God is intuitively held to be "that than which a greater—or a better or a higher—cannot be conceived".

Anselm was not the inventor of the formula "that than which a greater cannot be conceived" to designate God. His immediate sources are Boethius and Augustine; both had used what is in substance the same formula. Boethius had used it in identifying God as the Good in whom all goods participate:

For, since nothing better than God can be excogitated, who can doubt that he, than whom nothing is better, is good?[58]

An Augustinian of Anselm's quality could not have been unaware that, before Boethius, the Bishop of Hippo had made use of a comparable turn of phrase: God is "that than which none is superior," *quo nullus est superior*. As Augustine put it, whatever admits of a superior cannot be God; that which is seen to be superior to a rejected candidate must be subjected to the same criterion and the process continue until that to which nothing can be superior is reached.[59]

Nor did the family tree of the formula end there. Augustine may have read these words in Seneca;[60] he all but certainly had read them in Cicero.[61] In Seneca they refer to his god; in Cicero to the eternal cosmos. There is no reason to think that Cicero is the ultimate source of the formula which is to be found, for instance, in Ignatius of Antioch where it may represent an ancestry among Greek authors.[62] On just such hunting through his predecessors (even though only Boethius and Augustine are probable sources for Anselm) did the Abbot of Bec base the disclaimer that "there is nothing new" in his own work.[63] Given his creative use of old materials we shall grant this no more than did Anselm himself when, in another mood, he described the joy with which he received a light flooding his mind when he hit upon the argument of the *Proslogion*.[64]

Rejection of an argument of this type—for Anselm's reasoning is often taken to be the primary instance of what Kant called the "ontological" argument[65]—assumes that those who reasoned this way were pretending to unpack the real Being of God from a "concept" of God. The verbal forumula would be a definition of God and "real" (as distinguished from merely mental) being would be a property, illicitly derived from what had been accepted naively to be an "idea" of the divine Essence. Kant made his analysis and illustrated it with a precise analogue to the thus-interpreted "ontological" argument:

To posit a triangle, and yet to reject its three angles, is self-contradictory, but there is no contradiction in rejecting the triangle together with its three angles.[66]

This means that Kant thought of the notion and term "triangle" as parallel to the notion and term "God", this last expressed by the formula "that than which a greater cannot be conceived". He thought of the three angles with respect to "triangle" as parallel to real Being with respect to "God". Conceding that to accept either subject—triangle or God—while rejecting the affirmation of a necessary predicate of that subject would be "self-contradictory" (Anselm's "this cannot be"), Kant dismissed the whole dialectic as a mere playing with abstract ideas that need not have referents in the real world. Does this classical refutation of the "ontological" argument bear on Anselm's *Proslogion* reasoning? It does if and only if Anselm thought of his formula as a definition or a concept of God.

Now Anselm denied explicitly that his, or any created intellect can possess a concept of God:

> Therefore, Lord, not only are you that than which a greater cannot be conceived, but you are something greater than can be conceived.[67]

Whatever it may be, the *Proslogion* formula was not in Anselm's mind a definition of God. If not a definition, a concept expressed in words, what can this formula have been for Anselm? Two answers seem compatible with his use of the phrase. First, it can be taken as a "rule" to guide an intellect seeking to identify God. A putative "God" is truly God if and only if this rule can be verified in his regard: Nothing greater can be conceived. Second, put a slightly different way, the formula can be understood as a reference-fixing phrase. It does not tell us what God may be (what positive content could be assigned to this negative expression?) but it does provide a reliable guide in excluding pseudo-gods and thus in fixing by exclusion the correct reference of the Name.

Anselm did not claim that the truth "God is" compels our assent because it is "known of itself" (as Aquinas argued that he had done) on the ground that the predicate "is", or "being", can be discovered within the subject: "that than which a greater cannot be conceived" (as Kant interpreted the meaning of late echoes of the *Proslogion*). He had rather assumed that to impose a name correctly is to express a truth about a real being and also that some things are of more value than others. Juxtaposed in the *Proslogion* manner, these assumptions permitted him to indict the fool for a violation of the principle of non-contradiction when he said in his heart "God is not".

If the fool's assertion commits him to contradiction, might it not be argued that, whereas sentences about creatures may be contradictory, no contradiction can be as extreme as that between the necessarily true: "God is" and the impossible: "God is not"? In fact, this very conclusion was drawn by a mediaeval "inceptor" in theology and his argument makes it clear that, like Anselm, he too assumed the axiomatic value of the principle of non-contradiction, the expression of what we can know about reality in true sentences, and the hierarchical structure of all that is real. Roger Nottingham, O.F.M., went very far indeed when he claimed in his inaugural lecture on the *Sentences* that he could demonstrate the truth of the sentence "God is" from any instance of contradiction.[68] Perhaps the circumstances account for his brashness; Roger was lecturing in the presence of Oxford regent masters in order to establish his competence to join their ranks. He was not the last young scholar who took pleasure in providing his elders with an academic shock. In this case, his dialectical sleight-of-hand that derives from the *Proslogion* goes well beyond Anselm, yet never names him.

Still, Roger's elaborate dialectic does nothing that Anselm's brief argument had not invited him to do. It set up the world of real beings with parallel and contradictory degrees of non-being; where negations and affirmations can be fitted onto the same scale, there is the world of contingency, the world in which possibles are susceptible of actualization, but cannot be both possible and actual at the same time because, as contradictory, the two states are mutually exclusive. As between two contingent, contradictory sentences, there is a necessary relationship, grounded in the principle of non-contradiction: In the real world, one of the two must be verified and thus, one of the two sentences must be true. In this world, the assertion "God is not", the worst of all contradictions, implicitly includes any lesser contradiction; as Roger put it, an atheist must concede the consequence:

If God is not, then "a" is "b".[69]

This is not the time and place to pick our way through the dialectical minuet by which Roger Nottingham leads us from "any instance of contradiction to the truth that 'God is' "[70] but it is not irrelevant to cite his assertion that:

"God is not" not only includes a single contradiction, but it includes every imaginable contradiction. And thus it follows that "God is not" includes greater contradiction than does any other [saying] which does not include "god is not".[71]

The value of any argument must rest on its assumptions, its logical form, and on whether it fulfills the intent of its author. Anselm has asked us to cash a correspondence theory of truth as presiding over the imposition of names, to accept a perception of the world as hierarchical in justification of our language of "greater" and "better," and to allow the principle of non-contradiction. He thought the hierarchical character of the cosmos an empiric datum although, to be sure, he felt no need to anticipate the experiential procedures of Roger Bacon and Albert the Great. More important than these is Anselm's intention: He aspired to take us from faith to understanding, not from atheism to belief.

Since this was his goal, Anselm did not think it appropriate to enter into discussion with Gaunilo under the formality that the monk from Marmoutier had proposed when he wrote, not without wit, *Pro insipiente*, "In Behalf of the Fool". For a fool is beyond the reach of reason and Gaunilo was so little a fool that he could both contrive a refutation that deserved an answer and seek understanding from within faith. He was, in short, in Anselm's view a "Catholic" and it was to the Catholic, not to the fool, that Anselm addressed his response.

To bring faith to a degree of understanding is all that Anselm's argument was designed to do. This is not what Aquinas thought unaided reason can do with respect to divine Being, nor is it what Kant argued that pure reason cannot do with respect to God, soul, and immortality. Neither in their assumptions nor in their setting are the arguments that Kant termed "ontological" the *Proslogion* argument of Anselm; what Kant refuted is not Anselmian. If it is not too blunt to be tolerable, we must say that the *Proslogion* does not belong in collections of "proofs for the existence of God".

Anselm thought that the inner cogency of his reasoning would survive even the loss of faith. Whether this persuasion is justified or not poses a psychological rather than a philosophical enigma. If Anselm was right, once a believer had followed the *Proslogion* argument, he could never become a complete fool. Perhaps; but the trial remains one that the Prior and Abbot of Bec, the Archbishop of Canterbury and Primate of England, Saint and Doctor of the Church, was never called upon to face.

NOTES

1. F. S. Schmitt, "Zur Chronologie der Werke des Hl. Anselm von Canterbury," *Revue Bénédictine* 44 (1932) p. 350: "*Proslogion:* Wohl um 1077-1078 geschrieben. Die Kontroverse mit Gaunilo ist in den nächst folgenden Jahren anzusetzen." Anselm had been named Prior in 1062 or 1063; he became Abbot in 1078; for the text of the *Proslogion* see *S. Anselmi Cantuariensis opera omnia*, ed. F. S. Schmitt (Seckau: Abbatial Press, 1938) t. 1, p 89-122.

2. René Descartes, *Discours de la méthode;* see *Oeuvres de Descartes*, edd. C. Adam and P. Tannery (Paris: Cerf, 1902) t. 6, p 8, 11. 18-29: "Ie ne diray rien de la Philosophie, sinon que, voyant qu'elle a esté cultiuée par les plus excellens esprits qui ayent vescu depuis plusieurs siecles, & que neanmoins il ne s'y

trouue encore aucune chose dont on ne dispute, & par consequent qui ne soit douteuse . . . ie reputois presque pour faux tout ce qui n'estoit que vraysemblable.

3. *Ioannis Duns Scoti opera omnia,* ed. C. Balić (Vatican City: Vatican Polyglott Press, 1950) t. 2, p 208, 1. 16: ". . . potest colorari illa ratio Anselmi de summo bono. . . ," p 210, 1. 12: "Vel aliter coloratur sic . . ."

4. K. Barth, *Fides quaerens intellectum. Anselms Beweis der Existenz Gottes* (München: Chr. Kaiser Verlag, 1930); English translation of this work by I. W. Robertson, *Anselm: Fides quaerens intellectum* (London: SCM Press, 1960).

5. C. Hartshorne, *Anselm's Discovery: A Re-examination of the Ontological Proof for God's Existence* (La Salle, Illinois: Open Court, 1965).

6. Anselm refers in the Prooemium of the *Proslogion* to his search "si forte posset inveniri unum argumentum" as against the "multorum concatenatione contextum argumentorum" that had marked his *Monologion,* ed. cit. p 93, 11. 5 and 6; see also Eadmer's *Vita* on this point; *The Life of St Anselm, Archbishop of Canterbury by Eadmer,* ed., intro., notes and transl. by R. W. Southern (Oxford: Clarendon Press, 1962) p 29 informs us that: "Post haec incidit sibi in mentem investigare utrum uno solo et brevi argumento probari posset id quod de Deo creditur et praedicatur . . ." yet Hartshorne and N. Malcolm are in a long tradition when they distinguish a proof in Chapter III from another in Chapter II.

7. See remark on this phenomenon (as M. J. Charlesworth exemplified it) by the late A. C. Pegis in his magistral study, "St. Anselm and the Argument of the 'Proslogion'," *Mediaeval Studies* 28 (1966) p 229.

8. *Proslogion,* Chapter II, ed. cit. p 101, 11. 3-7.

9. It may be noted that whereas the formulae of 1.4 ("quia es sicut credimus" and "hoc es quod credimus") may blur this distinction inasmuch as the first phrase can be read as "that you are *as* we believe," that is, that you are *necessarily,* there can be no doubt but that the succeeding lines distinguish between what is understood to have merely mental existence and what is understood to have real existence as well.

10. Ibidem, 11. 7-15.

11. Ibidem, p. 101. 1. 15-p 102, 1. 3.

12. Gaunilo, *Pro insipiente* 6, ed. cit. t. 1, p 128, 11. 26-30.

13. Eadmer, *Life of St Anselm,* ed. cit. p 31.

14. Aquinas cited Anselm by name and rejected the *Proslogion* argument as a demonstration of divine Being in his early *Scriptum super libros Sententiarum,* lib. 1, d. 3, q. 1, a. 2, argument 4 and response; without naming Anselm the mature Aquinas repeated this rejection in both the *Summa theologiae* 1, 2, 1, argument 2 and response, and the *Summa contra gentiles* 1, 10; see also the *De veritate* 10, 12 and the *Expositio super librum Boetii De trinitate* 1, 3; Aquinas interpreted the argument as tantamount to a claim that divine Being is *per se notum quoad nos,* a situation that would render demonstration *superflua* and "impossible," *demonstrari non potest,* formulae from the *Summa contra gentiles.*

15. John Locke, *An Essay concerning Human Understanding* 4, 10, 7 was noncommittal on the validity of a "proof" from the "idea of a most perfect being," but in a paper entitled "Deus," cited by Peter King, *The Life and Letters of Locke,* vol. 2, p 138, rejected it unreservedly on the ground that "real existence can be proved only by real existence;" se R. I. Aaron, *John Locke* (Oxford: Clarendon Press, 1937, 1955, 1971) p 242; it may be noted that the reformulation of the

argument with the expression "most perfect being" is of mediaeval origin and must have been known to Locke through Descartes if not directly through a mediaeval author.

16. Immanuel Kant, *Critique of Pure Reason*, Transcendental Dialectic, Book II, Chapter iii, Section 4, A 592-602, B 620-631, where he named Leibniz and Descartes as the mistaken authors of the "Ontological Proof of the Existence of God," and in addition to the argument cited below, n. 60, held that existence is not a predicate and that one hundred real thalers contain no more than do one hundred imaginary thalers.

17. Alexander of Hales, *Summa theologica*, tr. 1, q. 1, c. 2, a. 1 (Quaracchi: Coll. S. Bonaventurae, 1924-1948) t. 1, p 42 had already made the reformulation: "optimum est optimum; ergo optimum est . . . 'optimum' est 'quo nihil est melius."

18. Bonaventure, *Commentaria in iv libros Sententiarum*, 1, d. 8, pars 1, a. 1, q. 2, and *Quaestio disputate de mysterio trinitatis*, 1, 1, 1, 29, texts to be found in his *Opera omnia* (Quaracchi: Coll. S. Bonaventurae, 1882-1902) t. 1, p 155 and t. 5, p 48 respectively, this Franciscan held first, that the "truth" of divine Being is evident in itself and also evident in proof; second, he joined Alexander (who had been his master) in outdistancing Anselm is formulating a "brief" argument: "si Deus est Deus, Deus est;" he also set up consequences of the same form on "optimum" and "ens completissimum."

19. Descartes, *Meditationes de prima philosophia*, ed. cit. t. 7, p 160-170, "secundae responsiones; Rationes dei existentiam probantes. . ." *Principia philosophiae*, pars i, 14, t. 8, p 10, 11. 12-15: ". . . percipiat idea trianguli necessario contineri tres ejus angulos aequales esse duobus rectis . . ." pars iv, p 34, 11. 21-24: ". . . plus parfait que ie n'estois, et mesme qui eust en soy toutes les perfections dont ie pouuois auoir quelque idée, c'est a dire, pour m'expliquer en vn mot, qui fust Dieu."

20. G. W. Leibniz, *New Essays concerning Human Understanding* 4, 10, 7, tr. A. G. Langley (New York: Macmillan, 1986) p 502-505; see *Neue Abhandlungen über den menschlichen Verstand /Nouveaux essais sur l'entendement humain*, edd. W. von Englehardt and H. H. Holz (Frankfurt am Main: Insel-Verlag, 1961) t. 2, p 434-441.

21. G. W. F. Hegel, *System der Philosophie, Erster Teil. Die Logik* Sämtliche Werke (Stuttgart-Bad Cannstatt: Fr Frommann Verlag, 1964) Bd. 8, p 149-151; Hegel's remarks are notable for their recognition that Aquinas had sought in the argument what Anselm had not intended to provide.

22. For a useful collection of papers on the *Proslogion* argument from various points of view, buttressed by an extensive bibliography, see J. Hick and A. C. McGill, *The Many-faced Argument* (New York: Macmillan, 1967).

23. W. James, *Pragmatism* (Cambridge, Ma.: Harvard University Press, 1975) on the "tough-minded," "tender-minded" terminology see p 13, 14; on Kant, ibidem, p 269: "Kant's mind is the rarest and most intricate of all possible antique bric-a-brac museums . . . not one single conception which is both indispensable to philosophy and which philosophy either did not possess before him, or was not destined inevitably to acquire after him . . . The true line of philosophic progress lies, in short, it seems to me, not so much *through* Kant as *round* him . . .;" on Hegel, having named Plato, Locke, Spinoza, Mill, Caird, and Hegel, James had harsh words for them all: ". . . these names are little more than reminders of as many curious personal ways of falling short. It would be an

obvious absurdity if such ways of taking the universe were actually true." ibidem, p 25.

24. On this fundamental point see the percipient remarks by G. R. Evans, "St. Anselm and Knowing God," *J.T.S.* NS 28 (1977) p 434, 435: "In the *Proslogion* alone [of Anselm's works] prayer and argument are brought together in a single work . . .," also, p 442: "Here, in a single work, Anselm is trying to know God directly through prayer, and to establish what can be known about him by means of plain argument . . ."

25. Ed. cit. t. 3 (Edinburgh: 1946) I. *Orationes sive meditationes.*

26. See discussion of this double concern, A. C. Pegis, art. cit., note 7; although Richard of Saint Victor declined to use the *Proslogion* argument to establish the divine Being, he was ready to apply the formula in grounding the divine attributes: *Richard de saint-Victor. Opuscules theologiques,* ed. J. Ribaillier (Paris: J. Vrin, 1967) p 241 "La perfection divine se définit par la formule anselmienne: *id quo majus, id quo melius cogitari potest.*" (SIC).

27. On Anselm's logical expertise see the laudatory (in my view totally justified) estimate by D. P. Henry, "Saint Anselm as a Logician," *Sola ratione.* Anselm-Studien für Pater Dr. h. c. Franciscus Salesius Schmitt OSB zum 75. Geburtstag am 20. Dezember 1969 (Stuttgart-Bad Cannstatt: Fr. Frommann Verlag, 1970) p 13, 14.

28. *Proslogion*, Chapter I, ed. cit. p 100, 11. 18, 19.

29. Ibidem, Chapter IV p 104, 11. 5-7.

30. The five works by Boethius are his *Philosophiae consolatio, In Isagogen Porphyrii commenta,* editio prima, *Introductio ad syllogismos categoricos, Commentaria in Topica Ciceronis,* and *In librum Aristotelis de interpretatione commentaria,* editio prima; the two by Augustine are his *De trinitate* and his *Tractatus in evangelium Ioannis.*

31. See below, notes 68-71 for the contention by Roger Nottingham O. F. M. in mid-fourteenth century that the denial of divine Being includes all other (lesser) contradictions.

32. See Anselm's response to Gaunilo, ed. cit. t. 1, p 130, 11. 3-5.

33. See, for instance, Rev 12,9; 13,14; 19,20; 20,3; 20,8; 20,10; Anselm complained in the *De veritate* IX, ed. cit. t. 1, p 188 that although everyone speaks of the truth of signification, few consider the truth that resides in the being of things (1. 27 ff.); between these two "truths" Anselm located the mode in which a morally good act is "true" and the morally deficient act "false:" "Since nothing is to be done by any one except what he ought to do, by the very fact that any one does anything he states and signifies that he ought to do it. Now, if he ought to do what he is doing, he states a truth; if he ought not, he lies" ibidem, p 189, 11. 4-7.

34. *Proslogion*, Chapter II, ed. cit. p 101, 11. 3-4; cf. ibidem, Chapter I, p 100, 11. 15, 16: "Non tento, domine, penetrare altitudinem tuam, quia nullatenus comparo illi intellectum meum."

35. Ibidem, Chapter I, p 98, 1. 4; Chapter XVI, p 112, 1. 20.

36. Ibidem, Chapter XVI, p 113, 11. 1-4.

37. Ibidem, Chapter XVI, p 112, 1. 22.

38. Ibidem, Chapter XVIII, p 114, 11. 2-5; cf. Ps 50,7 (51,5).

39. Ibidem, Chapter XXV, p 118, 1. 14, Chapter XXVI, p 121, 11. 7, 8, 11, 12.

40. Ibidem, Chapter XVI, p 112, 11. 24-27.

41. Ibidem, Chapter XIV, p 111, 11. 16-21.

42. Work cited above, note 27.

43. Aristotle, *Categories* 11; 14 a 15 ff. *Metaphysics* 4, 2; 1004 a 9 ff.

44. William of St Thierry and Bernard of Clairvaux counted this one of Abelard's most offensive errors; see Bernard's *Tractatus de erroribus Abaelardi*, PL 182, 1055 A-1061 B where he complained "We now have in France a novel 'theologian' in exchange for the old school-master who, when he was young, did his trifling in the art of dialectic, but who now does his raving on Sacred Scripture . . . His 'theology' is more accurately a 'foolology'!" Needless to say, the future was with Abelard.

45. Augustine, *De doctrina christiana* 2, 12, 17; PL 34 43.

46. Augustine, *De trinitate* 15, 2, 2; PL 42 1058.

47. The classical place in Augustine is the long noetic examination in the *De libero arbitrio* 2, 2, 5-2, 16, 41; Pl 32 1242-1263 where the Bishop of Hippo began with the Psalmist's fool, advanced through the perception of a series of axiomatic truths (Ibidem, 2, 10, 28, PL 32 1256) to the reasoned conviction that the fool is wrong and God is; these Augustinian "seeds" were cultivated by Boethius, *De trinitate* (dedication to his father-in-law, Symmachus, "Vobis tamen etiam illud inspiciendum est, an ex beati Augustini scriptis semina rationum aliquos in nos uenientia fructus extulerint" The Loeb Classical Library edition of *The Theological Tractates* and *The Consolation of Philosophy*, edd. H. F. Stewart and E. K. Rand (Cambridge, Ma.: Harvard University Press, 1946) p 4); the most influential combination of axiomatic intuitions with close reasoning to achieve the repose of "intellectus" is the *Quomodo substantiae (De hebdomadibus)*, ed. cit. p 38-51.

48. Aristotle's *Metaphysics*, in which he provided an indirect demonstration that it is not possible "for the same thing to be and not to be," (4, 4; 1005 b 35 ff.) was not available to the Latin world until the thirteenth century.

49. Aristotle's essays and the translations of them and commentaries on them by Boethius constituted a major part of the texts known as the *Logica vetus*, "The Old Logic."

50. Anselm, *Epistola de incarnatione Verbi* 1, ed. cit. t. 2, p 9, 10, wrote of "illi utique nostri temporis dialectici, immo dialecticae haeretici, qui non nisi flatum vocis putant universales esse substantias . . . Qui enim nondum intelligit quomodo plures homines in specie sint unus homo: qualiter in illa secretissima et altissima natura comprehendet quomodo plures personae, quarum singula quaeque perfectus est deus, sint unus deus?" In a letter to Fulco, ed. cit, t. 3, p 279, 11. 4-7, Anselm named him: "ROSCELINUS clericus dicit in deo tres personas esse tres res ab invicem separatas, sicut sunt tres angeli, ita tamen ut una sit voluntas et potestas . . . et tres deos vere posse dici, si usus admitteret."

51. E. Gilson, "Sens et nature de l'argument de saint Anselme," *Archives d'histoire doctrinale et littéraire du moyen age* 9 (1934) p 7: Au fond, l'insensé pense comme Roscelin: c'est un nominaliste.

52. *Proslogion*, Chapter IV, ed. cit. p 103, variant at all. 20, 21: "Nullus quippe intelligens id quod sunt ignis et aqua, potest cogitare ignem esse aquam secundam res, licet hoc possit secundum voces . . ."

53. Ibidem, 11. 18, 19: "Aliter enim cogitatur res cum vox eam significans cogitatur, aliter cum id ipsum quod res est intelligitur."

54. This is the general pattern of argument bequeathed above all by Boethius in his *Quomodo substantiae* cited above, note 47; the text of the *Monologion* is to be found in the same volume as that of the *Proslogion*, ed. cit.

55. *Monologion*, Chapter IV, t. 1, p 16, 11. 1, 2: "Qui enim dubitat quod in natura sua ligno melior sit equus, et equo praestantior homo, is profecto non est dicendus homo."

56. *De veritate* X, ed. cit. t. 1, p 190, 11. 1-4: "Considera quia, cum omnes supradictae rectitudines ideo sint rectitudines, quia illa in quibus sunt aut sunt aut faciunt quod debent: summa veritas non ideo est rectitudo quia debet aliquid. Omnia enim illi debent, ipsa vero nulli quicquam debet; nec ulla ratione est quod est, nisi quia est."

57. *Monologion*, Chapter XXVI, ed. cit. p 44, 11. 3-19 and ibidem, Chapter XVI p 30, 11. 8-11.

58. Boethius, *Philosophiae consolationis* liber 3, prosa 10, ed. cit. p 268: "Nam cum nihil deo melius excogitari queat, id quo melius nihil est bonum esse quis dubitet?"

59. Augustine, *De libero arbitrio* 2, 6, 14, PL 32 1248: "Fateor Deum, quo nihil superius esse constiterit;" comparable turns of phrase were often under his pen, see *De doctrina christiana* 1, 7, 7, PL 34 22: ". . . quo nihil melius sit atque sublimius . . ." ". . . nec quiquam inveniri potest qui hoc Deum credat esse quo melius aliquid est . . ." *Enarratio 3 in psalmum 32*, 2, 15, PL 36 393: "Melior te vis esse; novi, omnes novimus, omnes volumus; quaere, quod est melius te, ut inde efficiaris melior te;" *Epistola* 155, 4, 13, PL 33 672: "Quid autem eligamus, quod praecipue diligamus, nisi quo nihil melius invenimus? Hoc Deus est . . . Tanto enim nobis melius est, quanto magis in illum imus, quo nihil melius est;" see also *Confessionum* liber 7, 4, 6.

60. L. Annaei Senecae, *Ad Lucillium naturalium quaestionum libri vii*, 1, pro-logus, ed. Fr. Haase, (Leipzig: Teubner, 1893, p 159: ". . . quid est deus? . . . sic demum magnitudo sua illi redditur, qua nihil maius excogitari potest . . ."

61. M.T. Cicero, *De natura deorum* 2, 7, 18 The Loeb Classical Library edition, p 140, 142: "Atqui certe nihil omnium rerum melius est mundo nihil praestabilius nihil pulcrius, nec solum nihil est sed ne cogitari quidem quicquam melius potest;" this reference was given to me by Professor David Mosher, Scarborough College and the University of Toronto.

62. Ignatius Antiochenus, *Ad Magnesios* 1 and 7, The Loeb Classical Library, p 196: ". . . hēs ouden prokekritai . . ." and "ho estin Iēsous Christos, hou ameinon ouden estin."

63. Anselm, *Epistola ad Lanfrancum*, ed. cit. t. 3, p 199, 200 "defends" himself against a charge of novelty, ". . . omnino nihil ibi assererem, nisi quod aut canonicis aut beati AUGUSTINI dictis incunctanter posse defendi viderem . . . ea me non a me praesumpsisse, sed ab alio assumpsisse ostendendo."

64. Eadmer, *Vita sancti Anselmi*, ed. cit. p 30: "Et ecce quadam nocte inter nocturnas vigilias Dei gratia illuxit in corde ejus, et res patuit intellectui ejus, immensoque gaudio et jubilatione replevit omnia intima ejus . . ."

65. No Kantian term has been more widely accepted, in this case, with Kant's meaning, i.e. that arguments of this type begin with *logos*, "thought," and purport (illicitly) to end with *ontos*, the genitive of *ōn*, "being."

66. I. Kant, loc. cit. see above, note 16.

67. *Proslogion*, Chapter XV, ed. cit, t. 1, p. 112, 11. 14, 15.

68. "The 'Introitus ad sententias' of Roger Nottingham, O.F.M." ed. E.A. Synan, *Mediaeval Studies* 25 (1963) p 259-279; Roger also claimed to be able to demonstrate that "God is" from any necessary proposition by a dialectic that is comparable to that by which he argued from an instance of contradiction.

69. *Introitus*, ed. cit. p 279, par. 39.

70. His argument consists in an inference from the opposite of the consequent to the opposite of the antecedent; it assumes a complicated presentation of the world of real beings and its opposite, an intelligible structure of graded non-being; God is at the summit of real being and his opposite is not the contingent non-being of a possible, but the absolute non-being of impossibility.

71. Ibidem, p 279, par. 36: "... *deum non esse* non solum unicam tantum contradictionem sed includit omnem imaginariam contradictionem. Et ita sequitur quod *deum non esse* majorem includit contradictionem quam aliquod aliud quod *deum non esse* non includit ..."

The Sin of Folly*

ANNIE KRAUS

The final and highest cause of wisdom, which Thomas Aquinas rightfully contrasts with folly, is the absolute existence of the interior divine life of love. Human wisdom is constituted through participation in God's wisdom.[1] But what is the final and highest cause of *stupor* (dullness), folly, enabling us to understand it in its deepest origins and proper nature?

In the second article of his question *De Stultitia* (Of Folly), Thomas emphatically describes folly as a sin *(peccatum)*. He concludes that folly likewise has a final and highest cause which must be opposed to that of wisdom. At the very beginning of his question, Thomas calls language to witness for his definition of folly and we follow in his steps as we try to advance toward this final cause, having recourse to language. Latin, and German itself, with its encompassing and descriptive etymological treasures, coincide to a great extent with Thomas' understanding. However, we are equally indebted to the Hebrew, a language which, in its etymology, reaches to the depths of linguistic origins and enables us to fully define "folly". In the final analysis, this influenced Thomas' definition.

The following quotation from Jeremiah points to the profound agreement of Thomas with Holy Scripture. In 5, 21 Jeremiah complains about the perversity and stubbornnes of his people, exclaiming: "Hear this, O foolish and senseless (literally, without heart, this being the organ of understanding) people, who have eyes but see not, who have ears but hear not." This can be compared with *habet sensum* with its inner appeal for responsibility in Thomas' definition. Everyone has senses, which he can use when he so wills. Looking at Acts 7, 51 we find that Thomas took his definition of "folly" directly from this source: "You stiff-necked people *(stupor)*, uncircumcised in heart *(hebetudo cordis)* and ears *(obtusio*

---

*Translation from the German by Mrs. Nora Quigley and L. Frizzell.
"Folly" translates *Dummheit* and *Stultia*.

sensuum), you always resist the Holy Spirit!". This is *sapientia* which, according to Thomas, is rightfully contrasted with stupidity and which, as gift of the Holy Spirit, is its sole and ultimate conqueror.

Especially from the philosophical viewpoint, knowledge of language is of utmost importance. Philosophers are concerned with the whole of being (existence) and its foundations (principles) and must consider all details offered to them. Language belongs in a special way to human nature as a *zoon logon echon* and it contains a "fossilized philosophy". Therefore, we are entirely justified in referring to the teachings and language of the Bible and to the evidence of Hebrew etymology as a precious source for knowledge of the origin and essence of folly. Here we find a surprising conformity between Latin and German etymology for the word "stupid". The idea of folly developed by Thomas agrees with the German etymology and, contrary to commonly held opinions today, confirms the definition that folly, in its proper sense, is not rooted in the intellect but is a fault of the will,[2] that is, relates to the heart. It is the heart, the core and all-encompassing depth of the human being as person (which means the human being in his integral wholeness) which makes the most intimate, fulfilling and qualifying decision, namely: to accept or to reject God. This corresponds to the biblical understanding wherein "the foolish man declares in his heart" (that is, in his will): "There is no God" (Ps 14, 1;53, 2). He does not say this in his intellect since on the grounds of the law of causality the evidence of a highest cause cannot be denied (see also Rom 1, 20, according to which the human being can arrive at knowledge of God already through his creatures).

The Concept of Folly in the Old Testament
(Foolishness and Wickedness)

The concept of folly as a (serious) sin is characteristic of the Old Testament.[3] This is true, not only in the sense noticed in numerous texts but it becomes even more evident when we consider the frequently used root words: *nebhalah* and *nabhal* which can be identified with words meaning foolishness and wickedness as well as meaning "a fool" and "a wicked person." Foolishness is in itself wickedness and the fool a wicked person. The pertinent dictionaries interpret *nebhalah* as "insensitivity to God's law" and this conforms to Thomas' definition of "dullness of the heart." The words "stupid," "dishonourable" and "wicked"[4] denote negatively the same values which correspond to that which Thomas emphasized positively by contrast[5] with knowledge (intelligence) and virtue. The opposite of this refers here to (sinful) not knowing (folly) and depravity.[6]

Linguistically, therefore, foolishness becomes an extremely serious sin. This is corroborated further by the fact that foolishness and wickedness are often used as identical concepts, a fact also indicated by the medieval use of the word *tumpheit* (dumbness)[7]. In defining the concept foolishness as a sinful refusal to know God and as a willful, sinful wickedness, theological and biblical dictionaries refer especially to Psalms 14, 1 and 53, 2 wherein it says: "The fool says in his heart 'There is no God'." So, in accord with Thomas, stupidity is looked upon as a matter of the (perverted) heart or will.

The basic words *nabhal, nebhalah* and a great number of other words for "stupid" lie between the words *ʾewil* (wrong) and *beliyaʿal* (Belial), which express the weightiness of *stupor*. We can mention only a few of these words but it is interesting to note how accurately they correspond to significant English words: *pethi*[8] = inexperienced, simple, easily tempted; *nabhub*[9] = empty-headed; *baʿar*[10] = beastly stupid or dull; the important and frequently used word *kesil*[11] =impudent, inconsiderate, in a religious sense insolent, obstinate, wicked, sacrilegious.[12] *Kesil* belongs to the root form *kesel* which means impudent[13] together with another stem *kesel* = loin, fatty loin muscles alongside the kidneys[14] which originates in *ksl* = to be foolish, and this in turn comes from the root word for sluggish (to be obese?).[15] *Kesil* is frequently used in the sense of Gr. *aphron* = unreasonable, reckless.[16] Here the word *holeloth*[17] must be added; it comes from *halal* = to be deluded "as a result of the moral insensitivity of a foolish person."[18]

The Demonic Element of Folly (Belial)

The Hebrew word most often used for stupid is *nabhal* and it can be found in the well known 1Sam 25, 25: "Let not my lord regard this ill-natured *(beliyaʿal)* fellow, Nabal,[19] for as his name *(Nabal,* fool) is, so is he." The proximity of Belial and *nabhal* brings out the correlation of these words and in one step takes us to the abyss from which folly arises and into which it can lead: the syllables of both *beli* and *nabhal* originate in the root *blh* and imply negation.[20] It is no accident that Martin Buber translates Ps 14, 1 thus: "The empty person *(der Nichtige)* says in his heart 'There is no God' ".[21] These two negatives, initially denoting only a lack, a weakness and a deficiency (matching the mere diminishing of the senses or a weakness implied in the English word dumb), express the deceptive denial of truth and being, and also the hostility which characterizes the essence of folly. Scripture characterizes Belial in this same way; he is simply called the "enemy" (Matt 13.25.28.39 etc.), not only the "father of lies" but, as logically follows, "a murderer from the beginning" (John 8,44). So already we find in these primitive expressions the devastating historical power of folly: destructiveness as an active denial which belongs to folly as sin in the same way as active acceptance relates to wisdom as virtue. But whoever perverts the heart which establishes human existence and participates in it will end in oblivion. *Nabhal,* fool means the one who became nothing! And so Martin Buber is justified in saying: "The empty person says in his heart: 'There is no God.' "

In this connection it is very important to remember that the word *nabhal* originated in the verb *nabhel* which means: 1. to wither; 2. the decay of earth and mankind (compare this with the expression *dummern* = to smell of decay); 3. to be futile, to be foolish.[22] Therefore, the Hebrew language gives us an etymological connection between foolishness and things pertaining to the domain of death.[23] The biblical definition of the concept "foolishness" is related to *nabhel* = withered, *nebhelah* = cadaver, carrion.[24] Wilhelm Caspari thinks that those passages where *nabhel* is translated as "decaying"[25] are sufficient proof that *nabhal, nebhalah* mean "conveyor of destruction," "corruptible." This destructiveness seems to be applied in Old Testament community thought to what is a public danger and sacrilegious activity of fools. "The *nabhal* is . . . one who is under the influence of terrifying powers . . . who within the community of Yahweh . . . causes the individual's separation from Yahweh. Therefore, through rashness like *kesil* or *aphron,* he forfeits his salvation;"[26] no one should associate with such an individual.[27] The word *nebhelah* (cadaver, carrion) was used because of its relationship to sacred law describing the death of unclean animals which was thought to be caused by demonic powers.[28] Thus the connotations of the phenomenon of folly are established etymologically. They point to the abyss of death, to death in hell.[29] But this etymological reflection on the deadly demonic power of folly as serious sin, as Thomas defined it, must be investigated in light of the original relationship of *nabhal* and Belial. With the realization that the definition of Belial is closely connected with the concept of foolishness (i.e. *nebhalah)* as an ethical-religious category, which is proven by their common root *blh,* the demonic element of folly, which makes it into a sin and a vice, is fully expressed.

In Holy Scripture the entire range of meaning for the word dumb corresponds quite closely to the German, which is wider than the Latin words which were used infrequently but very emphatically by Thomas. However, these were exceeded by the abundance of different connotations in Hebrew, the language of revelation which approaches the endless reaches of the Absolute and which serves as the final explanatory basis for everything we have so far pursued concerning the nature of folly as a abyss itself. In agreement with the Latin word *stupor* the range of meanings reaches from ʿ*ewil*, to be sturdy and corpulent,[30] (which was probably the original meaning for dumb and signified a clumsy, obese, pudgy beast) to Belial, the useless, the corrupt, that which cannot rise up (that is, cannot reach God).[31] *ʾEwil* is the linguistic, metaphysical location of the gross, degenerated heart[32] which harbours bad and foolish thoughts and is bemoaned repeatedly in the Bible and the *hebetudo cordis* of St. Thomas. The fact that the word Belial *(beliyaʿal)* derives from the agricultural domain seems significant because here again, and from the ground up, the relationship of wisdom and foolishness with things corporeal seems to be emphasized, that is the "a priori" connection of spirit (in this case unspiritual or contra-spiritual) with body.[33]

Therefore, it is Belial who makes the human being clumsy and stubborn and imprisons him in matter. Because obese and dumb appear as closely related concepts it seems that the Bible already indicates a basic connection between stupidity and materialism. Thomas does the same when he states (q. 46 a. 3) that folly is the daughter of *luxuria*.[34] The heaviness of *stupor* which Thomas and the Hebrew etymology stress in common is based on this characteristic of persistent opposition to God; it aims toward that which opposes God as "Spirit" (John 4,24), namely the material, as far as it is perceived as something contrary to the spiritual, "materialistic." The origin of this *stupor* as sin, which works against God as Spirit of love, who (as *vis unitiva et concretiva*) bestows being must be a hate which wills non-being and death itself. In Scripture we find harsh expressions about this heaviness of the fool who is stubborn and stone-like,[35] whose "life is worse than death" (Sir 22,11). It is the *stupor* of a hellish death to which Belial, the God-denying *vis separativa et abstractiva* of folly, condemns the foolish man, forcing him into the narrowness of a loveless ego. The initial element of heaviness hints at the *mysterium iniquitatis* which characterizes sinful folly and which bases its existence on an arrogant refusal of love.

Scripture contrasts this God-sundering heaviness of sinful *stupor* with the lightness, the flexibility and penetrating power of wisdom[36] which is spirit and breath. When we read that wisdom is "more mobile than any motion" (Wis 7,24), this recalls the words of Thomas a Kempis "love flies" (*The Imitation of Christ*, Book III, ch. 5). In reading that wisdom is "so pure, fine and clear that it pervades and permeates all things" (Wis 7,22.23.24), we are reminded of the tangible, "tasting" knowledge of *sapientia* and also of a quotation from Isidore in q. 46 a. 1: "Sapiens autem habet sensum subtilem et perspicacem." Wisdom is the "breath of God's power" (Wis 7,25) whose "Spirit has filled the world and which holds all things together" (Wis 1,7). This proves itself to be *vis unitiva et concretiva*, the all-encompassing living and life-giving power of love, which as the "emanation of the Almighty" (Wis 7,25) alone can truly know and which—with the cardinal virtues (Wis 8,7) contains all the other virtues. Love is the basis for all moral virtues and also for intelligence[37] (or wisdom). According to Scripture, therefore, the depth of God's light, the inner divine life of love, wherein all true knowing (as life-giving love) is rooted ultimately, stands opposite the abyss of darkness, the death-inflicting hate of Belial, in whom the *stupor* of folly is grounded in all its terrifying reality. Through him folly becomes the cardinal vice with which all other vices are connected in the same way as all virtues are related to each other.

We deliberately ignore here the numerous places (especially in Sirach) where the word *nabhal* is interpreted with sociological overtones, as the opposite of propriety and common sense, especially because there it refers often to that "aliquid modicum," a trifle which would not drive Thomas to label a person as "dumb." Nor do we study the places where foolishness is interpreted as *pethi*, meaning inexperience. This involves that aspect of ignorance that can be alleviated by teaching. Even an intelligent person occasionally may be subject to it, and there can be a place for harmless, "natural," forgivable ignorance with sometimes even charming aspects. This is fundamentally different from the sinful, "supernatural" folly of the unbeliever. We are interested here only in the unity of knowledge and freedom (action) as it appears in countless instances in the Bible relating to linguistic, metaphysical foundations. Evidently, the constantly present intellectual impulse is completely assimilated into the affective, ethical-religious experience of biblical man. Wherever in the Sapiential Literature, especially in *Proverbs*, the basic theme of foolishness is mentioned, we find the fool to be a malicious despiser of God, a sinner who tramples God's commandment underfoot[38] even though he understands it intellectually, and through his understanding knows of his Maker's existence (Rom 1,20). For the prophets the inseparable unity of knowledge (intelligence), love and active fulfillment of the commandment is contrasted with lack of knowledge (foolishness), hate and sinful transgression of the commandment (see Jer 4,22; Hos 6,3 etc.). Even when folly seems to be clothed in intellectual raiment,[39] there is a turning toward the practical order in such a way[40] that a confrontation between malice (foolishness) and wisdom is obvious. The word "stupid" (or foolish) is always used in its radical sense of active ethical failing, a moral offense against God, and this is the case for Thomas in his question. The Scripture texts mentioning the word fool in the sense of godless[41] are as numerous as those mentioning the word wicked.

In connection with such relation of concepts, Grimm's dictionary remarks on the transition from deaf (dumb) to enraged, raving; the word raving (which means mental insanity as well as emotional fury) encompasses the stupidity unleashed by the double impulse of an intellectual, objective lapse from truth as well as subjective enmity against it in deed, even murder (see Acts 7,54.57.58). The affective medium of this transition to rage as an aspect of becoming foolish is anger, for according to the Scriptures, anger beclouds the heart and senses. "Anger lodges in the bosom of fools" (Ecc 7,9). The rabbinical literature of the third century contains many sentences similar to the following: "When a man who is angry is a scholar, his learning leaves him". "Because our teacher Moses became angry he made mistakes". "Three times Moses became angry (Exod 16,20; Num 31,14; Lev 10,16) and the *halakhah* (the legal norm) was hidden from him".[42] Thomas also mentions in the third article of his question that anger disposes a human being toward folly in a physical way and thus he stresses again the sensual bent of the spirit. "Anger, by reason of its keenness, produces the greatest change in the nature of the body, therefore it conduces most to the folly which results from a bodily impediment."

As Thomas allows for the interchange of the concepts *ens—verum— bonum*, so can we interchange *non ens—non verum (falsum)—non bonum (malum)*, especially with reference to the words studied through Hebrew etymology. When we state that non-being, untruth (as the *mysterium iniquitatis*, the lie of the heart), malice are interchangable concepts, we mean that folly as a willed denial and perversion of being and truth is a lie,[43] a radical sin *(malum)*; in the same way as truth presupposes the (good) being, it presupposes the (evil) non-being. Therefore, its hating iniquity wills this non-being[44] just as wisdom lovingly wills being.[45]

Folly and Simplicity (Wisdom)

A distinction must always be made between folly and simplicity whether the latter is coupled with erudition or not. Since truth is in its fullest sense only as done in love, the simple can find its light insofar as wisdom, which leads to this light, is "easily discernible by those who love her, and is found by those who seek her" (Wis 6,12). The simple man who makes the right decision in his heart "will find her sitting at his door" (Wis 6,14). Simplicity is a characteristic of wisdom. This simplicity is connected with intelligence because only those who do the truth will come to the light (John 3,21); they will be able to see, which means become wise. We must not forget that the Latin *prudentia* comes from *providentia* which contains the root *videre*. As a guiding virtue, intelligence is the eye of the spirit. Seeing it leads to a desire always to see more, so that its "eye becomes light" (see Luke 11,33-36) and always more light; it is oriented toward the ever-expanding fullness of being and leads man finally to his fulfillment, to the light of the beatific vision. In contrast, the depravity of folly is a blindness of the spirit in an increasing narrowness (obtuseness) which leads into the emptiness which is a portent of hell. However, because the intelligent person responds to the loving claim of transcendental Being, he sees, obeys him and in this loving obedience speeds towards his own freedom, as love. The discernment of intelligence which fulfills itself in the *visio beatifica*, comes from hearing.[46] The eyes of those who obey are opened, and whoever listens will see. The egocentric spirit, enmeshed in his stupidity, not wanting to listen, blinds himself and allows himself to be drawn into the dungeon of his selfishness where his eyes are clouded and his body becomes heavy and dull. Such a person deprives himself of open eyes, of the wisdom which makes the "entire body" (person) light (see Luke 11,33-36), both illuminated and free (light as opposed to heavy).

Intelligence founded in love is *scientia* as well as *conscientia*, knowledge and conscience, while blind folly founded in non-love is a willingly induced deafness and an unscrupulous lack of knowledge. In its essence folly does not have a conscience, and that is its sin. The virtue of intelligence with its "shrewd assessment of situations"[47] must always, alert as love is (see Cant 5, 2), strive to realize truth at every moment so that "with time" it may become ever more intelligent. The true diligence of the intelligent person, who allows himself to be taught "through the law of life and knowledge" (Sir 45, 5) proves his constancy. Folly (sluggishness) in its infidelity with regard to truth and its claim for practical and concrete at all times, is in its *stupor* idle and lazy, "lazy as sin"—it remains dumb and in death. As signs of life, alertness and watchfulness are integral components of intelligence. This can be seen in the word *sapientia*, the tasting *(sapere)* as most intensive activation of the totality of body and soul. Only love's watchfulness over life leads to eternal life which, through the power of the Holy Spirit, we are able to share even while still on earth. Only love, to which the essence of alertness belongs, "remains" (1Cor 13, 8). Thus the admonition rings out: "Watch!" The parable of the wise, alert virgins and the foolish, sleeping virgins (Matt 25, 1-13) is especially pertinent for our theme. As understood throughout the New Testament, the admonition means "Love one another!"

In Belial we have found the final and highest cause of folly which is antithetical to the final and highest cause of wisdom, which is the essence of divine love. Etymology of the Hebrew word *nabhal* and other Hebrew words for stupid refer to this cause. Seen from this viewpoint, we can state that language makes not simply a fossilized philosophy but also a fossilized theology. In view of such a central anthropological phenomenon as folly, to which Thomas deliberately paid meticulous attention, it seems that attention must be paid to the profound dimensions of an anthropological discussion with the help of Holy Scripture and theology, especially since anthropology has become such an important aspect of philosophy in our day. In a parallel to the demon's familiar admonition to Socrates: "Socrates, make music!", which emphasizes the close connection of philosophy and muses, we may now, because of the metaphysical insights derived from the Hebrew language, also exclaim: "Philosophizer, cultivate theology!" This challenge was heeded by several great philosophers (Plato, for example) in order to bring their philosophical studies to their highest point.

Although we have become aware of the terrible power of Belial in our discourse based on Holy Scripture, this power which may dominate the dissolute heart can be conquered. In contrast to the pure spirit of angels, the human being remains a sensient spirit. As such, he experiences a dulling of his senses but not their destruction. In spite of the *hebetudo* of his heart (even if it is so weak), man retains his freedom to which he can return at any time; because of the power of grace, as it were with a shout *de profundis*, he abandons the sin of folly, entering the love of God. This love will undo the stiffness and stoniness of his heart and is always ready to give him a new heart of flesh and a new spirit (Ezek 11, 19; 18, 31; 36, 26). "For God is a friend of life."

NOTES

1. *S. Th.*, II-II, q 23, a 2 ad 1: . . . sapientia qua formaliter sapientes sumus est participatio quaedam divinae sapientiae . . .
2. The word "stubborn" *(stupor)* closely connected with "dumb," has its origins in rigidity and leads through the related idea of "obstinate" directly to a relationship with the will. For the word dumb and those words related to it, see especially *Deutsches Wörterbuch von Jakob Grimm und Wilhelm Grimm*, 16 volumes, Leipzig (1860-1954) and other related dictionaries, and my book *Der Begriff der Dummheit bei Thomas v. Aquin und seine Spiegelung in Sprache und Kultur* (Münster: Aschendorf 1971).
3. This can be verified, especially in Ps 38, 6 and Ps 69, 6.
4. Herbert Haag, *Bibellexicon*, Einsiedeln (1956), Art. "Weisheit," col 1702.

5. *S. Th.*, II-II, q 47, a 13 ad 2 etc.: prudentia non potest esse sine virtutibus moralibus; *ibid*, I-II, q 58, a 4c etc.: virtus moralis sine prudentia esse non potest; *Ver:* 5, 1 etc.: oportet omnem prudentem esse virtuosum; *S. Th.*, II-II, q 109, a 2 ad 2 etc.: intellectus et voluntas invicem se includunt.

6. See Edm. Kalt, *Biblisches Reallexikon* (Paderborn² 1939), under "Torheit": . . ." in the Old Testament *nebhalah* (foolishness) indicates . . . the insensitivity concerning God's law and is equivalent to the idea of wickedness (Ps 14, 1; 53.2); also . . . wickedness, blasphemy (Isa 32, 6) rape of a virgin (Gen 34, 7; 2 Sam 13, 12) and hardheartedness." Herbert Haag, *op cit.*, under "Tor," col. (1631): "The Old Testament interprets . . . foolishness . . . as the deficiency brought about by one's own fault which hinders the knowledge essential to a moral-religious existence (Ps 37, 6 . . .)." *Biblisches Handworterbuch*, edited by Paul Zeller (Stuttgart³ 1912) under "Tor": Foolishness is . . . a moral error connected with a lack of truth. Therefore, foolishness is a sin and, conversely, sin is foolishness when it misunderstands God's truth." (See *S. Th.*, II-II, q 119, a 3 ad 3 etc.). Edo Osterloh and Hans Engelland, *Biblisch-theologisches Handwörterbuch zur Lutherbibel und zu neueren Übersetzungen* (Göttingen 1954) under "Tor": ". . . with them (foolish people) it is not only a matter of lacking understanding, but rather the lack of the correct knowledge of God . . . The foolish person is one who has abandoned God; he has severed his relationship with him because of contempt; he denies God . . . he insists in this foolishness on trying to convince other people to abandon God" (Isa 32, 5f).

7. See, for instance, E. Kalt, *loc. cit.*: ". . . Frequently folly and wickedness are identical concepts (2Sam 3, 33; Job 30, 8) . . ." Also Jost Trier, *Der deutsche Wortschatz im Sinnbezirk des Verstandes. Die Geschichte eines sprachlichen Feldes*, Vol. 1: *Von den Anfängen bis zum Beginn des 13. Jahrhunderis* Heidelberg 1931) p 308: ". . . Wisdom is the knowledge concerning the facts of salvation, but at the same time a grasping of salvation and therefore a purely religious attitude. The opposite of this is dumbness which can mean the obstinate turning away from salvation (*ignorantia* of the gravest sort) and often it expresses audacity, wicked arrogance and wickedness."

8. See L. Koehler, W. Baumgartner, *Lexicon in Veteris Testamenti Libros* (Leiden 1953) p 788.

9. *nabhub* = hollow: Exod 27, 8; 38, 7; Jer 52, 21; translated to hollow-headed, stupid: Job 11, 12.

10. *ba'ar* = bestial, stupid: references in Koehler-Baumgartner, op. cit., p 140.

11. See Koehler-Baumgartner, op. cit., p 447.

12. Attention should be paid to the movement over to action, corresponding to German vocabulary.

13. See Ecc 7, 25.

14. For instance, Lev 4, 9; 7, 4; 3, 4; 10, 15.

15. See Koehler-Baumgartner, op. cit., p. 447.

16. Ibid.

17. See E. Kalt, *op. cit.*: ". . . the expressions *holeloth* (from *halal* = being blinded) and *sikluth* (from *sakhal* = act foolishly) . . . emphasize the contrast to a true wisdom in living (Qoh 1, 17) . . .".

18. E. Kalt, ibid.; see Jer 4, 22 etc.

19. It seems significant that the word *nabhal* could become a proper name; folly as sin is something individual and personal. This personal character is not lost even in a so-called collective sin or in the almost proverbial stupidity of the

masses because man is essentially a person and is to be addressed as such even when he is part of a collectivity or group. Only with this presupposition did Jesus go to the "multitude"—today we would say: to the masses—and not to an elite group of intellectuals.

20. The basic meaning of *blh* is "to be used up, worn out, decayed" and *beli* would then mean: "cessation, destruction, negation, without."

21. *Die Schriftwerke,* translated into German by Martin Buber (Köln 1962).

22. Koehler-Baumgartner, op. cit., p. 589f, *nabhal-nebhalah* gives the references. See the exact parallels in the German language by Grimm, op. cit., Vol 2, Art "Dumm," col 1514,8 and Vol 11, Art "Taub," col 165,6.

23. Wilhelm Caspari, "Über den biblischen Begriff der Torheit," *Neue Kirchliche Zeitschrift,* 39(1928) p 668-695.

24. Ibid. p 668.

25. Isa 28, 1; 4 and 40, 7f., see Caspari, op. cit., p 671.

26. Wilhelm Caspari, art. cit., p 676.

27. Jos 7, 15.

28. Wilhelm Caspari, art. cit., p 669, 670.

29. See Prov 9, 18: "Dame Folly's guests are in the depths of Sheol."

30. For *'ewil* = foolish, see Jer 4, 22; for *'wl* = to be fat, with which *'ewil* is connected, see Ps 73, 4. See also Koehler-Baumgartner, op. cit., p 19.

31. *Beliya'al* = the useless; what does not let rise, prevents growth; without arising, without flourishing (taken from the domain of agriculture). See Koehler-Baumgartner, op. cit., 130, see above references.

32. Ps 73, 7; 119, 70; see Hos 13, 6 etc.

33. See here the teachings of Thomas about the necessary *conversio ad phantasmata* of the human spirit.

34. The concept of *luxuria* as indecent, carnal desire may be expanded to include excess and unbridled pleasure-seeking, in conformity with the word *luxus* which is related to *luxuria.*

35. See Sir 22, 14-15: "What is heavier than lead, what else is its name but 'Fool'? Sand and salt and a piece of iron are easier to carry than a stupid man." Prov 27, 22: "Crush a fool in a mortar with the pestle along with crushed grain, yet his folly will not depart from him."

36. Wis 7, 22-26 enumerates the characteristics of wisdom.

37. *De Veritate* 14, 5 ad 11.

38. See, for instance, Prov 13, 19; 5, 23 etc.

39. For instance in Wis 1, 3: "perverse thoughts separate men from God"; and at related places in Ps 14, 1 and Ps 53. 2.

40. See Wis 1, 4; 5; Ps 14, 1 (and Ps 53, 2): "They are corrupt, they do abominable deeds (wickedness) and there is no one who does good."

41. Here we come to understand that, according to the Bible, it was looked upon as a curse and mortal insult to call someone else a "fool," that is, a "wicked person." See Matt 5, 22 and G. Kittel, *Theologisches Wörterbuch zum Neuen Testament* (Stuttgart 1933-1960) IV p. 844-847. Between the biblical usage of the word "godless" as an insult and the usage of that word today, as it is accepted in most of the world as an evident and positive declaration of value, there lies a deep abyss which permits us to recognize in folly the extent of historical fall of mankind into sin.

42. Strack-Billerbeck, *Das Evangelium nach Matthaus erlautert aus Talmud und Midrasch* (Munich 1922) p 277.

43. Corresponding to Belial as the "father of lies."

44. Corresponding to Belial, the "enemy," the "murderer from the beginning."

45. Corresponding to God, who in his love is the "friend of life" (Wis 11, 26).

46. German dictionaries observe that each of the five senses is capable of interchanging with another and this is understandable for this concept too.

47. See *S. Th.*, II-II, q 49, a 4.

The Vision of Synagoga in the Scivias of Hildegard of Bingen*

WILLEHAD PAUL ECKERT, O.P.

The illuminated Scivias manuscript of Rupertsberg has thirty-five miniatures. It had been the property of the Nassau Landesbibliothek in Wiesbaden but in 1945 it was taken to Dresden for safekeeping whence it disappeared. Some time in the nineteen hundred and thirties a photostat of the manuscript was made at the Benedictine Abbey. The nuns of the Abbey of St. Hildegard at Eibingen copied the Codex between 1927 and 1933. A reproduction of the miniatures was therefore possible. It has been added to the translation of Scivias, *Wisse die Wege*, by Maura Böckeler (Salzburg 1954). The illuminated Scivias manuscript of Rupertsberg originated in the twelfth century, probably about 1170-80. According to the ownership entry on the end-paper inside the front cover (already in the thirteenth century), the manuscript belonged to the convent at Rupertsberg near Bingen where the nuns of the Benedictine order had settled. Presumably the Codex was produced at Rupertsberg under the supervision of St. Hildegard of Bingen. When the cloister at Rupertsberg was destroyed by the Swedes in 1632 the nuns saved the manuscript and took it along to their convent in Eibingen which became their home until the secularization in 1802. In 1814 the Codex was acquired by the Nassau Landesbibliothek in Wiesbaden. Johann Wolfgang von Goethe saw it there. In "Kunst und Wissenschaft am Rhein und Main" he remarks on it: "An old manuscript containing the visions of St. Hiltgard." The Codex was one of the treasures of the Nassau Landesbibliothek.

If it is true that the Codex originated at Rupertsberg during the lifetime of the saint, as indicated by the ownership entry, then she must have influenced the painting of the miniatures also. The artist would have had to simplify the highly complex visions of the saint in their structure

---

*Translation from the German by Mrs. Nora Quigley and L. Frizzell.

when he or she reproduced them on the pages of the book. However, he seems to have executed a relatively true reproduction of the saint's intentions. In these miniatures the portrayal of *Synagoga* deserves our special attention. The *Synagoga* of the Rupertsberg Codex, in contrast to the usual Synagoga pictures of the high and later Middle Ages, does not wear a blindfold; her eyes are closed. Still, no impression of absence of eyes or even only blindness is conveyed. An unprepared observer, that is, a person who is not familiar with the text accompanying the picture, will feel inclined to describe the eyes as cast down because the *Synagoga* seems to look upon the persons sitting on her arms and within a sort of cloth on her body. Also, in contrast to the customary Synagoga pictures, the *Synagoga* of the Rupertsberg Codex wears a golden head band. There is no indication of a crown having fallen off her head. She carries her head high even though, generally, *Synagoga* bows her head. Other common features are also missing: the broken lance and the downward-pointing tables of the Law. These features are usually regarded as a sign that the time of the Law has ceased and the time of grace begun. The tables of the Law are portrayed in this miniature but *Synagoga* does not hold them in her right hand. Rather, her arms are crossed and her hands are tucked under. In the curve of her arm and between her breasts Moses sits enthroned. He holds the tables raised in his right hand. It is the attitude that he assumed when he descended from Sinai to show the people the commandments he had received from God. Moses wears the Jewish hat which was common in the portraits of patriarchs and prophets of the twelfth century and which became mandatory after the Fourth Lateran Council in 1215. In the miniature of the Rupertsberg Codex only Moses is characterized by this Jewish hat, indicating that it was through him the Law was given to the Jewish people. Obviously the Old Law is not simply abolished by the New Covenant; here the artist conforms to the vision of the Benedictine nun. Behind the figure of Moses a golden sun shines forth; God's splendor descends upon him. In the golden cloth draped under *Synagoga*'s arm three rows of male figures are visible. The uppermost tier contains only three figures, the middle one has five, and the lowest one four. The men in these three rows are quite old except for two who seem youthful. Here we find portrayed the prophets, King David (discernible by his crown), and, most importantly, Abraham (with a raised knife) and his son Isaac.

This portrayal is significant because it refers to the original components of the Church: the *Ecclesia ex Judaeis* and the *Ecclesia e gentibus*. This is parallel to the portrayals of the fourth and fifth centuries, for instance, in the mosaic of the apse of St. Pudentiana church in Rome. In the

Middle Ages this contrast was interpreted differently. Then the emphasis was no longer on the development of the Church from the Jews and from the Gentiles, but rather on the competitive faith-communities of Jews and Christians. Christ, as the second Solomon, judges between these competing faith-communities, represented by the feminine figures of *Synagoga* and *Ecclesia*. This fundamental idea is not ignored by Hildegard of Bingen. However she, or rather her miniaturist, stresses the saving interrelationship more strongly than in contemporary *Synagoga* representations. This is made especially clear in the portrayal of the Old Testament saints, Moses and the prophets, for Christ fulfills what they had promised. The image of *Synagoga*, standing erect and in a solid framework, is not unlike *Ecclesia* in dignity. With the framework the artist refers to the vision of the saint. She had seen *Synagoga* fortified by walls and thereby an example of the new city of God. It is striking of the image of *Synagoga* that her outer garment and countenance are painted in light purple and that under her garment is black. Her feet are bare and painted in an intense red which signifies blood.

This miniature depicts what Hildegard describes as the fifth vision in the first Book of *Scivias:* "Then I saw a feminine figure. She appeared to be in shadow from the crown of her head to the middle of her torso; from the torso to her feet was blood-red. A gleaming white and immaculate cloud floated around her feet (in the miniature this becomes a silvery background for the feet) but she was deprived of eyes. Her arms were crossed with the hands tucked under. She stood beside the altar, which is in front of the eyes of God, but she did not touch it. In her heart stood Abraham, in her bosom Moses, and in her lap the other prophets. All of them could be identified by their characteristic signs and they gazed in admiration at the beauty of the new bride. The woman was as large as a sturdy tower and on her head she wore a band that shone like the sunrise."

It is characteristic of the *Scivias* that the brief description of the vision is followed by the seer's lengthy commentary. This commentary is not introduced as her own interpretation but as an explanation which was accorded her in the form of a hearing *(auditio)*. In her commentary she refers to the voice of the Lord, that is, the voice from heaven which interprets the vision for her. This holds also for the vision of *Synagoga*. Referring to the voice from heaven Hildegard gives first a sketch of salvation history in three stages: "the circumcision coming from Abraham, the strictness of the Law, and the gentleness of grace". Then an interpretation of the salvation history outline follows. This is also quite characteristic of the seer's methods: initially she offers an introduction and then an explanation follows. The feminine figure which appears so dimly from the crown of the head to the torso is identified as the Synagogue. For Hildegard of Bingen, the Synagogue means the community of the Jews, those who lived during the time of the Old Testament as well as those from the New Testament times. This continuity is affirmed by the title of honour: "It is the Synagogue, the Mother of the Incarnation of God's Son". Such a formulation reminds us of the comparison between Mary, the Mother of God, and the Synagogue. Actually in this same twelfth century, Gerhoh of Reichersberg described Mary as *antiquae synagogae portio electissima*. [1]

Before the Son of God became man there were a number of hints and prophecies concerning his coming. But the fulfillment surpassed all these indications. In the view of the Epistle to the Hebrews, which stressed that full revelation came first through the Son, all the earlier prophecies are primarily preparatory in nature. When Hildegard speaks of an only indistinct knowledge in Old Testament times, she is supported by the outlook of the Epistle to the Hebrews. The pictorial expression of this is the light purple of the outer garment, that is, the upper part of the dress in the miniature which corresponds to the description of this portion of *Synagoga* being in shadows. Hildegard of Bingen has *Synagoga* looking in amazement upon the new bride, i.e., the New Testament people of God. With this interpretation she stands in a salvation history perspective as already developed in the eighth century by Venerable Bede. We find it in his commentary to the Canticle of Canticles. Unlike other authors of the high Middle Ages, we do not possess a commentary on the Canticle of Canticles by Hildegard of Bingen. There are so few quotations from the Canticle in her work that Friedrich Ohly (for whose research on the Canticle up to the twelfth century we are grateful)[2] hesitated to ascribe a particular interpretation of it to Hildegard. In his opinion, the Canticle remains marginal to her thought.[3] Indeed, we find proportionately few quotations from the Canticle in *Scivias*. But it is noteworthy that precisely at this point of the commentary a quotation from the Canticle appears. "Who is that coming up from the wilderness, all gaily clad and leaning upon her beloved?" (8:5).[4] This corresponds to the interpretation found already in Venerable Bede, who describes *Synagoga* looking in amazement upon the Church. For him, too, *Synagoga* means more than a preparation of the Church. He sees that Judaism and Christianity together form that *Ecclesia* which is the Bride of Christ, into which the Jewish people after Christ will enter together with the pagan peoples before the end of the world as an *unanima conjunctio credentium populorum*. In the fifth Book of his commentary to the Canticle of Canticles, he describes the amazement and questions of the Jews who are destined to be united with Christendom concerning the nature of the ascending Church. In the sixth Book of his Commentary, Bede has *Synagoga* invited to support the infant Church; this indicates that, in his interpretation, the competitive situation between the two communities was not intended in God's original plan of salvation. The competition arose from the overly strict adherence of *Synagoga* to the commandments of the Old Testament. This interpretation of Bede was accepted by many later Christian authors, including Hildegard of Bingen.

It is significant that, in her description of *Synagoga*, Hildegard uses only one quotation from the Canticle (which is given above), and this she refers to the Church. She specifically calls her "the new bride who, filled with good works, comes up from the desert of the pagans". The visionary refers the delight mentioned in the verse of the Canticle to the gifts of the Holy Spirit; the beloved of the Canticle is the Bridegroom, the Son of God. *Synagoga* and the Church are simultaneously bride and mother. The Synagogue is portrayed as the mother of many sons: the patriarchs, Moses, the prophets, and also contemporary Jews. The Church also is the mother of many children. In this vision Hildegard of Bingen identifies the children of the church as the saints. There is no mention of troubles in the Church in this vision, even though the seer can express herself very critically concerning the Church of her time, especially its outward manifestation. Here she prefers the contrast: on the one hand, the Church protected by the angels, and on the other, the prostrate *Synagoga* abandoned by God. This statement leads to the description of the black gown that *Synagoga* wears from the middle of her body to the blood-red feet which are surrounded by a pure white cloud. Black is a sign of the violation of the Law and of disloyalty; the color of the blood is an indication of the crucifixion. Here Hildegard of Bingen recalls Jesus' sermons of reprimand which accused his adversaries of having murdered the prophets. That is why Hildegard chooses the formula that the Synagogue murders "the Prophet of the prophets", for which she came to grief. However, through her demise, she is raised in the souls of the faithful to the brightest, clearest faith. This is symbolized by the white cloud floating around her red feet.

According to Hildegard's vision *Synagoga* is deprived of eyes. Here the artist was less severe than the visionary; as we have already mentioned, *Synagoga* in the miniature is by no means without eyes, her eyes are merely closed. Absence of eyes or closed eyes symbolize the same thing. In John's Gospel Jesus is, according to his own statement, the true light. Before him the community of Jews closes its eyes. The interpretation of hands folded under the arms is interesting. For Hildegard this is a sign of the aversion whereby the Synagogue found fault with the works of righteousness. Here we sense how much Hildegard lacked a Jewish mentor; otherwise she would not have made such an assertion. In this passage of her text she seems quite shocking. But this idea of *Synagoga's* negligence is found also in other passages of her text. Hildegard of Bingen thinks that the Synagogue understood the Law of God only outwardly, and never penetrated to its true meaning. This is a sign of negligence and that is how the seer interpreted it.

But then comes a description of *Synagoga* which demonstrates the visionary's respect for the Old Testament people of faith. If the previous section sounded polemical, the following one is full of admiration: "In the heart of the figure stands Abraham, because he was the beginning of circumcision in the Synagogue. Moses is portrayed in her bosom because he places the divine Law into the hearts of human beings. In her lap stand the prophets — (in the order God confided them to her) — to whom the revelation of God's instructions was given.

The seer has Moses, Abraham and the prophets gazing in admiration upon the beauty of the new bride. "The Synagogue herself is as large as a sturdy tower. Because she was filled with the power of the divine instructions she delineates the circumvallation and fortification of the noble, previously chosen City of God." This city of God is the new community of the Church. "On her head she wears a diadem which shines like the rising sun because, as the Church went out from her, so the miracle of the Incarnation of God's Only Begotten became manifest and the radiant divine powers and mysteries deriving therefrom were disclosed. Likewise in the early morning, the Synagogue was crowned when she received the divine commandments in Adam." Hildegard of Bingen traces the story of the Synagogue to the beginning of mankind. Thus she forms the Synagogue into an all-inclusive community. The visionary now applies the comparison with Adam to the Jews. Just as Adam originally accepted God's command and later violated it, so also the Jewish people accepted the divine Law and later rejected the Son of God. But the comparison goes further. Through his sin Adam was condemned to death but his downfall was not final. Because of Christ's death on the cross, Adam is rescued from the corruption of death.

This introduces the theme of Christ's descent into hell, which appears in every medieval Passion cycle and is abundantly portrayed in pictorial art. "Thus, through God's mercy, the Synagogue will arise before the last day and she will abandon her unbelief and attain true knowledge of God." The Commentaries to the Canticle of Canticles structured around salvation history (such as that of Venerable Bede) make their own the salvation-history theme of Paul's letter to the Romans which emphasizes the deliverance of all Israel before the end of time. This theme is further used in the play of Antichrist which originated during the time of the Hohenstaufen Kings at Tegernsee. This originates only a bit later than *Scivias*. According to this play all nations desert Christ and allow themselves to be led astray by the Antichrist. But *Synagoga* sees through his schemes before any of the others. She publicly exposes the Antichrist and unleashes his wrath. She suffers martyrdom and thus brings the end of the world; then Christ himself intervenes in history. This shows that Hildegard of Bingen was not alone in her vision which compares the death and resurrection of Adam to the destruction and new rising of *Synagoga*. The Old Testament is likened to the dawn, the New to the sun. The dawn yields to the sun; so the Old Testament stands back, while the truth of the Gospels endures.

With many other theologians Hildegard of Bingen contrasts literal (i.e. "of the flesh") observance of the Law during the time of the old covenant and the spiritual obedience of the new people in the new covenant. What was understood beforehand in the flesh is fulfilled in the spirit. Hildegard of Bingen stresses that "circumcision is not abolished by baptism but assimilated into it. . .the Old Law is not abolished but elevated to a higher level". Here the visionary infers that the Synagogue which became believing (i.e. believing in Christ) passes over into the Church. She describes the Incarnation of God's Son as the mercy of the Father to his daughter. Through the Incarnation the Synagogue is freed from the harshness of the solely external Law. Instead, she now receives the gentleness of the spiritual teaching. The speaker changes. At first God the Father himself speaks to the Synagogue but suddenly the Son speaks in his stead. He woos the Synagogue as his bride and laments that she shames him and marries the devil.

For her description of the Son's futile wooing of the Synagogue as his Bride, the seer draws on Old Testament parallels. She compares Jesus to Samson who was deceived by his wife. This comparison is unfortunate, as it is inaccurate. The point of comparison is the abandonment by a woman but Samson's marriage had already separated him from his people. Delilah came from the pagan people of the Philistines.[5] However, Jesus pledges himself to his people. He turns to the Jews as those to whom his Father has sent him. Samson, who allows himself to be seduced by his wife, is deprived of his eyesight by the Philistines, but not so Christ. Delilah triumphs over Samson. Hildegard of Bingen portrays the Synagogue as blind and humiliated. And it becomes even worse as she continues: "But after Samson's hair grew again, that is, after the Church of God gained strength with his power, the Son of God exiled the Synagogue and disinherited her children. The wrath of God crushed them through the pagans who previously had no knowledge of God." Here Hildegard of Bingen follows an anti-Jewish theme, but she immediately modifies the first comparison with another. She reminds us of King David and his wife Michal, daughter of King Saul, who gave her to another (1Sam 25,24) but David finally recalls her to his side (2Sam 3,15); so also the Son of God. Hildegard voices the conviction that Christ will welcome the Synagogue back at the end of time as she was closely connected with him in his Incarnation. "As Saul, who had banished David from his Kingdom, was slain on Mt. Gilboa, so Satan with the excessive haughtiness of his pride will collapse when the Son of Perdition dares to approach my Son in his elect. My Son will vanquish the Antichrist and will call the Synagogue back to the true faith just as David, after Saul's death, took his first wife back. Because at the end of time, when they see that the one who betrayed them is vanquished, they will return with great haste to the path of salvation." Finally, Hildegard of Bingen repeats the contrast between Synagogue and Church. For her, the Synagogue is the forerunner in the shadow of symbolic meaning, while the Church follows Christ in the light of truth.

Who was this visionary? Hildegard of Bingen was born in 1098 on the estate Bermersheim near Alzey, the tenth child of the nobleman Hildebert. From early childhood she was destined for the religious life. At the age of eight she was sent as an *inclusa* to the recluse Jutta of Sponheim where she received her education. Her teacher instructed her in the Rule of St. Benedict, in liturgy, and also in the liberal arts. In 1114 she received the habit of the Benedictine nuns from Bishop Otto of Bamberg. She lived in the Disibodenberg convent and there, having earned the confidence of her fellow nuns, she was appointed Superior. After 1138 she was called Magistra or Mistress. Between 1147 and 1152 she founded the convent at Rupertsberg and took care to have it legally registered with Archbishop Arnold of Mainz in 1158. In a letter guaranteeing protection received from Emperor Friedrich Barbarossa on April 16, 1163 at a court assembly in Mainz, she was named abbess for the first time. In 1165 she founded a filial convent, Rudesheim, at Eibingen. Hildegard of Bingen lived to an unusually great age, in spite of the many ailments she endured throughout her life. She died on September 17, 1179 in her cloister at Rupertsberg near Bingen.

From 1141 Hildegard recorded her visions and, with the help of the monk Volmar and the nun Richardis of Stade, she incorporated them into her survey of the creation and salvation of the world. Her book *Scivias* was examined by a commission assigned by Pope Eugene III in 1147-48. The commission, which traveled to the convent at Disibodenberg expressly for this purpose, acknowledged the visionary character of

Scivias and reaffirmed its assessment at the subsequent Synod of Trier. Thus was her calling as a visionary established. From the middle of the twelfth century Hildegard of Bingen was regarded as *Prophetissa Teutonica*. Therefore, her pronouncements had great weight. Her vocation as the German prophetess was made even more significant through her correspondence with the important people of her time. She showed herself to be a sharp critic of the evils of the time, as she perceived them. This correspondence was quite unusual for her time but even more so were her preaching journeys in the decade between 1160 and 1170, when she emerged from the solitude of her convent cell. On these journeys she condemned the weaknesses and mistakes of the time. She denounced the decadence of the clergy as well as the dangers of heresy (she spoke especially against the Albigenses) and warned against the trickery of diplomacy as used by the princes of her time, especially the Emperor Friedrich Barbarossa.

Her literary interests were broad; God's wisdom, theology of creation, observations of nature, anthropology, evaluation of the contemporary situation, etc. all found their place in her work. But a certain doom hung over her work since it is basically too late for its time. A new era was dawning, that of Scholasticism. In his New German Biography (9,131), Heinrich Schipperges is justified in pointing out the ineffectiveness of her work in the context of the spiritual upheavals of the time. "The unusually wide-ranging work of Hildegard remained ineffective for centuries . . . Already in the thirteenth century the universalism of her thought and activities no longer made any impression. Hildegard's symbolistic world-view was drowned by the neo-Platonic-Arabic Aristotelianism; her theological and philosophy-of-nature-constructed anthropology could not hold its own against the "new Aristotle," as he was assimilated into the schools of Salerno, Chartres and Toledo and as he came canonized in Thomistic scholasticism. Hildegard's whole literary output shrank to the pseudo-prophetic *speculum futurorum temporum*, compiled in 1220 by the prior Gebeno of Eberbach. Nevertheless, the humanistic scholar, Jacques Lefévre d'Etaples (Faber Stapulensis), showed an interest in *Scivias*. In 1513 he published the first edition of this work. But at many points he re-formulated the text into the humanistic Latin then in use. Hildegard's characteristic expressions and pictures suffered from the loss of their original forceful phraseology. In 1855 Migne used the text published by Lefévre d'Etaples as a basis for his *Patrologia Latina* (volume 197). It would be desirable to have a critical edition of Hildegard's work. Maura Böckeler has based her translation on the text of the Codex of Rupertsberg.

As a mystic also, Hildegard of Bingen stands more at the end of an era than at the beginning. Her visions are influenced by the traditional teachings of the Church and one finds little that is purely personal. In her mysticism the subjective, perhaps subjectivistic, impetus of late medieval mysticism (e.g. German Dominican mysticism) is missing. Giovanna de la Croce states: "Hildegard of Bingen's visions concerning the Church contain nothing personal. Not the inner life of the seer but the 'objective' truths which she observed, behind which she hides herself, stand the central point of her vision. But she thinks about and suffers for the Church, in which she is aware of her mission: to teach the truths revealed to her, to call people back to faith and to encourage them to a deeper and unconditional love."[6] This characterization is valid also for the vision of the Synagogue; it is defined by the outlook of the Church and bears witness to this outlook. Hildegard's critical judgments are prompted by her love for the Church. Today a reader might find her outlook one-sided and probably a Jewish reader would be offended by it. But it should be recalled that Hildegard with her criticisms stands within the horizon of the theology in her time. Her negative judgments were common property not only of this theology, also of much later theology. One could pass this over as the order of the day if another tone were not noticed in her work. Together with the best scholars of her time, Hildegard recognized the intrinsic solidarity of Church and Synagogue; she knew of the ultimate gift of salvation for all Israel. This hope with regard to ultimate salvation for all Israel was the basis for a relative tolerance for contemporary Jews in the Middle Ages.[7] However, tolerance toward contemporary Jews was limited and often retracted, so one must speak of a "teeth-gnashing" tolerance. Here it should be noted that Hildegard of Bingen was not only moved by eschatological hope, but also that she clearly stressed the importance of continuity in spite of all divisions.

The visions of Hildegard of Bingen betray that she had no Jewish partner with whom to converse. Her view was so closed that a true dialogue would hardly have been possible. Yet there are moments in her vision when she reaches beyond these limitations. Lastly, the respect which is a presupposition for a possible dialogue is evident at points. The visions of Hildegard of Bingen represent a not unimportant step in the history of contacts between Christians and Jews, which should lead finally to encounter and meeting.

NOTES

1. "De gloria et honore filii homines" P.L. 194, c. 1105A.
2. *Hohelied Studien.* Grundzüge einer Geschichte der Hoheliedauslegung des Abendlandes bis um 1200. (Wiesbaden: Franz Steiner Verlag 1958).
3. Op. cit., p. 250, note 2.
4. "Quae est ista quae ascendit de deserto, deliciis affluens, innixa super dilectum suum?" The phrase rendered "all gaily clad" (Ronald Knox version) occurs in Vulgate and Septuagint but not in the Massoretic text. The German reads "von Wonne überstömend," which may be translated "overflowing with delight" (Editor)
5. The anonymous wife is a Philistine woman (Jg 14) but it is not said that he married Delilah (Jg 16) (Editor).
6. "Hildegard von Bingen und das Mysterium der Kirche", *Erbe und Auftrag* 44(1968) p. 195-212, note 212.
7. This was observed already by M. Schlauch in her essay "The allegory of Church and Synagogue" *Speculum* 14(1939) p. 448-464.

Judaism and Conscience

MICHAEL WYSCHOGROD

Never has conscience been in the forefront of human thinking as it is today. A number of convergent influences account for this. There is the emphasis on individuality which is characteristic of Western civilization. The totalitarian states of the twentieth century have perhaps permanently damaged the moral reliability of all authority, thereby forcing greater reliance on individual conscience. The dehumanizing effects of mass society have brought about an attempt toward liberation from the collective by a turning inward in conscience. For these and other reasons, the contemporary religious world places great emphasis on conscience as the source of moral authority.

Judaism has not remained uninfluenced by these developments. As a religion particularly replete with a specific code of conduct, the gradual abandonment by most Jews of the Torah way of life was at least an implicit and mostly unformulated exercise of conscience as an act of dissent from established norms. Most Jews did not put the matter in these terms. Instead, it was seen as a transition into modernity or, in the case of American Jewish immigrants, as a necessary response to the demands of the New World. But somewhere in the soul of the Jews who for the first time partook of forbidden foods or put on an electric light on the Sabbath, there was an exercise of conscience which reassured the individual that what he was doing was not wrong. Gradually, these deviations from the norms of the past were institutionalized into various forms of liberal Judaism. But even here, an explicit doctrine of conscience did not appear. *De facto,* the reformers were undoubtedly guided by conscience in deciding what in the tradition was to be retained and what discarded. But they did not develop conscience into a doctrine.

In this respect, the reformers were very traditional. The Judaism they set out to reform did not have a doctrine of conscience as such. In fact, there is no classical Hebrew term for the concept nor has it ever figured prominently either in Jewish theology or in Jewish history. No Jewish encyclopedia I could find has an article on conscience. The topic is covered in almost every general encyclopedia, with the *Encyclopedia of Religion and Ethics* devoting part of its general article on conscience to the place of this concept in Judaism. Instead of dealing with conscience in Judaism, however, this article, in spite of its heading, deals with a general exposition of Jewish ethics as if ethics and conscience were the same. And the same is true of Jewish history. No great departures in the development of Judaism can be ascribed to faithfulness to a call of conscience as, for instance, the Reformation to the conscience of Luther. Whatever the dynamics of Jewish history may have been, the proclamation "Here I stand: I can do no other" is not familiar to Jewish ears. The conclusion to which we are forced then is that Judaism lacks a doctrine of conscience as it is generally understood from stoicism to scholasticism through the Reformation to the present.

At this point, we have a number of alternatives. We can argue that, appearances to the contrary notwithstanding, there is a notion of conscience in Judaism. Or we can maintain that there neither is nor can be a doctrine of conscience in Judaism because of the primacy of revelation. A third possibility, one closely tied to the second, is to claim that an ethics of conscience, by the inner logic of its case, tends toward the deification of man, as for instance in the case of Heidegger. And, finally, we can take the position that Judaism is indeed the poorer for its lack of a doctrine of conscience because without conscience man never transcends the hegemony of the "Great Beast," the term Simone Weil applied to the collective whose rule she found intolerable in Judaism. Even superficial consideration of these alternatives reveals that they are not totally mutually exclusive, though of course some are more difficult to combine than others. None of them is without an element of the truth, though again there is more truth in some than in others. It is this complexity that makes the problem of conscience so fascinating for Jewish theology.

I

Is there a notion of conscience in Judaism? We have already found that there is no term for it in classical Hebrew; in contemporary Hebrew the term *Mazpun* is used, the root of which means "hidden or inward." But the absence of a word in itself, while important, is not totally decisive. The idea as such may exist, even if there is no particular word to express it. Are there any instances in classical Jewish literature that might reasonably be interpreted as evidence that the notion of conscience is not totally foreign to the tradition?

In the twenty-fourth chapter of the First Book of Samuel we read the very moving episode of David's adventure in the cave of En-Gedi. David's relations with Saul had been going from bad to worse and Saul was determined to capture his erstwhile favorite and kill him. When he is told: "Behold, David is in the wilderness of En-Gedi" (1Sam 24,2), he mobilizes three thousand of his best warriors for the search. David and his men seek refuge in a cave, presumably a rather large one. Suddenly, Saul appears in the cave alone, to attend to his natural functions. David's men, seeing in this development the hand of God who had promised David victory over Saul, urge David not to miss his opportunity. But David replies: "The Lord forbid it me, that I should do this thing unto my lord, the Lord's anointed, to put forth my hand against him, seeing he is the Lord's anointed" (24,7). Therefore, instead of killing Saul, he cuts off a piece of the king's garment, without the king being aware of it. But instead of being proud of his restraint, David begins to feel an inner discomfort. "And it came to pass afterward, that David's heart smote him, because he had cut off Saul's skirt" (24,6). It seems rather difficult to avoid the conclusion that we are dealing here with the phenomenon of conscience. Having performed an action, David learns through inner suffering that what he did was not right. Even in the decision not to kill the Lord's anointed, we can detect the voice of conscience, especially since David is urged by his men not to miss his opportunity. We thus seem to have in this incident an example of conscience vetoing a contemplated course of action as well as disapproving of one already committed. In fact, David's pangs of conscience for cutting the king's garment may even have been intensified by the prior victory his conscience had scored over his men's more activist advice. By cutting Saul's garment, David deprives conscience of the total victory it demands even if, from a more balanced point of view, David had more reason to be proud of his restraint than ashamed of the minor transgression.

And then there is the other episode in the life of David when the voice of conscience seems to play a role. David had seduced Bath-Sheba and she had become pregnant. Since her husband was away at war, David summoned him from the front so that it might be supposed that the child she was to bear was his. But Uriah refuses to visit his wife because, he reasons, at a time when his comrades are in battle he cannot "go into my house, to eat and to drink, and to lie with my wife" (2Sam 11,11). He returns to his comrades without having seen his wife. David, seeing no other alternative, orders Uriah's death in battle, after which Bath-Sheba becomes his wife. And then the biblical writer continues:

And the Lord sent Nathan to David. He came to him and said to him, "There were two men in a certain city, the one rich and the other poor. The rich man had very many flocks and herds; but the poor man had nothing but one little ewe lamb, which he had bought. And he brought it up, and it grew up with him and with his children; it used to eat of his morsel, and drink from his cup, and lie in his bosom, and it was like a daughter to him. Now there came a traveler to the rich man, and he was unwilling to take one of his own flock or herd to prepare for the wayfarer who had come to him, but he took the poor man's lamb, and prepared it for the man who had come to him." Then David's anger was greatly kindled against the man; and he said to Nathan, "As the Lord lives, the man who has done this deserves to die; and he shall restore the lamb fourfold, because he did this thing, and because he had no pity."

Nathan said to David, "You are the man. Thus says the Lord, the God of Israel, 'I anointed you king over Israel, and I delivered you out of the hand of Saul; and I gave you your master's house, and your master's wives into your bosom, and gave you the house of Israel and of Judah; and if this were too little, I would add to you as much more. Why have you despised the word of the Lord, to do what is evil in his sight? You have smitten Uriah the Hittite with the sword, and have taken his wife to be your wife, and have slain him with the sword of the Ammonites. Now therefore the sword shall never depart from your house, because you have despised me, and have taken the wife of Uriah the Hittite to be your wife.' Thus says the Lord, 'Behold, I will raise up evil against you out of your own house; and I will take your wives before your eyes, and give them to your neighbor, and he shall lie with your wives in the sight of this sun. For you did it secretly; but I will do this thing before all Israel, and before the sun.' " David said to Nathan, "I have sinned against the Lord." And Nathan said to David, "The Lord also has put away your sin; you shall not die" (2Sam 12,1-13).

Particularly significant for our purpose is Nathan's parable. Instead of merely delivering God's condemnation, Nathan's parable draws from David a moral judgment that emanates from his deepest moral self. It is David who condemns himself, who passes judgment over the rich man's outrageous robbery of the poor man's single possession. This outrage is so great that David pronounces the hypothetical culprit worthy of death, even if from the normal legal point of view no capital crime has been committed. And when Nathan thunders his unforgettable "Thou art the man," it is answered by an unequivocal "I have sinned against the Lord," a confession without explanation or mitigation but bold, simple and clear, the usual tone of a guilty conscience. Here again it is difficult to escape the conclusion that we are dealing with the phenomenon of conscience, even if the word is not used.

The third text of interest to our inquiry is drawn from rabbinic literature. Here, of course, the law is central and one would not expect the notion of conscience to play a prominent role since, as almost every writer on this subject correctly insists, from the point of view of the established legal order conscience can be an unsettling and disruptive force that the law cannot handle and toward which, therefore, the law must remain, at the very least, reserved. The law is objective and impartial and excludes, generally speaking, motifs of compassion or pity. "And a poor man," we are told in Exodus (23,3), "thou shalt not favor in his cause." And the Mishnah in *Kethuboth* (9,2) adds: "In legal matters no compassion is shown." This is the attitude one would expect in legal literature; it can come as a surprise only to those who have no feeling for the force of impartiality as a dimension of justice. And yet, this is not the whole story. We read the following in the tractate Baba Meṣiʿa of the Babylonian Talmud (83a):

> Some porters negligently broke a barrel of wine belonging to Rabbah son of R. Huna. Thereupon he seized their garments; so they went and complained to Rab. "Return them their garments," he ordered. "Is that the law?" he enquired. "Even so," he rejoined: " 'That thou mayest walk in the way of good men.' " (Prov 2,20). Their garments having been returned, they observed, "We are poor men, have worked all day and are in need: are we to get nothing?" "Go and pay them," he ordered. "Is that the law?" he asked. "Even so," was his reply: 'and keep the path of the righteous.' "

Having broken their employer's barrel of wine negligently, the laborers are legally responsible for the damage they caused. But Rab waives this "that thou mayest walk in the way of good men." But this is not sufficient, for he orders the laborers paid for the day's work. Here the law yields to something beyond it, something that cannot be codified but only perceived in the unique situation that presents itself and in which the moral agent must make a judgment taking into account the law but also an inner voice which he cannot suppress. The likelihood is that here we are dealing with something very much akin to conscience even if it is not called that or developed into an explicit doctrine.

And yet, we cannot leave this part of our discussion without giving due weight to the negative moment of the problem. David's feeling of remorse after he had cut Saul's garment is not, after all, a major event of Jewish theology. The difficulty with the theme of conscience in Nathan's exhortation to David is that while classical conscience is a voice that speaks within man, Nathan is the other who addresses David as spokesman of God and therefore, even if we agree that the content of his message is an appeal to conscience, to the extent that Nathan speaks from the outside he represents the heteronomous and not the voice of conscience. It is particularly strange that the same David whose conscience speaks up in defense of Saul's garment remains silent in the Bath-Sheba episode and that it takes a prophet to make David see the magnitude of his transgression. It would not be difficult to invoke psychological explanations for this difference; however successful these may be, they cannot obscure the fact that in the decisive transgression of his life, David's conscience, as the voice that speaks inwardly, remains silent and must be awakened by an outer voice. And finally, the case of the broken barrel of wine, too, is not quite a perfect example of the functioning of conscience. Whose conscience does this episode illustrate? If anyone's, it is Rab's but he is judging another, not himself. Can we speak of conscience when it is the injustice of another instead of the self that is the issue? Traditionally, conscience has been understood as that voice which censures the agent's own misdeeds, either before or after the fact. Whether it is the same conscience which speaks when I wax indignant at the crimes of another or whether there is a fundamental difference between my sense of justice turned outward and my self-condemnation turned inward, is a serious problem of moral phenomenology. That there is a difference between perceiving evil in another and in myself was illustrated by David's readiness to condemn the rich man of Nathan's parable without, at the same time, perceiving the magnitude of his own transgression. We must, therefore conclude that Rab's otherwise admirable decision is a problematic illustration of the voice of conscience.

We leave this section then with a mixed verdict. There are examples of conscience in Jewish literature but they are not in clear, bold relief.

II

Why did the conscience fail to achieve an unequivocally central role in Jewish thought? The question becomes particularly pressing once we realize that no plausible sociological explanation seems to be forthcoming. From the sociological point of view, conscience begins to play a prominent role in situations in which social cohesion is threatened and the individual is thrown into himself. He no longer receives the kind of support that is characteristic of societies in their vitality when value structures are intact, unquestioned and function to their optimum as instruments of social control. With the relativization of such value structures, with the appearance of competing systems soliciting the loyalty of the individual, choices of a rather fundamental kind have to be made from within the resources available to the individual. The fact that the notion of conscience makes its appearance in the ancient world not at the height of Greek philosophy, with Plato and Aristotle, but rather toward the end in Cicero and Seneca is, of course, a case in point. Can this sort of analysis help us with our problem? It does not seem so. If our problem were only the absence of conscience in biblical Judaism, the case would be different. We could then attempt to argue that biblical Judaism precedes the period of social dissolution during which one would expect to find the appearance of conscience. But the fact is, of course, that conscience fails to become important throughout Jewish history, a history which includes periods of decline and dissolution as well as growth and cohesion. It seems quite clear that the periods immediately following the destruction of the second Temple or the expulsion from Spain were times of serious social dissolution, permeated as they were by the disappearance of age-old institutions. Nevertheless, even at such times, we do not find the appearance to any serious extent of conscience as a motif in Jewish thought and this leads me to believe that the explanation, if any, must be other than sociological.

The explanation is theological. Judaism is based on obedience to God. In conscience it is not after all God who is being heard but man. The Jew, however, is required to listen to God and not to man.

To make this a bit clearer, we must now focus briefly on the phenomenon of conscience. Here, as so often elsewhere, the phenomenon under discussion is often confused with various theories about the phenomenon so that we no longer remember where theory begins and phenomenon ends. Perhaps it would therefore be better to start with some theories about conscience rather than conscience itself. It would appear that theories of conscience fall into two general categories: the autonomous and the heteronomous. For the autonomous theory of conscience, man recognizes in conscience what is right and what is wrong. This recognition is not a hearing of an external judgment, it is not a yielding to the inscrutable will of God, but an internal act of recognition of the moral truth, somewhat analogous to the recognition of the truth of a mathematical proposition or a principle of logic. The difference, of course, is that even for the autonomous theory of conscience we must distinguish between the general moral sense by means of which we apprehend universal moral principles and conscience which is largely, if not exclusively, particular, passing judgment on specific and concrete situations whether of the past or the proposed future. Whatever problems may lurk in the transition from the universal to the particular, and they are not inconsiderable, it remains true for the autonomous theory that by listening to the voice of conscience we do not simply abdicate our will and our sense of the right to another, but that in the deepest sense, it is our moral judgment that makes itself heard in the specific situation. From this point of view, conscience is an affirmation of our sense of the right, very often in conflict with the judgment of society, the church or possibly even God if and when his command conflicts with the dictate of conscience. Philosophically, this is an affirmation of an ethical humanism, of the moral self-sufficiency of man who in the final analysis must make his own judgments in his own light in deference to his humanity.

It is not difficult to see that understood in this way, the doctrine of conscience is not easily reconcilable with an ethic that looks to the word of God as its criterion of the right. The divine word is not a projection of, nor is it continuous with, man's moral sense. It is the judge of man's moral sense and as such it is the judge of man's self-deification. We will soon touch on an important contemporary *reductio ad absurdum* of this attitude in Heidegger's interpretation of conscience. But, it may be asked, is this the only possible interpretation of conscience? Can conscience not be thought of as the voice of God speaking to man in solitude and addressing to him the divine command? The answer is of course that it can and has been thought of in this way. Interestingly enough, it is in Karl Barth, the most authentic voice of the Reformation in our time, that we find a definition of conscience that is most sensitive to this aspect of the problem. Barth writes:

> Conscience . . . conscientia . . ., the knowing with God of what God knows, has to be understood strictly as the conscience freed and raised by God . . . and not a universal and always effective human disposition and capacity. Freedom of conscience is not, therefore, the permission, which in the 18th and 19th century sense we all have, to think what we consider fine and desirable. It is rather the power, which God imparts to those who accept His revelation, to think what in His judgment is right, and therefore true and wise.[1]

Barth is fully aware that as an expression of "what we consider fine and desirable," conscience is natural theology in the realm of the ethical and just as the God of natural theology is a humanly constructed idol, so conscience understood as a human faculty will yield only man's view of what is fine and desirable and not God's. Barth therefore sees conscience not as a universal human faculty shared by all men to the extent that they are men and rational, but as a special gift of God to those who accept his revelation by means of which they are able to determine what is right in God's view and not theirs. In this heteronomous view of conscience, there is no fundamental difference between obedience to God when God directly addresses man and listening to the voice of conscience in which also it is the voice of God that is being heard.

If this view of conscience were a tenable one, there would indeed be no conflict between conscience and revelation and Judaism could incorporate such a view of conscience without difficulty. Unfortunately, however, the heteronomous interpretation of conscience is not altogether tenable. To demonstrate this we must however abandon the realm of theories of conscience, with which we have been dealing until now, and direct our attention to the phenomenon of conscience itself. Before we do this, we must make one further observation concerning Barth's treatment of this topic. Because of the deep Reformation roots of his thinking, one could expect conscience to receive considerable emphasis in the thought of Barth. Instead, it plays a rather minor role. While it is true that the *Dogmatics* is incomplete with several of the more ethical volumes missing, it is difficult to believe that conscience could move into a position of centrality when so little groundwork has been laid for it in the more dogmatic volumes. I prefer to believe that the secondary role played by conscience in Barth's thought is an organic development. Where conscience is a more or less independent and internal human power that discriminates right from wrong, we can expect it to play a leading role in theology. But if conscience is a "power which God imparts to those who accept His revelation," then we must not be surprised to find it playing a distinctly secondary role to the study of God's revelation in Scripture. It is the divine word that must then be the focus of interest and while conscience may mirror the word and even perhaps to some extent interiorize it, it can never establish itself as an independent source of authority superior to or even equal to scripture. The reason that Barth cannot pay much attention to conscience is that he cannot ultimately take seriously that which is only human. In the form in which conscience appears in Barth, as an echo of the divine word, it is doomed to leading a shadow existence adjacent to the power and clarity of the divine word.

But let us now return to the phenomenon of conscience. Is the heteronomous interpretation of it persuasive or is it much more plausible to argue that conscience is essentially a phenomenon of autonomy, a turning by man to himself and a trusting of his own powers? There is much to recommend the latter alternative. Very often conscience asserts itself, as we have already seen, as a rejection of another's will, be he a person or an institution. When we hear the voice of conscience we are not, after all, merely hearing the command of another, as Abraham obeyed God at Mount Moriah. No one maintains that in the episode of Abraham's readiness to sacrifice Isaac, we are dealing with conscience. Here we have as clear-cut an instance as we could imagine of obedience, of a heteronomous command that conflicts with everything that Abraham's moral sense tells him is right and which nevertheless is obeyed. We learn here that the command of God pulverizes conscience and that, instead, obedience characterizes Abraham's relationship with God. All this, by contrast, serves to emphasize the prominence of the dimension of autonomy in the experience of conscience. Conscience is not a voice from the outside which speaks to us to censure our actions. Were it that, it could be disregarded with much greater ease than is the case. In conscience it is we who speak to ourselves and the censure is so painful precisely because it is self-inflicted, as we found when Nathan's parable produced David's self-condemnation. Very often conscience begins to make itself felt only after a long series of condemnations emanating from the outside have proven fruitless. Only when the condemnation no longer appears external but is transformed into my voice, my condemnation, do we speak of the appearance of conscience and this is the reason that, *prima facie*, a heteronomous interpretation of conscience seems to go against the facts.

And yet the heteronomous interpretation of conscience also reflects part of the truth. While it is true that in conscience it is a voice that, in one sense, is part of myself that is speaking, it is also true that this voice is experienced as condemning some past or future enterprise to which I have been committed and which, to that extent, represents the project that I am. The purpose of the call of conscience is to deflect me from the direction my project has taken and, as such, it is a force that is not part of my project but at odds with it. If we are to avoid confusing conscience with the general moral sense, we must distinguish those instances where a person, from the very beginning, has a moral insight by which he organizes his life and in the service of which he labors, from those instances, in which sometimes quite suddenly, an excruciating "no" is pronounced over an act, an undertaking, a life-choice which has been progressing on its path and which now collides with an unforeseen obstacle. The voice that pronounces this "no" cannot simply be the same person's whose enterprise comes under its judgment. At the risk of contradicting what we said earlier, we now argue that in conscience we discover that we are not in fact fully our own masters, that just when we have charted a course we saw fit, something or someone beyond us with a will and project quite his own can pronounce an unexpected condemnation. At times we may try very hard to evade the condemnation, to lose ourselves in a variety of concerns and rationalizations designed either to justify ourselves or at the very least to concentrate our attention on other matters so that our guilt recedes to the periphery of attention, finally, we hope, to disappear. But very often all this is of no avail. We feel a presence that will not disappear, that begins to speak again when the noises of the world abate and when we are with ourselves, constrained once again to listen to a voice that is another's, yet also our own.

It is here, it would seem, that we have reached the heart of the mystery. In conscience heteronomy and autonomy blend into a dialectical unity. The voice of conscience is both the voice of another calling us to our responsibility and it is also the discovery that this voice at the same time seems to be coming from within us, from the deepest levels of our being where we are what we really want to be and in which there is an immediate affinity to the heteronomous dimension of conscience. On this level, he who demands and he of whom the demand is made are no longer in conflict but in harmony. Nevertheless, it is vital to realize that this is never a harmony of identity. It is a harmony in which both moments of the dialectic remain alive. There is the resistance and even rebellion of the human against the demands of the heteronomous authority and there is also the submission in autonomy to an almost self-legislated right through which man becomes a being of freedom instead of a sullen slave.

Whatever the possibilities for reconciling autonomy and heteronomy in conscience may be, the fact of the matter is that for the biblical tradition, especially in Judaism, the autonomous aspect of conscience seemed to have loomed larger and this explains the absence of any serious notion of conscience in a tradition that turned to the divine word for its inspiration.

III

Our argument until now has led to the conclusion that, within certain limits, an ethics of conscience has the potentiality of drifting into a Godless proclamation of human independence. Equipped with a built-in ethical compass, man can rely on himself to discover the good, not only universally and abstractly, but also in the concreteness of the existential situation in which conscience makes itself heard in judging the right of specific instances. Antithetical as such a view may be to the biblical notion of man's dependence on the word of God as the source of

ethical direction, it still does not represent the full flowering of conscience as the basis of human autonomy. The reason for this is that the
autonomous direction of conscience we have been discussing until now
constitutes an autonomy relative to the divine word; in relation to the
moral law, conscience remains a sense that points beyond itself to the
good or the right which is not of man's making and which is perceived
or sensed by conscience but not created by it. To the extent therefore
that conscience retains its essentially moral character, it falls short of
total liberation of man from subordination to structures which rule over
him, even if these are now rational moral structures and not the
sovereignty of God. It was not until our century that an interpretation of
conscience makes its appearance in the work of Heidegger which reveals
for the first time the consequence that follows a totally secular interpretation of the phenomenon. Heidegger's importance lies in the sophistication of his categories which enable him, in a sense, to do full justice to
the phenomenon of conscience without unduly impressing upon it any
extraneous categories that obscure the phenomenon before it can introduce itself on its own terms. "The ontological analysis of conscience," he
writes, "on which we are thus embarking, is prior to any description and
classification of Experiences of conscience, and likewise lies outside of
any biological 'explanation' of this phenomenon (which would mean its
dissolution). But it is no less distant from a theological exegesis of
conscience or any employment of this phenomenon for proofs of God or
for establishing an 'immediate' consciousness of God."[2] Lest this be
taken to exclude the theological but not the moral function of conscience, we soon read the following: "What does the conscience call to
him to whom it appeals? Taken strictly, nothing. The call asserts
nothing, gives no information about world events, has nothing to tell."[3]
And should we finally be perplexed by the question as to *who* it is that is
calling us in conscience, we are told: "In conscience *Dasein* calls itself."[4]

    With conscience deprived of its theological locus, its message emptied
of any content whatsoever and its origin located in the very being to
whom the call is addressed, it nevertheless remains a phenomenon of
the most basic importance to Heidegger. The reason for this is that
through conscience man lifts himself out of the mode of existence that is
the life of the collectivity or the crowd into which he has been driven
inauthentically. The one aspect of conscience that Heidegger seems to
respect is its appeal to man in his aloneness, its refusal to attempt
making itself heard over the noises of the crowd with its false en-
thusiasms and superficial interests. Just as guilt emerges in Heidegger
shorn of its genesis in wrongdoing and transformed into a fundamental
ontological characteristic of human existence, so conscience is no longer

connected with any wrong done or contemplated but becomes a means through which man learns to take his destiny into his own hands by coming to terms with his anxiety which all inauthentic existence is desperately escaping. And yet this emptying of conscience of its content does not result in a formalism in the sense in which Kant's categorical imperative is a law whose content is nothing more nor less than the very form of law itself. Since the idea of law seems to be of no interest to Heidegger, the thrust of his interpretation of conscience is in the direction of the uncanny. Law, after all, provides man with a measure of existential security not only by directing his freedom but also by providing some measure of continuity with the rest of creation even if, as Kant insists, the law governing man's moral life is in significant respects different from the law that governs the rest of the universe. Heidegger's purpose is to heighten the sense of the uncanny which for him characterizes man's being-in-the-world as a being who is never fully at home in the world and who is redeemed from total absorption in the world by a voice which speaks in silence, which has no message and which is essentially a soliloquy, an act of calling itself. That conscience understood in these terms has something of the uncanny about it should surprise no one.

We can now see how far we have come since our main problem with conscience was its autonomy which we found to be in conflict with the biblical ethics of obedience. If Heidegger's interpretation of conscience is the end of the road we embarked on when we decided to explore the implications of an autonomous conscience, we now find that this is a road that leads us out of the realm of the ethical altogether. We need not insist that Heidegger's interpretation is in some way the logically necessary outcome of the doctrine of an autonomous conscience. Nevertheless, at the very least it is one of its risks, which goes a long way toward explaining Judaism's reserve toward the notion.

IV

And yet, is not Judaism the worse for its lack of concern with conscience? We now understand that for biblical theology it is the divine word that is at the center of attention and we also understand the potential implications contained in a doctrine of autonomous conscience for the development of an ethical humanism or even an a-ethical humanism as in the case of Heidegger. And it is therefore not difficult to see why the Jew who looks to the God of his fathers will remain skeptical of all doctrines of human self-reliance, whatever their particular form may be. And yet, can we leave the matter at that, without a sense of uneasiness? Must the believing Jew sacrifice his conscience in obedience to God? Must he give up an ultimate individuality when he embraces the covenant which is more national than individual and must he, together with Buber, reject the Kierkegaardian single one for a relation with God that is always social and in which the ultimate aloneness before God yields to the community of Israel which is ruled by law rather than conscience, by the public more than the private? Perhaps conscience is the Isaac in each one of us which, though we love, we must be prepared to offer on the altar of divine sacrifice. And yet, it is very difficult to teach that the Jew owes nothing to his conscience. Is not the very act of obedience to God ultimately dependent on a dictate of conscience? At the genesis of the God-man relationship there must somewhere be a recognition by man that it is right to obey him whose command he hears and whose word becomes binding by a submission on the part of man that is affirmed in the depth of human existence where the command is heard. Without such an autonomous act of submission, men are the puppets of God and the divine command a façade behind which a divine determinism orders the objects of the world, among which man is merely one.

Today, the community of Israel is more and more a gathering of individuals chosen in faith. It is strange that the bitter assault on Judaism launched by Simone Weil in our century came at a time when her criticisms were least justified. The spirit of the Great Beast of our day hovers over the mass of Jews whose uprootedness from the sacralities of the past reduces them to a degree of contemporaneity that makes their participation and absorption into the mass public of the day natural and inevitable. The minority of Jews that clings to its past, by this very act resists the current and disengages itself from the real Great Beast of our time. To some extent it is much more probable today than ever before that a Jew who remains faithful to the covenant in this day and age is acting out of conscience instead of social conformity.

To resist the profound forces that work to level differences between one faith and another, one community and another, is no easy task and it is for this reason that the faithful Jew, whether he likes it or not, is forced into a degree of individuality much greater than ever before. In this environment, as an individual swimming against the stream, the Judaism of our day can no longer dispense with conscience as part of our theological arsenal. If the effect of this is that we thereby move into the age of conscience, it is a risk that we must be willing to accept because to insist on a Judaism that remains deaf to this voice is even more perilous.

The alternative is to argue that when conscience and the law conflict one must follow the law. In the terminology of the scholastics, this is the problem of whether an erring conscience binds. If an erring conscience does not bind, then one must disregard its dictates when it errs, that is, when the voice of conscience commands a course of action that is in conflict with what is objectively the right or the will of God. But since an erring conscience does not announce itself as erring, it follows that the person whose conscience errs is convinced that the course of action commanded by his erring conscience is in conformity with the right or the will of God. To teach that it is his duty to act against his erring conscience is to maintain that a person whose conscience errs must do that which appears to him wrong or contrary to God's will and that is always wrong. In the words of St. Thomas:

> Erroneous conscience binds even in things intrinsically evil. For conscience binds, as has been said, in this, that if someone acts contrary to his conscience, it follows that he has the will to sin. Thus if someone believes that to omit fornication is a mortal sin, when he chooses not to fornicate, he chooses to sin mortally, and therefore, sins mortally.[5]

It follows, therefore, that as far as St. Thomas is concerned, conscience binds unconditionally, whether or not it is in error, a fact that may surprise those who connect conscience with the Reformation more than with scholasticism. In any case, it is clear that this is a position almost compelled by the logic of the case, if we are to take conscience seriously at all. Otherwise, if conscience is to be obeyed only when it is right, there must be some authority other than conscience to distinguish those cases when conscience is right from those in which it is wrong, a state of affairs essentially destructive of the authority of conscience. If conscience is to have *any* authority, it must have *all* authority and this is precisely what St. Thomas gives it, alarming as it may sound to maintain that conscience must be obeyed even when it counsels that which on other grounds is patently wrong and contrary to the divine law understood objectively. But since the individual can act only as the divine law appears in his light, as understood in his mind and mediated by his sensibility, in the final analysis he must obey the command as he hears it, in the depth of his conscience.

Must we end on such an anarchic note? Can we do no wrong if we think our action to be right? It is true that we must obey our conscience but it is our responsibility to have a conscience in good working order. This in turn involves two aspects. First, there must be the genuine willingness to listen to conscience, not only to what we want to hear but to what conscience is actually saying, however painful its message may be. And, second, there is the necessity for exposing conscience to those events and documents which constitute the record of Israel's relation with God, immersion in which shapes the conscience of the Jew. Human conscience in general and Jewish conscience in particular are not formed in a vacuum. No man is naturally endowed with an unerring conscience which miraculously leads him to the right irrespective of the knowledge available to him or unavailable to him. Without in any way diminishing the significance of conscience, we maintain that it can be sensitized and developed by the tradition of revelation to which the people of Israel are witness and without which Jewish conscience is impoverished and isolated, cut off from its source of historic sustenance. The study of Torah is therefore a fundamental dictate of Jewish conscience. And because this is so, while no person is guilty for following his conscience, he may be guilty for not giving a hearing to the voices of his tradition which speak to him across the ages and which at least purport to echo the voice of Sinai. Whether they will be perceived by him as such is a matter between him, his conscience and God. But that he ought to try to listen is a dictate of conscience.

NOTES

1. *Church Dogmatics,* volume 1, part 2, pp 696-697.
2. *Sein und Zeit* (Tübingen, M. Niemeyer 1963 [1927]) p 313.
3. Ibid. p 318.
4. Ibid. p 320.
5. In *Epistolam ad Romanos,* c. 14, 1. 2 (Opera Omnia, ed. Vives, 20, 1876) p 580 quoted in Xavier G. Colavechio, *Erroneous Conscience and Obligations* (Washington, D.C.: Catholic University of America, 1961), p 81.

On the Mystery of Eating:
Thoughts Suggested by the Writings of
Rav Abraham Isaac Kuk

HERBERT WEINER

The fact tends to fade from the consciousness of people for whom the gathering and ingestion of food is no problem. But, after breathing, eating is the most necessary aspect, the *sine qua non* of existence. Why then should it not be an object of man's earnest spiritual as well as physical concern? And any anthropological survey of the taboos, rituals and ideas associated with food by ancient—and some modern—folk cultures can assure us that it is. "You are what you eat" may be a popular "new-age" phrase, but it would be perfectly understandable in the context of older ages who saw the act of eating as decisive, not only for health but for a proper relationship with the cosmos.

The Hebrew tradition is certainly aware of the spiritual and moral aspects of eating. The earliest pages of the Bible link man's problems with Adam's consumption of forbidden fruit. Isaac insists on being fed before offering his blessings to Jacob and Esau. That God's blessing also waits upon proper feeding, we can deduce from the lengthy listings of permitted and forbidden foods, the strictures of the Passover diet and the intricate sacrificial offerings on the Temple altar—"my offering, my bread, the pleasant smell of my roast, shall you be careful to offer in its season" (Num 28, 2).

Post-Biblical tradition extends and elaborates the linkage between the dining table and holiness. Philo offers an intriguing description of a meal in a first century Dead Sea community. After returning from work in the fields, the members of the community immerse themselves in ritual baths and don white robes before entering the dining room. The meal begins with a solemn blessing over bread by the High Priest, then proceeds in a silence broken only by scriptural readings. To the members of this commune, the table was an altar and the consumption of food a highly important religious rite. One reason for the formation of these communities was their feeling that the Temple authorities in Jerusalem were not sufficiently observant of the biblical tithing laws which "freed" the produce of the fields for consumption. The ultimate punishment which could be visited upon a member of this sect was excommunication from the only community which could assure him of a ritually pure diet.

The great rabbinic schools of the post-Temple era poured vast energy into the details of proper (Kosher) and improper foods, method of preparation, purity of cooking utensils, order of blessings, too, for they taught, "The table is an altar." It would be difficult to overestimate the role "gastronomic" Judaism plays in traditional Jewish life. To this day, the orthodox "smikha," ordination, is basically a document testifying that its recipient is a qualified authority in all matters related to the kitchen.

Given this emphasis on the importance of what and how one eats, we might expect an occasional word of explanation. But this is rarely forthcoming in either biblical or Rabbinic tradition. The Bible does link the prohibition against forbidden foods with the goal of being "qdoshim"—"holy" or "set-aside." But why one food is "proper" and another an "abomination" is not discussed. It is assigned to the category of "gzerah"—divine edict whose reason is known only to God.[1]

Judaism's esoteric tradition, later known as the "inner wisdom" or the "Qabbalah" did venture reasons for these intricate laws. Circles associated with the teaching of the sixteenth century Qabbalist, Rabbi Isaac Luria, the Holy Ari (lion), talk about the "fallen sparks" imbedded in all creation, including food, animals and vegetation. The proper ingestion of food "raises the sparks" and aids in the "Tiqqun"—the "repair" of the world. This theme occupies a central place in the imagination of the Hassidic movement started in the eighteenth century by Israel, the Baal Shem Tov—the "master of the good name." The nineteenth century German historian, Heinrich Graetz, is quite choleric in his description of the new movement which he regarded as a retreat into superstition and folly, a throw-back to the ancient Essenes. But Graetz did notice that the new Hassidic sect and the ancient Essene community both centered around the personality of a "Ṣaddiq," a "righteous" leader who, dressed in white, presides over his community at the communal dining table. To this day, there are places where one can visit a Hassidic "tisch"—"table" for the "third meal" which ushers out the Sabbath. The twilight, the songs of yearning expressing "dvequt"—"clingingness," the words of the Rebbe, the rapt expressions of the Hassidim, illustrate the phrase "a table wreathed in mystery" used in a hymn composed for the Sabbath by the Holy Ari. At such a table, Hassidim will watch their Rebbe eat—watch as if they were observing a rite upon which the very existence of the universe depended. And this, indeed, is their feeling, for, has the psalmist not written "the righteous man is the foundation of the world." Therefore, the feeding of the Ṣaddiq is a "feeding" of the universe. On his plate the Rebbe will leave some remnants— *"shirayim"*—which the Hassidim devour as if they were partaking in a high mystery. And, for those who understand, the eating not only of *"shirayim"* but of all food can be a holy mystery.

It is to this "mystery" that Rabbi Nachman of Bratzlav, the great-grandson of the Baal Shem Tov alludes when he says: "There are two kinds of divine service—inner and outer. Torah study and prayer are 'inner'. Eating and drinking are 'outer.' And the 'outer' service is of a category higher, more shining, more praiseworthy than the inner" (Liqutei Moharan). And again: "There are people who eat so as to have strength to learn (holy Torah). There are also people—and they are of a higher level—who learn so as to know how to eat" (Liqutei Moharan).

The mystery of eating is discussed by many Hassidic masters, since most of them presided at a *"Tisch."* Non-Hassidic Rabbis are more reticent as to the "hidden" meanings of eating. They are content to concentrate on *"Nigleh,"* the "revealed" laws regarding prohibited and permitted foods, the instruction for proper slaughtering, the ingredients and measures used for Temple sacrifices, etc. But the "hidden" reasons behind these laws are rarely probed. A brilliant exception is the first Chief Rabbi of Palestine, Abraham Isaac Kuk (1865-1935).

Rabbi Kuk and The Way of "Hakhlala"

In Israel today, the name Abraham Isaac Kuk is associated with the photograph of a bearded face, luminous, somewhat sad eyes and a broad brow, usually encircled by the fur *"shtreimel"* favored by the ultra-orthodox community. The association also includes stories about how this "tolerant" Chief Rabbi ignored the criticism of the orthodox community by dancing with "free-thinking" pioneers on their Kibbutzim. In fact, there was nothing liberal or tolerant about Rabbi Kuk's attitude toward Jewish laws. But the main characteristic of his teaching is what his son, Rabbi Zvi Yehudah Kuk, calls *"Hakhlala"*—a verb built out of the Hebrew word *"kᵉlal,"* meaning an over-all principle, an inclusive generality.

"He was a vessel who received all streams of Judaism—the legal, the mystical, the poetic, the national. And his Torah was a teaching of "allness", of a *"Hakhlala"*, an "including which tried to see every part within a larger whole", Rabbi Zvi Yehudah Kuk explains. This insistence on *"Hakhlala"* could extend to those parts of the Jewish people who seemingly diverged from main-line Jewish religious belief. "Even Atheism—the denial of God," wrote Rabbi Kuk, "has a temporary right to existence, for it is needed to purge a religious faith that has accumulated negative adhesions through a narrowing of spiritual perceptions . . ." This was the kind of statement that popularly associated the Chief Rabbi with "tolerance", a word which, in actuality, he linked with weakness of faith.

The white-bearded, twinkling-eyed Rabbi Zvi Yehudah Kuk likes to wave his hands in a series of widening circles to explain his father's call to a vision of an organic "allness" wherein levels of reality are enwrapped "circle within circle", detail within a whole, and that whole within a large whole.

To grasp this wholeness is to approach truth. The more "whole" the more true. The converse also holds. The less whole, the more partial, the less true. This applies to everything—the function of a cell in the body, the view of a particular political party, the faith of a religion, and even the great antimonies of good and evil, life and death, past and future. All are like limbs on an upside down tree which can be traced upward to the trunk and roots which include all contradictions within the larger unity, the *"Kᵉlal."*

This "allness" is alive—alive, pulsing, heaving, rising, falling. It is not only alive but joyously vibrant, its parts adhering to each other "with friendship", every detail linked to the whole so that whatever affects one part, affects the whole, lifts it or lowers it.

The over-all direction is "upward" back toward the infinite source, the *"Ein sof"* from which it descended. This accent can be helped or hindered by man, who occupies a unique position in the universe. The universe, because it includes the *"ein sof,"* the infinite, is without boundary. Still, this wholeness has its center, man—who is the microcosm of the macrocosm. Man is not only an image of the All. He is also a centering receptacle into which all elements of the universe stream, and out of whom they radiate. Man is the central cog in an ecological cosmos where every part involves every other part. But no part is more crucial to the over-all direction of the whole than man, whose balancing and arranging of elements and energies crucially affects the totality.

So, all is dynamically alive, vibrating with joyous energy, and at the center of this sparkling ocean is man. It is a vision quite similar to the view offered by modern physics with its perception of matter as dancing configurations of energy. But Rabbi Kuk uses one word to describe this totality of energy which does not belong to the vocabulary of the physicist. That word is "good". All is not only alive, not only suffused with light and joy. It is also, at least in its over-all, inner truth, completely good. It is completely good because it comes from a completely good source.

That, of course, is quite an assertion in the face of earthquakes, cancer, Auschwitz, or simple human nastiness. Rabbi Kuk's "justification" draws on the usual attempt to explain evil as an illusion or categorization marred by limited human perception. But it also draws heavily on the mythological imagery of the Qabbalah describing a primal explosion which causes a "breaking of the vessels" and a concomitant "falling of sparks with the broken shells". The result is a universe beset by chaos and demoniac forces which draw their power from the holiness of the fallen sparks. It is a universe whose original harmony is shattered; a universe out-of-order, yearning for restoration.

Man has been assigned the task of effecting this restoration or *"tiqqun"*. He does this by separating sparks from shells and raising them back to the source so that the primordial harmony—*Adam Qadmon*—will be restored. This "fix" or *tiqqun* can be effected by an action, a word or a deed. Eating offers one of the most important opportunities for the *tiqqun*. Hence, the preference expressed in Rabbi Nachman of Bratslav's words for those "who study in order to know how to eat."

Every person can "lift" the sparks embedded in the domain of "mineral", "vegetable", and "animal" through his eating. But the eating of the Ṣaddiq, the "righteous one" is particularly efficacious in its effect on the universe.

The Ṣaddiq's soul is connected to the souls of his community. As the old Hassidic song goes, "When the Rebbe eats, all his Hassidim eat". He is the soul of their souls. He is also the "all inclusive soul" of mankind.

Therefore, his eating is watched with trepidation, but also with eagerness. For, since the Ṣaddiq's will is identified with the will of the Creator, and also tied to the will of every soul in his community, his eating merges the wills of his followers with the will of God. So, the Hassid is happy, the Rebbe is happy, the world and God—all are happy. For, happiness is the result of a harmonization of personal will with the will of the Creator. The mystical dimension of eating derives from a sense of personal participation in this cosmic harmonization. But is there more?

I believe there is, but it is a mystery more concealed, revealed only, in Rabbi Kuk's words, to those "who enter into the secret of the Lord, who know what can be alluded to only by a wordless sign."

These are the words with which Rabbi Kuk closes a passage which he links to the biblical sentence, from the Book of Ruth: "Boaz ate and drank and made his heart good" (3,7). "Good" adds Rabbi Kuk, "with words of Torah."

Of course, to dine in the company of those who discuss Torah and turn the table into an altar is "good". But Rabbi Kuk's allusion would take us beyond this recommendation into a more recondite mystery. The concept to which the Rabbi alludes is found in Hassidic literature and has its roots in the early sources of Qabbalistic tradition like the Book of Creation. There we are told that the basic building blocks of the Universe are the Hebrew letters. Qabbalistic tradition uses this idea to visualize all matter as being composed of Hebrew letters (the letters referred to are the source of the actual letters in Torah, that is, configurations of energy which descend to become materialized in the written or spoken letters. We meet this idea of food deriving its taste and power for nourishment from Hebrew letters in many sources, among them, Rabbi Nachman of Bratzlav, who in his youth tried to swallow food without tasting it—an attempt to ingest the letters (the energy) directly. An allusion to what Rabbi Nachman's style of eating was after, can be found in a passage attributed to him. "And he who can quicken the sparkling of the letters which are in all creation, in everything—his joy will then come only from the sparkling of the letters which are in the food and drink. And this is the reference of 'And Boaz ate and drank and it was good for his heart'. 'Good for his heart.'—that refers to the sparkling of the letters. Good refers to light.' And Boaz saw the light, that it was good' " (Liqutei Moharan 19).

Have we exhausted the mystery of eating as it is conceived by Rabbi Kuk or is there still more alluded by the "wordless sign"?

"When prayer," writes Rabbi Kuk, "which reveals the primordial will for absolute and holy good is related to food, it raises the configuration of all the sparks. And when their life unites with the life treasury of the eater, the holy flame, which shines and is warm with holiness rises, is adorned with all good, in the light of the light of life, and becomes bound up in the bundle of life with God, Lord of the Universe . . ."

To see life as a flame, consuming and being consumed—is that not part of the mystery involved in eating? For, does not everything eat everything? The earth is consumed by the plants; the plants by animals; animals by man. And what about man? Hebrew legend tells of an heavenly altar upon which the souls of the saints are offered. For, is it not written: "The Lord your God is a consuming fire" (Deut 4,24)—the actual translation should be "an eating fire."

The chain of life, essentially, is a chain of eating whereby the lower or smaller is consumed by the larger which is consumed by the still larger with the final consumer being death—or Life, the Life of lives, God. The thought comes to mind—the Ḥad Gadya sung at the conclusion of the Passover service, about the kid eaten by the cat which is bitten by the dog and so on till all is consumed by the angel of death. Is it the simple child's rhyme for which it is sometimes taken, or even an allusion to the history of nations swallowing each other? Why not take it at its face value—a song about eating—eating which when we contemplate it as mystery, seems to lift the veil from core truth of existence—that to live is to consume and to be consumed. Life is a flame of offering and if we would come close to its core, we must offer ourselves. Life is a consuming flame and it will consume us as we consume others. The secret, therefore, is not whether we will consume or be consumed but whether we will "eat" or be "eaten" for a high and holy purpose, for that which truly matters in the Ultimate Conscience of the universe which we call God.

> "And the Light of Israel will be fire,
> and its Holy One a flame. . . " (Isa 10,17)

Part II

The foregoing is offered as background for translations of Rabbi Kuk's writings which I call "Meditations". I call them that in the hope that they will be used just that way—to invoke an insight of soul as well as mind. That is the only way, I believe, to "receive" most of what "the teacher", the "Rav" as he is called in Israel today, has to offer our generation. Most—but not all. For those writings which deal with legal Rabbinic problems, or with concrete socio-political issues of the day, can bear direct prosaic translation and reading on the level of the discursive intellect. But other writings were products of an inner surge, an almost compulsive need to convey an insight, a vision of the hidden dynamics at play in history, in the world, in the cosmos. At such moments, Rabbi Kuk might scribble his thoughts on a scrap of paper, a notebook, whatever was at hand. These effusions were rarely edited and therefore retained a measure of prolixity and repetition. Pruning these outpourings while retaining evidence of their contact with primal inspiration is a challenge not easily met by those who want to be "transmitters" of Rabbi Kuk's literary heritage. The two major "transmitters" of this heritage are Rabbi Zvi Yehudah Kuk, who, among other works, has edited a two volume prayerbook with commentary culled from his father's writings. The other major editor is Rabbi David Ha-Cohen. Known during his lifetime in Israel as "The Nazarite"—an appellation evoked by his long blonde hair, "fasts of silence," restrictions of diet and other more private "vows". The carefully schematized arrangement of Rabbi Kuk's thought which the Nazir called "Lights of Holiness," is described by Professor Gershom Scholem as "a veritable *theolgia mystica* of Judaism equally distinguished by its originality and the richness of its author's mind."[2] Rabbi David HaCohen has also edited a collection of Rabbi Kuk's thoughts in the "hidden" meanings of the dietary laws and Judaism's attitude toward vegetarianism.

My translations are drawn with gratitude and apology from the works of these two transmitters.

I

THE ALL-EMBRACING GLANCE

The eye that is open
Sees life spreading throughout all Being
In its wholeness and its detail

It beholds and perceives the ascent and descent of the parts;
With intelligence it unites man's soul, understanding, and will
To the whole of existence in a vision
That encompasses the slumbering, lower powers
And reaches toward the heights.

The master of such a vision
Is seized by the inner life of all that he encounters,
Be it near or far.
When he eats, drinks, is occupied with any bodily matter,
He perceives waves of life flooding toward him
From out of the Allness,
Asking to be lifted, through him, with him.
And he, loving all,
Stirred with compassion,
Filled with the glory and the beauty of strength,
Wants all to be lifted.

From "The Lights of Holiness"

II
FROM LEVEL TO LEVEL

Divine energy manifests itself by degrees level after level.
In mute mineral matter, in plants, in animals, this energy
Has not yet achieved its consummate articulation.
It lacks the light and variegated expression of intelligence.
It achieves this level through the eating of a person who,
    guided by divine light and high knowledge, will expend
    his strength with intelligence and integrity.

When the strength which comes to a man through his food,
Is transmuted into intelligence suffused with holy light,
A portion of creation is lifted with him.

Prayerbook

III
THE SPARKS

The life sparks encountered in eating
May be lowered or lifted

Prayer—which reveals the primal desire for utter goodness,
For high and holy goodness—
Can, when associated with the meal,
Raise the configurations of sparks,
Unite their life
With the storehouse of life in the person that is eating
So as to form a holy torch,
A flame, shining, warming in its holiness
Adorned with all manner of goodness,
Alight with the light of life,
Bound up with the bundle of life,
With God, Lord of the Universe.

From "The Lights of Holiness"

IV
THE BREAD OF SADNESS

When one eats only to satisfy the physical appetite,
sadness increases, that sadness hinted at by the words,
"They who eat the bread of sadness."
For the sparks which could rise, instead fall, and are saddened
by this descent.
The person eating senses this sadness. Through various
Transformations of feeling and transposition of letters,
this sadness makes itself known within his inner soul.

From "The Lights of Holiness"

V
THE EATING OF ṢADDIQIM

A high soul descends into the chosen, the holy ones of Israel when they
approach food. And this is "The Table set before the Lord."
These Ṣaddiqim, whose saintliness sustains the universe, wish to quicken
themselves with all the sparks of holiness hidden in food.
Even before the act of consumption, the joy of their souls awakens a like joy in
the holy sparks which respond and move with increased strength and
happiness.

At the time of eating, joy sparkles throughout the depths.
During the course of the meal, it ascends even higher.
"And Boaz ate and drank and it did his heart good."
—"It did his heart good"—through the letters of Torah which are the real
substance of eating and drinking as is known to those who enter into the secret
of the Lord, who know the silent signs.

From "The Lights of Holiness"

NOTES

1. Father L. Frizzell has kindly drawn my attention to several non-Rabbinic sources where "reasons" for permitted and forbidden foods are offered. For example, the Letter of Aristeas #130-168, edited by M. Hadas, *Aristeas to Philocrates* (New York: Ktav 1973)p 153-167, and Philo (Legum Allegoria III, 100-131).

2. Gershom G. Scholem, *Major Trends in Jewish Mysticism* (New York: Schocken 1961) p 354.

A Jewish View of the World Community

JACOB B. AGUS

The ideal of uniting all mankind in one society is today gaining ever wider acceptance. When many millions of people see on their television screens our "cool, green earth," as it appears to the astronauts, who can doubt that we are all passengers on one ship, condemned to the same fate?

Whatever happens in one part of the globe affects all of mankind, for good or ill. If the threat of a nuclear war hangs over the heads of all men, the promise of the good life gives hope to the most wretched on our blood-stained planet.

Yet, even if the vision of "one world" should be embraced most ardently by all men, there is no assurance that it will be realized. So long as people adhere to their present scale of values, all advances toward the goal of unification are likely to be frustrated. Zechariah counselled his people to love truth and peace, putting truth ahead of peace (8,19). To attain universal peace, we need a high degree of sophistication in soul-searching, utilizing all the resources of our religious traditions, along with the insights and institutions of the behavioral sciences. We have to recognize the areas of ambiguity in our noblest ideals, the shadows and penumbras that appear, whenever a lamp is lit in the dark.

This essay is a contribution toward this end. It consists of two parts, a brief historical review of religious humanism in the Jewish tradition and an analytical study of the theological concepts bearing upon this theme.

I

The unity of mankind is a central theme of the Hebrew Scriptures, from cover to cover. All men and women are derived form one couple, Adam and Eve. Only one language was spoken prior to the building of the tower of Babel. In the end of time, mankind will again be one, walking together "in the light of God", abandoning the implements of war for the arts of peace, and basking together in the heavenly radiance of redemption (Isa 40, 2-4; Mic 4, 1-5).

However, the consummation of this hope is dependent upon the acceptance by all men of monotheism, in some form (Zeph 3,9; Zech 14, 16; Isa 49, 1-6; 56, 6-8). The pristine unity of mankind was due to a kind of pre-Abrahamite monotheism which, according to Jewish tradition, lasted until "the generation of Enosh," when idolatry became the fashion of the day. (Maimonides, Introduction to his Code, *Mishnah Torah*). Similarly, the redeemed, all-embracing society of the end of history will be marked by a universal acceptance of the sovereignty of God—"on that day the Lord will be One, and his Name One" (Zeph 3,9). This change in theological nomenclature will mark a deep transmutation of the human spirit—"and the earth shall be filled with the knowledge of the Lord as the waters cover the sea" (Isa 11,9). It is the universal acknowledgement of the Fatherhood of God, in heart and soul, that will make possible a genuine sense of brotherhood. Any advance in the horizontal expansion of the ideal society is dependent upon growth in the vertical dimension of life, the realm of ideals that leads from man to God. The prophets were not interested in mere formalistic successes, external patterns of organization that do not reflect genuine values of the spirit. Hence, their insistence that the social-political unity of mankind is dependent on its spiritual unity.

In order to serve as the spiritual vanguard of humanity, Abraham and his "seed" were selected and charged with special obligations—"that all the families of the earth will be blessed in thee" (Gen 12, 1-3). In the Mosaic polity, the people Israel are designated as "the first-born son" of the human family, or as "a kingdom of priests and a holy nation" (Exod 4,22; 19,6). It is the task of priests to bring laymen to the service of God; they must not dwell apart, in cloistered solitude, but teach all men to serve God together" (Commentary of Sefornu on Exod 19,6). Thus, from the beginning, Israel was regarded as "the people of God," or as God's "treasure-people," in this special priestly sense.

The literary prophets recognized the tension between the ideal, holy community and the empirical people of Israel, but they insisted that Israel could not but remain forever the nuclear community of the future, since it was constituted by an "eternal covenant" (Isa 55,3; Jer 33,25). They foresaw two processes whereby the empirical people will be made suitable for its role—first, only a "remnant" of Israel will truly "return" to the Lord; second, some non-Israelites will "associate" themselves with the holy community (Isa 10, 21; 66, 21; Jer 16,19; Zech 2,15). With these reservations, the prophets regarded the living Israelites of their day as the heirs of the Promise and the "heartland" of the future Kingdom of God.

In the exilic period, the winds of assimilation swept away the marginal Israelites. The thin ranks of "the loyal remnant" were, however, inspired by a holy zeal to cherish every aspect of the tradition. Ezra and Nehemiah drew up a "sure covenant" (Neh 10,1) and considered only those who adhered to it members of the holy community. Their loyal followers separated themselves from "the uncleanliness of the nations of the land" (Ezra 6,21). No effort was made to convert the Gentile wives of Jewish spouses, or their offspring. It appears that at that time, the *halakhah* of conversion had not yet been formulated.[1] Also, the loyalists were scornful of the piety of the common people, "the people of the land" (*ʿam haʾares*) (Ezra 4,4; Neh 13, 14-22). In the book of Daniel, written during the early days of the Maccabean uprising against the Syrian government and its allied Jewish "Hellenizers," the author speaks of the Kingdom being reserved for "the saints of the most High" (Dan 7,22). Thus, the biblical canon contains a minimal as well as a maximal definition of "the people of God".

In pre-rabbinic literature, we encounter a wide spectrum of attitudes ranging from the total rejection of all but a few "elect" to the inclusion of all who shun idolatry and abide by the principles of ethics. The Qumran sectarians maintained that only those who belonged to their own society were "children of light." All others were doomed to destruction. In the "Wisdom of Solomon," the righteous saints are elevated to the status of the "sons of God" (2, 16.17). The author of the "Psalms of Solomon" was probably a quietistic Pharisee, who looked forward to the imminent arrival of the Messiah. He foresaw "sanctified nations" surrounding the House of Israel (17,40). The narrowest and most pessimistic view was probably the one held by the author of IV Ezra, who witnessed the destruction of the second Temple. Sirach speaks of every nation being governed by an angelic prince with Israel, the "first born" in the family of nations, being ruled by the Lord Himself (17,17). This widely held view is asserted also by the author of the Book of Jubilees, who in a fit of malice, adds that these national angels were instructed to mislead their human charges (15,31).

When we come to Philo, we encounter a bright and generous spirit. He speaks of a category of *gerim*, sojourners or proselytes in spirit, who belong to God, though they are not "sons of the Covenant."

". . . the sojourner is one who circumcizes not his uncircumcision, but his desires and sensual pleasures and the other passions of the soul. For in Egypt, the Hebrew nation was not circumcized. . . . But what is the mind of the stranger, if not alienation from belief in many gods and familiarity with honoring the One God and Father of all?" (*Quaest. in Exod.* II,2., commentary on Exod 22,21).

In describing every day as a possible holiday dedicated to God, Philo speaks of "the blameless life of righteous men, who follow nature and her ordinances . . . All who practice wisdom, either in Grecian or barbaric lands, and lead a blameless and irreproachable life . . . as behooves true 'cosmopolitans' . . ." (*De Specialibus Legibus*, II, 12,42).

In his essay on Moses, Philo describes the prophet as addressing a message of repentance to all men. Of those who respond by renouncing idolatry, he writes, "They have shown the godliness of heart which above all leads to friendship and affinity, and we must rejoice with them. . . " (*De Virtutibus*, XXIII, 175). In the Testaments of the Twelve Patriarchs, forgiveness is exalted as an absolute ideal and the redemption of the Gentiles is predicated as a direct consequence of Israel's redemption.[2] Jewish propaganda for the Gentiles to give up idolatry, sexual offenses and other moral sins, lest they be destroyed by an eschatological catastrophe, is reflected in the Sybilline Oracles.[3]

If we take a survey of the world-community from the standpoint of a Hillelite Pharisee in the year 65c.e., it would be about as follows:

(a) The righteous Israelites, who are destined for heaven and the resurrection, and the World to Come. These include the "righteous proselytes," *gere haṣedeq*.

(b) The "middle people," i.e. Israelites, who are neither saintly nor wicked. Here, the Hillelites differed from the Shammaites who asserted that such people must traverse through hell, even if only for a moment, in order to obtain forgiveness (Rosh Hashanah 16b). The Hillelites maintained that God forgives "the middle people," his Grace being offered freely to those who make some effort to win favor in his sight.

(c) The "wicked" Israelites, *posh'ey yisrael*, who may be consigned to hell for a maximum of 12 months. We are not quite certain of the contemporary reference of that designation (Rosh Hashanah 17a).[4]

(d) The malicious heretics, for whom there is no hope, particularly if they cause others to stumble. The Hillelites, prior to the destruction of Jerusalem, did not include the Jewish Christians, much less the Gentile Christians in this category, as is evident in the book of Acts (5,34 and 23:9).

(e) The sectarian groups, Samaritans, Essenes, Zealots, Jewish-Christians, Gnostics, who are judged individually. (No *minim* among the nations: Hullin 13b. Aruch Hashalem V, 169).

(f) The Gentiles who have taken the first steps on the way to conversion, refraining from the final step, on account of one reservation or another. This type of semi-convert is probably the subject of the stories, dramatizing the difference between Hillel and Shammai (Shabbat 30b). Hillel's policy was to promote conversion by proceeding from the love of man, to the observance of the commands of Torah, and thence to the love of God—"Love mankind and bring them closer to Torah" (Abot I, 12); also, after stating the Golden Rule to the would-be-convert, Hillel said, "the rest is commentary; go and learn." (Shabbat 31a). Those Gentiles who accepted certain practices, like the Sabbath-laws, were apparently looked upon with favor by Josephus (*Apion* II,39), but with distinct dislike by the Talmud (Sanhedrin 58b).

(g) The "pious among the nations of the world," who share in the World to Come and may even provide the norms of piety, whereby Israel is to be judged (Test. of Benjamin 10,10; Tos. Sanhedrin, 13). "Any one who denies idolatry is called a Jew" (Megillah 13a).

(h) Gentiles who undertake to abide by the Seven Laws of Noah belong to the invisible congregation of the Lord, but Israelites are not obligated to include them among the beneficiaries of their philanthropy. But, if they avow their acceptance of these laws, before a court of three learned men *(ḥaberim)*, then they become part of the fellowship of Israel, in respect of all types of communal charity (Aboda Zara 64b; Tossafot *ad hoc*).

(i) Gentiles who continue to practice the rites of idolatry for a variety of external reasons, but whose hearts are not in it, are not really guilty of idolatry, for "God looks to the heart" (Hullin 13b). This recognition of an inner reality that no man can judge was frequently quoted by the medieval rabbis, who might condemn certain rites as idolatrous and certain beliefs as false, without stigmatizing as idolatrous the people who practice those rites or hold those opinions. (See the letter of Moses Maimonides to Rabbi Hisdai the Sephardi).

(j) Gentiles who cherish Wisdom and preoccupy themselves with the demands of their particular inherited faith, providing that faith incorporates the Noachide principles; also, those who entertain no creedal principles whatever and yet make their contributions to the various arts of civilization; all such men may well reach the highest levels of holiness, "like the High Priest," even if they have never heard of the God of Israel (Sanhedrin 59a).

(k) Masses of people, who fall in no particular category, and who are judged individually on the principle that "the Lord does not spoil the reward of any of his creatures" (Baba Kama 38b).

(l) The heathen idolators, who are willfully guilty of moral perversions, and sin against the laws which the Lord implanted in creation (Rosh Hashanah 17a).

These twelve categories include virtually all the people with whom the Hillelite Pharisees were acquainted. There is a great deal of vagueness in regard to all the Gentiles of categories (f) to (l). Perhaps, this was intentional, since the Jewish Sages did not presume to judge the nations. In contrast to Paul and his disciples, we find in the Talmudic apocalypse that the Lord himself judges all nations (Aboda Zara 2a). Rabbi Akiba was rebuked for his suggestion that the Messiah will share in judging the nations (Hagigah 14a).

Of particular interest are the so-called "fearers of the Lord" in the New Testament and Greco-Roman literature, *(phoboumenoi ton theon* or *sebomenoi)* and the category of a semi-proselyte, *ger toshav* or *ger hasha'ar*.[5] In the Talmud, the category of *ger toshav* was said to consist of those who in the presence of three Associates, undertook to abide by the Noachide principles (Aboda Zara 64b). But, the question is discussed by second century rabbis in a manner which shows that they were debating only a theoretical issue. The status of one who was baptized, without undergoing circumcision, or who was circumcized without being baptized, was debated by rabbis at the beginning of the second century (Yebamot 46a). The assumption in the Talmud appears to be that the status of *ger toshav* applied only when the Jubilee year was observed. Hence, it existed only before the destruction of the Kingdom of Israel. (This is the opinion of Rashi, Gittin 36a. The Tossafot disagree).

Schürer suggests that baptism may have been required even of those who did not undergo full conversion (*History,* 1891 Eng. ed. IV, p. 323). G. F. Moore argues that there was no valid category of "semi-proselytes" in rabbinic law. Yet, the widespread phenomenon of 'fearers of the Lord' in the Roman world is well attested. Prof. H. A. Wolfson speaks of so-called "spiritual proselytes."[6] The local authorities of the various Synagogues in the Diaspora must have set their own standards to regulate the admission of interested worshipers to this marginal status; such authorities were accustomed to act of their own accord in those areas where the Palestinian rabbis were deliberately vague. Prof. Salo W. Baron concludes, "There is little doubt that Diaspora Jewry went farther than the Palestinian Sages in the reinterpretation of the biblical provisions to fit the exigencies of their own environment."[7]

We note also the category in the Talmud of "attached converts," *gerim gerurim,* or "converts en masse," as Moore defines it. Rashi's interpretation that they are self-converted converts, who had not been accepted by a Jewish court, appears to be more correct (Aboda Zara 3b). That it was indeed a supreme *miṣwah* to bring people "under the wings of the *Shekhinah*" can scarcely be disputed. Well-known is the teaching that the Israelites were exiled in order that converts might be added unto them

(Pesahim 87b). The sacrifices of the unconverted Gentiles were accepted in the Holy Temple, while those of Jews who have offered oblations to idols, or who have violated the Sabbath in public, were not accepted (Shabbat 69b).

In theory, the Jews clung to the vision of the unity of mankind in time to come. While they were accused of "hatred of the gods" and "hatred of the human race," they demonstrated in Rome under the slogan, "Oh, heavens, aren't we brothers, the sons of one father and mother. In what do we differ from every other nation and tongue?" (Ta'anit 18a). To be sure, there were times, when contemporary hostilities produced some bitter outbursts of hatred and contempt. Nahman Krochmal, in *Moreh Nebukhai Hazeman*, chapter 14, cites many authorities for the proposition that some unworthy *aggadot* were inserted into the Talmud by copyists. But, on the whole, such lapses in faith and love, were rare. In normal times, the tannaitic Sages insisted that all acts of charity, from feeding the hungry to visiting the sick to burying the dead, must be extended to all men equally in order to multiply the ways of peace (Gittin 61a; Tosefta, Gittin, Ch. 3; Tossafot on Shabbat 19a; Berakhot 17a). Under stress, the community tended to polarize—while some Jews withdrew into a shell, shutting out of sight the world that was so harsh to them, others kept alive the outgoing, universalist orientation of prophetic Judaism.

The standard Prayer Book, which attained its final form in the Gaonic period, kept alive the hope for the universal society. In the prayer of *"Aleinu,"* which concludes each of the three daily services, the first paragraph extols the unique privilege of the Jew as the servant of "the supreme King of Kings, the Holy One, blessed be he." The second paragraph of the same prayer articulates the hope for the establishment of God's Kingdom on earth, "when the world will be perfected under the reign of the Almighty, and all mankind will call upon thy name, and all the wicked of the earth will be turned to thee." The two paragraphs constitute one prayer, since it is the role of Israel to serve as a "light to the nations," the vanguard of redeemed humanity.

Of all the festivals of the year, it is the High Holidays in particular that celebrate the advance of mankind toward this goal. Rosh Hashanah, the beginning of the year, marks the anniversary of the birth of Adam and Eve, the parents of all men and women, and Yom Kippur is the day of forgiveness for all sins. The liturgy on these Days of Awe reaffirms the undying hope of Israel.

"And therefore, O Lord our God, let Thine awe be manifest in all Thy works, and a reverence for Thee fill all that Thou hast created, so that all Thy creatures may know Thee, and all mankind bow down to acknowledge Thee. May all Thy children unite in one fellowship to do Thy Will, with a perfect heart. . . " (Silverman edition, *High Holiday Prayer Book*, 1939, p. 152).

This consummation is conjoined with the hope for the vindication of Israel's destiny—"and therefore, O Lord, grant honor to thy people who serve thee. . . .". The particular "hope of Israel" was inseparable from the universal hope for the conversion of all men. Even in the ideal future, historic groups will preserve their identity, as in the vision of Isaiah—" 'Blessed be Egypt, my people, and Assyria, the work of my hands, and Israel, mine inheritance' " (Isa 19,25).

During the medieval period, Jewish thought moved along three parallel streams—rationalistic, romantic and mystical. Each of these currents contributed to the enrichment of the ideal of a world-community.

Rationalistic Judaism transferred the focus of religious life from the inscrutable Will of God to the well-being and spiritual greatness of humanity. The purpose of the prescribed commandments was to train the individual in the disciplines of the good life and to promote an ideal society. Many of the rituals were historically conditioned—that is, they were designed to protest against certain idolatrous practices (Maimonides, *Guide for the Perplexed*, III, 32). In the course of time, and without any supernatural breakthrough, the messianic age will arrive, and all mankind will be converted to "the religion of truth" (Maimonides, *Hilkhot Melakhim*, XI).

Even now, the service of God is open to all men, with the "philosopher-saints" of all faiths coming closer to the vision of God than those who are simply loyal to the rites of the Talmud (Maimonides, *Guide*, III, 51). And the ultimate test of religious experience is a life of "steadfast love, justice and righteousness" (with reference to Jer. 9,23; *Guide*, III, 54). Maimonides' ideas were applied in Jewish law *(halakhah)*, by the much quoted legalist, Menahem Hameiri as follows—"But everyone who belongs to 'the nations disciplined by religion' (*umoth hagedurot bedat*) . . is not included in this (the laws against idolators), and is to be regarded as a full Jew in respect of all this."[8]

Romantic Judaism, which operated with biological categories, conceived of all of humanity as one living organism, with Israel as its living heart. As the heart supplies all the organs with fresh blood, so it is Israel's task to inspire all nations with the love of God.[9]

The mystical current added the notion of the scattering of Holy Sparks throughout the world and the consequent need of redeeming these sparks. The purpose of prayer was "to uplift the *Shekhinah* from the dust" and thereby bring about the salvation of Israel and of mankind.

The doctrine of "Holy Sparks" scattered in all creation implied that God could be served even in so-called "secular" ways, an implication that Israel Baal Shem Tov converted into the core of the mystical mass-movement of Hassidism. And Martin Buber revealed the contemporary relevance of this doctrine in his "I-Thou" philosophy of interpersonal relations — namely, we address "the Eternal Thou," when we turn in love to every "Thou" that we encounter in life.

With the secularization of the messianic hope in modern times, the vision of a world-community was pursued along two different lines. The classical Reform theologians taught that mankind will be united through a process of religious enlightenment. Indeed, it was the special "mission" of the Jewish people to lead in the conversion of all men to a pure, rational form of "ethical monotheism." This advance in the ethical-spiritual domain will make possible the ultimate fulfillment of Isaiah's vision. And the role of the Jew, by virtue of his history as well as his faith, is to teach men to overcome ethnic bias and theological exclusiveness. Modern humanism, with its stress on rational and esthetic values, is itself a divine thrust in the direction of the Kingdom. God works through history, his wonders to perform, and in the Nineteenth century, who could doubt the reality, the certainty, yea the inevitability of progress?[10]

After two world wars, the Holocaust and the Vietnam disaster, the easy optimism of the Nineteenth century is all but gone. But, the nuclear umbrella has turned the humanist utopia into an indispensable instrument for the sheer survival of the human race.

The Zionist movement was similarly moved by the messianic ideal. But, while the Reform theologians identified Jewry as a religious community, the Zionists, in keeping with the European nationalist awakening, conceived of world-Jewry as a people *(Volk)*, or a nation. The Jewish Faith is indeed inseparable from the life of the Jewish people, but the substance of Jewish loyalty, previously framed in religious terms, was now identified with the feeling of belonging to the historic community of Israel. In the Zionist view, the Jewish people can regain its vitality and creativity only in its own ancient homeland. When it is no longer threatened by the twin-headed hydra of annihilation and assimilation, the Jewish people will regain its ethical-spiritual genius, and will bring its own peculiar contribution to the treasure-house of mankind's culture. The nature of Israel's mission is conceived differently among Zionist Socialists (Hess, Boruchov), Zionist liberals (Aḥad Haʿam), and the Orthodox (A. I. Kuk). In any case, Israel's rejuvenation is conceived in Zionism, as in classical Reform, within the context of dedication to the building of the world-community.

In the second part of this essay, we proceed to describe the theological concepts underlying the prophetic vision of a world-community.

II

God loves all men; yet, in all generations, there are those who may be designated "people of God," in a special and meaningful way. I do not refer to the exalted role or an *ish-Elohim*, a prophet like Elijah or Elisha, but to the more widespread and limited meaning that Abraham had in mind when he explained his fear that Yire*ath Elohim*, the fear of God, might be lacking in Egypt. In the large company of "people of God," there would be embraced all who advance the various causes that are calculated to bring into being the Kingdom of Heaven, *malkhut Shamayim*. It comprises therefore in the last resort an invisible company of men and women, whose genuine worth only God can tell. (The command to sanctify the Holy Name is incumbent upon Noachides as well as Israelites. Sanhedrin 74b). But, it would also include organizations and historic communities, insofar as these groups are truly dedicated to the task of forming the vanguard of mankind's advance toward the perfection of the messianic age. This general description in itself is far too simplistic to serve a useful purpose; indeed, it is loaded with many booby-traps, as an examination of the optimistic philosophies of the past will amply demonstrate.

The crucial task is to distinguish between syncretism and spiritual openness. The ancient Romans used to invite the gods of the cities that they set out to conquer to take up residence in their Pantheon. This practice was typical of the syncretistic mentality of the pagan world. In contrast, our Scripture condemns King Solomon for allowing his wives to build altars in Jerusalem to their respective gods (1Kgs 11:4-9). In the Greco-Roman world, the Jews refused to join their neighbors in the amalgamation of gods and rituals. But, they opened their hearts and minds to the philosophic endeavors of their age. Syncretism is the cheap way of achieving unity by mingling the outer symbols of faith; it transpires on the outer, ceremonial plane; it robs each faith of depth, flattening religion out into a meaningless mumbo-jumbo. The emergent compromise is like a babel of tongues, loud, vulgar and devoid of the power to grip the imagination of mankind.

Shunning the attractions of syncretism, our Sages sought "to gather the Holy Sparks" that God had scattered among all peoples and faiths. According to the Qabbalists, it is for this purpose that Providence had scattered our people among the nations.[11] The "sparks" are gathered through an intensification of our own strivings for holiness. In the

Nineteenth century Krochmal interpreted the uniqueness of Jewish history in terms of this dedication of our people to the worship of the all-embracing totality of Spirit — an ambition that can ever be approached, but never entirely fulfilled.[12] In history, the world is unredeemed, and all of us are called to "prepare the way" for redemption. In what follows, the implications of this position are outlined.

It is in three ways that the Divine Power enters into the human world, namely — Creation, Revelation and Redemption. In the biblical view, the history of mankind which begins with an act of Divine creation, will culminate in the attainment of complete redemption, this process being directed and accelerated through the gifts of revelation. In creation, God's Power is manifested; in revelation his will; in redemption, the Divine thrust to help man transcend his own personality and the pattern of values in his social order. Each of these phases of divine activity is continuous. Of creation, the Prayer Book describes God as "renewing in his Goodness daily the works of creation" (*Daily Prayer Book* ed. Hertz, p. 109. Psalms 104 and 24); of revelation, we learn of God as ordaining fresh laws daily (Genesis Rabba 64,4); he is addressed in prayer as "the Redeemer", in the present sense, performing wonders "every day, morning, evenings and afternoons." (Present tense is used in the Amida, seventh benediction, Hertz *Prayer Book*, p. 140. Based on Pesahim 117b). In Jewish theology, this threefold interpretation of the essence of faith was adumbrated in the teaching that there were three essential principles of faith — belief in God, in Torah, and in Providence (J. Albo, *The Book of Principles*, trans. J. Husik and S. Duran, *Sefer Magen Avot*). Franz Rosenzweig speaks of the three currents of metaphysical reality — Creation, Revelation, Redemption, with creation taking place between God and the world, revelation between God and man, and redemption between man and the world.[13] This brilliant schematization is certainly helpful, but we must remember that every Divine impulse partakes of all three categories. God's Will is revealed in creation as well as in revelation, and to perceive his Will is to take the decisive step on the highway of redemption. Yet, these phases of the Divine are sufficiently distinctive for us to be able to discuss them separately and to analyze their implications for the concept of the nuclear community of "people of God."

We take up the doctrine of revelation first, since it provides a clue to the twofold nature of God's activity—his universality and particularity. In the sphere of revelation, his will was manifested in a general way through the gifts of intelligence and conscience which he has implanted in the hearts of all men. We have referred previously to the Noachide principles. A more inclusive characterization of universal revelation would be the category of wisdom *ḥokhmah*. And in ancient times, wisdom included ethical and even religious values. Aristotle and Plato insisted on a distinction between shrewdness, or cleverness, and genuine wisdom. And the book of Proverbs asserts, "the beginning of wisdom is the fear of the Lord" (Prov 9,10. Prov 1,7, *da'at* is translated as "knowledge" in J.P.S and R.S.V. A better rendering is "understanding"). In contemporary terms, we would say an existential commitment to ethical values or an intuitive perception of their validity is the first principle of wisdom. Manifestly, the category of wisdom is a universal possession of mankind.

We note that Torah and Wisdom share in this quality of "the fear of the Lord" *(Yire'at Adonai)*. It is the "beginning" of Wisdom and the "end" of Torah (Deut 10,12). Rabbi Akiba said: "Man knows that he is made in the image of God". Indeed, this awareness is the spontaneous expression of man's true being for, as another Sage put it, "all is in the power of heaven, except the fear of heaven" (Berakhot 33b).

The notion that the content of revelation is law is one of those half-truths, which confounded scholars since Paul. While law is the detailed articulation of revelation, as it unfolded through the ages in the minds of prophets, priests and sages and in the life of the people, the dynamic intent of the law is the training of people in the ways of holiness—to fear God, to love him and to walk in his ways (Deut 10,12). So, a third century Palestinian rabbi asserts that only the first two Commandments were directly revealed by God — i.e. the essence of revelation is God's self-revelation in human freedom and in the shunning of all that is less than God, or idolatry (Makkot 23b). Maimonides defines the purpose of the Law as being the cultivation of an ethical life for the individual and an ethical order for society (*Guide* III, 28). At the same time, the Law is designed to foster the love of God and the fear of God (ibid, III 29 & 52). Both purposes are one, since man fulfills himself only in the highest moments of holiness. Revelation takes place at the cutting edge of man's quest of truth; it is a confirmation of previously revealed values and an aspiration for his "nearness;" it is the source of the hunger for truth, goodness and wisdom.

In our Holy Scriptures, wisdom was regarded as a divine gift, akin to the inspiration and fervor of prophecy. Wisdom dwells with God; it is the principle of creation (Prov 8,22-31). Sirach extols it as the indwelling harmony that holds all things in thrall (Sir 24,1-34). Philo maintains that it is an illusion for man to imagine that he himself is the source of his thoughts. All noble thoughts flow from God, and man's part consists in rendering his mind receptive to Divine inspiration.[14] For this reason, the

Hellenistic Jews believed that Greek wisdom was divine in origin; they speculated that Pythagoros, Plato and Aristotle may have been disciples of the Hebrew prophets (Josephus, *Apion.* I, 22). In the Talmud, the Sage is regarded as the latter-day successor of the prophet (Shabbat 119b). The thought is even projected that a sage, *ḥakham,* is better than a prophet (Baba Bathra 12a).

The Talmudic sages recognized that wisdom is a universal category, while Torah is the special possession of the Jewish people (Lamentations Rabba, 2). On seeing a Gentile sage, a Jew is obligated to thank the Lord for his sharing his wisdom with a creature of flesh and blood (Berakhot 58a). The true Sage learns from all men (Abot 4,1). On the other hand, Torah is not found among the nations (Lamentations Rabba, 2). Reacting against the claims of the early Christians that they alone understood the true meaning of the Pentateuch, some of the Sages insisted on the unity of Israel and Torah with hyperbolic rhetoric—to wit, Israel and the Torah are wedded, and a Gentile who studies Torah is committing adultery, as it were (Pesahim 49b; Sanhedrin 59a).

What is the relation of Torah to Wisdom? While in the several streams of Jewish thought, this relationship was conceived in different ways, the assumption is well-nigh universal that Torah and wisdom cannot be mutually contradictory (Abot 3,21—no piety without wisdom). While Torah is trans-rational, deriving from Divine inspiration, it is never anti-rational.[15] Indeed, Torah itself is "a lower representation of the wisdom that is above" (Genesis Rabba 17,5). Hence, the ideal scholar should be learned in all forms of wisdom as well as in Torah. The members of the Sanhedrin, we are told, were supposed to be familiar with "the seventy languages," and even with the arts of witchcraft, though the practice of witchcraft was strictly forbidden (Sanhedrin 17a, 68a).

In medieval Jewish philosophy, the rationalists, beginning with Saadia, maintained that the principles of Torah and speculative wisdom were virtually identical. Torah presents us with conclusions, which reason would reach only through a long and arduous effort.[16] For Maimonides, all passages in Torah which do not accord with the dictates of reason must be interpreted figuratively.[17] Still, he recognized certain "necessary beliefs" for the masses of the people.[18] He believed in *creatio ex nihilo*, because this question could not be determined by reason; when the scales are balanced, we have to allow the nisus toward perfection within us to tip the scales in favor of the doctrine of creation—a doctrine "which makes Torah possible".[19]

A neo-Platonist, like Gabirol, did indeed set will above reason. A romanticist like Judah Halevi maintained that Torah brings the Israelite to a state of responsiveness to the "Divine Quality" that is far superior to any level of insight available to philosophers.[20] But, even Halevi insisted that God could not command us to believe aught that is contrary to reason (*The Kuzari* I, 89). The Qabbalists did affirm the existence of a realm of Divine Being, where all was paradoxical—infinity and finitude were commingled, limits were reached and not reached. Powers were divided and undivided—the principle of "the excluded middle" being honored in the breach almost consistently. That supernal realm was conveyed to chosen souls by means of revelation, and it could be conveyed from master to disciple only through the magic of personal charisma, "like one who lights a candle by a candle, without the first candle being diminished in the slightest".[21]

Yet, even Nahmanides, one of the greatest luminaries of Qabbalah, asserted that man must not believe anything that is contrary to reason. In summing up his explanation why Jews could not accept the Christian faith, he pointed to the irrationality of Christian theology, as he saw it.

"The core of the true dispute among us is not the concept of the Messiah . . . but the crux of the issue and the reason for the argument between Jews and Christians is the fact that you impute to the Deity things which are exceedingly repugnant . . . For what you state, and this is the essence of your faith, reason cannot accept, nature does not permit, and the prophets never implied. Also, the belief in miracles cannot be extended to cover such a phenomenon . . . The thought of a Jew and a man cannot tolerate such a belief, hence you argue for naught and your words are wasted, for this is the essence of our disputes" (*Sefer Havikuah Leharamban*, 12).

Nahmanides had in mind the popular conception of Incarnation in the Church of his day; yet, he also laid down a general principle that "the thought of a Jew and man" sets limits to the content of faith.

In a book written by another participant in a disputation that took place a century and a half later, the author agreed that two different religions may coexist at one time, and be equally true (J. Albo, *Book of Principles* vol. 1, ch. 25). Yet, he refused to accord this concession to Christianity, on the ground that its teachings contradicted the clear principles of reason (ibid, vol. III, ch. 25).

In the age of Enlightenment, Moses Mendelssohn identified Judaism with "the religion of reason" and in a well-known letter he suggested that convergence between Judaism and Christianity would be possible only after the Christian faith had been reinterpreted along rationalistic lines.[22] Today, we know that there is much more to religion than reason can fathom.

As Pascal put it: The heart has its reasons that are too big for the mind, while the logic of the mind is too small for the heart.

Yet, it remains true that Torah and wisdom must advance hand in hand. Even a non-philosophical Talmudist, like Elijah Gaon of Vilna, had asserted "that Torah and wisdom derive from one source, and for every measure of wisdom that we lack, we miss ten measures of Torah" (quoted in *ʿAliyot Eliyahu*). God comes at us from several different directions at once, and we must take account of every form of revelation in our effort to seek his nearness. This synthetic adventure is possible because neither the body of revelation we possess nor the insights of wisdom available to us are closed and complete. To the modern mind, history is a very present reality. We see revelation as being an ongoing quest, as well as a possession. We seek "the nearness of God," but we can move ahead only so far. Our goal is to understand the Absolute and feel his Presence in our bones, as it were, but we cannot possess the Absolute.

What is the relevance of these reflections to our vision of the world-community? It is the distinction between the terms, "people of God" and "people of the Covenant." In the Talmud, a faithful Israelite is designated as a "son of the Covenant" *(ben berit)*. While the recipients of wisdom share in Divine Guidance, they do not necessarily belong to the people of the Covenant. Through the special obligations that a historic people or a newly constituted *ecclesia* assumes, it establishes private signs and symbols that become charged with holy significance for their members. People need houses as well as the great outdoors in order to feel at home in the universe; when a house is built, the outside universe is shut out, but only for certain times and seasons. And it is an act of Divine revelation that prompts us to build homes of the spirit for our collective existence.

In the biblical period, Covenants were made by patriarchs and kings, in the Name of God and for his sake. Joshua renewed the Covenant, so did kings Hezekiah and Josiah, and Ezra instituted the "sure Covenant" (Josh 24,24; 2Chr 29,10; 2Chr 34,31; Ezra 10,3; Neh 10,1). The account of Ezra's reforms does not speak of a fresh theophany; yet, there was a clear awareness in rabbinic literature that Ezra was a second Moses, as it were (Rosh Hashanah 19b; Sanhedrin 21b; Koheleth Rabba 1,8). For what we do for God, is in essence of God. In the Talmudic period, whatever legislation the Sages enacted, the people were supposed to regard as a Divine commandment. So, the reading of the *Megillah* on Purim and the lighting of candles on Hanukkah are preceded by a benedition in which we thank God "for hallowing us by his Commandments and enjoining us to perform these rites."[23] Similarly, all benedictions recited prior to tasting food were formulated by the Sages; yet, we are told that any one who partakes of food, without reciting the prescribed benediction, "robs the Holy One, blessed be he, and the congregation of Israel" (Berakhot 55b; Tosefta Berakhot, 4). The sages allowed that "the pious among the nations shared in the World to Come," but they insisted that new proselytes could not set conditions or eliminate some items from the Covenant (Tosefta Sanhedrin, 13,2; Sifra, Kedoshim, 8).

Now, the Covenant-principle can be generalized. An *ecclesia*, or any historic community, that is dedicated to God is a covenant-community. It becomes an instrument of God who works in history through communities as well as through individuals. The mark of his revelation in both cases is a hunger for "the knowledge of God" and a thirst for his nearness. But while the individual's quest of God is spontaneous and open-ended, that of the historic community is articulated in institutions and rites, in a so-called covenant.[24]

While the designation "people of God" became problematic and invisible, the meaning of a covenanted people remained concrete and empirical. Already, the prophets assumed that the Israelites will truly become God's people only at a future date. While the talmudic Sages were certain that the Israelites were God's children, in a special sense, they interpreted this relationship in a non-biological sense. The same Rabbi Akiba who glorified Israel "for their being called sons of the Place" asserted that the Ten Tribes were cut off entirely from the body of Israel. Is not this attempt to dissipate the aura of the archetypal image of the Twelve Tribes a bold affirmation of the rabbinic understanding of the meaning of Israel? Since the exiled northern tribes did not submit to the Torah, which interprets the meaning of the Covenant, they did not belong to *Kenesset Yisrael*, the congregation of Israel. As a matter of fact, the cold realism of the Sages did not calm the messianic expectations of the popular imagination. In the folk-legends of redemption, the Twelve Tribes continued to play a central role.

The Jewish individual could not assume that he was numbered among "the people of God." For no man is proof against sin. So, King David, pictured as a saint in the Talmud, was wont to say, "I know that God rewards the righteous in the World to Come, but I cannot tell whether I shall be among them." Jacob too was ever anxious lest sin cause him to lose the favor of God (Berakhot 4a). If these super-saints could not be certain of belonging to "the people of God," how could ordinary mortals arrogate such a title to themselves? The Talmud stigmatizes the smug

Pharisee, who imagines he has fulfilled every Commandment, quite as bitterly as the Gospel of Luke. To be human is to be potentially wicked or saintly, for one's intention makes the difference. So, if a person says the wedding-formula to a girl, "on condition that he is a perfect saint", she is married to him, since he might have repented fully. Similarly, if his condition be "that he is thoroughly wicked", she is married to him, since he might have meditated an act of idolatry. A person must think of himself as being neither wicked, nor saintly, but somewhere in the middle, with the next act being decisive. Rabbi Judah the Patriarch was wont to weep over this uncertainty of man's status—"it is possible for man to acquire his world in one hour". We walk before God on a razor's edge. "Do not trust yourself until the day of your death." Even Moses could not depend upon his merit; he had to plead for the free act of God's grace.

On the other hand, every person, Jew or Gentile, can bring nearer the Divine Presence by an act of *ḥesed*, steadfast love, and the Kingdom of God is established when the *Shekhinah* dwells securely on earth. A late Midrash portrays Elijah as asserting dramatically—"I bring heaven and earth to witness that whether a person be free or slave, man or woman, Jew or Gentile—according to his deeds the Holy Spirit rests upon him." The same idea is presented in a tannaitic source, in the name of Rabban Yoḥanan ben Zakkai. Rebuking the zealotry of his young disciples, he taught that while it is righteousness that uplifts Israel, the nations obtain forgiveness through deeds of steadfast love. Israel is bound by a covenant, with detailed specifications, while the nations can join the ranks of the favored through free acts of love.

The *miṣwot*-mentality of the Pharisees has been frequently abused, as if these progenitors of the latter-day merchants already conceived of heaven in cash-register terms.[25] To be sure, the Pharisees had to guard constantly against reducing religion to a cluster of external actions. And the best among them were always on guard. But, their emphasis on individual actions liberated the religious imagination from the temptation to play the role of God. They did not need to ask, "am I among the saved?" "am I and my people among his Children, or his Saints, or his Kingdom? "The Compassionate One seeks the heart" of his worshipers. All that we can do is to concentrate on the next decision in our lives. We should ask, "what is my *miṣwah* at this moment?" For this reason, the Talmudic rabbis allowed the feeling of belonging to "the people of God" to fade into the background, while they focused attention on seemingly trivial questions, the choices that one must make in his daily life.

This emphasis did not turn them into a closed fellowship, though at various times the danger of such a fixation loomed large on the horizon.

Of particular interest is the report of a discussion between Rabban Gamliel of Yavneh and the young Rabbi Akiba. The old patriarch expressed his anxiety that one could not be saved by the law, since even the slightest transgression might lead one to perdition. (This fear, of course, is echoed in the letters of Paul and in the letter of James). Rabbi Akiba argues in behalf of the contrary thesis, that the performance of even one *miṣwah* assures a person of sharing in the world to come (Sanhedrin 81a; Midrash Tehillim 15,7).

The emphasis on redemptive deeds balances the concept of a nuclear core of redeemed persons. The polarization between the "chosen" and the rejected is softened. We come to think of the Kingdom of God as a free and open society, which people enter and leave in accordance with the quality of their ethical life, day by day. For the protean, emergent Kingdom is composed of deeds, not of people. "There is no man who does not have his hour, and no thing that does not have its place" (Abot 4,3). A rabbi who impulsively exclaimed, "how ugly is this man!" underwent a long penance, until he learned that there were no "ugly men," just ugly deeds (Taanit 20b). Every good deed, the rabbinic Sages declare, creates a good angel, and every evil deed a demon—i.e. a divine law operates in the cosmos, which is akin to the Newtonian principles of momentum and the conservation of energy (Abot 4,11). Sometimes, the consequences of an action may not be felt for centuries. When King Solomon took Pharaoh's daughter to wife, the angel Gabriel put an obstacle in the river Tiber around which silt began to gather, forming the foundation for the city of Rome (Shabbat 56b). On the other hand, "the merit of the patriarchs" saved Israel from trouble again and again. In respect of great *miṣwot*, a person enjoys their fruit in his lifetime, while their healing essence endures until the world to come. While the messianic End is certain to arrive in any case, the time of the advent can be hastened by the multiplication of deeds of love.

In Augustine's "Civitas Dei," the world is divided between persons, the "city of God," comprising those who love God to the point of total selflessness and "the city of man," consisting of those who love themselves to the exclusion of God. People are categorized and polarized. And he does not make clear whether the former are an invisible congregation, transcending sectarian bounds, or simply a glorified characterization of the Catholic church. In Judaism, the living nucleus of the Kingdom of God is both the empirical people of Israel and the company of angels generated by the *miṣwot* of the past and the present. The Sages were certain that the living people of Israel was the heart of the emergent society of redeemed mankind, even while in theory they agreed that the pious of the nations shared in the world to come. They saw terrestrial history as an acting out of a scenario composed in the meta-historical realm, where angels arise daily to sing unto the Lord and then to sink into a river of fire, flowing from the divine throne; yet, two angels, Gabriel and Michael, stand above this flux, and Michael is the "prince" of Israel (Hagigah 14a).

This view that the Kingdom is being built by the deeds of the righteous was supplemented by the belief in the inexhaustible power of repentance. In this way, the rabbis guarded against the danger of externalization that threatened to alienate man from his own actions. Repentance is an inner transformation, a reorientation of man, in his deepest inwardness. So Maimonides defines the goal of repentance as follows—"that he who knows all secrets may testify about the penitent that were he exposed to the same temptation, he would not commit the sin of which he is guilty." Such a transformation is possible, because of man's rootedness in the Divine Being. The human soul cannot be completely cut off from its source and if one truly turns to God, all his sins vanish and he comes closer to God than the righteous, who have not sinned. Indeed, his very sins are turned into *miṣwot* (Yoma 86b). There is an infinite dimension to the human personality, since it embodies the "image of God;" hence every person is commanded to say, "for my sake was the world created" (M. Sanhedrin IV,5). Because of this outreach beyond all finite limits, the human potential for self-transcendence is incalculable. A beautiful legend tells of King Menasseh's repentance. The angels surrounded the divine throne, intent on preventing the penitential prayers of the renegade from reaching the Presence, but the Holy One dug a hole in his heaven and put his hand through it to receive the petition of the penitent and to reinstate him in his favor (Sanhedrin 103a).

Apart from the performance of so many *miṣwot*, faithfulness was the keynote of the religious personality. As Martin Buber pointed out, faithfulness or trust is the central motif in Judaism—not the propositional "belief that," but the existential "belief in." The first paragraph of the *Shema*, in which one undertakes to love God, with all one's heart amounts to "an acceptance of the yoke of the Kingdom of heaven." So, dedication to the building of the kingdom is re-affirmed twice daily. The vision of the future is not merely re-kindled on the High Holidays, when it forms the central theme of the liturgy, but it is echoed in everyday life. Before partaking of food or drink, the prescribed benediction (*beshem umalkhut*) includes a reference to the Kingship of God, a consummation that belongs to the messianic era. Rashi interprets the *Shema* itself as an affirmation of this hope—"the Lord, who is now our God, will become the One God of all men" (ad loc. Deut 6:4). The Sages interpret the meaning of loving God as being "to cause him to be beloved by all people" (Sifre to Deut 6:5). Here is a general formulation of the goal of all missionary enterprise—it is not to teach so many doctrines, but to live the kind of life and build the kind of world which result in God's being loved by more and more men. But, love is inseparable from faith and hope. Hence, the exaltation of the power of faith, in one of the earliest tannaitic works.

Instructive for our purpose is the comment of an eighteenth century rabbi, Jacob Emden, who was a contemporary of Moses Mendelssohn, but who was so remote from the mood of the Enlightenment that he doubted whether the pious Maimonides could have composed so skeptical a work as the "Guide for the Perplexed." Commenting on the statement of the second century Palestinian Sage, Rabbi Yohanan the Shoemaker, "every community that is organized for the sake of heaven will endure and every community that is not for the sake of heaven will not endure" (Abot 4,14). Rabbi Emden wrote as follows:

"Certainly the Sage did not concern himself with communities that are not related to us, but with those new faiths and sects that derived from us. . . Indeed when we take account of the cults they (the Christians) supplanted, which worshipped stocks and stones and did not know God as the Absolute Power, administering reward and punishment in the hereafter, their (the Christian) church may truly be called an *ecclesia* for the sake of heaven. For they proclaim God to distant nations. . . They glorify the Lord, God of Israel and his Torah, even among people who have never heard about him. Therefore, their good intentions cannot be in vain. The Compassionate seeks the heart. . . Furthermore, Christian scholars are known for their dedication to research into the meaning of Holy Scriptures. By their studies in biblical history, many of them have added to its glory. . . "[26]

In this judgment, Emden ranks the Christian polity as a divine institution. It is dedicated to the Glory of God; it stresses purity of heart; it promotes the quest of truth and justice. Its capacity to endure and its role in history demonstrate that the God of history had assigned it a crucial role; it is indeed "a community for the sake of heaven". Yet, Emden would have been horrified at the suggestion that the establishment of the Christian polity had annulled the Covenant of the Jewish people. For Jews, to forsake their own covenant is an act of apostasy; but, they must remember that they are not the only "people of God"; other historic communities, as well as other individuals, share in this honor and in its concomitant responsibilities.

Emden's judgment of the Christian church ties in with Gamliel's opinion, at the trial of Peter and John (Acts 5,38.39) and the view of the

Pharisees at the trial of Paul (Acts 23,9) as well as Maimonides' judgment of the redemptive role played by Christianity and Islam in the history of the world.[27] Halevi too regarded Islam and Christianity as playing a redemptive, messianic role (*Kuzari* 4,23), though as an ethnic romanticist he asserted that the least son of Torah attains a higher level of piety than any non-Israelite (*Kuzari* 5,19).

It is interesting to note that the neo-Orthodox theologians of the Nineteenth century, Bernais and Hirsch, spoke of a general revelation in the hearts of men, as well as of the specific Sinaitic revelation. "The quest of truth and justice within you is the primary revelation of God within you." The latter theologian, for all his uncompromising extremism, regarded the French Revolution of 1789 as "one of the hours in which God entered history," in spite of the fact that at that time, as on so many other occasions, "the light of God in the hearts of men" was quickly fragmentized and perverted.[28]

In sum, insofar as revelation is a divine activity, it comes to us in three ways—primarily, through our own covenanted community, secondarily through the general revelation of human wisdom and thirdly as a challenge and a spur to reflection, through the work of other covenanted communities. We live within our own historic covenant, but we learn from the other two sources as well as from our own. In each case, our insights unfold in the course of history. It is particularly in the nature of wisdom to evolve and expand. The role of history in the growth of wisdom may be acknowledged without falling into the trap of an all-doubting historicism. We have to maintain the living tension between the different covenanted communities and the universal sphere of wisdom, which provides their common meeting ground. Said Rabbi Judah the Patriarch, "which is the right road that a man should choose?—That which is beautiful and good in his own eyes and beautiful and good to mankind" (Abot 2;1. The term "beautiful and good" is in Hebrew, *tifereth*, in Greek probably *kalos*). The very letters of the Hebrew word for truth, *'emet*, according to the Talmud, suggest that genuine knowledge derives from the conjunction of several viewpoints, for it consists of the first letter of the alphabet, the last letter and the middle one, suggesting that most issues in life need to be viewed from an affirmative, a negative and a synthetic standpoint (Shabbat 104a; Rashi ad loc).

Creation

Man was designed by the Lord to be a "partner of the Holy One, blessed be he, in the works of creation" (in promoting justice, Shabbat 10a; in observance of Sabbath, Shabbat 119b). His industry and inventiveness are God-given powers, for the promotion of the settlement of the earth, that it might be a paradise, not a wasteland. (A covenant was made regarding man's productive work: Abot d. R. Nathan, 11; Isa 45, 18; Gittin 41b). In contrast to the Greek legend concerning Prometheus and the fire he stole from the gods, the Talmud ascribes the discovery of fire to a special act of Divine favor. (God inspired the thought of rubbing two stones together in the mind of Adam. Pesahim 54a). Abraham is represented in the Book of Jubilees as an inventor of the plough (Jubilees, Charles' edition, 11,23). The secular art of medicine was praised by Sirach as being fully in keeping with the Will of God (Sirach, Charles' edition, 38,4). This attitude was contrary to the plain meaning of 2Chr 16,12. Both attitudes were preserved in the medieval era. (See Ibn Ezra's comment on Exod 21,19). It is a sin to idle away one's time and refrain from doing one's part in "the settlement of the world" (yishuvo shel olam). For this reason, gamblers are not considered worthy of serving as witnesses in a law-court (Sanhedrin 24b. Some would limit the law to professional gamblers). The talmudic sages were in many cases artisans, and they taught that the Shekhinah dwells only where good and loving craftmanship is at work (Abot 2; Abot d. R. Nathan 11). In modern parlance we should say, religion and culture go hand in hand.

In this area, as in revelation, the polarity of pluralism prevails. There is the particularistic culture of the Israelites and an emergent, universal culture. The Sages were acquainted with Hellenistic and Roman cultures, which laid claim to universalism. Some of the tannaitic Sages were willing to acknowledge Rome as a Power enthroned by God in order to introduce the arts of civilization and lawful order to the world (Shabbat 33b. Tanhuma, Tazria, 11). Those who disrupted this judgment questioned the motives of the Roman governors, not the worth of their achievements. A third century rabbi who visited the imperial city marvelled at the wonderful care which the Romans lavished on their marble statues, but he criticized their order of priorities when he saw the hunger and nakedness of the poor in that metropolis (Genesis Rabba 33,1; Tanhuma, Emor).

The range and character of universal culture was set over against the particular Hebrew culture that was so intimately interwoven with the Jewish faith (Rome and Jerusalem were seen as a polarity. Shabbat 56b). The "settlement of the land of Israel" (yishuv Ha'areṣ) was a supreme Command in Judaism, and the rabbis enacted many laws in order to promote that goal (Baba Bathra 101a; Gittin 8b; Kethubot 110b; Makkot 7a). So intimate was the bond between the Holy Land and the Torah that some modern scholars refused to acknowledge the universal dimension of the Jewish religion.[29] They asserted that the ethnocentric embrace of Hebrew culture prevented Judaism from becoming a world religion.[30] Actually, as we have seen, Judaism was an expansionist faith in the Hellenistic and early Roman period. But, concern with humanity as a whole did not diminish Jewish eagerness for the preservation and cultivation of their own national culture—their language, their land, their historical memories and associations. In fact, rightly or wrongly, they imagined that for the sake of humanity and universal culture, they are obligated to preserve their own cultural distinctiveness. A particular religion may well be associated with a particular culture in an intimate, organic way, even while it cultivates an openness and empathy for the cultures of other people and the vision of a universal culture.[31]

To be sure, there were times when the yearning for Zion reached fantastic proportions, as in the philosophy of Judah Halevi, who maintained that the Holy Land possessed a theurgic potency, which would be revealed in a revival of prophecy if a faithful Israel were once again settled in it (*Kuzari* II, 8). But, even Halevi remained true to the vision of a united mankind. He compared Israel among the nations to the heart in a living person; through the revitalization of the heart, all other organs will regain their vigor.[32]

Two questions arise in relation to the interaction of religion and culture. Should religions combat the rise of diverse ethnic cultures for the sake of a universal society, and if ethnic cultures are inescapable, should religions stand apart from them and subject them to criticism, or should they enter the secular world with a holy enthusiasm so as to sacralize the secular?

The first question was fiercely debated in western Europe in the nineteenth century. The founders of Reform Judaism insisted on eliminating the nationalistic residues in the Jewish religion, in order to render it worthy of serving in the vanguard of the world-religions of the future. So, they reduced the role of Hebrew in the liturgy, eliminated references to Zion, declared the dietary laws to be obsolete, and generally represented Judaism as the religion of reason and humanity. From Abraham Geiger to Leo Baeck, the Reform movement claimed that Jewry must preserve its faith as the nuclear religion of the future society of mankind.[33]

But history has a way of betraying those who cling tightly to its skirts. Today, classical Reform has lost its appeal to the Jewish mind. Modern Zionism affirms the worth of Hebrew culture, as well as of the Jewish religion. Yet, Zionism does not call for a return to the ghetto, or to a retreat from the humanist ideal. On the contrary, it is imbued with the faith that the revival of Hebrew life and culture in the land of Israel will contribute to the reinvigoration of western culture, which draws its inspiration from the Holy Scriptures. The universal ideal of a global society must be conceived in pluralistic terms, as an association of many and diverse ethnic cultures, all sharing in an emergent universal culture. The universal and the particular are not opposites but the two poles of one dynamic reality. In every generation, it is necessary to counter the absolutist claims of the proponents of each pole and to find the right balance between them.

As to the second question, concerning the interaction of religion and culture, we have seen in recent years the pendulum swing from Barth's "wholly Other" to Cox's "Secular City." Extremists draw attention, since they fall in with the alternation of popular sentiment. But, actually, it is obvious that to be effective religion must be intimately involved with the living culture of the moment and, at the same time, transcend it and subject its trends to relentless criticism. Religion performs the double function of celebrating the *status quo* and fueling the drive to transform it. It sanctifies the great ideals of society, yet if it has not lost its own vision of human destiny, it cannot but uphold standards and project social visions which loom far beyond the grasp of men at any one time.

The intimate association of Judaism with the empirical Jewish people provides a unique opportunity for the study of the interaction of a universal religion with a specific nationality. An ambivalent mood is generated, as dangerous as it is creative. The danger consists firstly in the temptation for outsiders to discount its message and to treat it as a form of sanctified ethnicism. Secondly, let it be admitted that the ethnocentric bias may indeed distort the message of faith. If the ancient proverb is true, "no one sees his own failings", how much more is this the case when one's communal interests are engaged. When a particular faith is organically bound up with a particular ethnic group and a political state, it is just as likely that religious values will be strangled by political interests as it is that politics and culture will be ennobled by the momentum of faith. On the other hand, when a faith is totally dissociated from culture and politics, it is just as probable that the faith will be "unspotted of the world", as it is that it will be ethereal and irrelevant, totally incapable of directing national policy.

For this reason, the Jewish faith-culture relationship, which is intimate and organic, and the Christian faith-culture posture, which is loose and indirect, are polar opposites; they should be juxtaposed and kept in a state of mutual challenge and tension. As in the realm of revelation, so in that of creation, God works through us, yet not through us alone, but also through the challenge to us of our neighbors's faith and that of the emergent society of mankind.

The emergence of the State of Israel did not transform essentially the character of Judaism as a historical blend of a universal faith and a national culture. Israel is a secular and modern state; yet, it is also the homeland of a widely scattered people, that defines itself by its religious faith. For this reason, it is perennially troubled by the recurrent question, "Who is a Jew?" And the Jewish people of the Diaspora, who may be in all respects other than religion totally integrated in the life of the nation of which they are part, nevertheless retain a particular affection for the land and people of Israel. Here, then, is a people that has been in the vanguard of progress in the western world, and yet in its social structure has somehow remained an anomaly. In its case, a universal religion and a particularist ethnicism were not bifurcated by the cutting edge of modern secularism, but on the contrary, both nationalism and faith were in modern times reinvigorated and re-combined. Because of its world-wide impact, Israel cannot run its affairs like any other secular state that is concerned only with its own security. Inevitably, it will strive to become a great center of man's quest for ultimate meaning and transcendent values. The momentum of history will impel it to serve as a force for interfaith and intercultural activities. And the faith of the Jews in the Diaspora will be challenged peculiarly by the concrete issues deriving from the realities of the Jewish state.

While the diverse loyalties of the Jews to God, to country, to humanity and to Israel are theoretically compatible, situations are bound to arise when these sentiments will pull in different directions. Thus, the Jew cannot afford to be complacent. Out of his inner turbulence, he must become sensitive to the subtle nuances of the ideals and beliefs that bind men together and generate the forces of history. And the example of the Jew will serve as a call to all peoples to transmute their parochial loyalties by the universal ideals of religious faith, to become "chosen people" with all the ardor and all the anguish that this task entails.

Redemption

It is frequently stated that while Jews think of redemption in terms of exterior, visible developments, Christians think of it in terms of interior spiritual transformations. The contrast is also viewed as one of national vindication versus the salvation of all mankind. In both cases, we deal actually with variations of intensity in one spectrum of hope, variations which however are exceedingly important in our day and age.

Let us begin with the common theme. Redemption involves a fresh ingression of Divine power. It is God that redeems. While man can help through his repentance and good deeds, he cannot redeem himself. The

Sages declare that if all Israelites were to attain the perfection of repentance, the Messiah would instantly arrive (Sanhedrin 97b). But, such a consummation is quite improbable, and repentance itself involves the help of God (Yoma 38b). So, even before the emergence of the modern concept of progress and man-made social advancement, a spiritual version of hopeful progress was implicit in the Judeo-Christian view of history. Yet, the distinguishing mark of that idea, in contrast to the modern concept of progress, was the central role of the trans-natural act of God. He is the Savior, in Christianity; "the Redeemer of Israel", in Judaism.

What is the negative significance of this belief? Manifestly, it implies that we must not assume the finality of any of our human achievements. The *Eschaton* involves both a physical and spiritual transformation. And there is an abundance of metaphors in Judaism for both aspects of redemption. But, in both domains, we are cautioned to remember that none of our physical achievements is more than a passing phase in the divine scheme of salvation. Our industry and technology may be essentially flawed, with a terrible, even if, invisible price being exacted for every inch of progress. We must be constantly on guard against the sanctification of techniques and the smug assumption that human progress can be quantified and calibrated. To be sure, we must strive for advancement along the plane of external, visible progress, overcoming the anguish of privation in food, shelter and amusement. But, such progress, we are cautioned, is ambiguous. We cannot redeem ourselves. Our collective achievements, for all their grandeur, cannot bring ultimate salvation.

In the interior domain, as in the realm of physical progress, we must acknowledge our insufficiency. Our values and ideals may have to be transcended in ways that we cannot foretell. In the impetuosity of his genius, Nietzsche spoke of rising "beyond good and evil"; Kierkegaard wrote of "the suspension of the ethical", and in the last decade we endured the follies of the so-called "death of God" theologians. The facet of truth in these extremist outbursts is the recognition of the non-ultimacy of even our highest ideals and noblest values. There is a dimension of depth in the life of the spirit, while our value-judgments tend to be flat and fragmentary. Our concepts of God, though not God in himself, need to be perpetually refined. Old concepts, like old shells, should be thrown back into the ocean of past history, where the natural processes of "recycling," will one day work their magic of resuscitation. Our perceptions of good and evil need to become ever more penetrating and critical, as our society becomes more complex; we should not be satisfied with a black and white checkerboard of human affairs.

By the same token, even our values and ideals may and probably will be overriden and, in due course, be supplanted by other attainments and norms, which will also be non-ultimate. In this way, man is kept from worshipping his own image in the mirror of time, much less the work of his hands.

Coming down to the events of our day, we need to maintain an open, yet critical, mind regarding the efforts of some of our youth to push beyond the old norms of personal and communal life, though we must insist on the compatibility of any new insights with the proven wisdom of the past. Any new Covenant "fulfills" but does not destroy the Old Law. We must not maintain that our patterns of the good life are absolute; at the same time, there are no breaks in the life of the spirit. The new emerges out of the old, creating new norms and generating new visions, but there is a deep continuity and essential unity, underlying all differences. Here, again, the course of revelation is instructive. Say the Sages, "all the prophets have delivered the same message, though not two prophets have spoken in the same style" (Sanhedrin 89a).

The youth-movement of our day flowed along the boundary between prophetism and apocalypse. At one end, it was critical of specific evils, but devoted to the grand ideals of the past, bitter but not despairing, visionary in its view of the high potential of their people, but not escapist. At the other end, it rejected the totality of existing society as irredeemably evil, embraced a revolutionary policy without any program, indulged in irrational fantasies and escapist utopias that reflected its despair and dreamlike irresolution. It was articulated in symbols of defiance and paradoxicality, an unculture, aptly called "counter-culture."

Religious leaders in both Judaism and Christianity have always had to contend against such quixotic movements of pseudo-messianism or chiliasm, which arose in times of widespread frustration. If authentic leaders keep the prophetic mood alive, they can hope to divert the energies of the apocalyptics into constructive and realistic channels.

In Judaism, the vision of redemption centers around the vindication of the destiny of Israel; in Christianity, redemption is of the individual, and the goal is to preach the message of redemption to all men. Again, the differences are in emphasis and centrality. The Jewish vision of the salvation of the people of Israel is viewed within the perspective of universal redemption, and the universalist outreach of Christianity allows for the role that an invisible *ecclesia*, "the people of God, have to carry out on the stage of human history". Yet, the differences are of immense significance.

In the Jewish view, the goal of redemption is not only an all-embracing universal society, but also the consummation of the particular cultures and dreams of the diverse nations and peoples. The universal goal must not be so construed as to preclude the fulfillment of the special qualities of each historic community. And if every individual is obligated "to say that the world was created for his sake", every individual nation is similarly enjoined to regard its own fulfillment as a supreme value. And just as in the case of an individual, the supreme importance of his own life is not interpreted as a license for selfishness; on the contrary, the motif of personal appreciation is embraced in the larger vision of a society of infinitely important selves, governed in justice and in freedom, so the particularist ambition of each people must be fitted within the concept of a universal society of peoples, abiding by a law that safeguards the rights of all.

Law, like love, is an expression of the Divine Will. While the rule of law is associated with harshness and privation in some literatures, including Qabbalah, it is viewed in the Pharisaic tradition as a sublime art, in which the Lord himself participates. The chief quality of the Messiah will be his supreme capacity as a judge. Hence, in the vision of the future, it is assumed that all nations will then be governed by a universal law. And the pioneering souls of the Kingdom of God may well be those who are even now engaged in preparing the world for the rule of law.

The application of universal law to the governance of mankind presupposes the attainment of three goals—first, the creation of a sense of community among the various nations of the world, second, the establishment of agencies for the investigation and determination of the true facts in every national dispute, third, the establishment of enforcement agencies. These three steps are needed in addition to the formulation of norms and principles comprising international law.

The third step can only be taken by governments, and we are still far from that consummation. But, the first and second steps can be taken by individuals, those who feel "called" to "improve the world through the Kingdom of the Almighty". A sense of world-fellowship or world-citizenship, as Philo put it, can only be built up by deeds which demonstrate our responsibility for one another as members of the human race. An international "peace corps" aided by governmental contributions on a generous scale, could be expanded in a generation to involve millions of people. The myriad deeds of helpfulness would generate in the course of time the feeling of belonging to "one world", a feeling which is still pale and feeble in our day. The Jews of the Diaspora and the reborn Israeli nation will, by reason of the impetus of history, as well as the promptings of their faith, ever strive for this consummation.

For the vision of a world-community is for the Jew the substance of his millenial history. It is the one hope that lends meaning to a hundred generations of travail. He has experienced the hurt inflicted by the barriers that divide mankind as thrusts of cold steel into his own flesh. Combining uniquely the roles of prophet and pariah, he stood at the center of the great issues that stirred the passions of the western world. The hydra-headed monster of Antisemitism was involved in all the struggles for the liberation of the mind of modern man from the burdens of ancient hates. Inescapable then is the place of the Jew in the vanguard of those who dream of a world redeemed from hate.

Along with such efforts to build a consciousness of humanity, we have to create agencies for the discovery of truth, in every international dispute. There can be no peace without truth. The first act of every tyrant is to take control of the investigative and publishing instrumentalities of the nation. These functions are vastly complicated when diverse national interests are in conflict. Who can rise above the distorting passions of ethnic loyalty, especially when secularized piety tends to merge with the deep streams of modern nationalism? Yet only those who are truly able to transcend the popular pieties of their time can be said to belong to the nuclear fellowship of the universal society of the future.

It is in the realm of redemption, that the recognition of mutual need is greatest in both Judaism and Christianity. So, Maimonides allowed that both Judaism and Christianity were "preparing the way" for the coming of the Messiah. In the nineteenth century, Formstecher, Rosenzweig and Kohler declared that the global destiny of Judaism was being fulfilled through the efforts of the Christians. Their scheme was based on the analogy between the sun and its rays—the sun is Judaism, the all-permeating rays are Christianity. Geiger clung to Halevi's analogy of the heart in a living organism, since he believed that the Jews had a special genius for religion. Kohler spoke of the Jewish faith as providing the standards as well as the source of progress toward a universal faith and a redeemed society. Still the bitter polemical note of medievalism was rarely overcome before our own generation. We still have to transcend the residues of bitter rivalry and sheer narcissism in the philosophies of the nineteenth century and return to fundamentals.

In the first place, we recognize that we do not know and cannot presume to know the course of redemption. The Talmudic sages excoriated those who "calculate the end" and those who "press the end".

Maimonides adds wisely that in these matters we shall know what the prophets meant only after the events of the Eschaton shall have taken place (*Hilkhot Melakhim*, XII). And Jesus, too, affirmed that no one knows the time of the End of Days (Mark 13,32; Acts 1,7).

In the second place, we have to transcend the rhetoric which foisted upon us mountains of misunderstanding. It is said that for Christians, the world is already redeemed, while for Jews, it is unredeemed. This is a specious juxtaposition. We might say with equal justification that for Christians, the world is in a "fallen" and corrupt state, while for Jews, the world is "very good". Actually, the tension in Judaism between an unfinished universe and a radiant vision of redemption was retained in the Christian philosophy of history, as presented in Augustine's "City of God," though Augustine rejected the chiliastic belief. A similar philosophy of history was contained in both faiths. The tannaitic Sages speak of the ongoing struggle between "the righteous who establish the world" and "the wicked who destroy the world", while Augustine speaks of the contention between the two cities; to the Jewish Sages as to the Christian Saint, the outcome was clear and firm (Abot 1,5; The City of God XII, 28). To be sure, Judaism and Christianity project different categories for the judgment of the course of history, but the categories are mutually supplementary at times, mutually challenging at times, and the variations within both faiths are so vast as to render meaningless the ancient controversies about the "fulfillment" of Scriptural verses.

Every creative act of God and every theophany is also redemptive. So, in many rabbinic passages, the Messiah was seen as another Moses, or another Adam. To many Christians, "the second coming" of Jesus was anticipated with the same ardor that the Jews displayed in regard to the Messiah. And in the major trends of Judaism, "the hope of Israel" is inseparable from the redemption of mankind. To a rationalist, like Maimonides, this result will come about through the normal developments of history, without any break in the laws of nature (*Hilkhot Melakhim* XII, 1); to a mystic, like Nahmanides, the End will be achieved through a miraculous intervention in the course of history.[34] To the truly religious person, the boundary between the natural and the supernatural disappears. In any case, during the messianic age, all redeemed mankind will form one universal society and "the covenant-people" will merge within the all-embracing "people of God." But, before the final consummation is attained, the diverse covenanted bodies must advance under their separate banners (Mic 4,5). Yet, they move toward the same goal, "when the Lord will be One, and his Name One". And as they advance along their own diverse paths, they must keep their minds and hearts open, so they can learn from one another. For the course of human history is studded with theophanies that are creative, revelatory and redemptive. The Deuteronomist, in our Massoretic version, calls upon the Israelites to discover their own true being by studying the careers of all nations and all epochs.[35]

The action of God in redeeming mankind, transpires in three dimensions — in release from suffering, in the overcoming of sin, in the attainment of a new scale of values. The pictorial representation of the messianic age in Judaism appears to stress the first more than the second, and the third dimension is in some versions reserved for the World to Come. Actually, the messianic vision of Judaism is complex and many-splendored, and the conquest of sin is central in all versions. If the Israelites repent truly, the Messiah will come and a "renewal of Torah" will take place.[36] The doctrine of the Second Coming in Protestant thought also emphasizes repentance and "rebirth."

A century or so ago, Friedrich Nietzsche articulated the inchoate feelings of his day by his vision of a progressive overcoming of the values of man by those of superman. He envisioned a transvaluation of all values, and he appealed to restless youth to take up the work of God in creating a nobler humanity, since, as he put it, "God is dead". His call sounded plausible to a generation shocked by Darwinian theories. But it led to the "youth-movement" at the turn of the century and then to Nazism. Today, we hear similar calls for new values, also similar declarations of the irrelevance of so-called "God-talk." But, values are intrinsically non-disposable. What we do need is a keener grasp of values and their application in our complex times. New values grow out of the inner impetus of old values, not by their dissolution. In the realm of nature, the plants of this season grow out of the organic matter that derives from the rotted bodies of previous years. But, in the realm of spirit, we can transcend the wisdom of the past only if we understand it from within first. Every new advance presupposes the assimilation of ancient insights; else, our progress is illusory, like walking up on a descending escalator.

In our contemporary setting, the three phases of redemption are still very current. For most people the three quests of redemption are secularized. Sin is simply failure and values are sought in a retreat to privatism, or in various forms of negativism. As to suffering, moderns pin their hopes on the progress of science. However, science cannot cure the discontent that derives from interpersonal relations. We may be able to still the pangs of physical hunger, but poverty as relative to deprivation is becoming more and more unbearable. For many people, the term sin has lost its theological significance, but if they are at all aware of social problems, they cannot but acknowledge that the malaise of our times is moral-spiritual. The smoldering volcanoes of hate in our urban centers and the bitter disaffection of our youth are fueled by a general feeling of loss of direction as well as by specific causes like war, unemployment and racism. And this absence of a sense of purpose is most disconcerting to us, as religious teachers, since it indicates the measure of our failure. Yet, each religious denomination can easily exculpate itself on the ground that its impact on the education of our youth is extremely marginal. In a society where church and state are separated, and properly so, can the several agencies of faith work together in providing a national *ethos* that is adequate to our times? I disagree most sharply with those who claim that we need a "theology of revolution", but equally, we cannot be content with the traditional role of unyielding conservatism, saying with Alexander Pope, "whatever is, is right."

In the maintenance and creation of new values, the pluralism of the redemptive work of God must be our basic axiom. As in the spheres of revelation and creation, the divine impact hits us from diverse and opposite sides. The Chariot of Ezekiel was lifted up by a wind that came from four directions at once. So, we have to cherish the basic values in our heritage, even while we listen hard to the new and strange music that assaults our ears. And our own way of life, wonderful as it is, may well not be the only way in which divine values are brought into society. Can a pluralistic ecumenism keep us from the sin of self-righteousness? It was this besetting evil of piety that constituted the main theme of the critique that Jesus leveled at the religious establishment of his day. The Sages of the Talmud agreed that the Pharisaic order, with all its greatness, was frequently guilty of false piety. This does not mean that Pharisaism was itself evil. On the contrary, it represented the institutional framework which served as the chrysalis out of which three universal faiths arose. But, every concrete body casts a shadow, when it stands before one source of light. The shadows disappear, though not altogether, when several lamps are lit at different points in the room.

In the Judeo-Christian tradition, God is identified now with one ideal, now with another. He is immanent in the moral order of life. —"Can it be that the Judge of the whole earth will not to justice?"; or, He is love; or He is freedom; or, "The seal of the Holy One is truth"; or, "The beginning of the Torah and its end are lovingkindness"; or, "the Name of the Holy One, blessed be he, is peace". But, while all these ideals are divine, we find that we arrive at a different posture in our social ethic, according to the primacy we accord to one or another of these ideals. Shall we stress freedom at the expense of equality, or compassion at the expense of justice, or truth at the expense of loving-kindness, or peace above all other values? These questions must always be open options to us, for God is the Source of all these values, and we become guilty of idolatry, when we substitute any ideal, no matter how lofty, for the fullness of his Being as the end of our worship. Virtually all the massive evils of our day, from Communism to Fascism to the shortcomings in our own society, may be traced to the exaltation of any one ideal to the point where it excludes the other relevant ideals. This is why the emphasis on pluralism is so salutary. Particularly so, in an age which deems itself to be living on the threshhold of the Apocalyptic Era. And is not the crux of our anguish today precisely this widespread mood of apocalyptic hysteria?

It has been noted that a healthy society is one in which the forces of conservation and utopianism are held in balance. Is it not reasonable to hope that in a pluralistic faith-society there is less likelihood of either danger materializing, either a rigid stand-patism or a runaway utopianism?

Speaking from but the vantage point of Judaism, I can say that the perennial problem in Jewish history was to keep the balance between messianism and pseudo-messianism. Without messianism we lose the gift of hope, but if we join the cry, "Perfection must come right now", we open the gates to social insanity. The Anabaptist movements of the Sixteenth century teach us a similar lesson. We, the exponents of the several religious traditions of America are called upon to generate that balanced mentality that will keep the equilibrium between a galloping utopianism and a sterile stand-patism in our domestic as well as foreign affairs. "Without vision, a people perishes", said Isaiah. In a democratic nation, free from the last of the ideological commissars, who is to scatter the seeds of spirit that will one day blossom in the flowers of ideals? Can the press, the radio, T.V., do this task alone? Can the schools do it alone? Would it be unfair to say that the recent coincidence of an explosive growth of higher learning and a massive temper-tantrum of America's youth prove that the schools have failed? In the domain of national rededication and reconciliation, we encounter the ultimate test of the ecumenical movement. Can we, working together, keep alive the inner values and the sense of national purpose of the American nation?— I have no doubt that we can, for our national sickness resulted from the breakdown in the creaking agencies of social transmission, not from the obsolescence of the values themselves.

The challenge of our youth confronts us in three areas—in the ideals of personal life, in the moral temper of the community and in the vision of national purpose. With all the unlovely outbursts of radicalism in recent years, we have to recognize a desperate groping for national integrity, a hunger for the genuine values of love and communalism. Perhaps, the strongest conviction of our radical youth is negativistic—somehow, we, the elders, have not been true to our own ideals. And this feeling is likely to persist. Even if we should establish equity in race relations, feed the hungry and end unemployment, we shall still have a vast problem of rebuilding the sentiment of dedication, of family loyalty, of pride in work and a sense of sharing in the greatness of the nation. And these qualities our nation possessed in far greater measure in the days when a larger percentage of its people lived at the level now called poverty.

In terms of personal values, the so-called "Protestant Ethic" needs to be broadened and deepened, not abandoned. As Max Weber recognized, the Protestant Ethic was also the Jewish ethic, but instead of being directed solely toward personal success, we need to direct it toward national well-being, especially since the four-day workweek may become a reality. We need to glamorize the humanist values of study, appreciation of art and music, and the cultivation of productive talents. Voluntary days of work in improving the environment can be planned by the religious agencies in order to build a sense of national pride. In particular, all agencies of religion face the problem of providing alternative measures of success and achievement. To be good and true in the sight of God is far more important than to amass worldly goods. Is this no longer true, because it has so long been commonplace? In one of the first books to reflect the disaffection of the young, "Frannie and Zooey," J. D. Salinger showed how a brilliant young actress was talked out of a nervous breakdown by the suggestion that an emissary of God might appear at any time, in the shape of a "fat old lady" to judge her performance. Inequalities in achievement will always mark a free society, and without a sense of spiritual values, massive tides of bitterness may well overwhelm the fragile texture of a civilized society.

Personal values need to be sustained by the bonds of fellowship. What the so-called "secular city" needs most is that intricate network of voluntary organizations, which has enriched the lives of small-town America. And those intertwined institutions were generated by the several covenanted communities. If the unchurched and the unsynagogued constitute today in many cities a seething mass of faceless individuals, some new social structures need to be devised by those who are churched and synagogued to reawaken the sense of personal worth. When Harvey Cox rhapsodizes over the joys of anonymity in the big city, he writes as an intellectual surfeited with public acclaim. He forgets that the biblical Adam demonstrated his humanity when he was able to name all living things. The attraction of communal living for the young is in part at least a frantic escape from loneliness, alienation and anonymity. There is need of an interfaith effort along experimental lines to encourage healthy forms of cooperative communities.

Finally, in respect of the world-community as a whole, we need to think of our collective mission, as members of the greatest industrial nation in the world. The problems are immense, but so are the spiritual rewards. Our national purpose in this space-age can be nothing less than to encourage the emergence of a world-community, viable in its population, with help for the backward peoples, and with security dependent ever more preponderantly on international agencies.

To achieve these ends, all of us that call ourselves "the people of God" must learn to labor together, shoulder to shoulder.

The last *mishnah* of Eduyyoth deals with the function of Elijah the Prophet. In a general way, all the Sages agreed that it was his function "to prepare the way" for the coming of the Messiah. But, how does he go about his work? Said one rabbi, he separates the true from the false; said another, he rectifies the evils and injustices of the past. But, the majority of the Sages, after due deliberation, concluded that reconciliation is more important than either the quest of truth or the demands of an abstract justice. Said they, "it is not his function to make clean or unclean, to repel or to bring near those who were repelled, but to make peace in the world". This is our task.

NOTES

1. Yehezkel Kaufmann, *Toledoth Haemunah Hayisrealit,* vol. VIII. p 283-300.

2. See R. H. Charles' *The Apocrypha and Pseudepigrapha of the Old Testament II,* Introduction p. 292-295; references on p 312 and 358.

3. Emil Schürer, *A History of the Jewish People* (New York 1891) vol. V p 291-292.

4. See A. Marmorstein's essay on *Poshey Yisrael.* H. J. Schoeps, *Jewish Christianity* (Philadelphia: Fortress Press 1969) concurs in the identification of this term as referring to the Ebionites.

5. See H. Strack and P. Billerbeck, *Kommentar zum Neuen Testament* on Acts 13,16 (vol II p 715-723).

6. H. A. Wolfson, *Philo: Foundations of Religious Philosophy in Judaism, Christianity and Islam* (Cambridge, Harvard 1947) vol. II p 364.

7. Salo W. Baron, *A Social and Religious History of the Jews,* Vol. I p 375 note 15.

8. The underlying philosophy of Menahem Meiri and his indebtedness to Maimonides is discussed in Jacob Katz, *Exclusiveness and Tolerance* (New York: Schocken 1962) p. 114-128.

9. Jehudah Halevi, *The Kuzari* II, 44.

10. Kaufmann Kohler, *Jewish Theology* (New York: Ktav 1968 reprint) p 323-324.

11. G. Scholem. *The Messianic Idea in Kabbalism* (New York: Schocken 1971) p 46.

12. N. Krochmal, *Moreh Nebuchai Hazeman;* Nathan Rotenstreich, *Jewish Philosophy in Modern Times* (New York: Holt, Rinehart and Winston 1968) p 48.

13. Franz Rosenzweig, *The Star of Redemption* (New York: Holt, Rinehart and Winston 1970) Part I. The original appeared in 1930.

14. *De Praemiis et Poenis* XX, 123; *Legum Allegoria* II, 69 (Leob Classics edition).

15. Saadia, *Book of Beliefs and Opinions* (translation by Rosenblatt), Introduction, 6; Maimonides, *Guide for the Perplexed* (translation by Pines) III, 31; Joseph Albo, *Book of Principles* (translation by Husik) (Philadelphia: J.P.S.A. 1946) III, 25.

16. *Book of Beliefs and Opinions* Introduction and 1, 3.

17. *Guide for the Perplexed* I, 36.

18. *Guide for the Perplexed* III, 28. See the commentary of Shemtov.

19. *Guide for the Perplexed* II, 23. His "will to believe" is really an appeal to join in the quest of God's nearness as in III, 51.

20. *The Kuzari* (translated by Hirschfield IV, 16). He regarded Islam and Christianity, for all the persistence of a pagan underground in their ritual, as closer to Judaism than philosophy—ibid. IV, 11, 12, 13.

21. Moses Cordovero, *Or Neerav,* an introduction to Qabbalah. Understanding is ranked as *The Third Sefirah* after Wisdom and Crown.

22. Mendelssohn's letter to the Duke of Braunschweig in January 1770; it is discussed in Ravidowitz's article in *Hatekufah* vol. 25 and 26.

23. Shabbat 23a, where two reasons are given: one legal, based on Deut 17; the other moralistic, based on Deut 32,7.

24. *Sifre,* ed. Ish Shalom, Voet-hanan, 32. The text adds, "like Abraham", suggesting the role of a missionary.

25. Strack and Billerbeck, *Kommentar* vol. IV p. 490.

26. Rabbi Jacob Emden, *Eṣ Abot,* published in 1756, a commentary on the Ethics of the Fathers.

27. *Hilkhot Melᵃkhim,* 10;14 (Constantinople edition).

28. See I. Heinemann, *Taʿamai Hamiṣwot* (Hebrew) II p. 95.

29. Charles Guignebert, *The Jewish World in the Time of Jesus,* (New York 1959) p. 157; G. F. Moore, *Judaism in the First Centuries of the Christian Era* I p. 233.

30. Strack and Billerbeck, *Kommentar* I p. 925; James Parkes, *The Foundations of Judaism and Christianity,* London 1960, p. 279.

31. Martin Buber, *Israel and the World,* New York 1963 p. 183-213.

32. Judah Halevi, Kuzari II, 44; II, 36. The Torah is the beginning of the manifestation of his Kingdom, III, 17.

33. Abraham Geiger's battle for Reform was conceived by him as a war of "liberation" from the fetters of nationalism. See *Abraham Geiger and Liberal Judaism* by Max Wiener, Philadelphia 1962, pp. 156, 60, 71. Leo Baeck's conception of Judaism as a ceaseless, dynamic revolution aiming at the unification of man and of thought is summed up in his essay, "The Character of Judaism" in *The Pharisees and other Essays* (New York: Schocken 1947).

34. See *Sefer Hageulah,* printed in *Kithvei Haramban* Jerusalem 1963 vol. I.

35. Deut. 32,8. In the Septuagint, each nation has its divine Prince, as in the Book of Daniel. And the Qabbalists assumed that the reason the Israelites were exiled was that they might gather the "holy sparks", wherever they are found.

36. Lev Rabba 13,3. Whether a "new Torah" or a "renewal of Torah" was to be given by the Messiah according to the Sages, is a moot point. See Strack and Billerbeck, *Kommentar* III p 577. Recent discussion is found in Urbach's *Ḥazal* (Jerusalem 1969) p 264-267.

Utopia and Reality in Martin Buber's Thought*

SHEMARYAHU TALMON

I

The question concerning the mutual relationship of utopia and reality pertains to a central aspect of Martin Buber's work. It is necessary, therefore, to preface our limited study of this issue with a few remarks that will place it, at least in broad outline, within the wider context of Buber's world.

In his work as writer and educator for nearly seven decades Buber concerned himself with all aspects of the humanities that were of interest to the European intellectuals of this day. It was on this foundation that he built his interpretation of the spirit and faith of Judaism and his socio-political thought, conceived at the height of German Jewry during the Weimar period, and developed further during the second phase of his life in Jerusalem.

Martin Buber's bibliography bears witness to an unusually rich spiritual heritage, which cannot be neatly packaged into a system. He incorporated into his work in a masterful way the major advances and crises of the twentieth century—in technology and sciences, the social sciences, education, philosophy, psychology and theology. The emancipation of European Jewry attained its finest realization in Martin Buber. He achieved in his own thought a ground-breaking symbiosis of the Greek and Jewish worlds, in which the particular values of Judaism blended with the universal values it shared with or received from the rest of the world. Through his thought and action Buber became the catalyst for a fruitful dialogue between Christians and Jews. The longed for living and striving in common of Christianity and Judaism found its symbolic expression for him in the vis-à-vis and togetherness of the

---

*Translation from the German by Dr. Eva Fleischner, the author and L. Frizzell.

great and proud cathedral of Worms and the lopsided, weather-worn tombstones of the Jewish cemetery, the "holy sand", rather than, as for Franz Rosenzweig, in the statues of the Strasbourg Cathedral, where *Ecclesia triumphans* faces the broken *Synagoga*. Christian thinkers and theologians to this day see in Martin Buber the most eminent interpreter of Judaism for the non-Jewish world.

We must beware, however, of making Martin Buber the "apostle of Judaism to humanity" (Gustav Landauer). The focus of his creative life lies in the Jewish people and in the Jewish faith; his educational work is aimed at the Jews of his day, whether in the Diaspora or in Israel. In the house of his grandfather, the rabbinic scholar Solomon Buber, the grandson acquired his love of Hebrew and his understanding of Hebrew philology, which later were to play a decisive role in his work of translating the Hebrew Bible into German. There in Lemberg, the young Buber encountered Hassidism for the first time. The study and exploration of that Jewish religious movement of renewal later became a central point of his socio-theological interest and of his entire spiritual life. The study of Judaism, the familiarity with Jewish writings and the meeting with Eastern European Jewry, so steeped in tradition, awakened in the young Buber a receptivity for modern Zionism as proclaimed by Theodor Herzl. Active in the Zionist movement already at the age of twenty, Buber worked until his death in critical loyalty for the realization of Zionist ideology, devoting himself especially to its spiritual-cultural interpretation. Buber's understanding of Zionism was rooted in a coming together of his anthropology and sociology—that is to say, his view of man and society—and his understanding of Jewry as an ethnic entity rooted in a confession of faith, whose historical-ideal resting point is the land of Israel. In the return to Israel, in the people's becoming rooted once more in the soil of this land, Buber perceived the grandiose background against which the "believing humanism"[1] which he taught would unfold within the resurrected national community. It was Buber's hope that in Israel his concept of a just, socialist society would be realized. He saw the heart of his model in the kibbutz, the Jewish collective village, and its communal structure.

Buber's social teaching and political ideology must be considered in the light of this panorama shaped by philosophical-sociological and theological premises and his own personal experiences.

II

Every thinker who is concerned not primarily with theory and abstraction, but with the actuality of human and social living, awakens in his hearers and readers the question: do his ideas relate to and build reality, or do they belong to the realm of wishful dreams which, at last in the immediate future, cannot be realized? This question becomes more acute when we are confronted with a "thinker out of faith", as Martin Buber called himself. "Faith," it is true, is rooted in human reality, hence oriented toward it; but faith also transcends reality, seeking to shape and reshape it in light of a value grounded in an idea-structure that reaches beyond what is real. A "thinker out of faith" cannot develop his concept of man and his world in untrammelled freedom. He cannot formulate a system simply on the basis of his own insights. His anthropology—his view of man, and his sociology—his doctrine of society, are tied to ideal conceptions which have their roots in the sphere of the more-than-human, the divine, hence in the realm of the not-yet-experienced in human action, that which cannot be experienced in history. Thus they belong in the realm of utopia. The human "here and now" stands in an inherent, insoluble tension to the hoped-for, awaited, ideal, future situation. But precisely this relationship of tension constantly calls for the attempt to lessen the distance between reality and ideal. The image of the future makes a demand on human beings in their historical limitation. The believer must work on himself and his group, must educate himself and his society so as to make it receptive to the ideal concept and the promise of its realization, if only in a yet undetermined future. This demand runs through Martin Buber's whole work. We shall consider it here under two aspects, pertaining to "social" and "political" problems. This division reflects one of Buber's basic attitudes. He made a clear distinction between the "social" and the "political" principle, since each fulfills different functions in human life. The "social" has an "administrative ordering" task in society; the "political", a task which rests in "power and domination" and stands above society. Buber sought to limit power and domination to an absolute minimum, in order to grant more room in human existence to the ordering principle, based as it is on the fundamental equality and equal claims of those who are ruled. This order is no utopia for him, no wishful dreaming. He conceives it as topical, that is, as realizable, depending on place and circumstances.

This orientation toward the topical can be clearly seen in two spheres: a) the way in which Buber understood the character and tasks of the purely social, non-political microstructures of human life—family, community, social organizations, unions, affiliations, etc. These configurations, partly natural in origin, he would call with Tönnies "communities," or, with Schmallenbach, "Bünde." b) his conception of the structure and task of the State as a political entity and the mutual relationship of states, i.e. of political macro-structures. He sought to understand how a desirable world order could be conceived and realized in history. We can point to this question here only in passing.

Our ultimate concern is the relevance of Martin Buber's thought to contemporary situations. Do his principles and ideas still keep their value today, or are they outmoded? The question is particularly relevant to a socio-political phenomenon which Buber foresaw long before it became actual: the relationship of Arabs and Jews in Palestine in the wake of the immigration of Jews in large numbers sparked by Zionism, which resulted in the building of new Jewish settlements and political institutions in the Land. More than fifty years ago Buber warned of a possible clash of these two ethnic groups, and set forth ideas and plans which, he believed, could prevent an open conflict and actually lead to peaceful cooperation.

III

What, then, is the relationship of utopia and reality?

Buber saw these concepts not as possible poles, but as alternating and mutually complementary phases in human life and in the existence of human communities, related to each other through the paths which lead now to one, now to the other. He developed this basic principle in greater detail in a book, which he first published in 1946 in Hebrew, and which then was translated into many languages. In English it is known under the title *Paths in Utopia* (London: Routledge and Kegan Paul 1949). The deliberate plural, "paths" reflects a readiness, which runs through the entire book, to recognize the validity of a variety of attempts to sketch an ideal image of society in all its complexity. Buber expresses a view which earned him the criticism of those social reformers of his day who were willing to recognize only *one* interpretation of history—the Marxist-scientific interpretation—and who believed in only *one* possibility of creating a new and just social order through the communist revolution. *Paths in Utopia* proclaims a counter-theory: the desired goal, the not-yet-experienced ideal social structure, may be reached by different paths and from a variety of starting points. Perhaps, yet more sharply: Utopia, the ideal Non-place, the ideal Non-land, cannot be achieved at all through *one* single system. Each society must fashion its own Arkadia and attain it through its own particular paths. This represents Buber's basic rejection of the Marxist-monistic manifesto, the exclusive demands of which he refused to accept.

In the confrontation with scientific-Marxist socialism, Buber does not do full justice to the differences in society—presupposed by this system—which must also find their expression in the diverse shapes of "revolution." But this fact does not lessen the basic difference between his view and that of his opponents, for whom he was a utopian dreamer. It seems as though Buber turns the tables on his critics. The belief that a new and just world order could be achieved through a concentrated revolutionary upheaval appears to him to be "utopian". The variety of human beings, and of societies and institutions requires a corresponding variety of efforts to build ideal social forms, which in a later stage can then be molded into a "community of communities", without losing their separate identities. He is convinced that only a differentiated, process-like development, not a one-time revolution, can promise the realization of a perfect and just community, one which has been born out of thought, not in dreams.

The concept "utopia", which plays such an important role in this confrontation, must be studied more carefully in its various interpretations if Buber's ideas and the attack on them by the representatives of "scientific-realistic" socialism are to be better understood. We must keep in mind that Buber, especially in his younger years, saw and described himself as a "revolutionary socialist". But his interpretation of this revolutionary world view differed radically from that of Marxist socialism, which experienced rapid growth after World War I. The "realized socialism" of the Soviet-Russian brand disappointed Buber deeply. The substitution of the domination by the proletariat for the domination of capitalism produced neither the ideal forms of a truly just society, which Buber saw as the goal of the revolution, nor that inner change in the human soul which for him, as for Saint Simon, Proudhon, Gustav Landauer and Edward Heinemann, was an indispensable mark of realized socialism. Communal social structures evolved by the State, such as the Russian *kolkhos,* did not witness to nor make possible the regeneration of community-forming forces, which for Buber represent the alpha and omega of the true socialist revolution. The Buberian version of socialist utopianism, furthermore, has little in common with the classical utopias. The latter were shot through with a primitivism that dreamed of social ideals which could be realized only outside an existing society. The wish-images that saw a new "Arkadia" in the making, or the effort in Europe and America of the nineteenth and twentieth centuries to duplicate the social structure of Polynesian Southsea islands, unburdened by the needs and problems of modern society, had no chance of realization under the very different conditions to which modern industrial society is subject. No wonder that such "hallucinations" elicited the mockery of modern revolutionaries and social planners.

Buber's thoughts follow different lines. As already mentioned, in contrast to Marxist ideologues he insisted, like Lorenz von Stein, on the independence of the "social" or "communal" life from that of the "State". This in itself stamps a socialist revolution of the Marxist type, conceived and led by the State, as a *contradictio in se*. The corruption of our societies, the stagnation of our cultures, and the deviations of existing political systems from basic norms, cannot be cured by having recourse to simple structural and organizational palliatives which fail to touch the person and the basic forms of social living. The soil must be plowed in depth. The creative person who can be expected to generate and sustain such an upheaval must be born anew. Like Gustav Land-auer, Buber too seeks to shape a person who will not accept the existing order because it is unsatisfactory and corrupt. The moral person, whose morality is the basis of his socialism, must try to diagnose the causes of human corruption and to identify ways and means for healing it. These will flow in part from the communal models of the past, and in part from the untrammelled power of thought, which presents an ideal utopian social structure in contrast to the defective "topical" one that already exists.

The insistence on man's personal commitment, and on the inner reshaping of the individual and of social forms, shows that the "utopian socialism" proclaimed by Buber actually can be totally identified with the "humanism" he defends. When we recall that Buber elicited values inherent in "utopian socialism" from the classical, partly the medieval, but primarily the biblical tradition—then it becomes clear that for him "utopian socialism" is in many respects identical with the biblical humanism which he presented as the foundation of a just, faith-centered community life. The "biblical" or "Hebrew humanism" derived from the Bible shares with "utopian socialism", as Buber understood the latter, a clear link to reality. Both grew out of the topical, out of the existing human structures, whose manifoldness and variety they accept without reserve. The realization of the utopian-exemplary social order-ing is made possible through the mobilization of positive powers present in topical societies. For this purpose a uniform program will not do. The utopian image of the social order of the future must not lose contact with the specifically topical. Without such contact we invent unrealizable tales and mirages, which are and remain utopian in the truest sense of the word, that is, can never become reality. Buber valued ideal con-structs such as those of Thomas More, and attempts to build extra-territorial small communities and brotherhoods, such as the Hutterite Brethren or the Dukhobors. But these cannot serve as models for a utopian socialism or a "theo-political humanism", which is concerned with the transformation of the large social structures. Buber shared with those extra-territorial utopians the criticism of state structures and the fear of political elements which might nip the generative, spontaneous, social and cultural forces in the bud. But this reservation must not lead to flight into a Never-never-land, to the creation of ideals outside society, whose influence would remain limited to the inevitable small number of members of such communities. True regeneration must take place within existing political structures. The political domain as such is not to be judged negatively. It is basically an essential autonomous component of society, with a positive role in the rhythm of social forces, as long as it is held within its bounds. The choice of secessionist elites—whose motto is "let those who can, save themselves"—should not become the basis of a true humanism or socialism.

Buber also considered another partial solution for social problems as inadequate, although it was valid as a preparatory stage: consumer-groups, production-unions, and cooperatives. Through communal structures, unions of this type may indeed correct some aspects of the economy which had gotten out of hand; but they do not bring about the necessary socialist-humanistic human transformation. The chapters in *Paths in Utopia* in which these "attempts" are described and validated concludes with the statement:

"A genuine and lasting reorganization of society from within can only prosper in the union of producers and consumers, each of the two partners being composed of independent and homogenous co-operative units; a union whose power and vitality for socialism can only be guaranteed by a wealth of Full Co-operatives all working together and, in their functional synthesis, exercising a mediatory and unifying influence. For this it is necessary, however, that in place of all the isolated experiments (condemned in the nature of things to isolation) that have made their appearance in the course of more than a hundred years of struggle, there should emerge a network of Settlements, territorially based and federatively constructed without dogmatic rigidity, allowing the most diverse social forms to exist side by side, but always aiming at the new organic whole." (*Paths in Utopia*, p 79).

In this brief summary we find the book's *raison d'être*. The detailed presentation of the history of utopian ideologies and movements, which is followed by an overview of the plans of Marx and Lenin for the "renewal of society" (p 80-128) was necessary, but not central to Buber's undertaking. All earlier explanations really lead us to "yet another experiment" (p 129-149) which stands at the center of Buber's interest and no doubt provided the catalyst for the concepts of *Paths in Utopia:* the construction of new communal forms in Palestine in the context of the Zionist settlement, predominantly the kibbutz.[2] In the description of the "Hebrew commune in its various forms," and in the analysis of the ideas and historical circumstances underlying it, Buber's deep sympathy for this experiment is evident. Indeed, he identifies with it as the "only all-out effort", in the past and present, "to create a Full Co-operative which justifies our speaking of success in the socialist sense" (p 141). Despite the problems which are inherent also in this experiment, Buber recognizes here the germ of a realized utopian socialism:

"Nowhere else in the history of communal settlements is there this tireless groping for the form of community-life best suited to this particular human group, nowhere else this continual trying and trying again, this going to it and getting down to it, this critical awareness, this sprouting of new branches from the same stem and out of the same formative impulse" (p 141-142).

Here, and only here, merge reality and utopian ideals of every shade which Buber previously considered in his work:

"In the spirit of the members of the first Palestinian Communes ideal motives joined hands with the dictates of the hour; and in the motives there was a curious mixture of memories of the Russian *Artel,* impressions left over from reading the so-called 'utopian' Socialists, and the half-conscious after-effects of the Bible's teachings about social justice. The important thing is that this ideal motive remained loose and pliable in almost every respect. There were various dreams about the future: people saw before them a new, more comprehensive form of the family, they saw themselves as the advance guard of the Worker's Movement, as the direct instrument for the realization of Socialism, as the prototype of the new society; they had as their goal the creation of a new man and a new world. But nothing of this ever hardened into a cut-and-dried programme. These men did not, as everywhere else in the history of co-operative settlements, bring a plan with them, a plan which the concrete situation could only fill out, not modify; the ideal gave an impetus but no dogma, it stimulated but did not dictate" (p 142-143).

In this passage Buber expresses concisely the essence of his conception of utopian socialism, and at the same time his rejection of Marxist-Leninist ideology which he characterizes as petrified, mechanistic, utopian-universal. He clearly opted for the Israeli model, for the realization of the utopian idea in microstructures of a just community. The "restructuring of society as a League of Leagues" is the "devouring of an amorphous society by the omnipotent State; Socialist Pluralism or so-called Socialist Unitarianism" (p 148). The active involvement in the gradual process of the creation of a new social order, on the basis of the teachings of the biblical prophets and in their tradition promises a realization of the ideal in historical time. This is to be preferred over an "absolute order imposed indefinitely for the sake of an era of freedom alleged to follow 'of its own accord' " (p 148). This is the dream of a communistic utopianism and will evolve by itself through a dialectical jump.

Buber affirmed the partial realization of utopian socialism in the form of the Israeli village communes, because he saw in them the microcosm of a larger just social order. In contrast to the self-centered utopian communes in other countries, whose members are concerned only with their own good and the good of their small community, the kibbutzim and moshavim, the Israeli communes and cooperative villages, represent an elite conscious of and faithful to its task toward the wider society. Their integration into this larger context removes the danger of utopian dreams and safeguards the link to reality:

"Even in its first undifferentiated form a tendency towards federation was innate in the Kvuza, to merge the Kvuzoth in some higher social unit; and a very important tendency it was, since it showed that the Kvuza implicitly understood that it was the cell of a newly structured society" (p 146).

The association of the Kibbutz Communes has the capacity of becoming a model for a realizable world community of communities, a *"communitas communitatum"* (p 147-148). With the birth of the kibbutz movement, utopian socialism began its "Gang in die Wirklichkeit", its march into reality. Here Buber wrote:

"On the soberest survey and on the soberest reflection one can say that, in this one spot in a world of partial failures, we can recognize a non-failure — and, such as it is, a signal non-failure" (p 142).

In concluding this brief and hence inadequate analysis of "utopian socialism" in the life of communities as presented by Buber, the underlying realism becomes clearly apparent. As already suggested, the reason for this may be that Buber started out, not from abstract models, freely invented by the mind, but from aspired social structures which *in nuce* become visible to the observer already in the present. Basically, Buber provided the kibbutz movement, which had grown up experimentally from the historical circumstances of early Zionism in Palestine, with an ideological base. He proved, as it were, that without intending to do so, these communities had realized an utopian image of society. In this case, reality seemingly preceded ideology. Or to put it differently, Buber's conception of utopian Socialism grew out of the actually experienced model of the kibbutz.

In contrast, the concept of a *communitas communitatum*, the community of peoples, is an abstract idea, lacking in tangibility because it originates only in the mind and, partly, in biblical eschatological visions. It is but a mirage of hope, whose potential for realization was not — perhaps could not be — adequately developed, since it did not evolve out of an actual experience, and therefore could not be tested by it.

IV

Let me add a few remarks about Buber's attempt to make his sociopolitical ideology relevant to the Arab-Jewish issue.

He considered the problem of the relationship of Jews to Palestinian Arabs, even before the establishment of the State of Israel, as being implanted in the historical Jewish question and as being intimately bound with Jewish ethics. He saw in the way that the relation to the Arab population would unfold the test of what he conceived as "Hebrew humanism." Already in 1921 he voiced the view, with little success, that the Jewish liberation movement — Zionism — must assume the task of fostering a parallel Arab liberation movement. He believed that it was possible to generate a positive attitude on the part of Arabs toward the Jewish renaissance if Jews would help bring about a counterpart to the Balfour Declaration for the Arabs. He argued that after Judaism had won it emancipation and, through Zionism, its autoemancipation, at least in the West, it should now see as its task helping others effect their own emancipation. For Buber this was not a utopian fantasy. He believed in its practicality. Out of his ethical-political stance he conceived a plan of economic development for both peoples, and tried, again without visible success, to awaken an echo for his ideas also in Arab circles. Later he applied his concept of the desirable federated communal structure to the Jewish-Arab situation, by proposing the formation of a bi-national State. When, because of the Jewish-Arab war of 1948, this plan lost all chance of success, Buber did not cling to his utopian idea and insist that it could be realized in the near future; that is to say, he did not close his eyes to reality. Rather than do that, he was prepared to modify his idea in view of realities. He then displayed the flexibility on which, in his appreciation, was founded the partial success of the kibbutz movement. He did so without giving up the hope for the full realization of the not-yet-attained peaceful and mutually beneficial co-existence of Arabs and Jews in the Land.

In 1958 he assessed the situation as follows:

> "I have accepted the form of Jewish community existence which arose out of the war, the State of Israel, as my own. The command to serve the spirit must be fulfilled by us in and through this State. . . Today it seems absurd to many, especially in the present situation among the Arabs, that we still think of a Jewish participation in a federation. But tomorrow, with a change in certain global political events independent of ourselves, this possibility may be regarded in a highly positive light. In so far as it depends on us, it is important to prepare the ground for this. Today there can be no peace between Jews and Arabs which is only a cessation of hostilities. It can only be a peace of close mutual co-operation."

This is the pivot of Martin Buber's ethical-political testament. Twenty years ago it sounded like a utopian fancy. Does it, today, have the ring of an attainable reality?

In the tension between the "already given" and the "not-yet-attained", Buber saw the most significant aspect of morality. Some thirty-five years ago, in a seminar at the Hebrew University in Jerusalem, he discussed the possibility of defining fundamental aspects of morality which may be considered to be unconditional and objective, and hence retain their binding validity in all human situations and in all societies, at all times. The attempt to establish a universally applicable scale of such primal moral values and demands failed. Buber proved to his hearers that, in light of the multifaceted nature of human life and the variability of human situations which affects the concepts of right and wrong, of good and evil, such an undertaking was doomed to failure from the outset. If, then, the "content" of morality cannot be defined objectively, what are the definitions of its scope and focus that address man as such, hence are universal and beyond particular human and social conditions? The only generally applicable constant which he worked out in his exposition was the following: morality is not the holding of but rather the striving towards the actualization of the spcific values. The moral person is always conscious of the distance between his particular what "is" and the fundamentally different what "should be". The tension between these two poles will spur him to self-examination and radical self-criticism. At the same time, such a person is inspired by the clearly perceived and unreservedly accepted task to realize as many of the absolute demands of the ideal image as the given situation permits. In the realm of history, the decisive nature of morality cannot express itself in the immediate realization of the idea, but rather is perceived as a straining to the ultimate goal. The courageous, yet cautious groping forward along the path to the goal is to be seen as the touchstone of the moral person, and the moral society. The unceasing striving toward the attainment of the ideal standards of individual behavior and social life is the crucible of human morality.

NOTES

1. See Martin Buber, *A Believing Humanism: My Testament* (translated with an introduction and explanatory comments by Maurice Friedman) (New York: Simon and Schuster, 1967).

2. For a presentation of major aspects of kibbutz life and ideology, see Yonina Talmon, *Family and Community in the Kibbutz* (Cambridge: Harvard University Press, 1972).

A Cycle of Holocaust Songs

MONIKA K. HELLWIG

I. *The Merits of the Fathers*

My father was a wandering Aramaean
Lord how long
It was easier in the throng
Light piercing shafts in laughter and song
   The first fruits of the land
Quiver of aspen leaves
It was only yesterday
We brought you, Lord,
Silence in silver fragments
On a cobbled street
Dying away the echo of feet
Swathed in the desert heat
Thirst draws like a magnet
On the endless trail
Unbroken light
The heavy burden of terrible glory
Lord how long
To the land of desire
The flowing of milk and honey
We bring you still
   The first fruits of our hope
Under the lash of quiet contempt
Sweating another's profit
To the last insult
Dancing fire in the blood
Yearning the great crossing
We bring you, Lord,
   The first fruits of our pain

Great is the Lord of Hosts
Riding the cherubim
   YHWH sees.

II. *Unless You have Stood at Sinai*

God thunders on his holy mountain
Cedars leap and torrents toss their foam
   Beware, Moses, come home.

The cloud has rested on the holy mountain
Terrible absence shining black
   Come down, Moses, come back.

Lightning flashes on the holy mountain
Fiery carriage swinging low
Cherubim raise their wings to the glory
   Don't climb, Moses, don't go.

In his temple all cry glory
Wilder the winds have never blown—
And Moses climbed the holy mountain
   Moses went up alone.

III. *David: The Duties of the Heart*

Why do you mock me, Lord,
On the slopes of the holy mountain
With the swing of the dancing girls
On a Saturday night
And the clinging delight
Of the ring of the laughing years
Of forgotten fears
On the slopes of the holy mountain.
Oh! laugh me not to scorn—

From the day I was born
With longing in my heart
You know me, Maker of men,
And ever again
The darkness fails to hide me from your ken.

You know my words
Before they flash from thought to song
My actions all along

Are written in your book.
Lord, read for me the riddle of my years
Along the crooked pathways
Where my heart was sold
And lead me, Shepherd, in the ways of old.
The rebels rise in hatred to destroy
But let your servitors be clothed in holiness
Your faithful ones
Shout merrily for joy.

IV. *Job's Question*

Night fell, or so they said,
But when I looked—
A seer in the crystal of my tears—
It was the sun that fell
From dazzling noonday heights
And sank
And toppled over the horizon vanquished.
Night did not fall.
It rose on every side
And round about
The darkness swarmed and surged,
Waves of primeval chaos.

The light shall shine in darkness,
So they said,
And darkness shall not smother it
But now I know it is not true—
Myself have seen
The jaws of night
That swallowed up the flaming sun,
Have heard the roaring
Of dark waters
Shatter the silent sky,
Have flung the anguished "why"
Into the void
Until it got itself with young
And tumbled back a thousand echoes.
I myself have felt
The aching agony
Eat up the flinching marrow of my bones
Piled like cold stones—

And cold it was;
It was the sun that fell
And slid from the horizon vanquished.
Cold the waters of chaos seep
Into the dry bones and creep
A deathly poison into flesh and sinew.
I myself have known
The chill embrace of death
That swallowed up the living breath
And rose on every side
And round about
The darkness surged and swarmed,
Waves of primeval chaos.

And who shall quell the dragon waves
And leash the wind?
One thing there is I wish I had not said,
Therewith a second that I shall not say again.

V. *Missed Passover: A Lamentation of Jeremiah*

Sadly at sunset under cloud and storm
Into a desert place apart in haste
I went in reckless pilgrimage to taste
The ancient hunger of my fathers
Who were poor.
How sure
Beyond the sleeping shepherd and his flock
Where lizards lurk between the cactus and the rock
The trail darts upwards to the place of bitter waters
In thirsty wilderness
Where sound and season roll away into the valley
And the silence speaks
The presence and the meeting and the death.
No breath
Can stir the evening, night fast falls
From heaven to earth, and the hyena calls
The terror summons to the sudden loneliness
Where all is dark
Nor star nor candle-spark
Comforts the hunger of the aching emptiness

Nor comes to bless
The watches of the lonely waiting with a stray caress.

Day dawns too soon
My desert blooms into a garden
Radiant with his footprints all around
Where fern and flower and fountain
Spring up from the ground
And pilgrim crowds jostling with thrust and throng
Chant forth with cheerful heedlessness
The Hallel song
Of hungry agony
For he has passed this way at night—
We looked and did not see.
YHWH is holy
Who can look on him and live?

VI. *Survivor: Shall these Bones Live?*

Alas, too late I came
To my favorite haunt under the juniper tree.
Another, a stranger, was there ahead of me
And how should he dare
To offer me consolation
When I wanted despair?
In the bitter atomic glare
Under the juniper tree
Lord, make an end of me;
I am a living curse
My fathers were no worse
My sons will be no better
Sheltered from heaven's favor
By the mushroom of fear in the sky.
Lord, let me die
For how can I walk
With divine intoxication
When the forty days' bread
Is sullen with irradiation
And my heart is filled with disgust?

Shame, horror and dust

Are on Horeb the holy mountain
And in the desert air
Quiet despair.
And yet the troubled prayer
Of the last longing in the heart
To walk the weary wilderness
Beyond the setting sun
To climb the death rocks
Of distrust
And once more thrust
With all the aching anger of the man I was
Towards the emptiness where YHWH used to be
And see
That YHWH does not speak in thunder or in storm
Nor in the roaring of destroying winds—
But in the breath that faintly stirs
The silence
Mid crushed bones
Of broken rebels
YHWH speaks.

My father was a wandering Aramaean
In this desert
YHWH speaks.

Bibliography of Msgr. John M. Oesterreicher

COMPILED BY LAWRENCE FRIZZELL

All entries from 1934-1937 appeared in *Die Erfüllung*.

1934 "Die Judenfrage" 1 (November 1934)p 7-17

"Sinai" 1 (November 1934) p 29-33

1935 "Solowjews Vision vom Antichrist" 1 (January 1935) p 10-23

Review: Die Protokolle der Weisen von Zion; Zum Ritual-
mordbuch von Christian Loge 1 (January 1935) p.41-47.

Dokumente: Die Flucht vor Gott 1 (March 1935) p 35-38.

Eine Berichtung: Albert Mirgeler und Johannes Oesterreicher 1
(March 1935) p 38-43

"Franz Rosenzweig: Ein jüdisches Schicksal" 1 (May 1935) p 7-20

Dokumente: Die Gefährdung des Christentums 1 (May 1935) p
29-34.

Periodical review: Der Christ in der Zeit; Die Überwindung eines
Mythos 1 (May 1935) p 38-43

Dokumente: Friede über Israel (Prague); Der Mensch (Ernst
Hello); Das nachbiblische jüdische Schrifttum; Ein Zeuge für
Christian Loge? 1 (July 1935) p 27-42

Periodical review: Rass, Volk, Menschheit, Kirche 1 (July 1935) p
42-45

"Hominem non habeo . . ." (Nüremberg laws) 1 (October 1935)
p. 3-13

"Die Juden und der Sozialismus": Ein Briefwechsel (Rudolf Fanta
und Johannes Oesterreicher) 1 (October 1935) p 16-26

Dokumente: "Rechtfertigung Gottes"; Vrede over Israel
(Amsterdam); Eine Schweizer Kundgebung; Vor der Liebe 1
(October 1935) p 27-41.

Periodical review: Das Urteil der katholischen Presse (Nuremberg laws) 1 (October 1935) p 42-46

1936 "Paulus und sein Volk" 2 (April 1936) p 7-16

"Die Mysterien des Glaubens" 2 (April 1936) p 24-27

Dokumente: Eine Stimme aus der katholischen Jugendbewegung;

"Im Schatten von Morgen"; Der Prügelknabe"; Der nie ver-
siegende Quell 2 (1936) p 29-35
Kritik: "Die Ansprüche der Judenmission"; Das Minderheitsrecht
für die Juden 2 (April 1936) p 35-43
Periodical review: Der Christ, der Deutsche und der Jude 2 (April
1936) p 43-44
"Die Mysterien des Glaubens" 2 (June 1936) p 70-75
Dokumente: Israel und das Werden der abendländischen Kultur;
Das Zeugnis eines Dichters (Hans Christian Andersen); Der nie
versiegende Quell; Im Namen der christlichen Gerechtigkeit 2
(June 1936) p 78-79 Kritik: Die Entleerung der Religion 2 (June
1936) p 89-92
"Die Mysterien des Glaubens" 2 (August 1936) p 120-124
Dokumente: Der nie versiegende Quell; Karl Kraus; Von der
Würde des Christentums und der Unwürde der Christen 2 (Au-
gust 1936) p 123-132
Kritik: Dr. Eberle zur Judenfrage 2 (August 1936) p 132-141.
Dokumente: Nationalismus und Antisemitismus; "Getrennte
Brüder"; "Zur Selbstprüfung der Gegenwart anbefohlen" (S.
Kierkegaard); Gericht und Erneuerung 2 (October 1936) p 175-
185
Kritik: Die spanische Revolution und die Juden; Der grosse Be-
trug des Antichrist 2(October 1936) p 185-199
Book reviews: Alois Hudal, Die Grundlagen des National-
sozialismus; Clemens Holzmeister (editor), Kirche im Kampf;
Friedrich Neumann, Die Judenfrage und der christliche Jude;
Erich Kahler, Israel unter den Völkern; Anton van Miller,
Deutsche und Juden; R. N. Coudenhove-Kalergi, Judenhass von
heute. 2 (October 1936) p 200-213
"Die Mysterien des Glaubens" 2 (October 1936) p 115-119

1937   "Credidi, propter quod locutus sum" (Pauluswerk) 3 (January
1937) p 3-7
"Die Juden und das Reich Gottes" 3 (March 1937) p 91-112
"Der gefallene Ismael" 3 (Summer 1937) p 124-131
"Dokumente: Paul Claudel"; Drei Briefe; Aus einer Predigt (Karl
Barth); Picards Bekenntnis zu Christus 3 (Summer 1937) p 191-202
"Vergäss ich dein, Jerusalem . . .!" 3 (Autumn 1937) p 209-210
(editor) "Die Kirche Christi und die Judenfrage" "The Church
    and the Jews" (New York: Paulist Press)

1943   *Racisme–Antisémitisme–Antichristianisme:* Documents et Critique
(New York: Editions de la Maison Francaise)
"The Blessed Virgin and the Jews," New York, 1943 (Radio
Replies 1946)

1944 "The mystical reality of the Old Testament," *Homiletic and Pastoral Review* 44 (August 1944) p 822-828

1946 "An epistle to Sholem Asch," *The Catholic World* 162 (February 1946) p 438-442

"The sacrament of strength" (sermon at Confirmation) New York

"The Blessed Virgin and the Jews," *Our Lady's Digest* 1 (September 1946) p 41-48.

1947 "Christ in Buchenwald," *The Catholic World* 164 (February 1947) p 443-447.

"Pro perfidis Judaeis," *Theological Studies* 8(1947) p 80-96 and *Cahiers Sioniens* 1(1947) p 85-101.

"Henri Bergson and the Faith," *Thought* 22(1947) p 635-678.

"Can a Jew be a Christian?" (New York: Catholic Information Society)

1948 "The Apostolate to the Jews: a Study of the Church's Apostolate to the Jews, its Theology, History and Present Methods," (New York: American Press, 1948)

"Life from the Dead," *Blackfriars* 29(October 1948) p 466-473.

1949 "Church Unity Sermons: The Conversion of the Jews," Peekskill (N.Y.); Graymoor, p 35-46.

"The Catholic Attitude towards the Jews," *Orate Fratres* 23(July 1949) p 385-402.

1950 "Seeds of Hope: Five Sermons on the Mystery of Israel 1945-1949," (St. Louis: Pio Decimo Press)

"The Jews: the Mirror of our Sins," *Cross and Crown* 2(1950) p 32-46.

"Max Scheler and the Faith," *The Thomist* 13(April 1950) p 135-203.

1951 "Rev. John M. Oesterreicher answers Mr. Blanshard," (New York: Carl Lopez Press)

"Our flight from God," *Journal of Arts and Letters* 3(1951) p 19-26

"Abraham our Father," *Orate Fratres* 25(1951) p 559-573.

1952 *Walls are Crumbling:* Seven Jewish Philosophers Discover Christ (New York, Devin-Adair) (London, Hollis and Carter)

Richard Baumann, *To See Peter:* a Lutheran Minister's Journey to the Eternal City (New York: David McKay) (translated by J.M. Oesterreicher)

"His vision of the Church," *A Newman Symposium* (editor Victor Yantelli) (New York: Fordham) p 76-86

1953 "Edith Stein on Womanhood," *Integrity* 7(September 1953) p 21-28

"Piety and prayer in the Jewish home," *Worship* 27(November 1953) p 540-549

1954 *Muren Storten In:* Zeven Joodse Filosofen vinden de Weg noor
Christus (Haarlem, N.V. Drukkerij de Spaarnestad)
"Why Judaeo-Christian Studies?" The inaugural lecture of the
Institute of Judaeo-Christian Studies.
"Mary of Israel," *Worship* 29(December 1954) p 2-15

1955 Sept Philosophes Juifs devant le Christ (Paris: Editions du Cerf)
The Bridge: A Yearbook of Judaeo-Christian Studies I (New York:
Pantheon Books)
"The Enigma of Simone Weil," p 118-158
"Introduction," *The Christian Imagination:* Studies in Religious
Thought by Justus George Lawler (Westminster (Md.) Newman
Press) p vii-xii
"Can a Jew be a Christian?" *Australian Truth Society Record,* June
10, 1955

1956 *The Bridge:* A Yearbook of Judaeo-Christian Studies II (New York:
Pantheon Books)
"The Community of Qumran," p 91-134

1958 *The Bridge:* A Yearbook of Judaeo-Christian Studies III (New York:
Pantheon Books)
"The Hasidic Movement," p 122-186
Review of Abba Hillel Silver, *Where Judaism Differed,* p 354-363

1960 "Foreword" to *A Study of Hebrew Thought* by Claude Tresmontant
(English translation) (New York: Desclee) p ix-xiv

1961 *Siete Filosofos Judios encuentran a Cristo* (Madrid: Aguilar)
The Bridge: A yearbook of Judaeo-Christian Studies IV (New York:
Pantheon Books)
"The Swastika Reappears," p 344-352
Contribution to "Umfrage zum Konzil" *Wort und Wahrheit*
(Freiburg, Herder 1961) p 646-648
"Pope John and the Jews," (Garrison [N.Y.] Graymoor)

1962 *Der Papst und die Juden* (Recklinghausen; Paulus Verlag) *The Gospel
of Jesus Christ* (editors, Roland E. Murphy, John M. Oesterreicher
& David Stanley) Seton Hall University Press
"Fulfillment," The Gospel of Jesus Christ, p 21-34

1963 *The Israel of God* (Englewood Cliffs: Prentice-Hall) "Israel's misstep and her rise: the dialectic of God's saving design in Romans
9-11." *Studiorum Paulinorum Congressus Internationalis Catholicus,*
1961 (Rome: Pontifical Biblical Institute) I p 317-327.

1964 *Auschwitz, der Christ und das Konzil* (Freising: Kyrios Verlag)
"Das Konzil und die Juden," *Judenhass—Schuld der Christen*
(editor Willehad Eckert) (Essen: Verlag Hans Driewer) p 380-398
"The Brotherhood of Christians and Jews," South Orange (N.J.)
Institute of Judaeo-Christian Studies

"The Council and the Jews," *Catholic Mind* 62(March 1964) p 42-56
"Israel's Misstep and her Rise—the Dialectic of God's Saving
Design in Romans 9-11" *The Bible Today* 12(April 1964) p 768-774

1965 "Speaking of the Jews" *The Bible Today* 13(October 1964) p 864-868.
Auschwitz, the Christian and the Council (Montreal: Palm Publishers)

1966 *L'Eglise, Israel de Dieu*: Elements vétéro-testamentaires de la foi
dans l'Eglise (Paris: Mame)
"The Church and the Non-Christian World: Man's many Religions," *Homiletic and Pastoral Review* 66(March 1966) p 478-486

1967 *Five in Search of Wisdom* (Notre Dame [Ind.]; Notre Dame Univer-
sity Press)
"Das Zweite vatikanische Konzil: Erklärung über das Verhältnis
der Kirche zu den nichtchristlichen Religionen"
Das Zweite Vatikanische Konzil, Dokumente und Kommentare (editor
Herbert Vorgimler) (Frieburg: Herder) Part II, p 406-478.
"Commentary on the Declaration on the Relationship of the
Church to non-Christian Religions," *American Participation in the
Second Vatican Council* (editor, Vincent A. Yzermans) (New York:
Sheed and Ward) p 595-614.
"Jewish comments on the conciliar statement about the Jews,"
Concilium 28(1967) p 97-110.

1968 *Der Baum und die Wurzel*: Israels Erbe—Anspruch an die Christen
(Freiburg: Herder)

1969 Japanese edition of *Walls are Crumbling*.
"Introduction and Commentary: Declaration on the Relationship
of the Church to Non-Christian Religions," *Commentary on the
Documents of Vatican II* (ed. Herbert Vorgrimler) (New York:
Herder & Herder) III p 1-136
"SHALOM: the Encounter of Christians and Jews and the
Catholic Educator," Institute of Judaeo-Christian Studies.

1970 *Brothers in Hope: The Bridge*, Judaeo-Christian Studies V (New
York: Herder and Herder)
"Deicide as a theological problem," p 190-204
"The Theologian and the Land of Israel," p 231-243
"The Declaration: One Year Later," p 263-275
"Jewish Aid to Biafra," p 276-283
"In Praise of Law," p 284-290
"A Statement of Conscience," p 291-295
"The Hangings in Iraq," p 296-300
"The Burning Mosque," p 301-302
Book review: David Flusser, *Jesus*, p 320-333
"Salute to Israel" (Teshuvah Paper #1), South Orange, Institute
of Judaeo-Christian Studies

1971 *The Rediscovery of Judaism:* A re-examination of the Conciliar statement on the Jews (South Orange, Institute of Judaeo-Christian Studies)
Die Wiederentdeckung des Judentums durch die Kirche (Freising, Kyrios Verlag)
"Internationalization of Jerusalem?" (Teshuvah Paper # 2), South Orange, Institute of Judaeo-Christian Studies

1972 "Jerusalem the Free" (Teshuvah Paper # 3), South Orange, Institute of Judaeo-Christian Studies

1973 "Passion Jesu heute," *Passionsspiel heute?* Notwendigkeit und Möglichkeiten, (Stephan Schaller and others), (Freising, Kyrios Verlag) p 65-74
"Christianity threatened in Israel? An examination of Archbishop Ryan's charges," *Midstream* (January 1973) p 3-16

1974 "Unter dem Bogen des Einen Bundes," *Judentum und Kirche* (ed Clemens Thoma), Theologische Berichte III (Einsiedeln; Benziger) p 27-70
John M. Oesterreicher and Anne Sinai (editors) *Jerusalem* (New York: John Day)
"Berrigan's bankruptcy" *Jewish Frontier* 41(February 1974) p 6-8
" 'Abba!' Jesu Olberggebet als Zeugnis seiner Menschlichkeit," *Das Vaterunser:* Gemeinsames im Gebet von Juden und Christen (editors Jakob Petuchowski & Michael Brocke), (Freiburg; Herder) p 209-230

1975 "Anatomy of Contempt": A critique of R.R. Ruether's *Faith and Fratricide* (Teshuvah Paper # 4), South Orange, Institute of Judaeo-Christian Studies

1976 Contribution to the Symposium in *The Sunflower* by Simon Wiesenthal (New York: Schocken Books) p 175-183

1977 "The challenge of the Holocaust" (Review essay of *Auschwitz: Beginning of a New Era?) America* 137(June 11, 1977) p 525-527
"The Covenant of Israel: Old, New and One," *America* 137(October 29, 1977) p 282-283

1978 " 'Abba, Father!' On the Humanity of Jesus," *The Lord's Prayer and the Jewish Liturgy* (editors Jakob Petuchowski & Michael Brocke) (London: Burns and Oates) p 119-138
"For love of Zion I cannot be silent: a theological affirmation," *Christian News from Israel* 26(1978) p 119-121, 171-174

Works in Progress:

(1) *The Chimneys Are Smoking Still,* Reflections occasioned by Pope John Paul II's Pilgrimage to Auschwitz

(2) *The Grace of Remembrance,* Questions Raised by the Holocaust

(3) *God At Auschwitz?* The Jewish Tradition on God Suffering with the Suffering Israel

(4) *The Unfinished Dialogue: Martin Buber and the Christian Way,* Based on Lecture given at the Occasion of the Buber Centennial, at Tantur, Israel

(5) "The Secret of God's Reign" to be published in *God and Temple:* Reflections on Samuel Terrien's *The Elusive Presence*

Index of Texts and Terms

HEBREW, ARAMAIC AND GREEK TERMS

SUBJECT AND AUTHOR INDEX